R: **JONATHAN HICKMAN**

TS: **NICK DRAGOTTA** [#17-18, 20-21, 23], **GABRIEL HERNANDEZ WALTA** [#19]
& **ANDRÉ ARAÚJO** [#22]

TISTS: **CHRIS SOTOMAYOR** [#17-18, 20] & **CRIS PETER** [#19, 21-23]

TERER: **VIRTUAL CALLIGRAPHY'S CLAYTON COWLES**

ARTISTS: **MIKE CHOI & GURU-EFX** [#17, 19-21], **KALMAN ANDRASOFSZKY** [#18, 23]
AND **RYAN STEGMAN & MARTE GRACIA** [#22]

EDITORS: **JOHN DENNING & JAKE THOMAS**

E EDITOR: **LAUREN SANKOVITCH**

EDITOR: **TOM BREVOORT**

COLLECTION EDITOR: **JENNIFER GRÜNWALD**
ASSISTANT EDITORS: **ALEX STARBUCK & NELSON RIBEIRO**
EDITOR, SPECIAL PROJECTS: **MARK D. BEAZLEY**
SENIOR EDITOR, SPECIAL PROJECTS: **JEFF YOUNGQUIST**
SENIOR VICE PRESIDENT OF SALES: **DAVID GABRIEL**
SVP OF BRAND PLANNING & COMMUNICATIONS: **MICHAEL PASCIULLO**

EDITOR IN CHIEF: **AXEL ALONSO**
CHIEF CREATIVE OFFICER: **JOE QUESADA**
PUBLISHER: **DAN BUCKLEY**
EXECUTIVE PRODUCER: **ALAN FINE**

WRITE
ARTIS
COLOR AR
LET
COVER A
ASSISTANT
ASSOCIAT

URE FOUNDATION

UNIFIED FIELD THEORY: STAN LEE & JACK KIRBY

FF BY JONATHAN HICKMAN VOL. 4. Contains material originally published in magazine form as FF #17-23. First printing 2012. Hardcover ISBN# 978-0-7851-6314-5. Softcover ISBN# 978-0-7851-6315-2. Published by MARVEL WORLDWIDE, INC., a subsidiary of MARVEL ENTERTAINMENT, LLC. OFFICE OF PUBLICATION: 135 West 50th Street, New York, NY 10020. Copyright © 2012 and 2013 Marvel Characters, Inc. All rights reserved. Hardcover: $24.99 per copy in the U.S. and $27.99 in Canada (GST #R127032852). Softcover: $19.99 per copy in the U.S. and $21.99 in Canada (GST #R127032852). Canadian Agreement #40668537. All characters featured in this issue and the distinctive names and likenesses thereof, and all related indicia are trademarks of Marvel Characters, Inc. No similarity between any of the names, characters, persons, and/or institutions in this magazine with those of any living or dead person or institution is intended, and any such similarity which may exist is purely coincidental. **Printed in the U.S.A.** ALAN FINE, EVP - Office of the President, Marvel Worldwide, Inc. and EVP & CMO Marvel Characters B.V.; DAN BUCKLEY, Publisher & President - Print, Animation & Digital Divisions; JOE QUESADA, Chief Creative Officer; TOM BREVOORT, SVP of Publishing; DAVID BOGART, SVP of Operations & Procurement, Publishing; RUWAN JAYATILLEKE, SVP & Associate Publisher, Publishing; C.B. CEBULSKI, SVP of Creator & Content Development; DAVID GABRIEL, SVP of Publishing Sales & Circulation; MICHAEL PASCIULLO, SVP of Brand Planning & Communications; JIM O'KEEFE, VP of Operations & Logistics; DAN CARR, Executive Director of Publishing Technology; SUSAN CRESPI, Editorial Operations Manager; ALEX MORALES, Publishing Operations Manager; STAN LEE, Chairman Emeritus. For information regarding advertising in Marvel Comics or on Marvel.com, please contact Niza Disla, Director of Marvel Partnerships, at ndisla@marvel.com. For Marvel subscription inquiries, please call 800-217-9158. **Manufactured between 9/24/2012 and 11/5/2012 (hardcover), and 9/24/2012 and 5/5/2013 (softcover), by QUAD/GRAPHICS, VERSAILLES, KY, USA.**

10 9 8 7 6 5 4 3 2 1

FUTURE F

OUNDATION

YOU ARE WHATEVER
YOU WANT TO BE

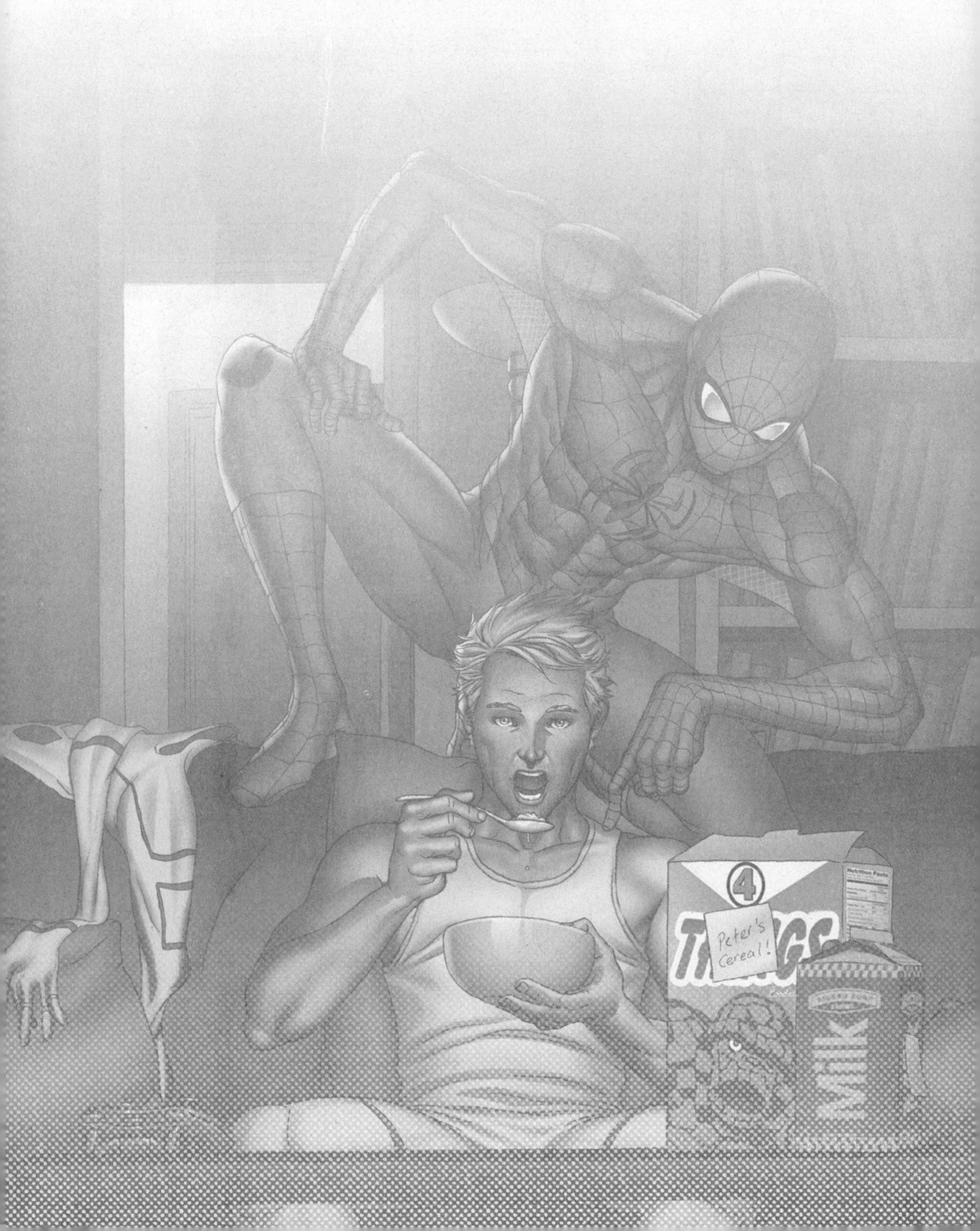

Peter's Cereal!

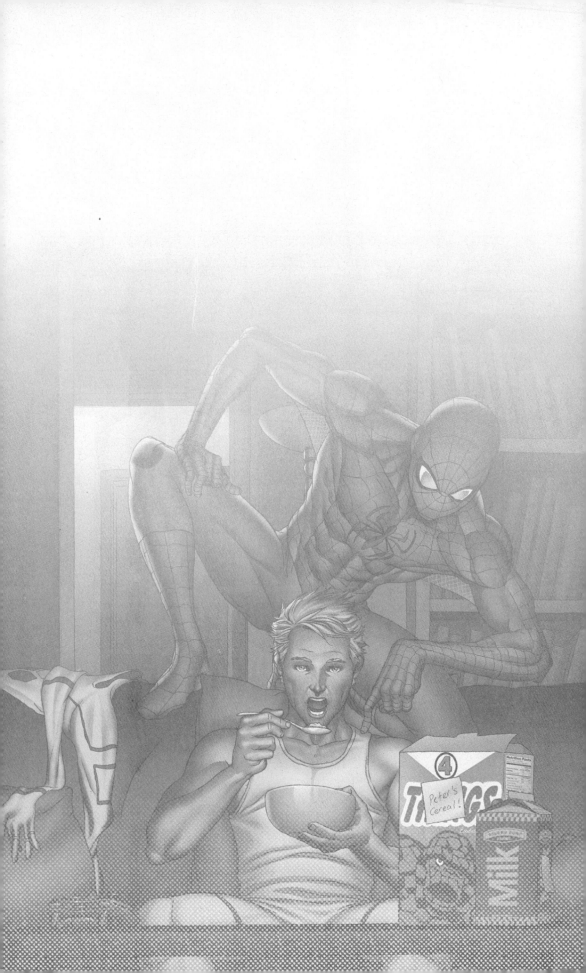

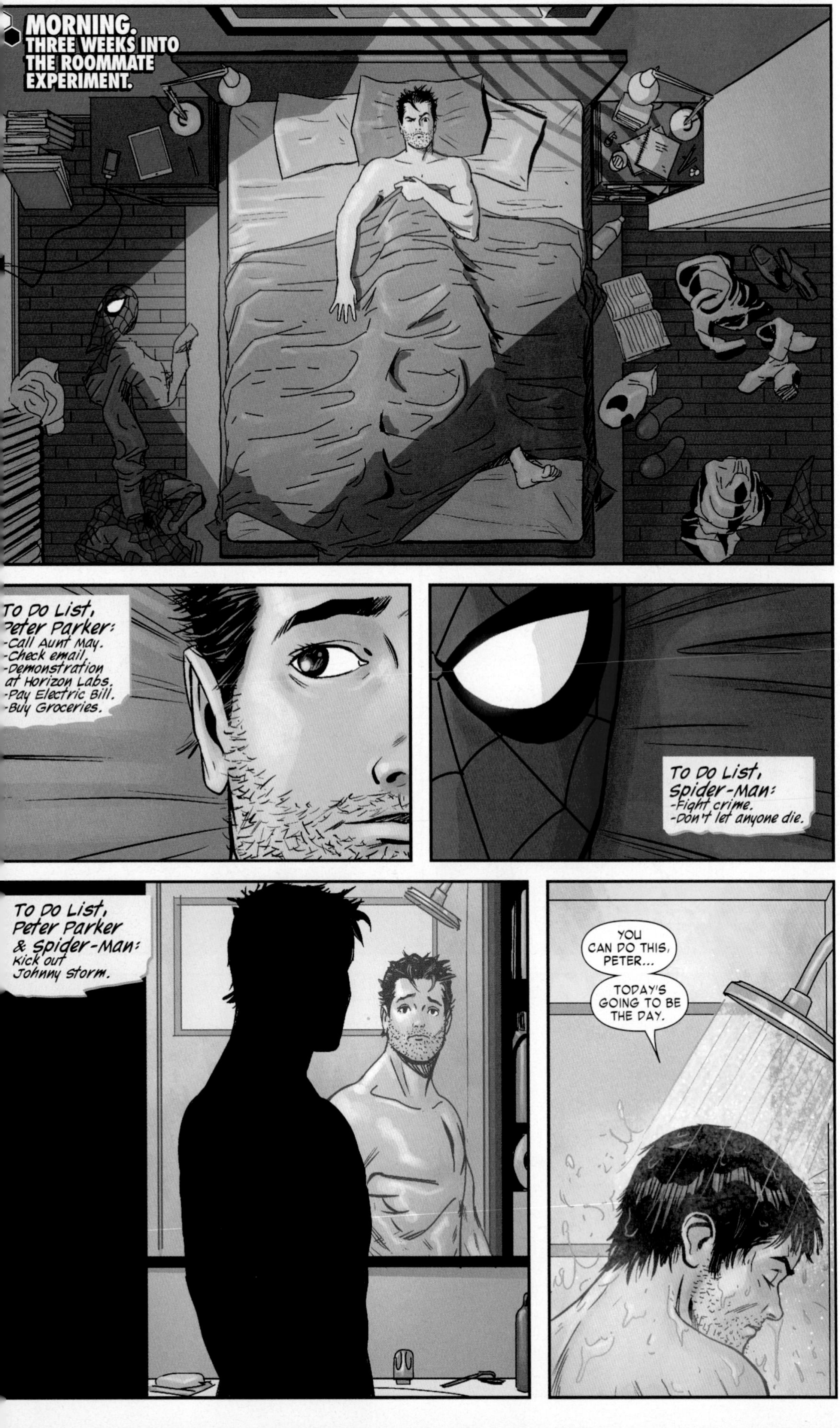
MORNING. THREE WEEKS INTO THE ROOMMATE EXPERIMENT.
To Do List, Peter Parker: -Call Aunt May. -Check email. -Demonstration at Horizon Labs. -Pay Electric Bill. -Buy Groceries.
To Do List, Spider-Man: -Fight crime. -Don't let anyone die.
To Do List, Peter Parker & Spider-Man: Kick out Johnny Storm.
YOU CAN DO THIS, PETER...
TODAY'S GOING TO BE THE DAY.

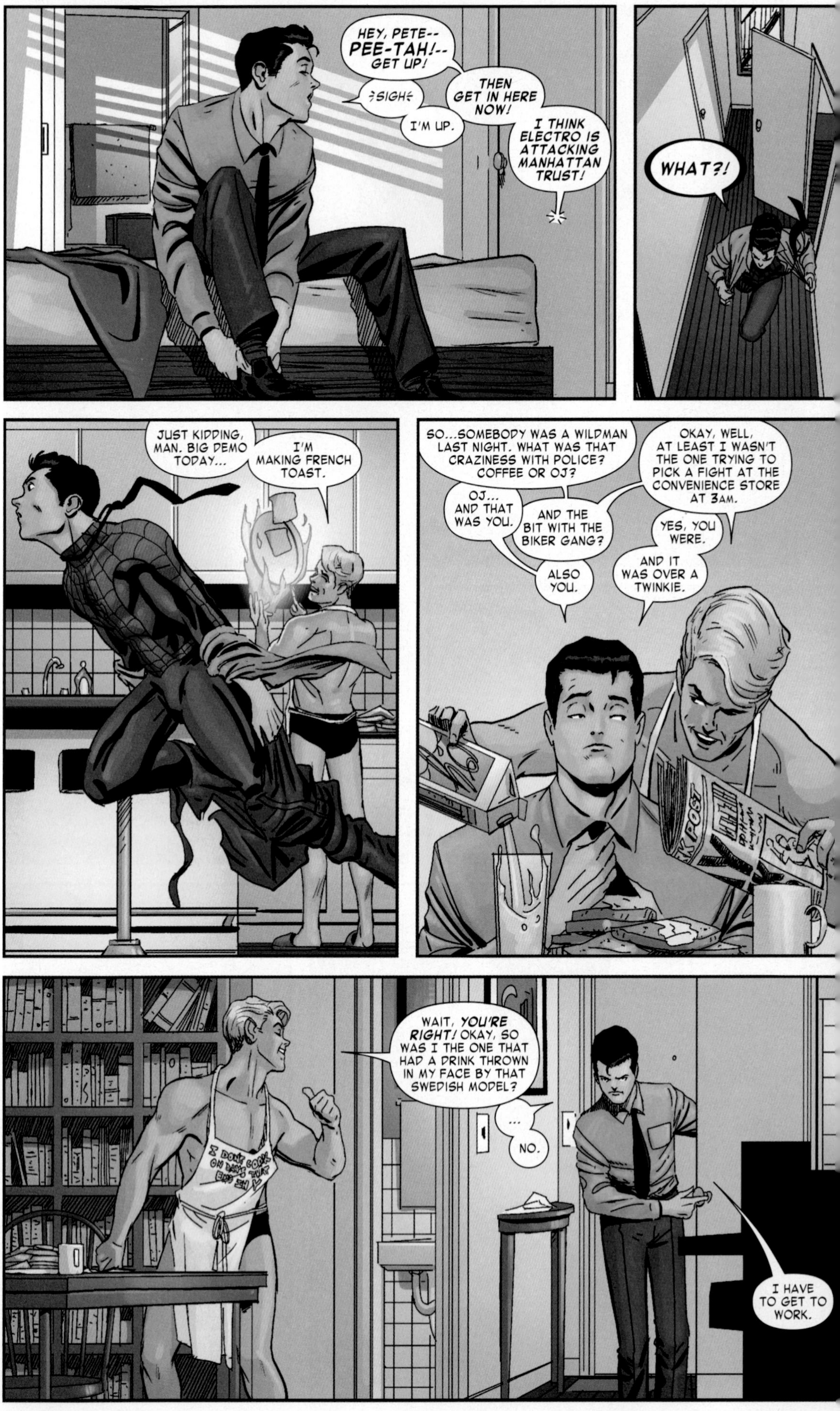
HEY, PETE-- PEE-TAH!-- GET UP!
⇒SIGH⇐
I'M UP.
THEN GET IN HERE NOW!
I THINK ELECTRO IS ATTACKING MANHATTAN TRUST!
WHAT?!
JUST KIDDING, MAN. BIG DEMO TODAY...
I'M MAKING FRENCH TOAST.
SO...SOMEBODY WAS A WILDMAN LAST NIGHT. WHAT WAS THAT CRAZINESS WITH POLICE? COFFEE OR OJ?
OJ... AND THAT WAS YOU.
AND THE BIT WITH THE BIKER GANG?
ALSO YOU.
OKAY, WELL, AT LEAST I WASN'T THE ONE TRYING TO PICK A FIGHT AT THE CONVENIENCE STORE AT 3AM.
YES, YOU WERE.
AND IT WAS OVER A TWINKIE.
WAIT, YOU'RE RIGHT! OKAY, SO WAS I THE ONE THAT HAD A DRINK THROWN IN MY FACE BY THAT SWEDISH MODEL?
...
NO.
I HAVE TO GET TO WORK.

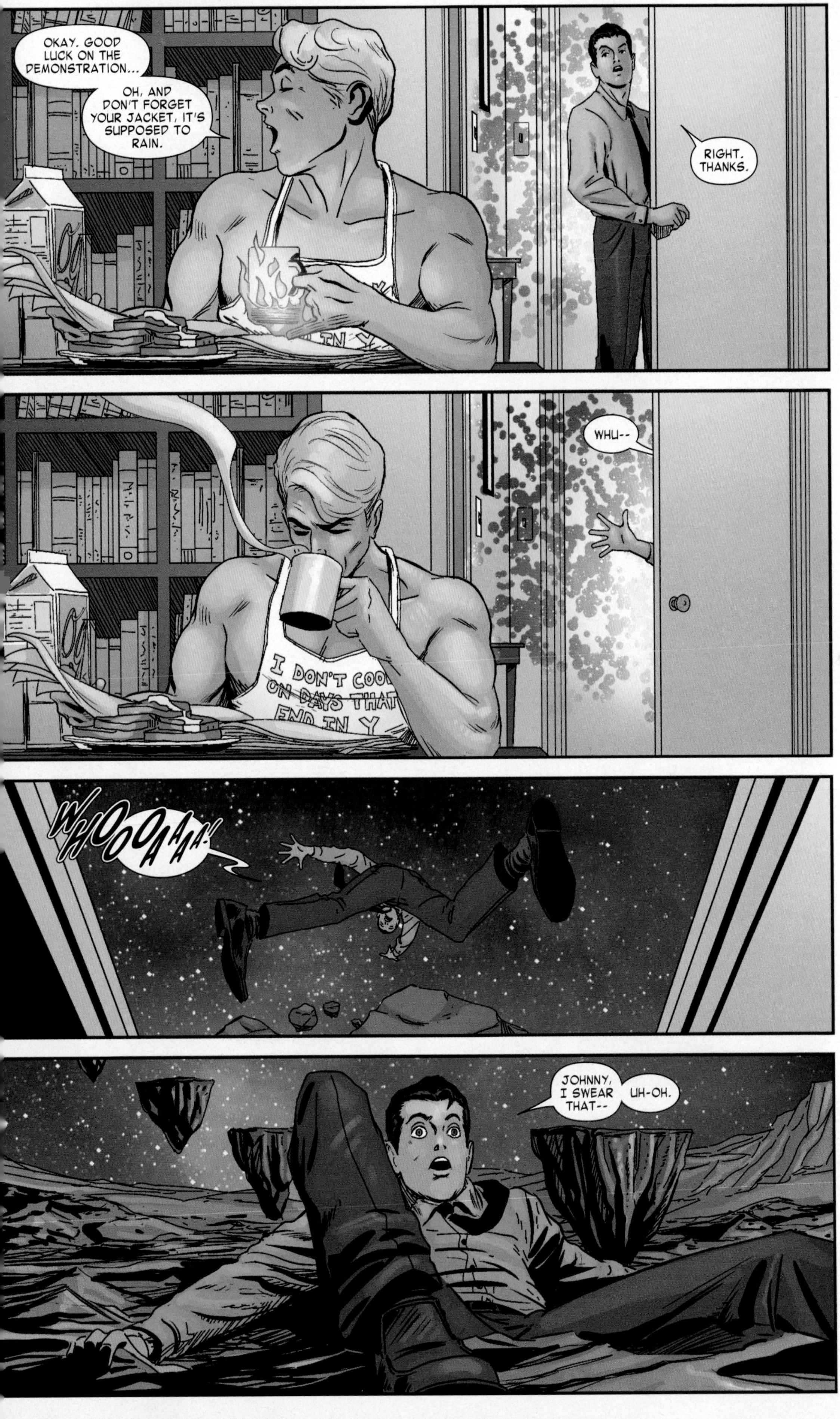

OKAY. GOOD LUCK ON THE DEMONSTRATION...
OH, AND DON'T FORGET YOUR JACKET, IT'S SUPPOSED TO RAIN.
RIGHT. THANKS.
WHU--
I DON'T COOK ON DAYS THAT END IN Y
WHOOOAAAA!
JOHNNY, I SWEAR THAT--
UH-OH.

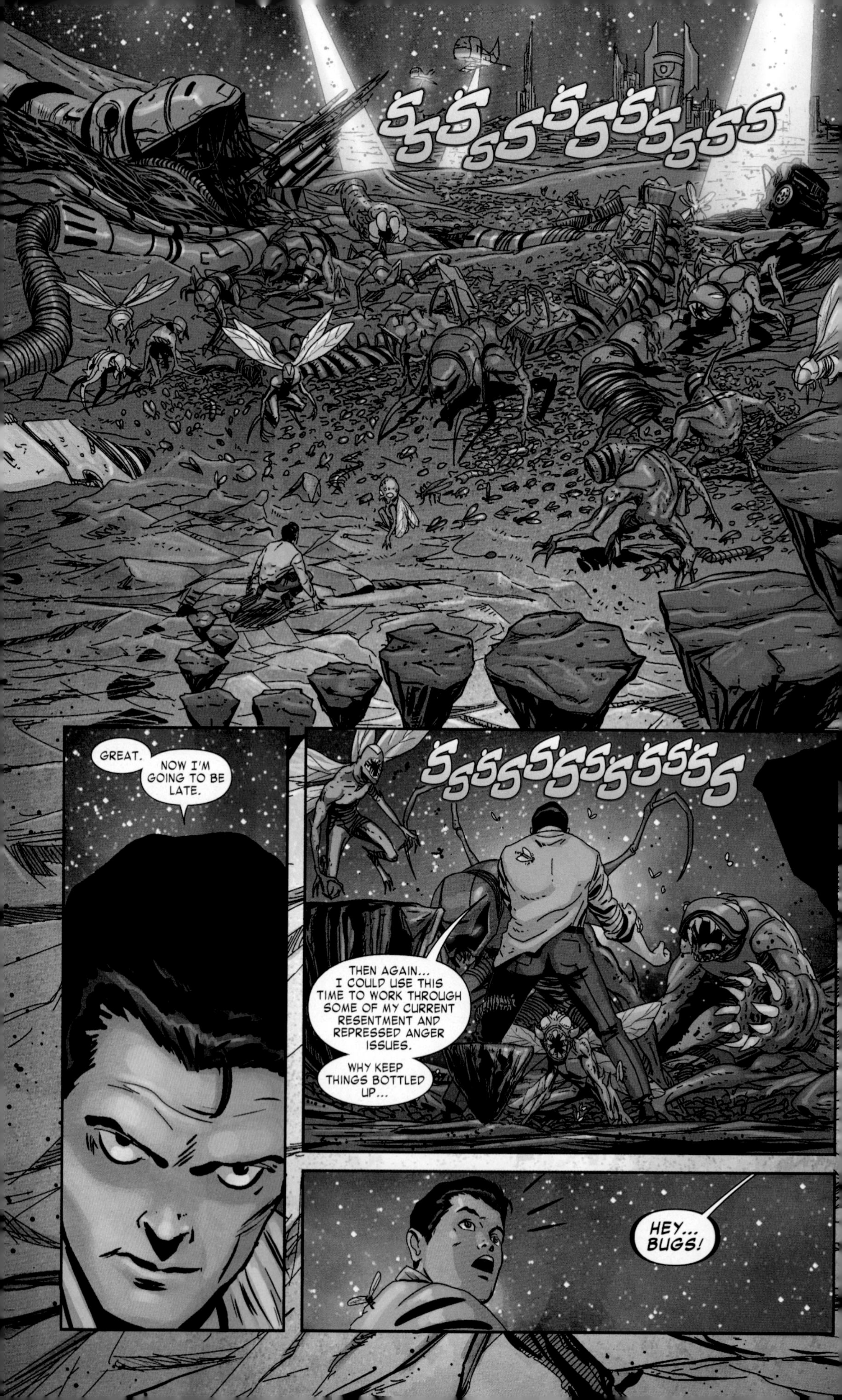
SSSSSSSSSSSSS
GREAT.
NOW I'M GOING TO BE LATE.
SSSSSSSSSSSSS
THEN AGAIN... I COULD USE THIS TIME TO WORK THROUGH SOME OF MY CURRENT RESENTMENT AND REPRESSED ANGER ISSUES.
WHY KEEP THINGS BOTTLED UP...
HEY... BUGS!

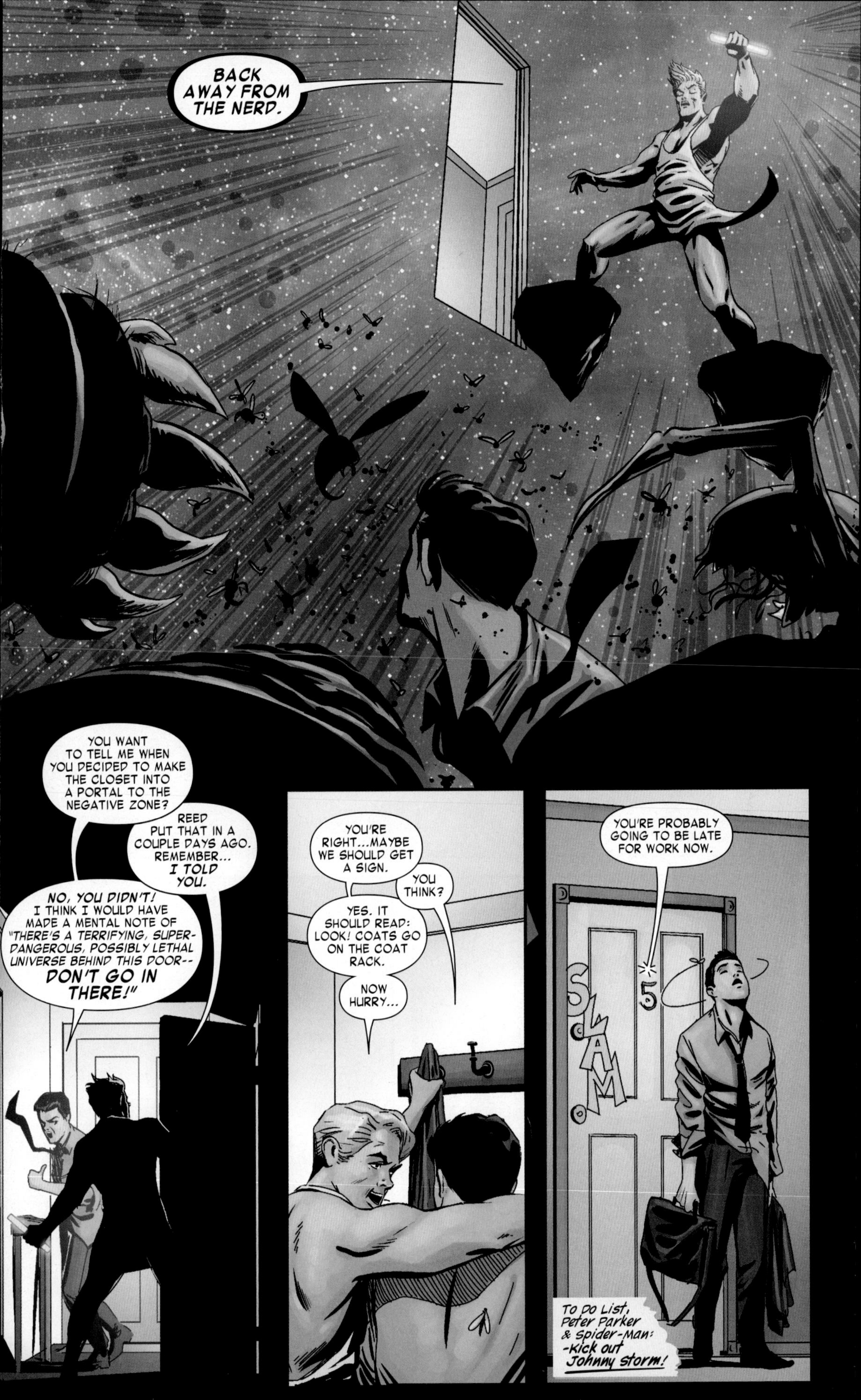
BACK AWAY FROM THE NERD.
YOU WANT TO TELL ME WHEN YOU DECIDED TO MAKE THE CLOSET INTO A PORTAL TO THE NEGATIVE ZONE?
REED PUT THAT IN A COUPLE DAYS AGO. REMEMBER... I TOLD YOU.
NO, YOU DIDN'T! I THINK I WOULD HAVE MADE A MENTAL NOTE OF "THERE'S A TERRIFYING, SUPER-DANGEROUS, POSSIBLY LETHAL UNIVERSE BEHIND THIS DOOR--DON'T GO IN THERE!"
YOU'RE RIGHT...MAYBE WE SHOULD GET A SIGN.
YOU THINK?
YES. IT SHOULD READ: LOOK! COATS GO ON THE COAT RACK.
NOW HURRY...
YOU'RE PROBABLY GOING TO BE LATE FOR WORK NOW.
SLAM
5
To Do List, Peter Parker & Spider-Man: -Kick out Johnny Storm!

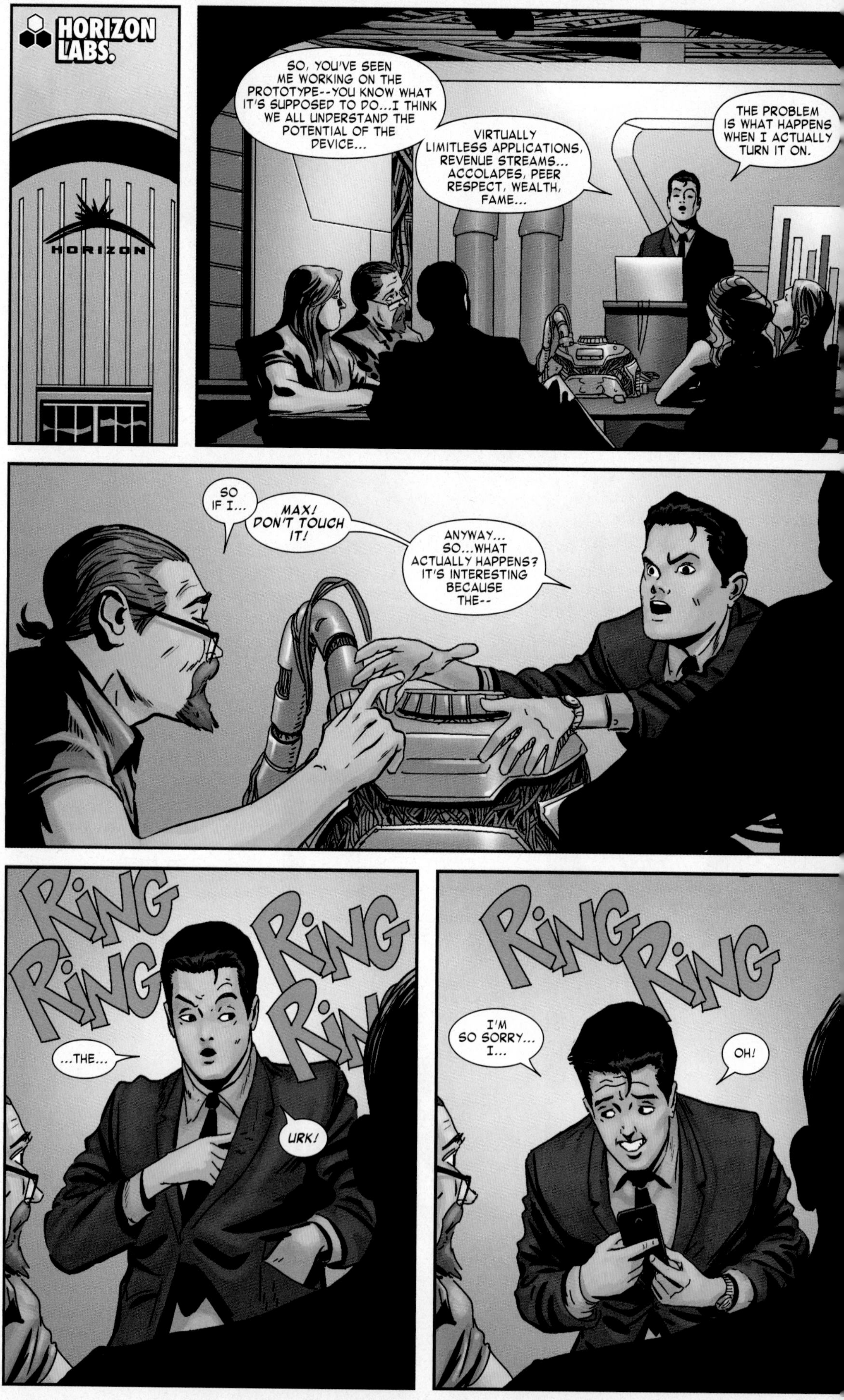
HORIZON LABS.
HORIZON
SO, YOU'VE SEEN ME WORKING ON THE PROTOTYPE--YOU KNOW WHAT IT'S SUPPOSED TO DO...I THINK WE ALL UNDERSTAND THE POTENTIAL OF THE DEVICE...
VIRTUALLY LIMITLESS APPLICATIONS, REVENUE STREAMS... ACCOLADES, PEER RESPECT, WEALTH, FAME...
THE PROBLEM IS WHAT HAPPENS WHEN I ACTUALLY TURN IT ON.
SO IF I...
MAX! DON'T TOUCH IT!
ANYWAY... SO...WHAT ACTUALLY HAPPENS? IT'S INTERESTING BECAUSE THE--
RING RING RING RING
...THE...
URK!
RING RING
I'M SO SORRY... I...
OH!

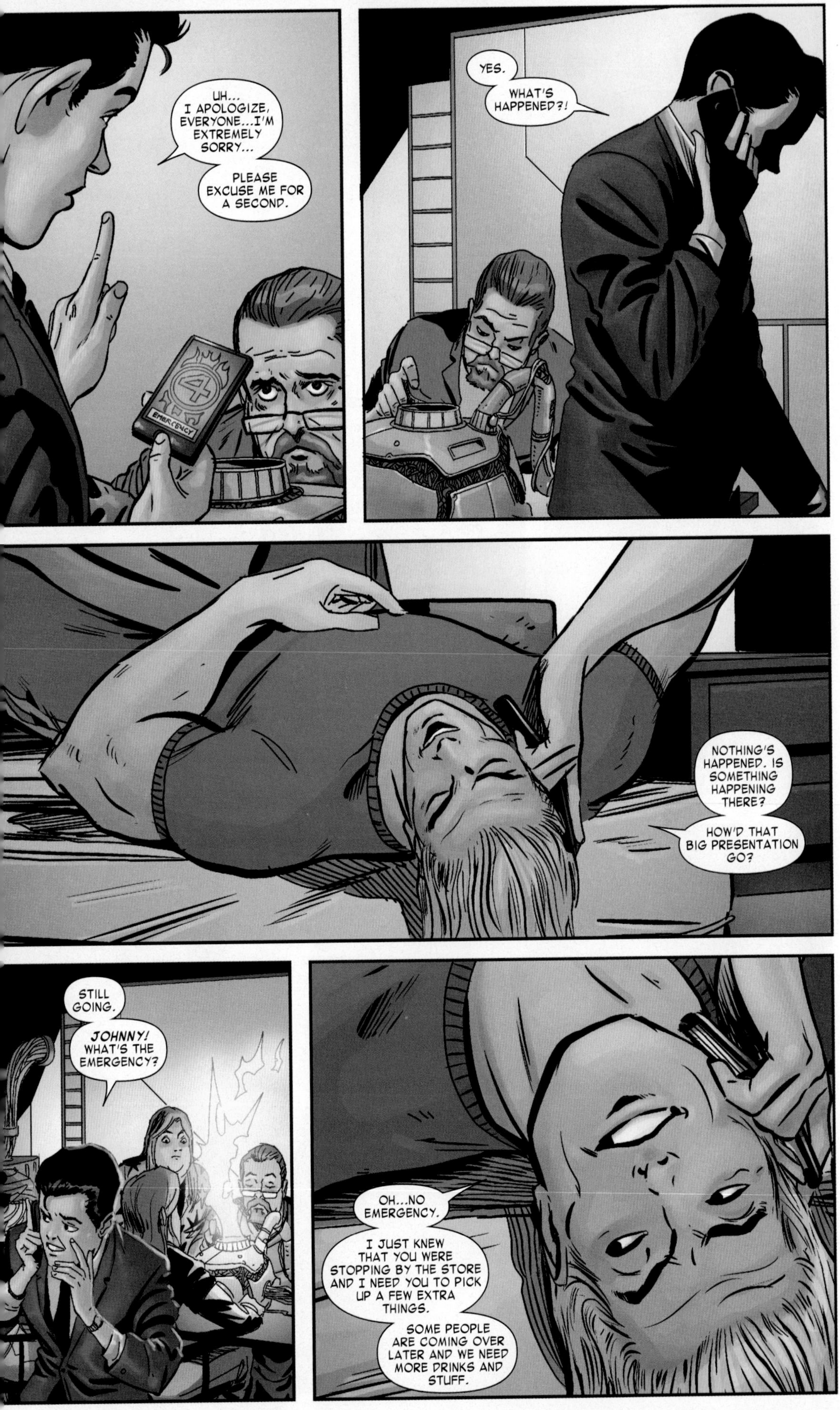
UH... I APOLOGIZE, EVERYONE...I'M EXTREMELY SORRY...
PLEASE EXCUSE ME FOR A SECOND.
EMERGENCY
YES.
WHAT'S HAPPENED?!
NOTHING'S HAPPENED. IS SOMETHING HAPPENING THERE?
HOW'D THAT BIG PRESENTATION GO?
STILL GOING.
JOHNNY! WHAT'S THE EMERGENCY?
OH...NO EMERGENCY.
I JUST KNEW THAT YOU WERE STOPPING BY THE STORE AND I NEED YOU TO PICK UP A FEW EXTRA THINGS.
SOME PEOPLE ARE COMING OVER LATER AND WE NEED MORE DRINKS AND STUFF.

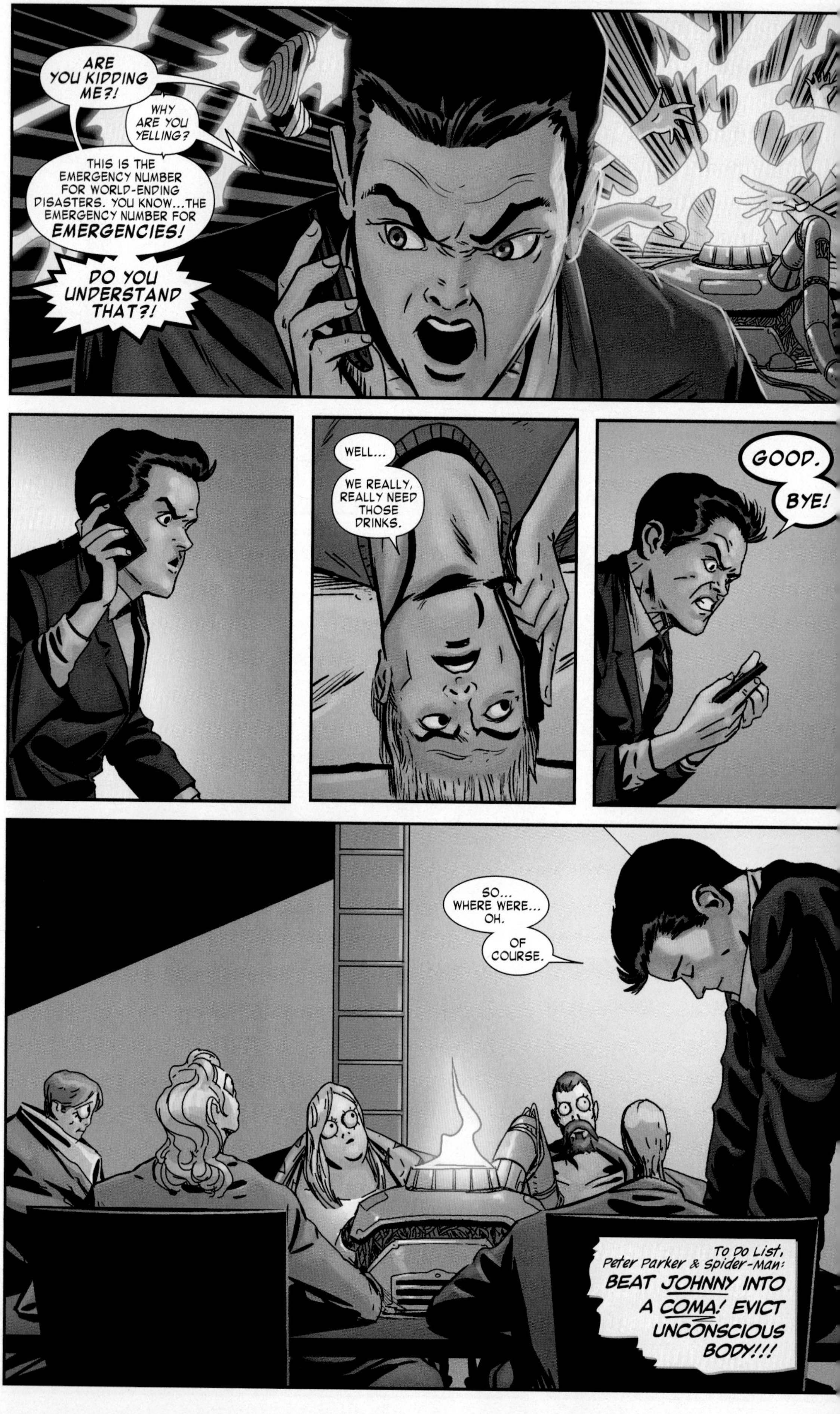
ARE YOU KIDDING ME?!
WHY ARE YOU YELLING?
THIS IS THE EMERGENCY NUMBER FOR WORLD-ENDING DISASTERS. YOU KNOW...THE EMERGENCY NUMBER FOR EMERGENCIES!
DO YOU UNDERSTAND THAT?!
WELL...
WE REALLY, REALLY NEED THOSE DRINKS.
GOOD.
BYE!
SO... WHERE WERE... OH.
OF COURSE.
To Do List, Peter Parker & Spider-Man:
BEAT JOHNNY INTO A COMA! EVICT UNCONSCIOUS BODY!!!

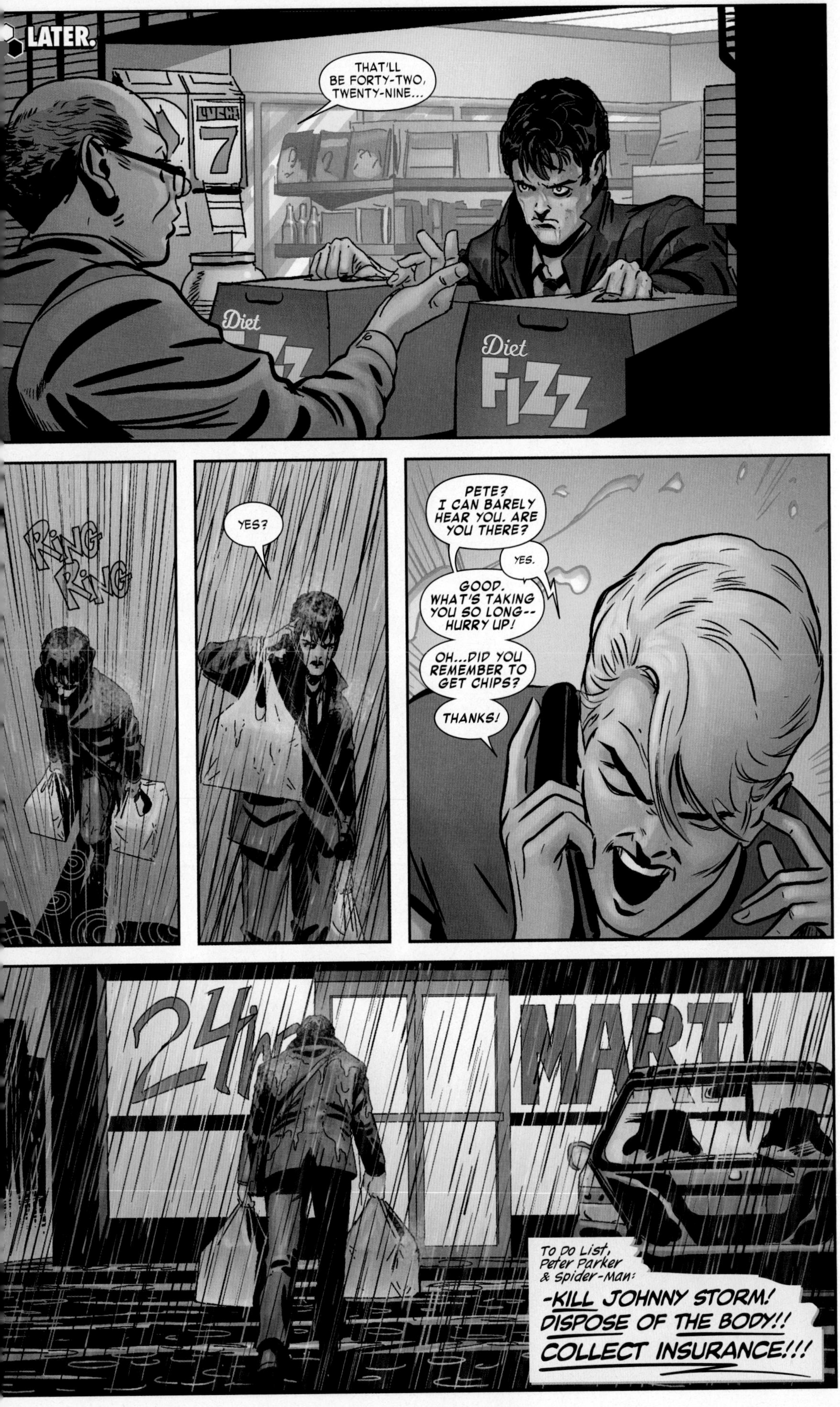
LATER.
THAT'LL BE FORTY-TWO, TWENTY-NINE...
Diet FIZZ
Diet FIZZ
RING RING
YES?
PETE? I CAN BARELY HEAR YOU. ARE YOU THERE?
YES.
GOOD. WHAT'S TAKING YOU SO LONG-- HURRY UP!
OH...DID YOU REMEMBER TO GET CHIPS?
THANKS!
24hr MART
To Do List, Peter Parker & Spider-Man:
-KILL JOHNNY STORM!
DISPOSE OF THE BODY!!
COLLECT INSURANCE!!!

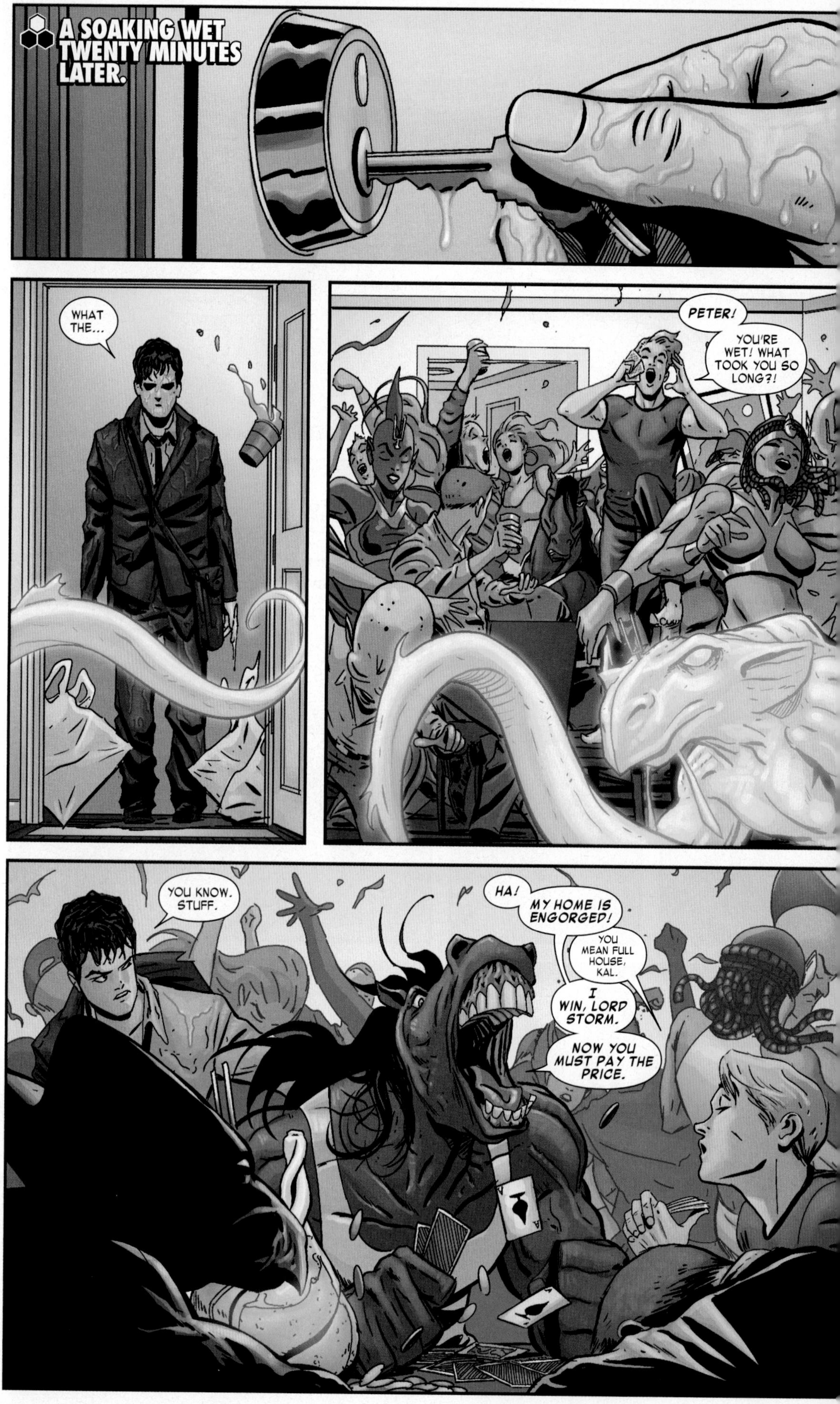
A SOAKING WET TWENTY MINUTES LATER.
WHAT THE...
PETER!
YOU'RE WET! WHAT TOOK YOU SO LONG?!
YOU KNOW. STUFF.
HA!
MY HOME IS ENGORGED!
YOU MEAN FULL HOUSE, KAL.
I WIN, LORD STORM.
NOW YOU MUST PAY THE PRICE.

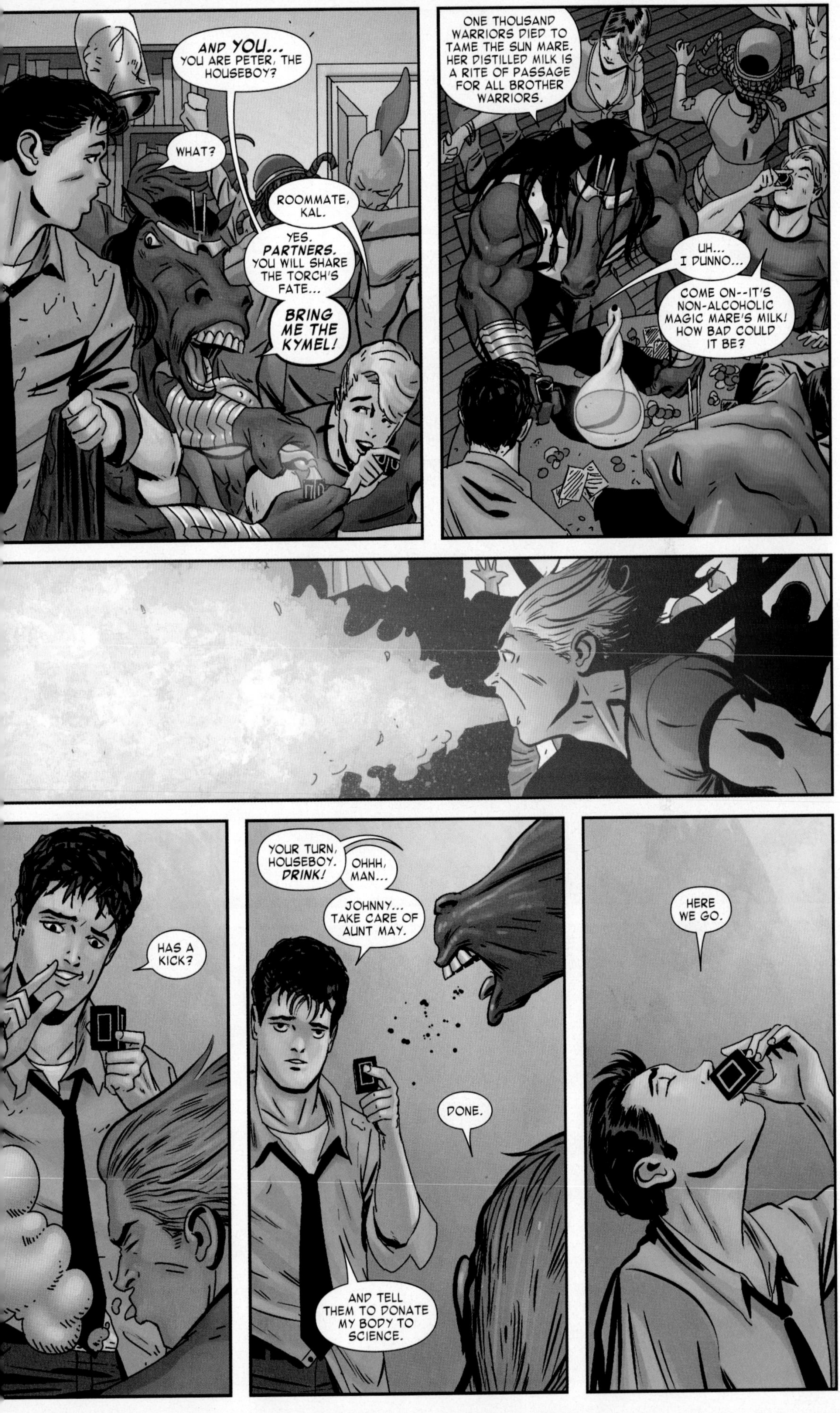
AND YOU... YOU ARE PETER, THE HOUSEBOY?
WHAT?
ROOMMATE, KAL.
YES. PARTNERS. YOU WILL SHARE THE TORCH'S FATE...
BRING ME THE KYMEL!
ONE THOUSAND WARRIORS DIED TO TAME THE SUN MARE. HER DISTILLED MILK IS A RITE OF PASSAGE FOR ALL BROTHER WARRIORS.
UH... I DUNNO...
COME ON--IT'S NON-ALCOHOLIC MAGIC MARE'S MILK! HOW BAD COULD IT BE?
HAS A KICK?
YOUR TURN, HOUSEBOY. DRINK!
OHHH, MAN...
JOHNNY... TAKE CARE OF AUNT MAY.
DONE.
AND TELL THEM TO DONATE MY BODY TO SCIENCE.
HERE WE GO.

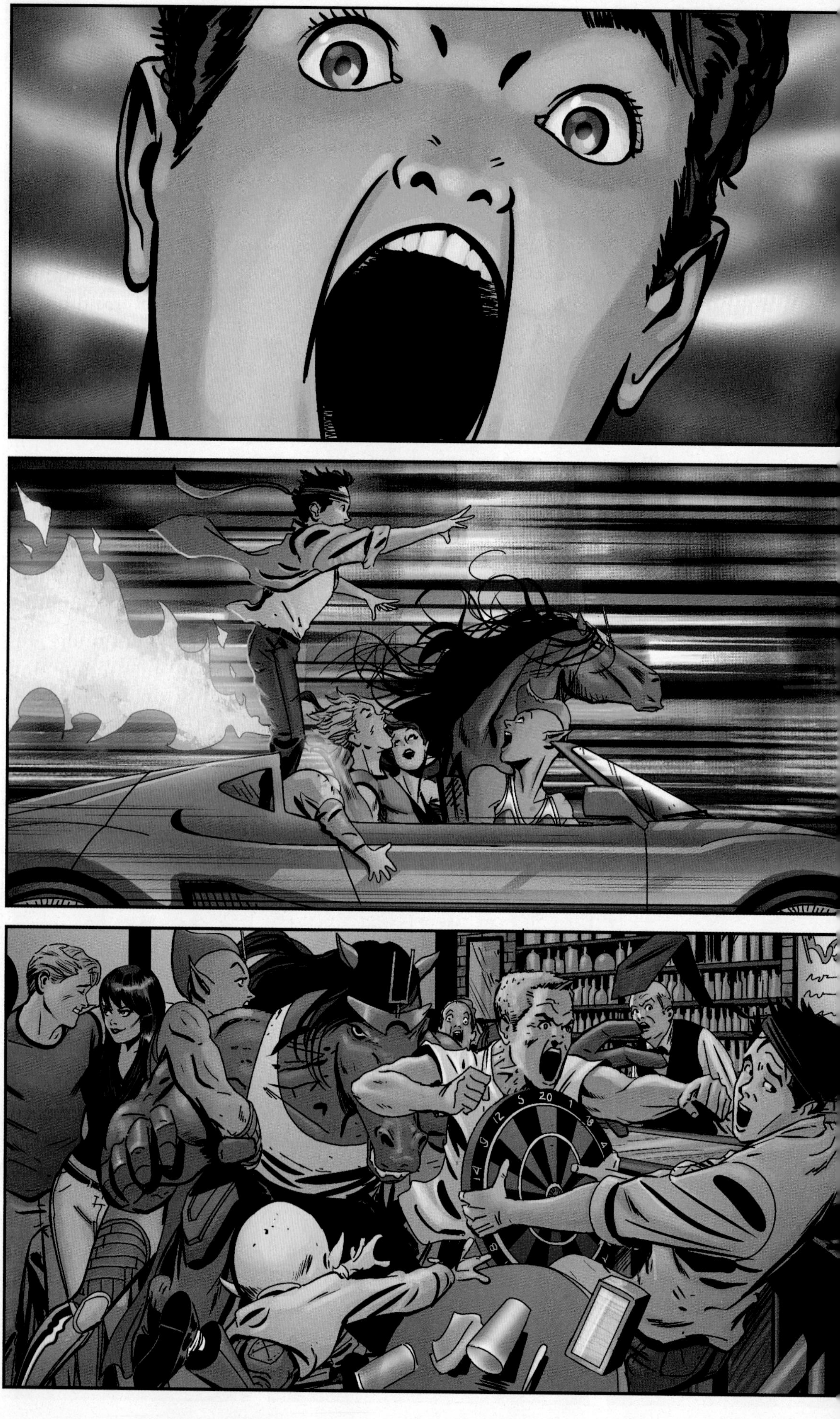

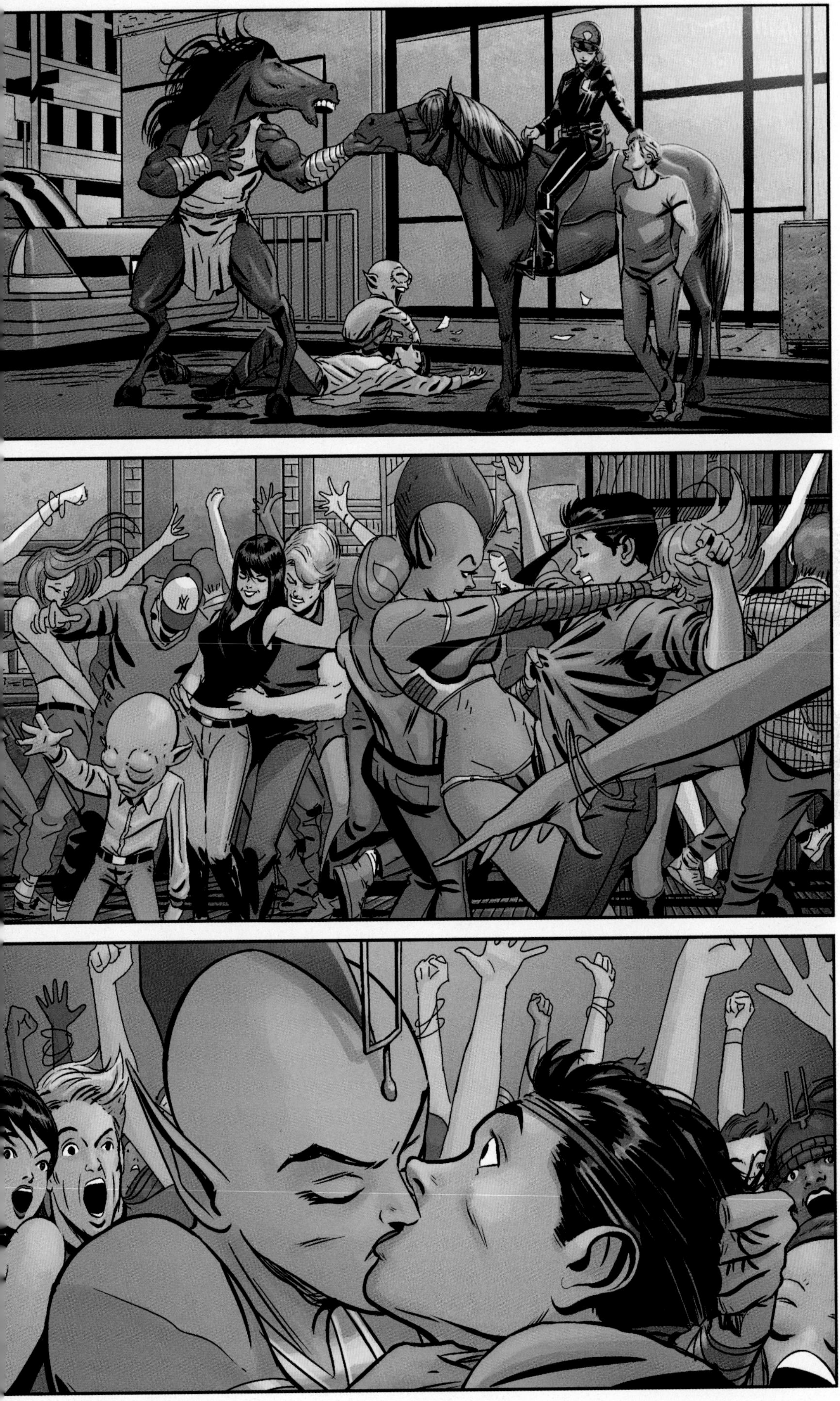

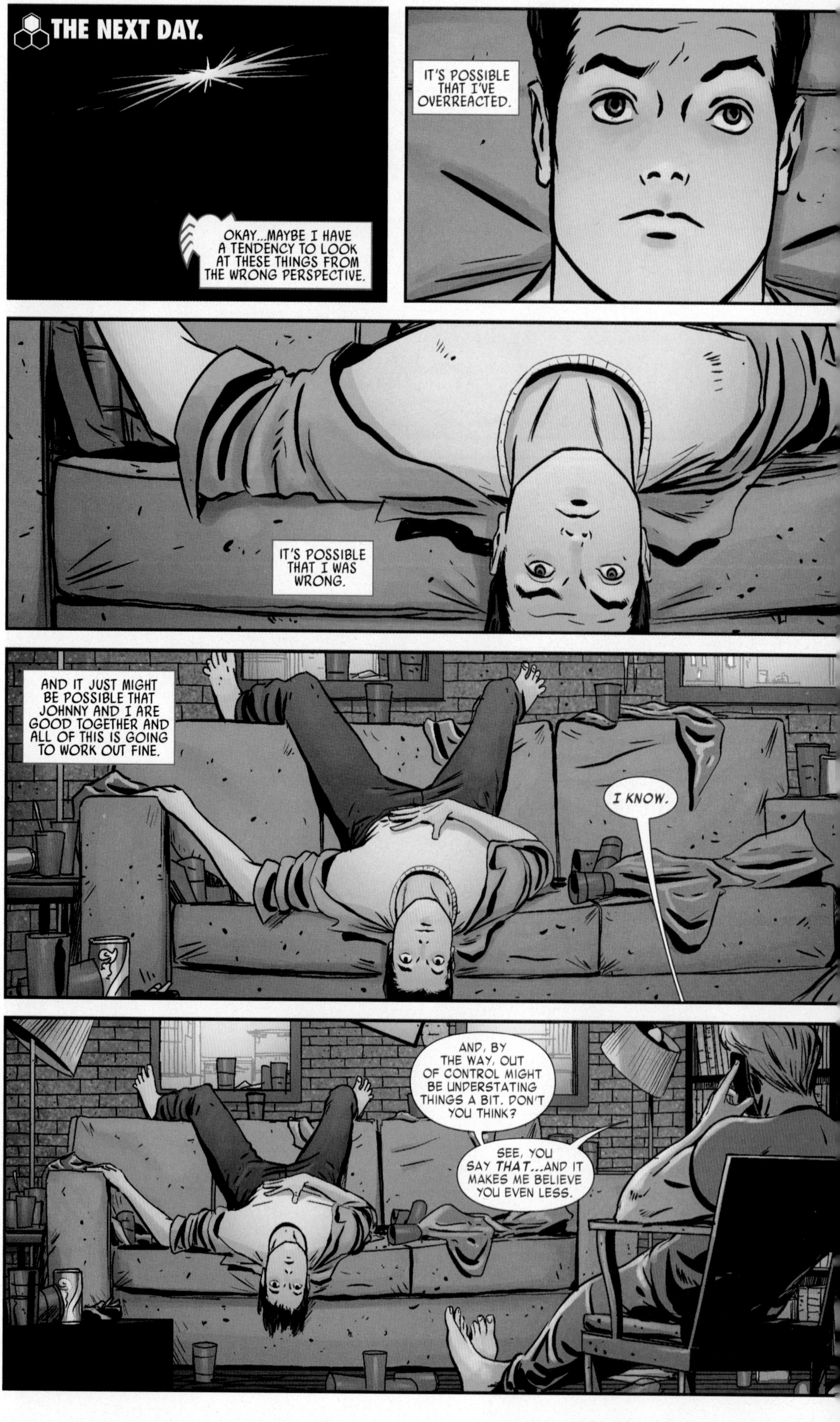
THE NEXT DAY.
OKAY...MAYBE I HAVE A TENDENCY TO LOOK AT THESE THINGS FROM THE WRONG PERSPECTIVE.
IT'S POSSIBLE THAT I'VE OVERREACTED.
IT'S POSSIBLE THAT I WAS WRONG.
AND IT JUST MIGHT BE POSSIBLE THAT JOHNNY AND I ARE GOOD TOGETHER AND ALL OF THIS IS GOING TO WORK OUT FINE.
I KNOW.
AND, BY THE WAY, OUT OF CONTROL MIGHT BE UNDERSTATING THINGS A BIT. DON'T YOU THINK?
SEE, YOU SAY THAT...AND IT MAKES ME BELIEVE YOU EVEN LESS.

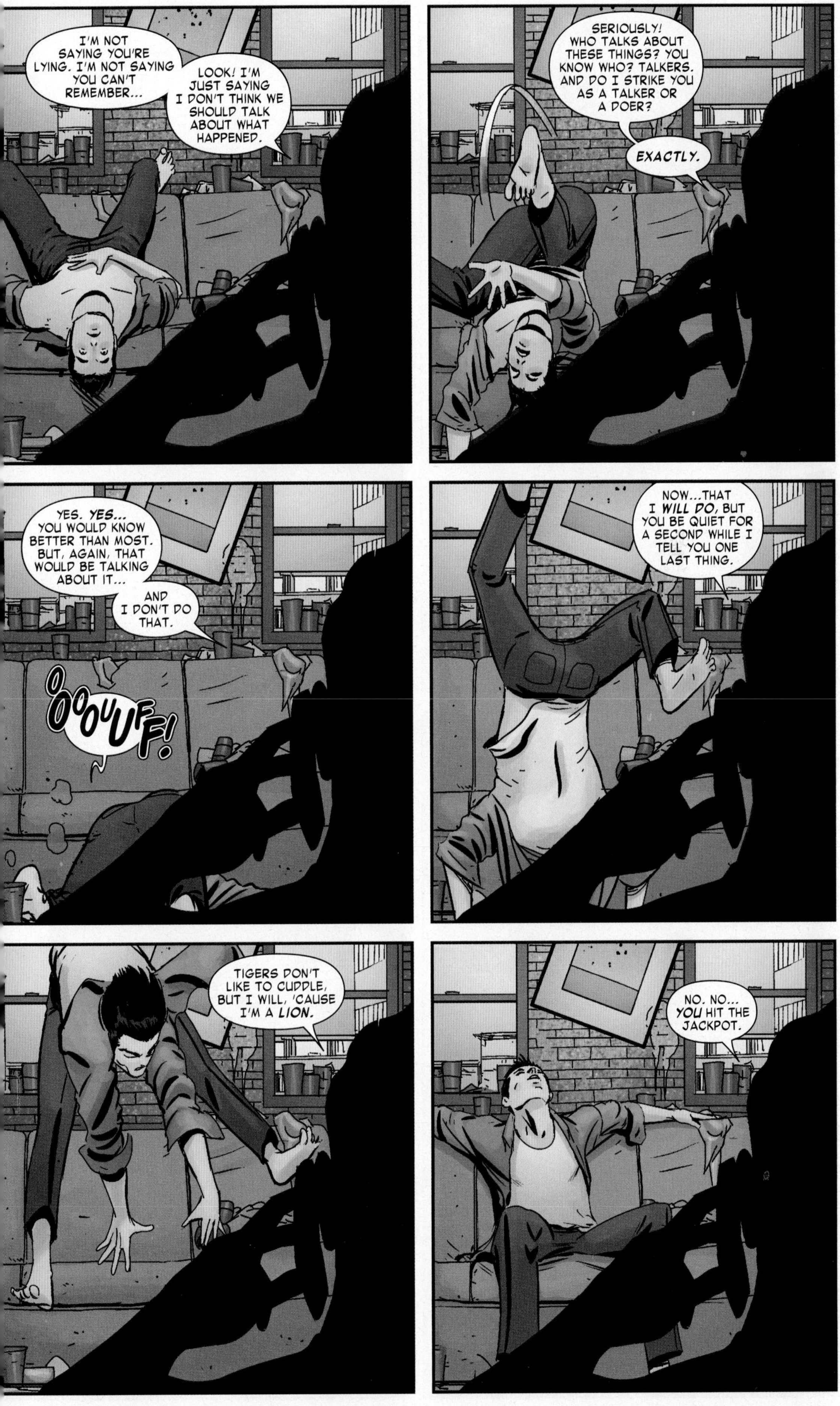
I'M NOT SAYING YOU'RE LYING. I'M NOT SAYING YOU CAN'T REMEMBER...
LOOK! I'M JUST SAYING I DON'T THINK WE SHOULD TALK ABOUT WHAT HAPPENED.
SERIOUSLY! WHO TALKS ABOUT THESE THINGS? YOU KNOW WHO? TALKERS. AND DO I STRIKE YOU AS A TALKER OR A DOER?
EXACTLY.
YES. YES... YOU WOULD KNOW BETTER THAN MOST. BUT, AGAIN, THAT WOULD BE TALKING ABOUT IT...
AND I DON'T DO THAT.
OOOUUFF!
NOW...THAT I WILL DO, BUT YOU BE QUIET FOR A SECOND WHILE I TELL YOU ONE LAST THING.
TIGERS DON'T LIKE TO CUDDLE, BUT I WILL, 'CAUSE I'M A LION.
NO. NO... YOU HIT THE JACKPOT.

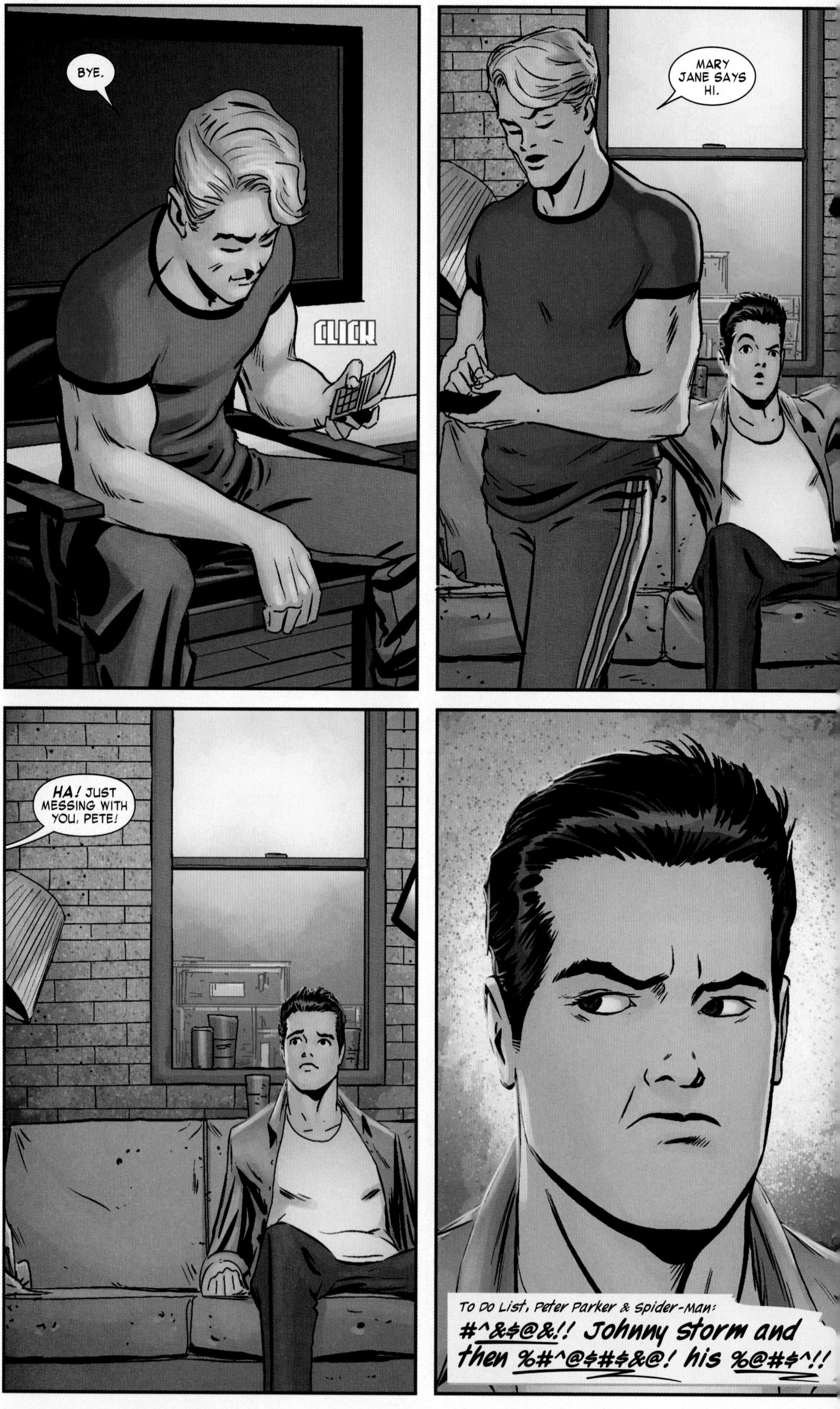
BYE.
CLICK
MARY JANE SAYS HI.
HA! JUST MESSING WITH YOU, PETE!
To Do List, Peter Parker & Spider-Man:
#^&$@&!! Johnny Storm and then %#^@$#$&@! his %@#$^!!

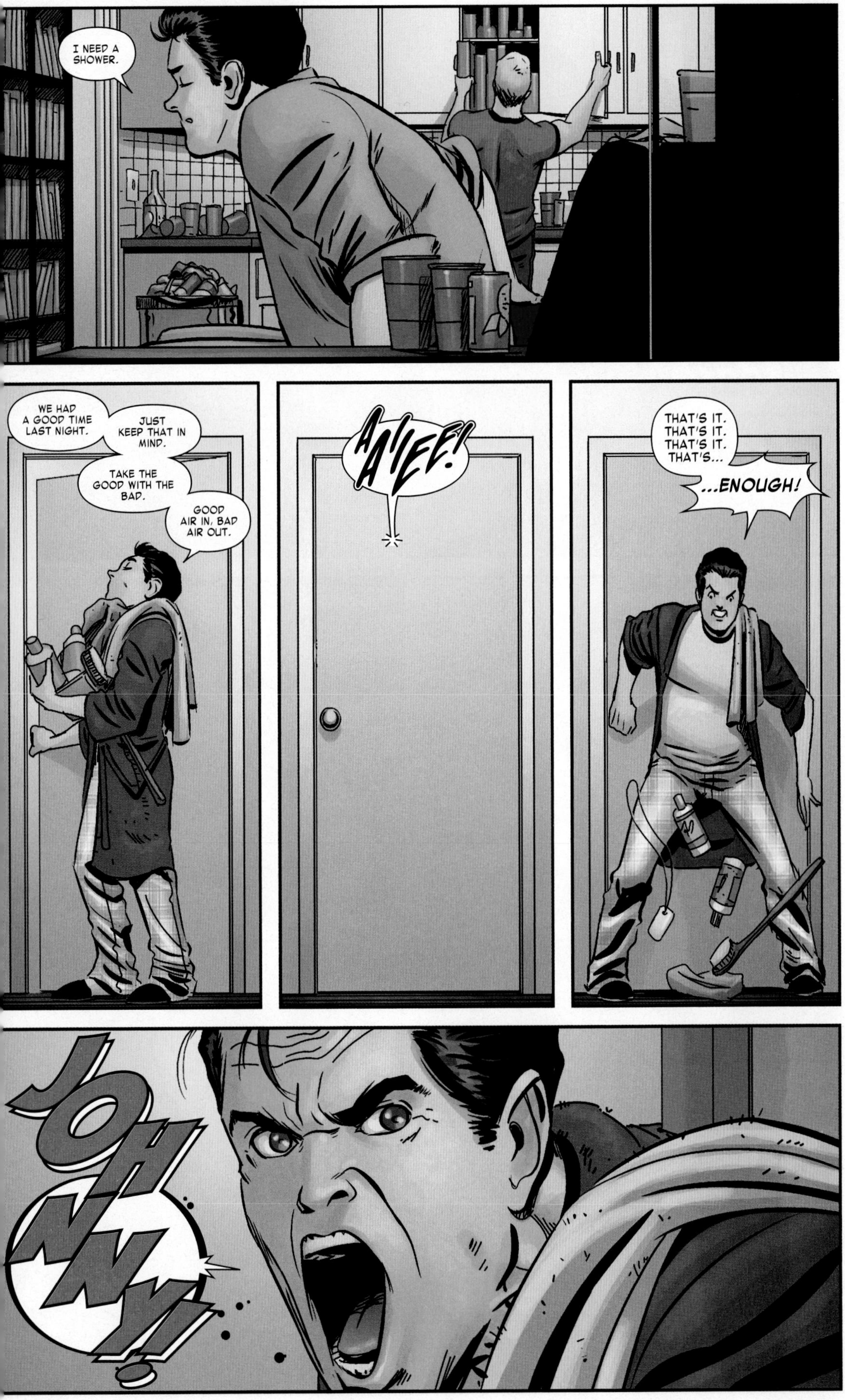
I NEED A SHOWER.
WE HAD A GOOD TIME LAST NIGHT.
JUST KEEP THAT IN MIND.
TAKE THE GOOD WITH THE BAD.
GOOD AIR IN, BAD AIR OUT.
AAIEE!
THAT'S IT. THAT'S IT. THAT'S IT. THAT'S...
...ENOUGH!
JOHNNY!

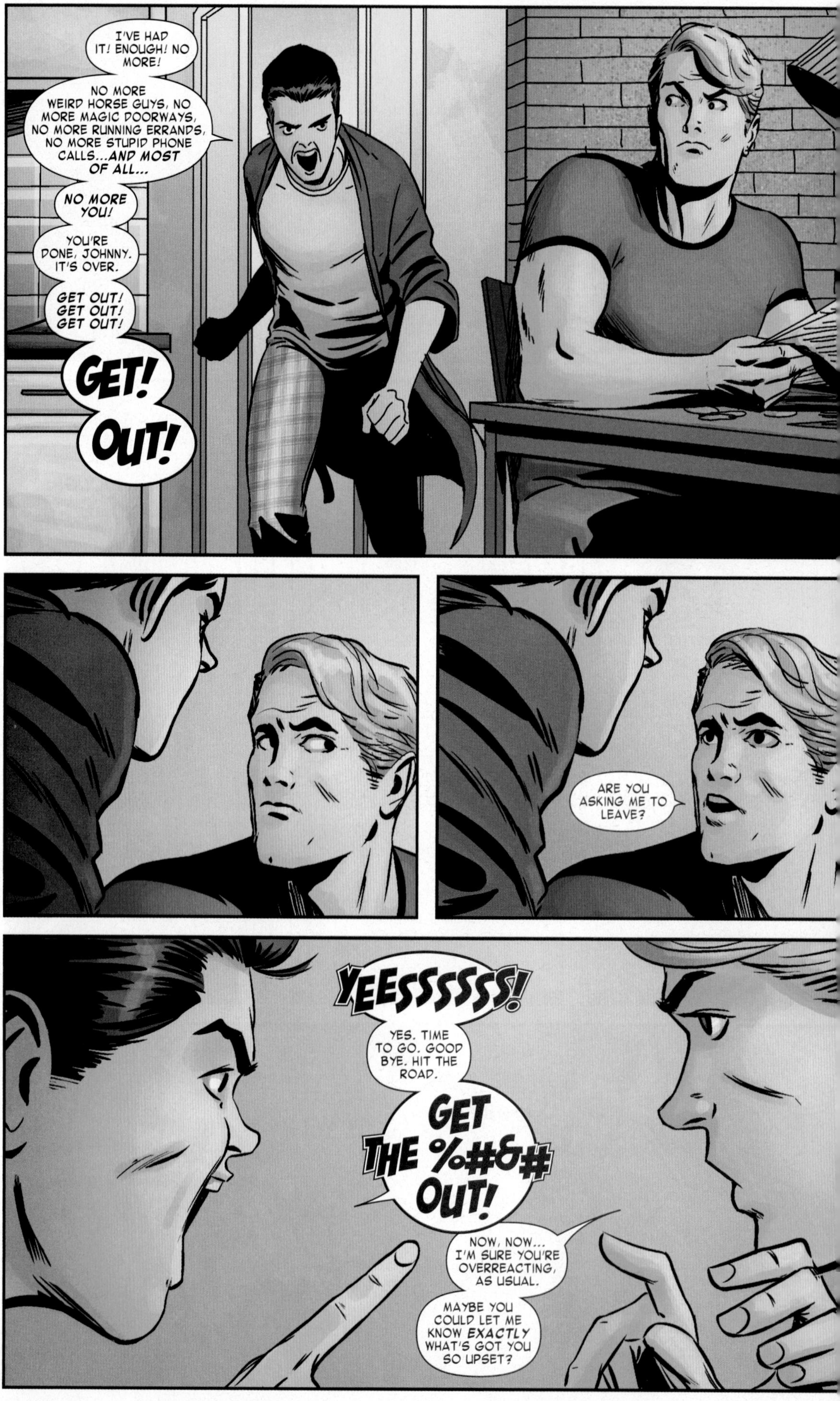
I'VE HAD IT! ENOUGH! NO MORE!
NO MORE WEIRD HORSE GUYS, NO MORE MAGIC DOORWAYS, NO MORE RUNNING ERRANDS, NO MORE STUPID PHONE CALLS...AND MOST OF ALL...
NO MORE YOU!
YOU'RE DONE, JOHNNY. IT'S OVER.
GET OUT! GET OUT! GET OUT!
GET! OUT!
ARE YOU ASKING ME TO LEAVE?
YEESSSSSS!
YES. TIME TO GO. GOOD BYE. HIT THE ROAD.
GET THE %#&# OUT!
NOW, NOW... I'M SURE YOU'RE OVERREACTING, AS USUAL.
MAYBE YOU COULD LET ME KNOW EXACTLY WHAT'S GOT YOU SO UPSET?

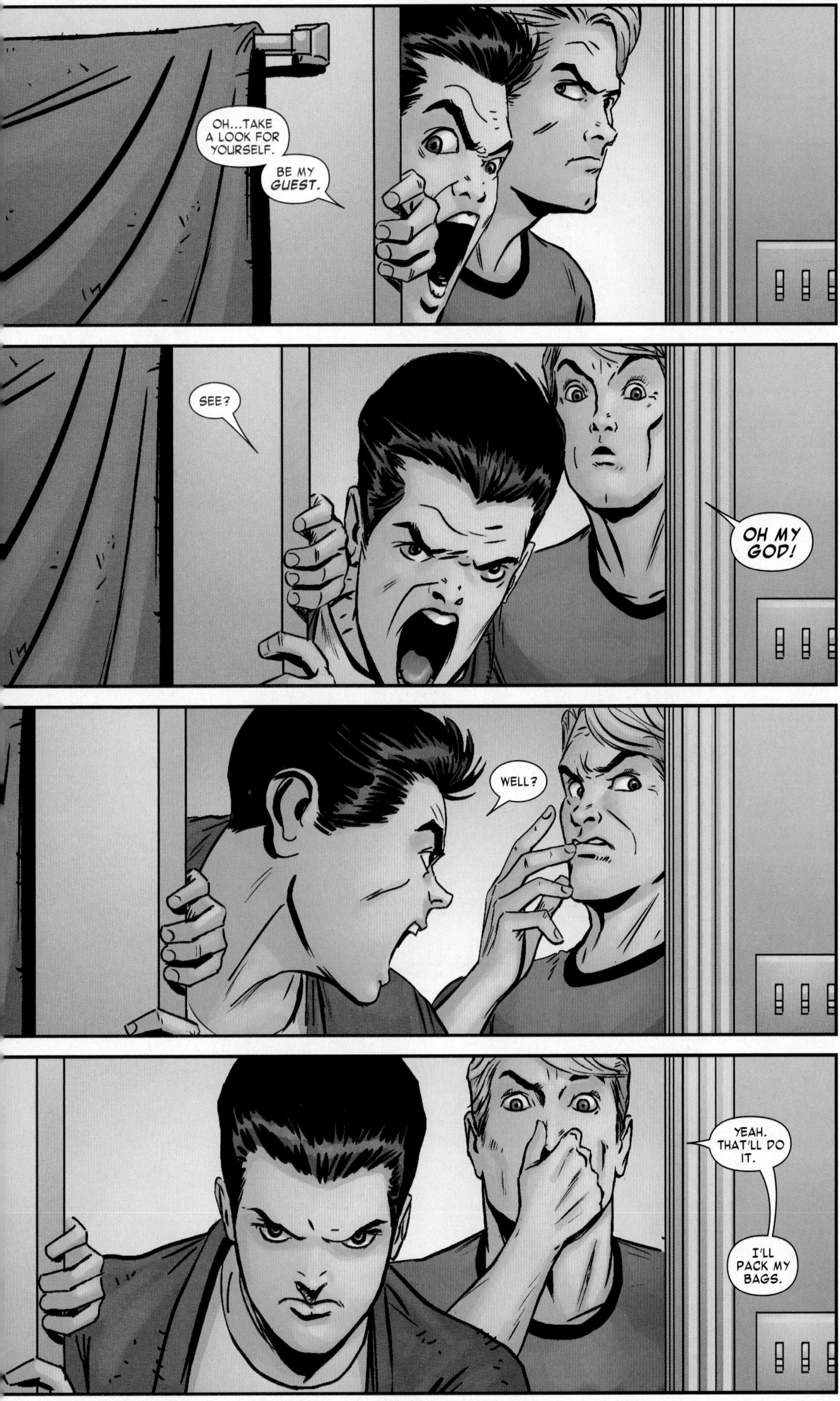
OH...TAKE A LOOK FOR YOURSELF.
BE MY GUEST.
SEE?
OH MY GOD!
WELL?
YEAH. THAT'LL DO IT.
I'LL PACK MY BAGS.

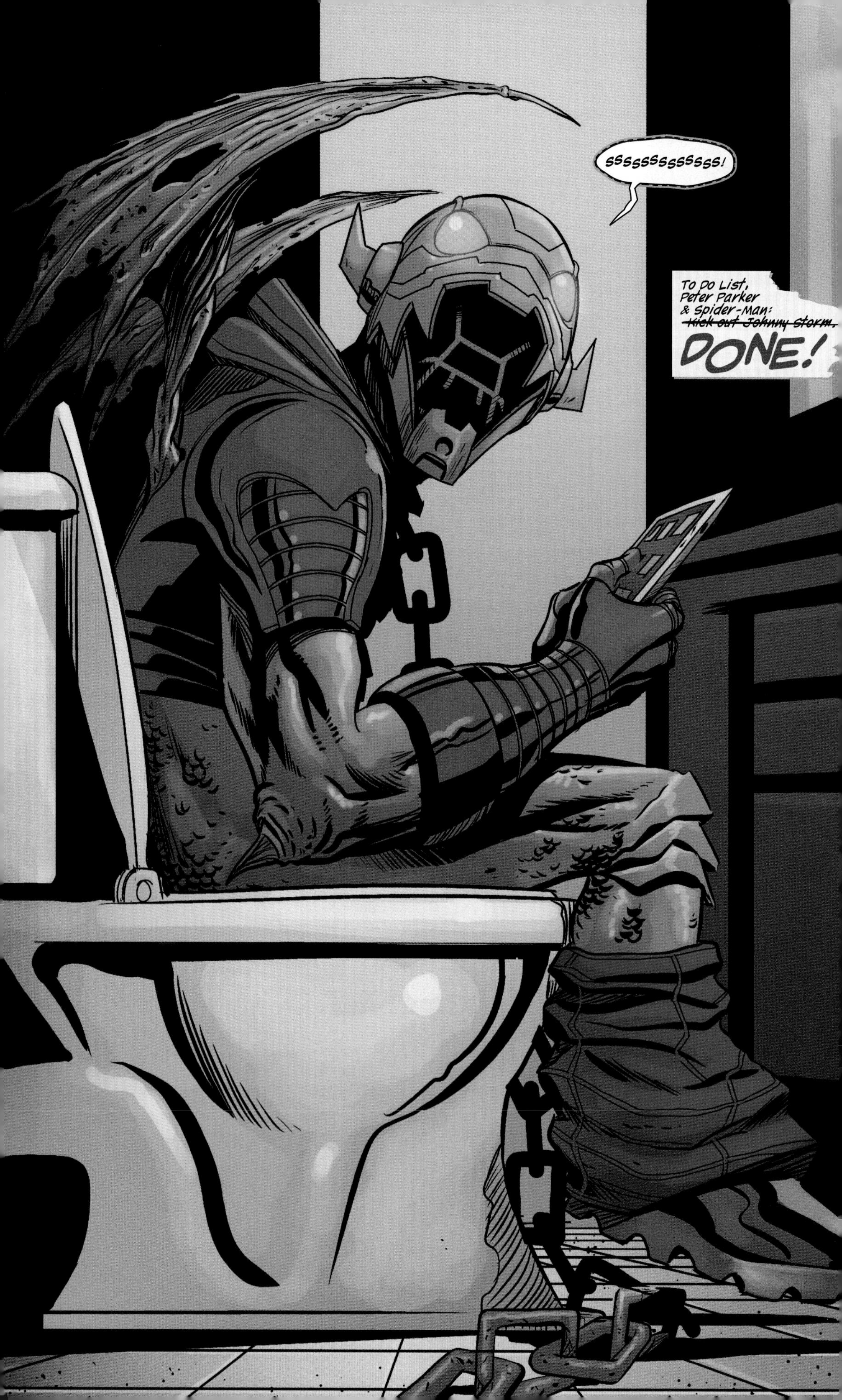
SSSSSSSSSSSSSS!
To Do List, Peter Parker & Spider-Man:
Kick out Johnny Storm.
DONE!

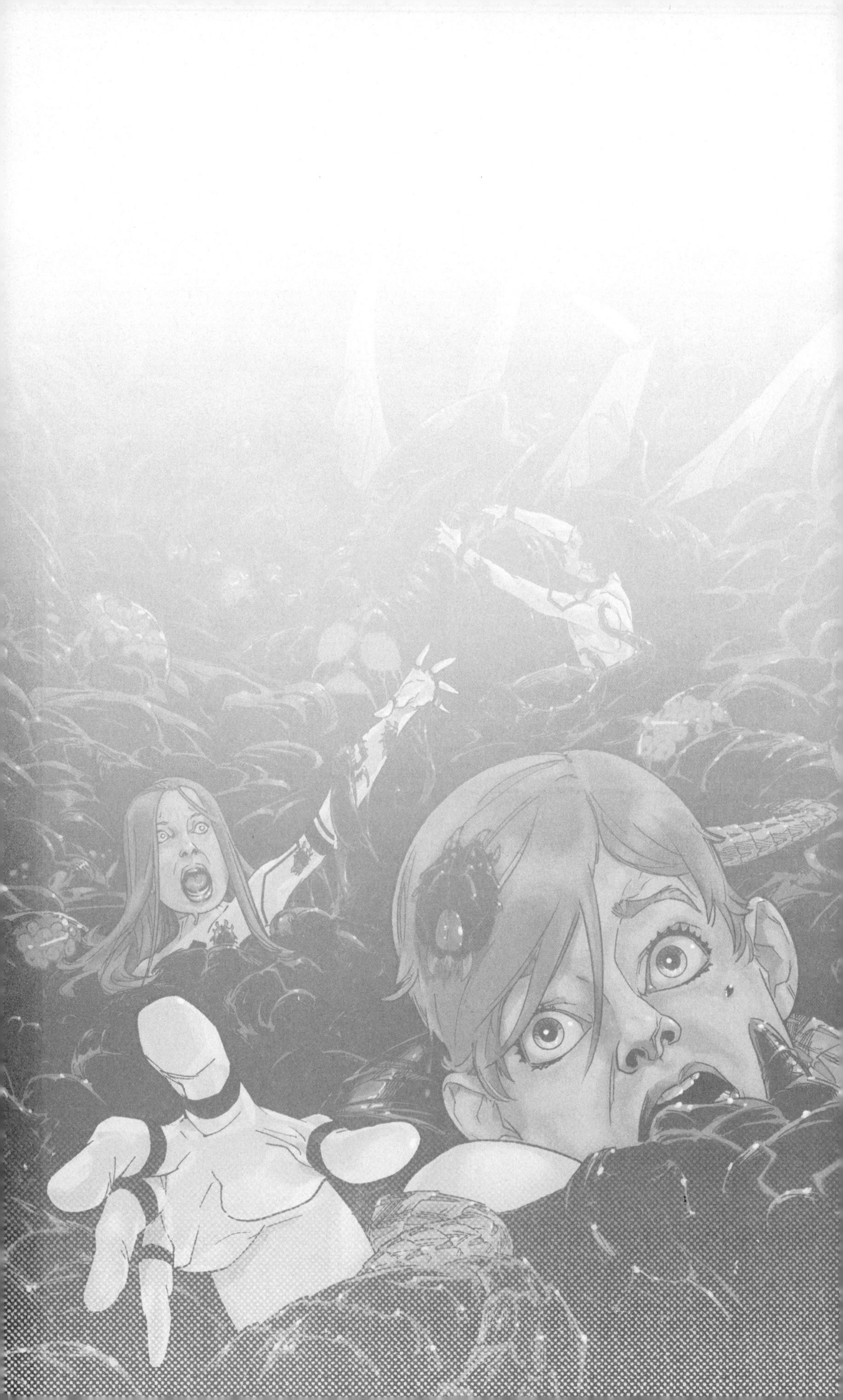

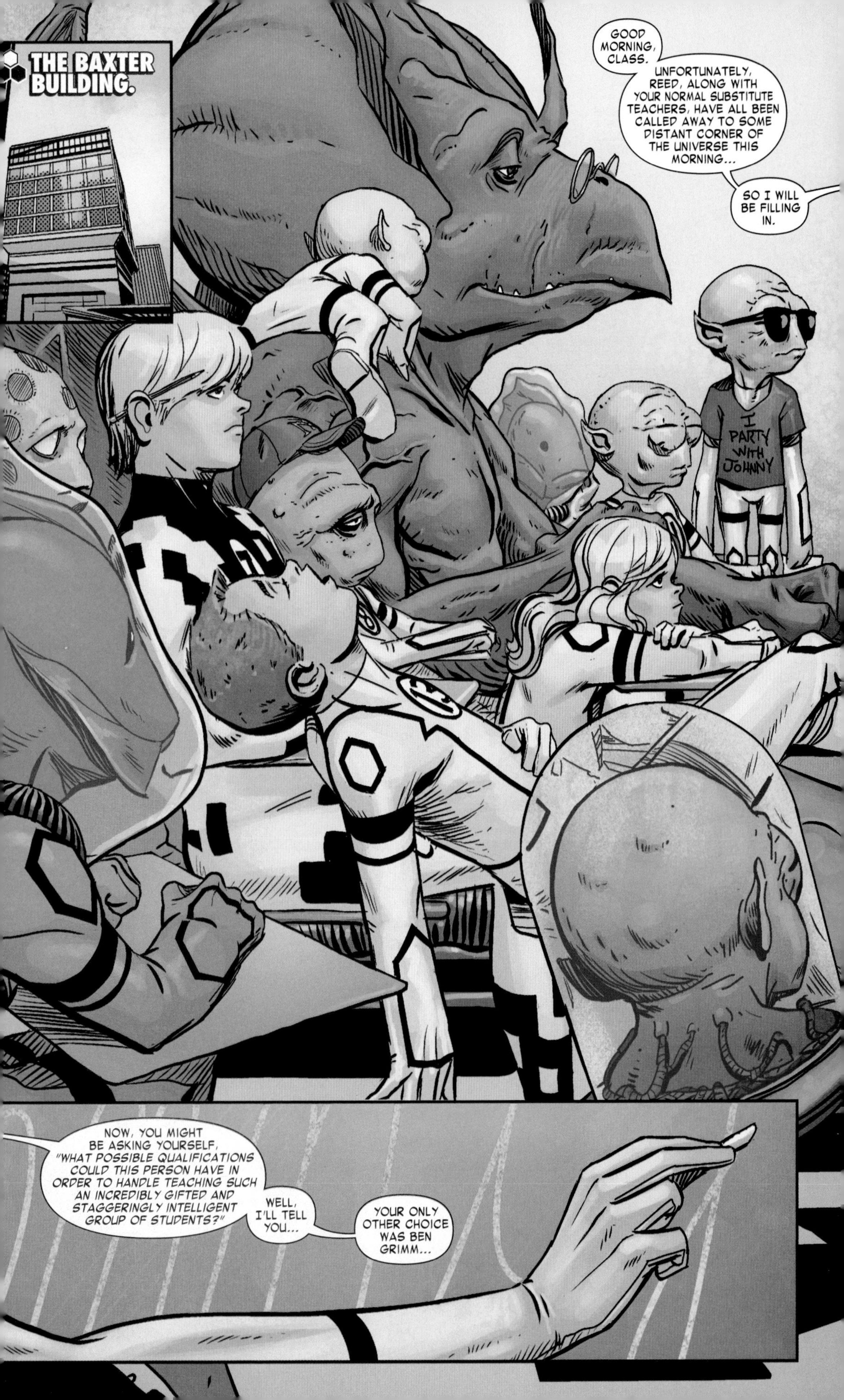
THE BAXTER BUILDING.
GOOD MORNING, CLASS.
UNFORTUNATELY, REED, ALONG WITH YOUR NORMAL SUBSTITUTE TEACHERS, HAVE ALL BEEN CALLED AWAY TO SOME DISTANT CORNER OF THE UNIVERSE THIS MORNING...
SO I WILL BE FILLING IN.
I PARTY WITH JOHNNY
NOW, YOU MIGHT BE ASKING YOURSELF, "WHAT POSSIBLE QUALIFICATIONS COULD THIS PERSON HAVE IN ORDER TO HANDLE TEACHING SUCH AN INCREDIBLY GIFTED AND STAGGERINGLY INTELLIGENT GROUP OF STUDENTS?"
WELL, I'LL TELL YOU...
YOUR ONLY OTHER CHOICE WAS BEN GRIMM...

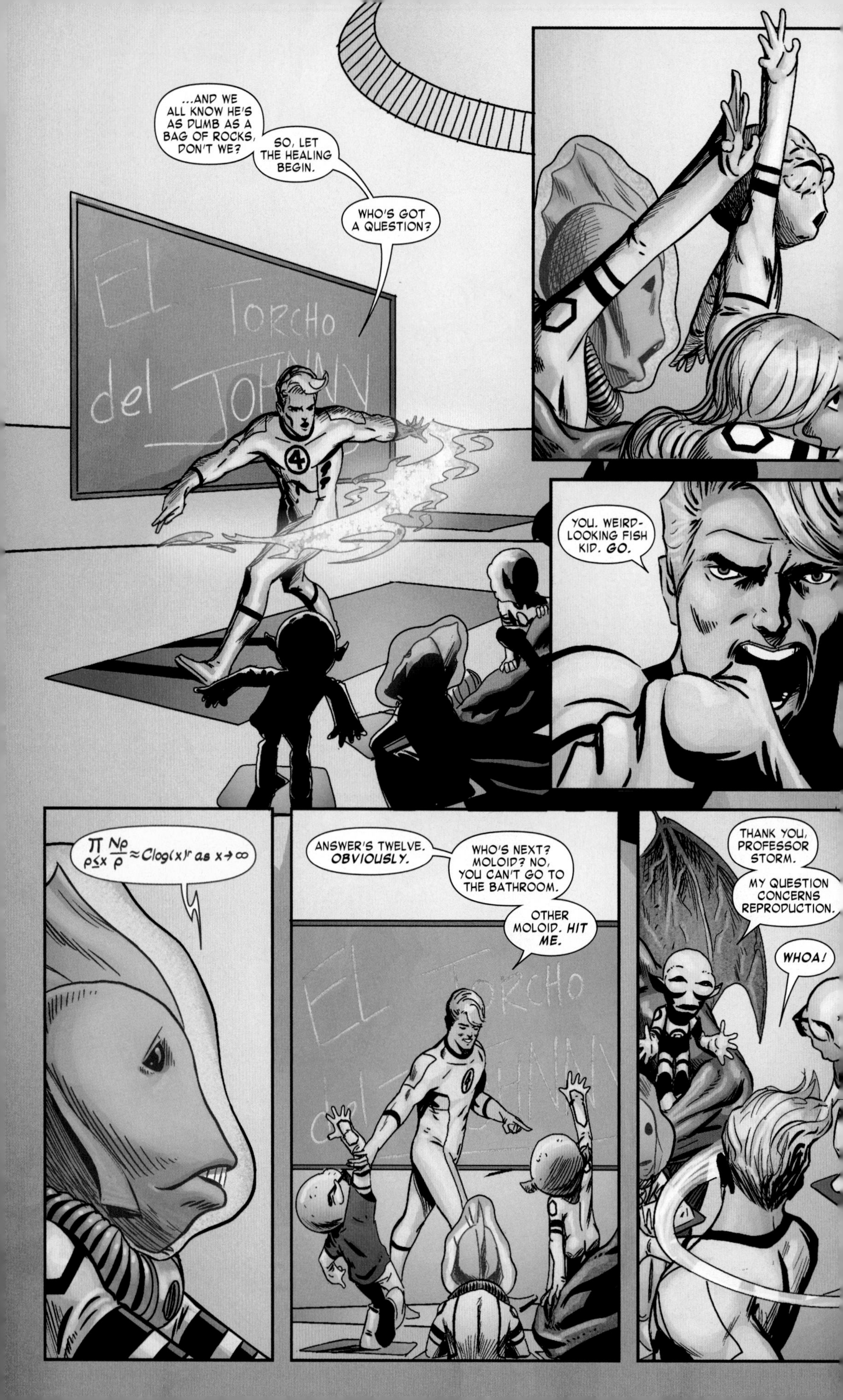

...AND WE ALL KNOW HE'S AS DUMB AS A BAG OF ROCKS, DON'T WE?
SO, LET THE HEALING BEGIN.
WHO'S GOT A QUESTION?
EL TORCHO del JOHNNY
YOU. WEIRD-LOOKING FISH KID. GO.
$\prod_{p \leq x} \frac{N_p}{p} \approx C \log(x)^r$ as $x \to \infty$
ANSWER'S TWELVE. OBVIOUSLY.
WHO'S NEXT? MOLOID? NO, YOU CAN'T GO TO THE BATHROOM.
OTHER MOLOID. HIT ME.
THANK YOU, PROFESSOR STORM.
MY QUESTION CONCERNS REPRODUCTION.
WHOA!

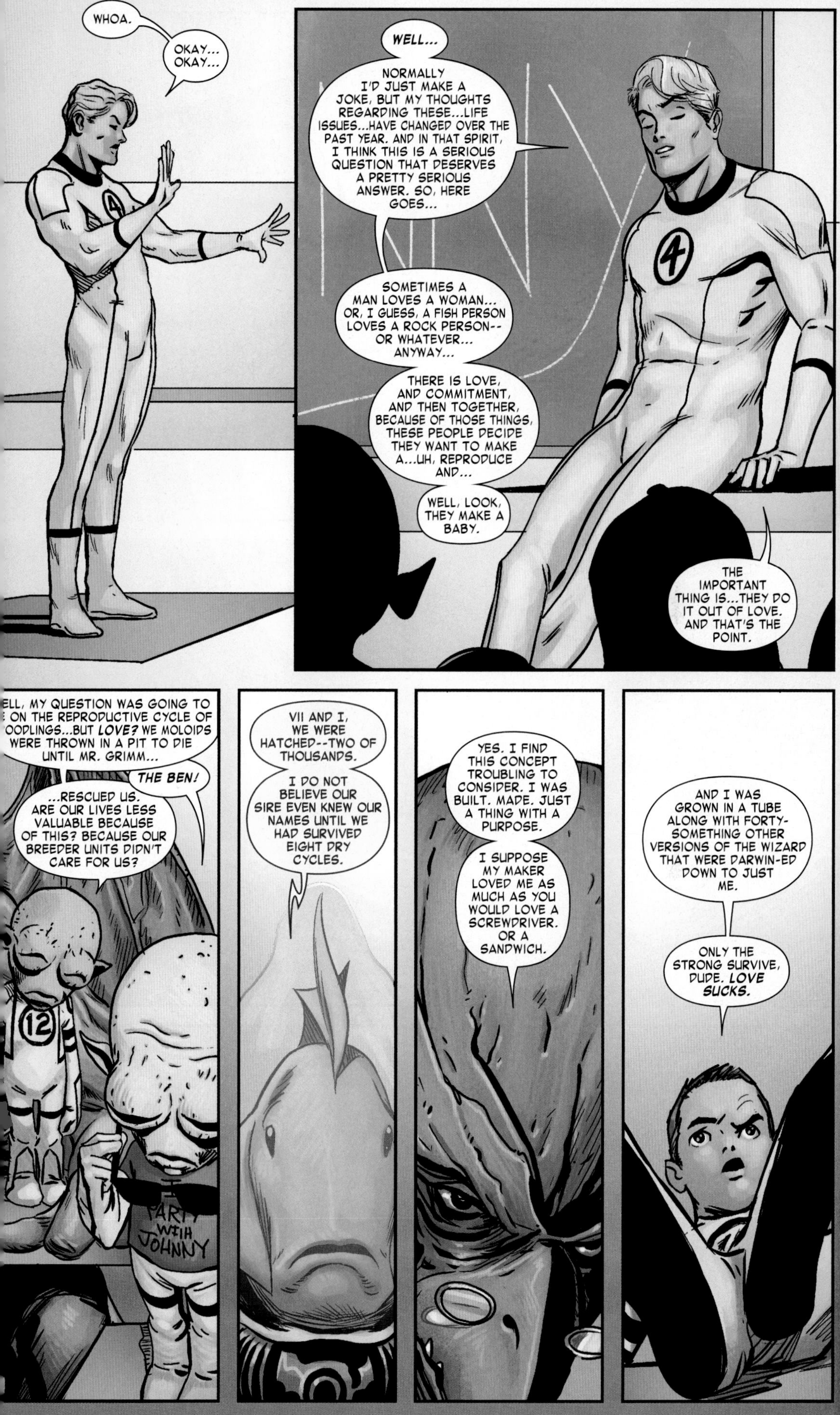
WHOA.
OKAY... OKAY...
WELL...
NORMALLY I'D JUST MAKE A JOKE, BUT MY THOUGHTS REGARDING THESE...LIFE ISSUES...HAVE CHANGED OVER THE PAST YEAR. AND IN THAT SPIRIT, I THINK THIS IS A SERIOUS QUESTION THAT DESERVES A PRETTY SERIOUS ANSWER. SO, HERE GOES...
SOMETIMES A MAN LOVES A WOMAN... OR, I GUESS, A FISH PERSON LOVES A ROCK PERSON-- OR WHATEVER... ANYWAY...
THERE IS LOVE, AND COMMITMENT, AND THEN TOGETHER, BECAUSE OF THOSE THINGS, THESE PEOPLE DECIDE THEY WANT TO MAKE A...UH, REPRODUCE AND...
WELL, LOOK, THEY MAKE A BABY.
THE IMPORTANT THING IS...THEY DO IT OUT OF LOVE. AND THAT'S THE POINT.
ELL, MY QUESTION WAS GOING TO E ON THE REPRODUCTIVE CYCLE OF OODLINGS...BUT LOVE? WE MOLOIDS WERE THROWN IN A PIT TO DIE UNTIL MR. GRIMM...
THE BEN!
...RESCUED US. ARE OUR LIVES LESS VALUABLE BECAUSE OF THIS? BECAUSE OUR BREEDER UNITS DIDN'T CARE FOR US?
12
PARTY WITH JOHNNY
VII AND I, WE WERE HATCHED--TWO OF THOUSANDS.
I DO NOT BELIEVE OUR SIRE EVEN KNEW OUR NAMES UNTIL WE HAD SURVIVED EIGHT DRY CYCLES.
YES. I FIND THIS CONCEPT TROUBLING TO CONSIDER. I WAS BUILT. MADE. JUST A THING WITH A PURPOSE.
I SUPPOSE MY MAKER LOVED ME AS MUCH AS YOU WOULD LOVE A SCREWDRIVER. OR A SANDWICH.
AND I WAS GROWN IN A TUBE ALONG WITH FORTY-SOMETHING OTHER VERSIONS OF THE WIZARD THAT WERE DARWIN-ED DOWN TO JUST ME.
ONLY THE STRONG SURVIVE, DUDE. LOVE SUCKS.

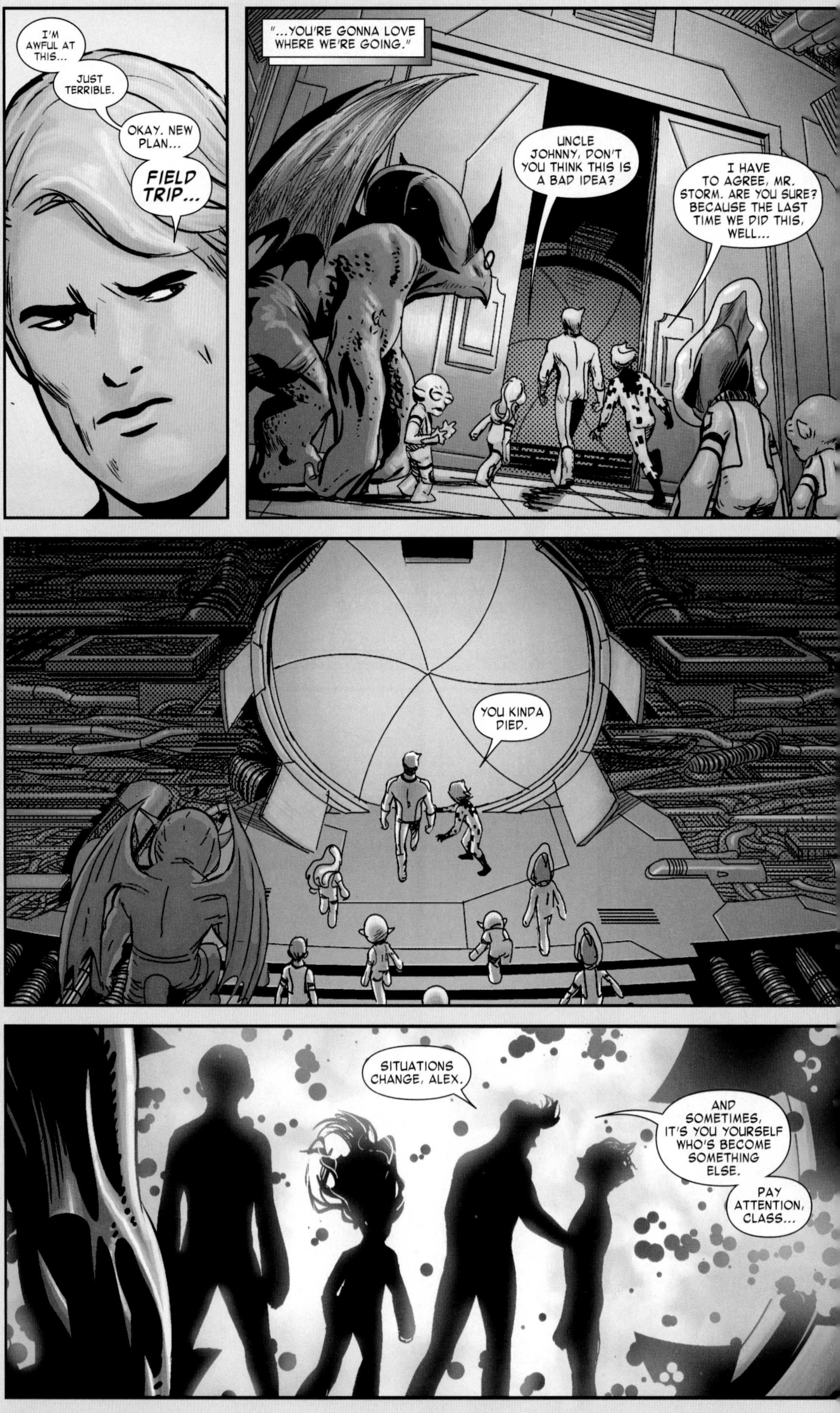

I'M AWFUL AT THIS...
JUST TERRIBLE.
OKAY. NEW PLAN...
FIELD TRIP...
"...YOU'RE GONNA LOVE WHERE WE'RE GOING."
UNCLE JOHNNY, DON'T YOU THINK THIS IS A BAD IDEA?
I HAVE TO AGREE, MR. STORM. ARE YOU SURE? BECAUSE THE LAST TIME WE DID THIS, WELL...
YOU KINDA DIED.
SITUATIONS CHANGE, ALEX.
AND SOMETIMES, IT'S YOU YOURSELF WHO'S BECOME SOMETHING ELSE.
PAY ATTENTION, CLASS...

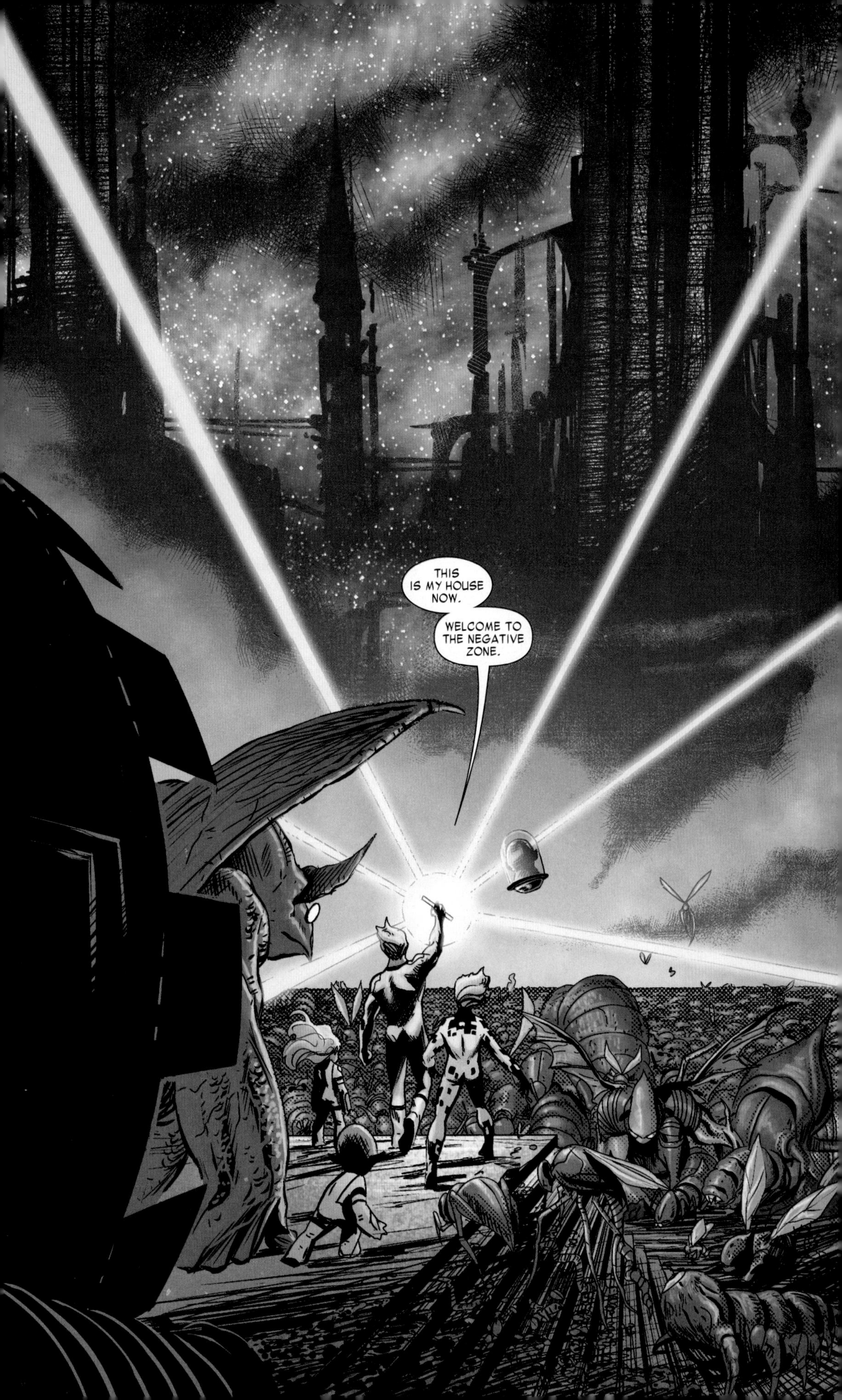
THIS IS MY HOUSE NOW.
WELCOME TO THE NEGATIVE ZONE.

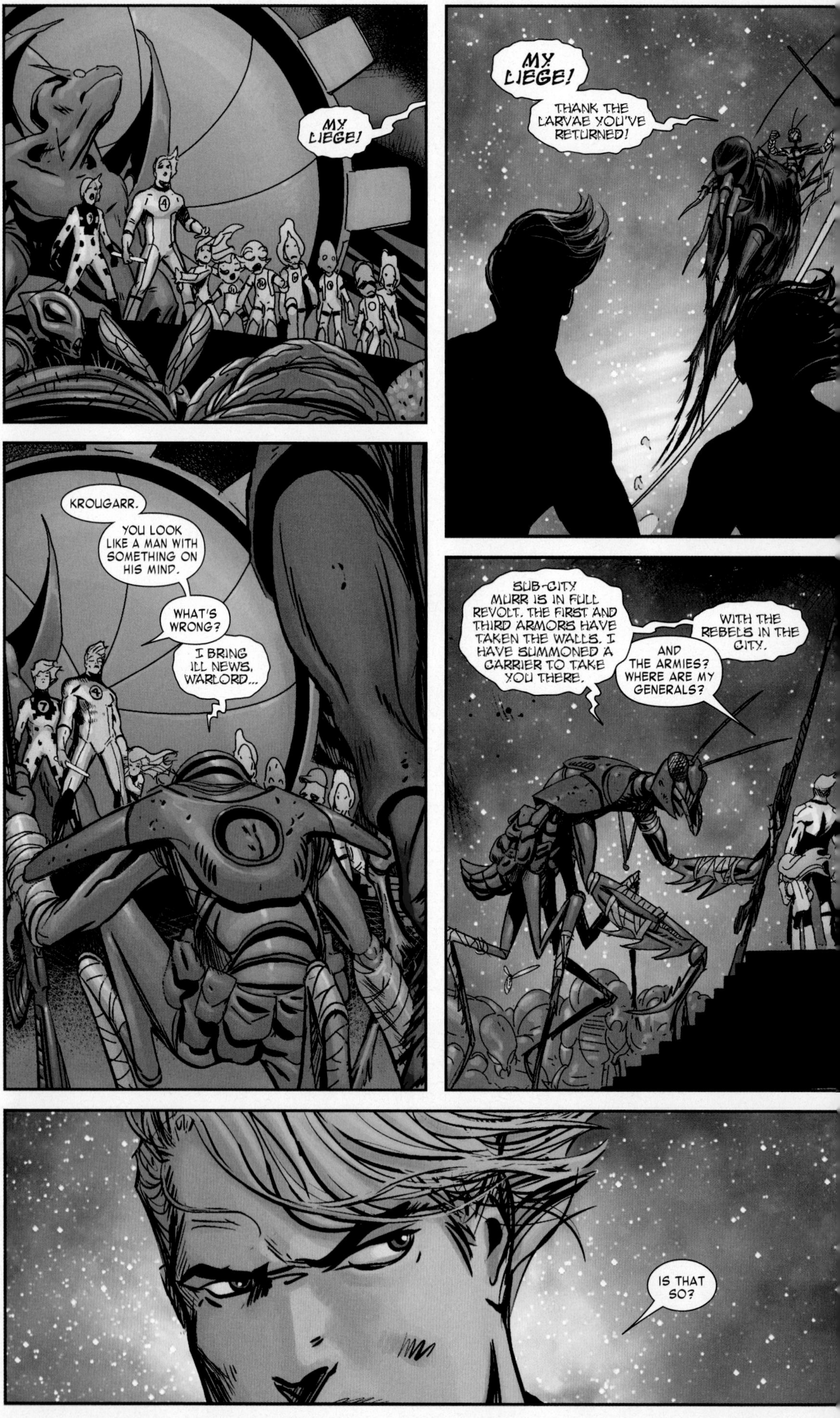
MY LIEGE!
MY LIEGE!
THANK THE LARVAE YOU'VE RETURNED!
KROUGARR.
YOU LOOK LIKE A MAN WITH SOMETHING ON HIS MIND.
WHAT'S WRONG?
I BRING ILL NEWS, WARLORD...
SUB-CITY MURR IS IN FULL REVOLT. THE FIRST AND THIRD ARMORS HAVE TAKEN THE WALLS. I HAVE SUMMONED A CARRIER TO TAKE YOU THERE.
AND THE ARMIES? WHERE ARE MY GENERALS?
WITH THE REBELS IN THE CITY.
IS THAT SO?

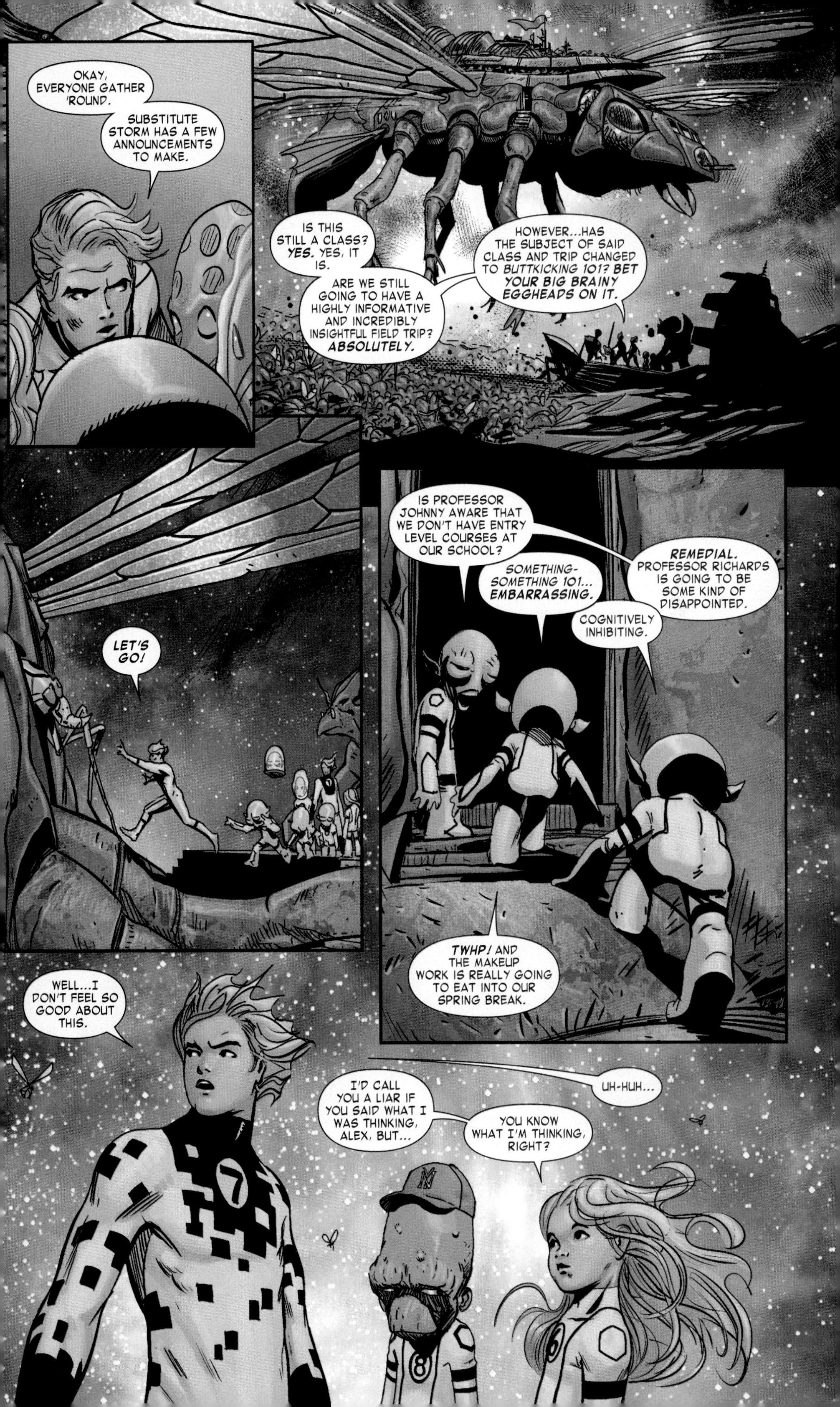
OKAY, EVERYONE GATHER 'ROUND.
SUBSTITUTE STORM HAS A FEW ANNOUNCEMENTS TO MAKE.
IS THIS STILL A CLASS? YES. YES, IT IS.
ARE WE STILL GOING TO HAVE A HIGHLY INFORMATIVE AND INCREDIBLY INSIGHTFUL FIELD TRIP? ABSOLUTELY.
HOWEVER...HAS THE SUBJECT OF SAID CLASS AND TRIP CHANGED TO BUTTKICKING 101? BET YOUR BIG BRAINY EGGHEADS ON IT.
LET'S GO!
IS PROFESSOR JOHNNY AWARE THAT WE DON'T HAVE ENTRY LEVEL COURSES AT OUR SCHOOL?
SOMETHING-SOMETHING 101... EMBARRASSING.
REMEDIAL. PROFESSOR RICHARDS IS GOING TO BE SOME KIND OF DISAPPOINTED.
COGNITIVELY INHIBITING.
TWHP! AND THE MAKEUP WORK IS REALLY GOING TO EAT INTO OUR SPRING BREAK.
WELL...I DON'T FEEL SO GOOD ABOUT THIS.
UH-HUH...
I'D CALL YOU A LIAR IF YOU SAID WHAT I WAS THINKING, ALEX, BUT...
YOU KNOW WHAT I'M THINKING, RIGHT?

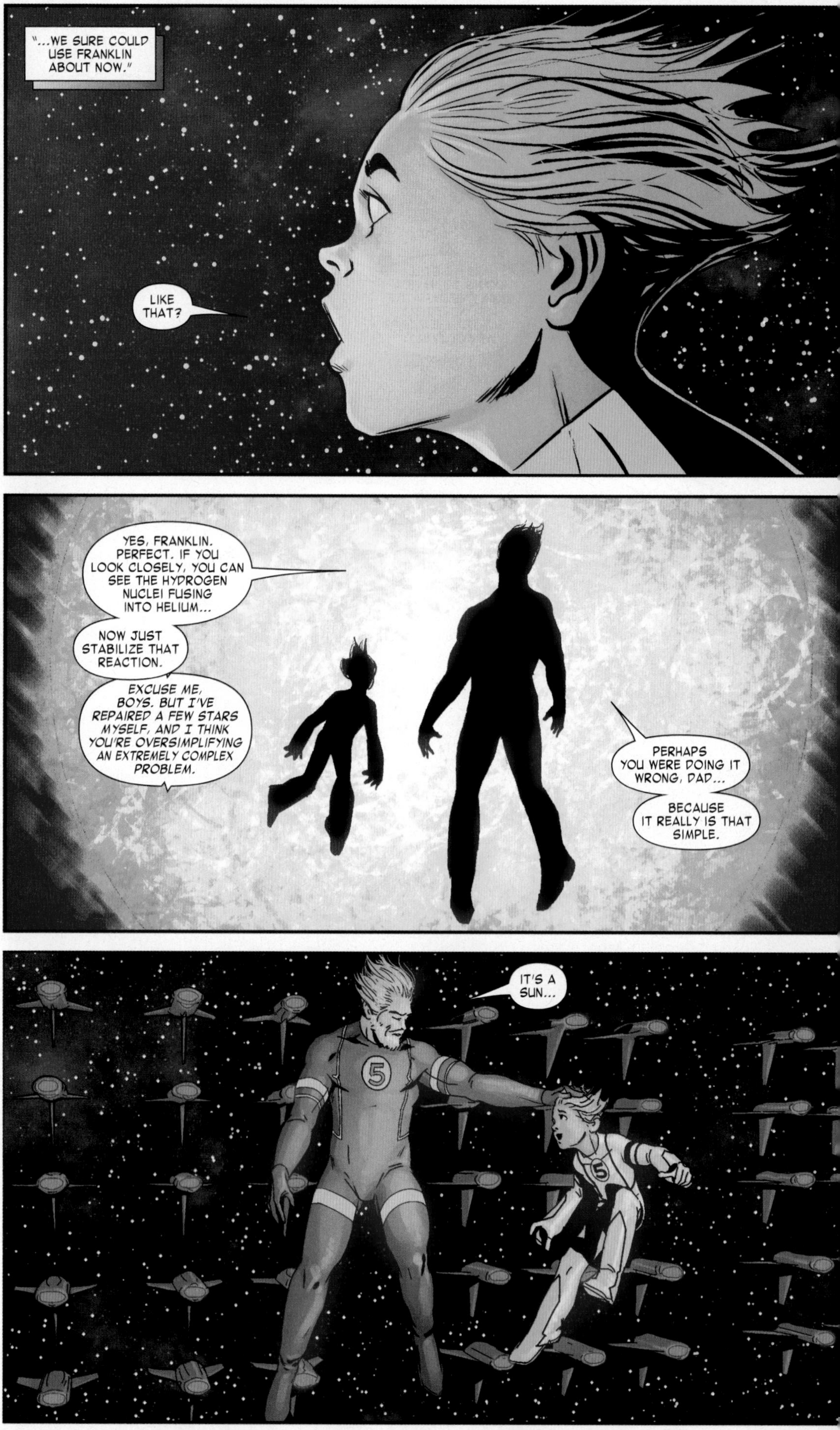
"...WE SURE COULD USE FRANKLIN ABOUT NOW."
LIKE THAT?
YES, FRANKLIN. PERFECT. IF YOU LOOK CLOSELY, YOU CAN SEE THE HYDROGEN NUCLEI FUSING INTO HELIUM...
NOW JUST STABILIZE THAT REACTION.
EXCUSE ME, BOYS. BUT I'VE REPAIRED A FEW STARS MYSELF, AND I THINK YOU'RE OVERSIMPLIFYING AN EXTREMELY COMPLEX PROBLEM.
PERHAPS YOU WERE DOING IT WRONG, DAD...
BECAUSE IT REALLY IS THAT SIMPLE.
IT'S A SUN...

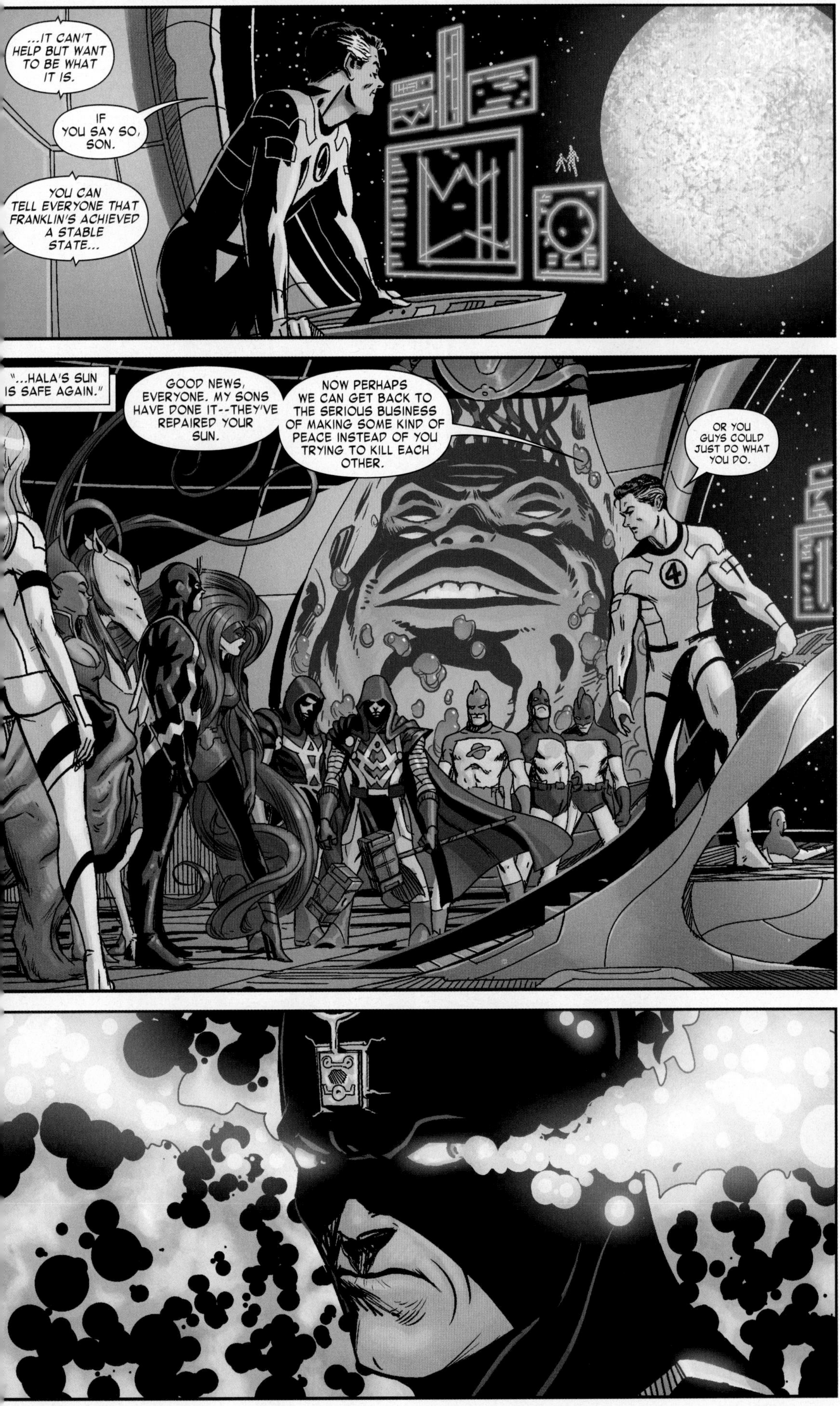
...IT CAN'T HELP BUT WANT TO BE WHAT IT IS.
IF YOU SAY SO, SON.
YOU CAN TELL EVERYONE THAT FRANKLIN'S ACHIEVED A STABLE STATE...
"...HALA'S SUN IS SAFE AGAIN."
GOOD NEWS, EVERYONE. MY SONS HAVE DONE IT--THEY'VE REPAIRED YOUR SUN.
NOW PERHAPS WE CAN GET BACK TO THE SERIOUS BUSINESS OF MAKING SOME KIND OF PEACE INSTEAD OF YOU TRYING TO KILL EACH OTHER.
OR YOU GUYS COULD JUST DO WHAT YOU DO.

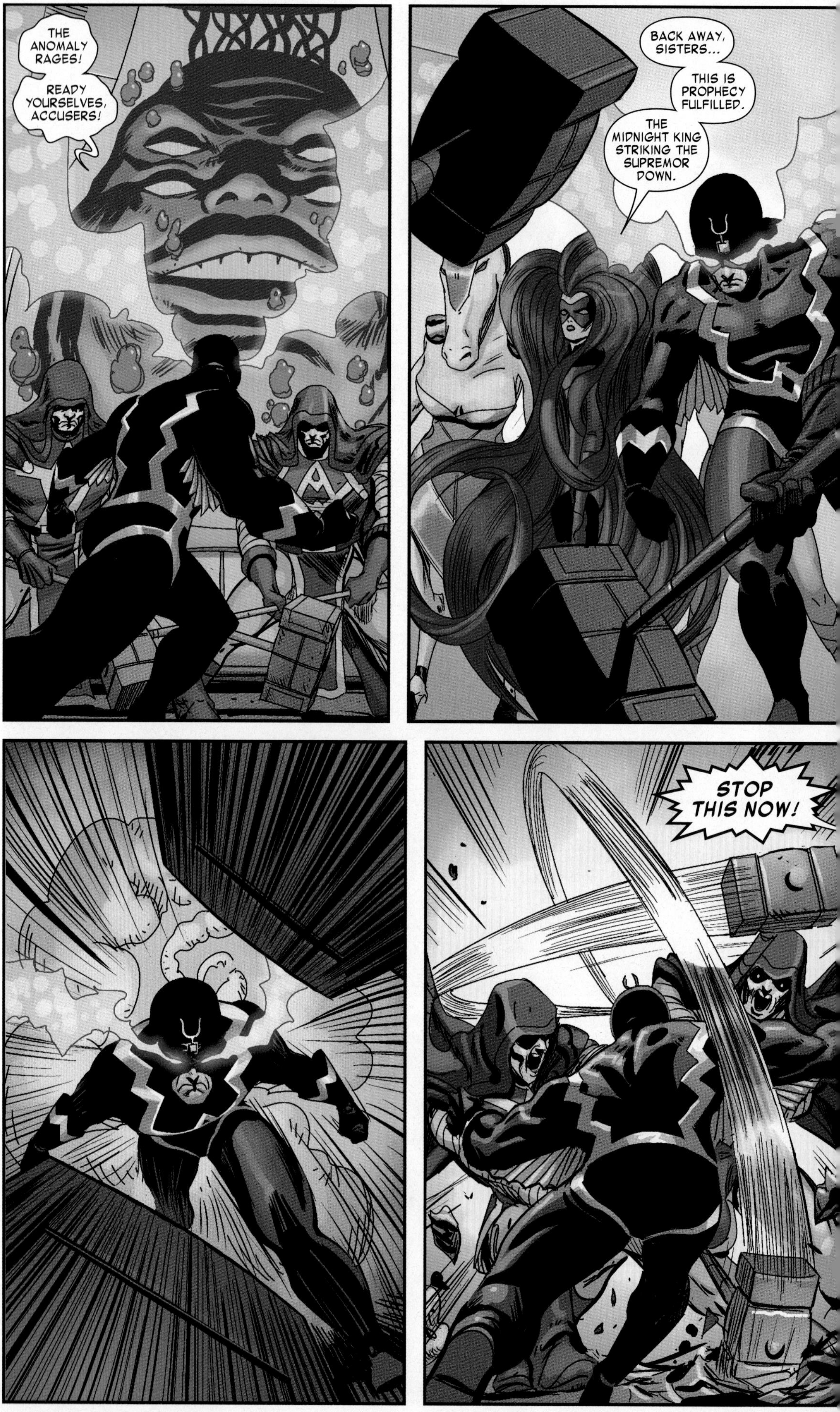
THE ANOMALY RAGES!
READY YOURSELVES, ACCUSERS!
BACK AWAY, SISTERS...
THIS IS PROPHECY FULFILLED.
THE MIDNIGHT KING STRIKING THE SUPREMOR DOWN.
STOP THIS NOW!

WE NEED TO SPEAK, GOOD KING.

HEY, *MOM!* DID YOU SEE THAT?

I MADE THE STAR HAPPY AGAIN.

I DID. YOU WERE *AMAZING!*

FEEL FREE TO SPEAK IN HERE, BLACK BOLT.

NOTHING CAN ESCAPE THIS CUBE, AND I WOULD NEVER ALLOW YOUR WORDS TO HARM ME.

YOU DARE TO--

OH, DON'T BE MAD.

I DARE MANY THINGS. IT'S A CHARACTER FLAW.

WHY DON'T YOU LOOK AT ME? CLOSELY.

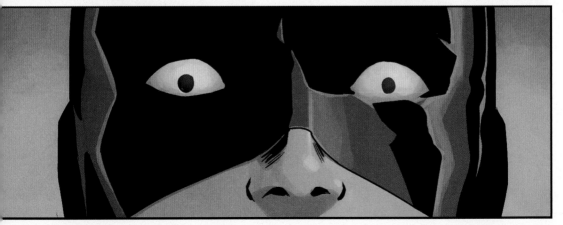

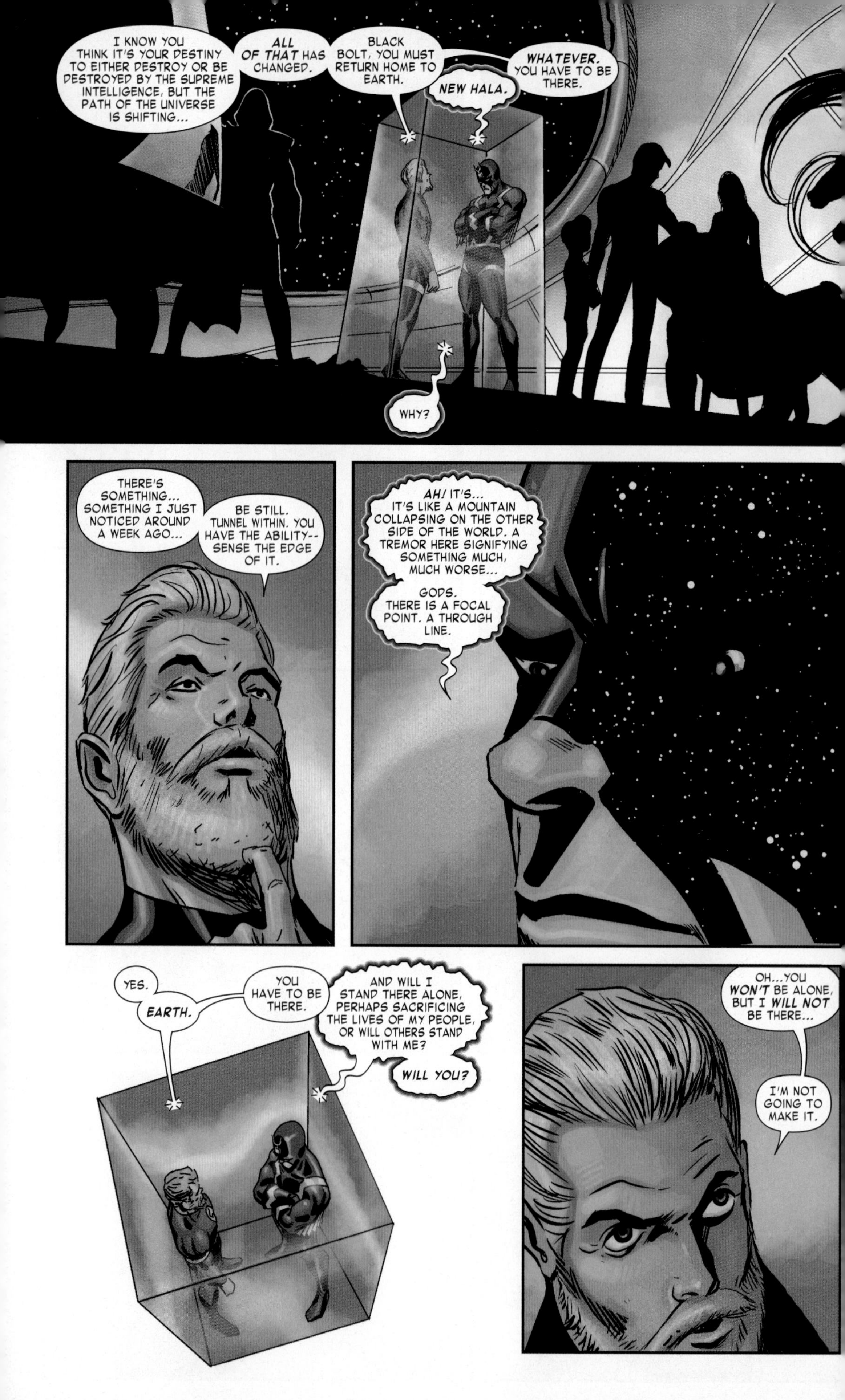
I KNOW YOU THINK IT'S YOUR DESTINY TO EITHER DESTROY OR BE DESTROYED BY THE SUPREME INTELLIGENCE, BUT THE PATH OF THE UNIVERSE IS SHIFTING...
ALL OF THAT HAS CHANGED.
BLACK BOLT, YOU MUST RETURN HOME TO EARTH.
NEW HALA.
WHATEVER. YOU HAVE TO BE THERE.
WHY?
THERE'S SOMETHING... SOMETHING I JUST NOTICED AROUND A WEEK AGO...
BE STILL. TUNNEL WITHIN. YOU HAVE THE ABILITY-- SENSE THE EDGE OF IT.
AH! IT'S... IT'S LIKE A MOUNTAIN COLLAPSING ON THE OTHER SIDE OF THE WORLD. A TREMOR HERE SIGNIFYING SOMETHING MUCH, MUCH WORSE...
GODS. THERE IS A FOCAL POINT. A THROUGH LINE.
YES.
EARTH.
YOU HAVE TO BE THERE.
AND WILL I STAND THERE ALONE, PERHAPS SACRIFICING THE LIVES OF MY PEOPLE, OR WILL OTHERS STAND WITH ME?
WILL YOU?
OH...YOU WON'T BE ALONE, BUT I WILL NOT BE THERE...
I'M NOT GOING TO MAKE IT.

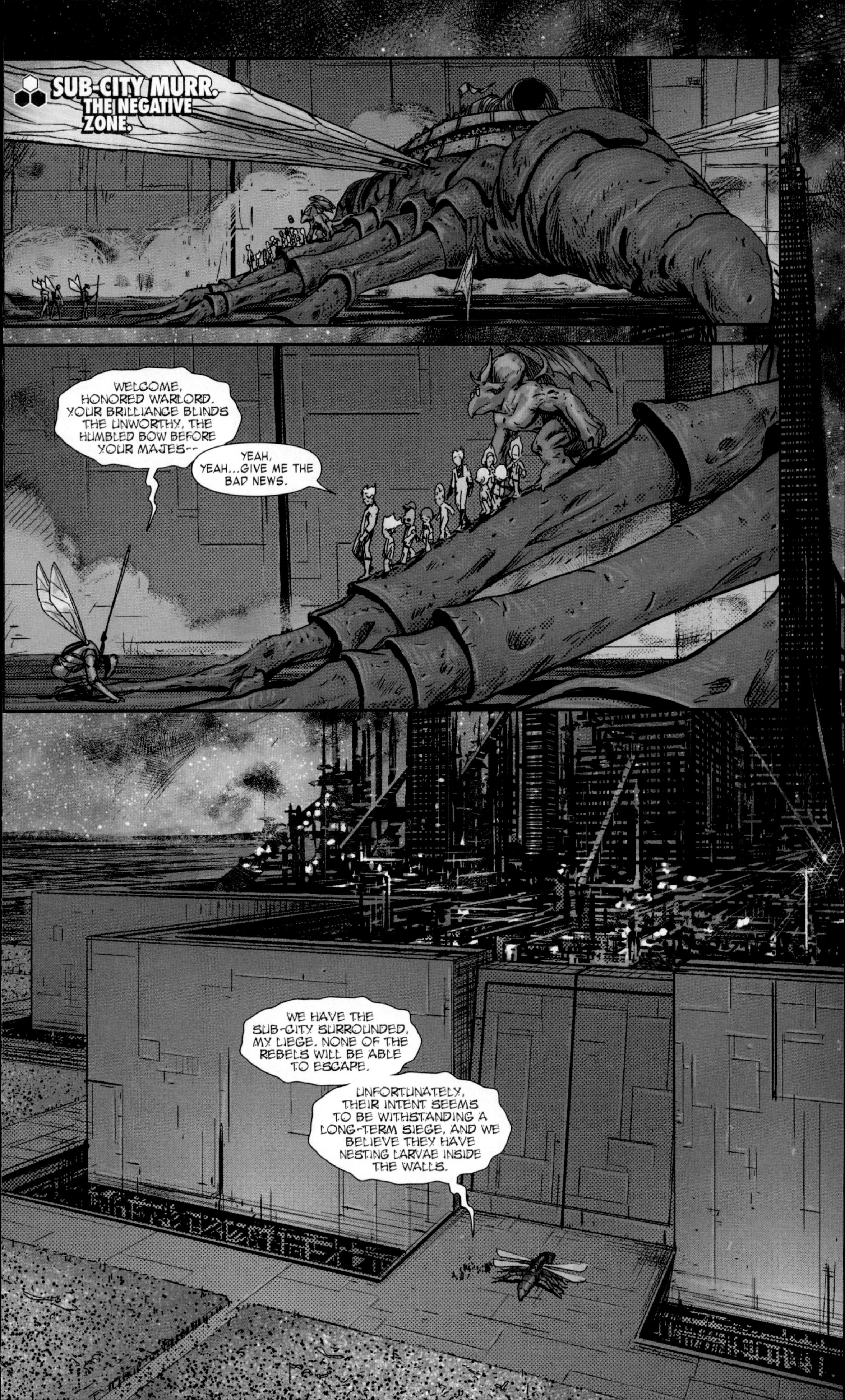
SUB-CITY MURR. THE NEGATIVE ZONE.
WELCOME, HONORED WARLORD. YOUR BRILLIANCE BLINDS THE UNWORTHY, THE HUMBLED BOW BEFORE YOUR MAJES--
YEAH, YEAH...GIVE ME THE BAD NEWS.
WE HAVE THE SUB-CITY SURROUNDED, MY LIEGE. NONE OF THE REBELS WILL BE ABLE TO ESCAPE.
UNFORTUNATELY, THEIR INTENT SEEMS TO BE WITHSTANDING A LONG-TERM SIEGE, AND WE BELIEVE THEY HAVE NESTING LARVAE INSIDE THE WALLS.

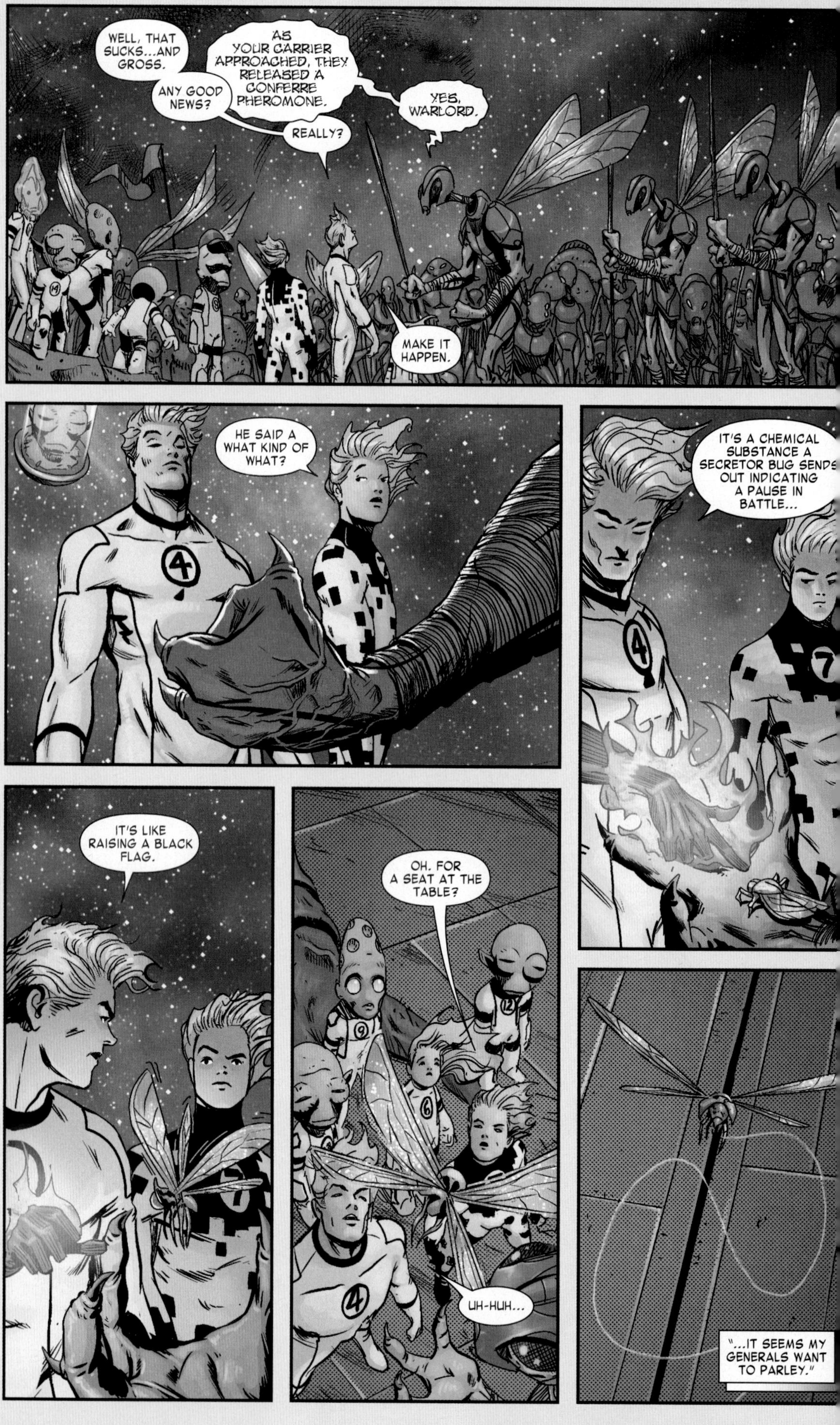
WELL, THAT SUCKS...AND GROSS.
AS YOUR CARRIER APPROACHED, THEY RELEASED A CONFERRE PHEROMONE.
ANY GOOD NEWS?
YES, WARLORD.
REALLY?
MAKE IT HAPPEN.
HE SAID A WHAT KIND OF WHAT?
IT'S A CHEMICAL SUBSTANCE A SECRETOR BUG SENDS OUT INDICATING A PAUSE IN BATTLE...
IT'S LIKE RAISING A BLACK FLAG.
OH. FOR A SEAT AT THE TABLE?
UH-HUH...
"...IT SEEMS MY GENERALS WANT TO PARLEY."

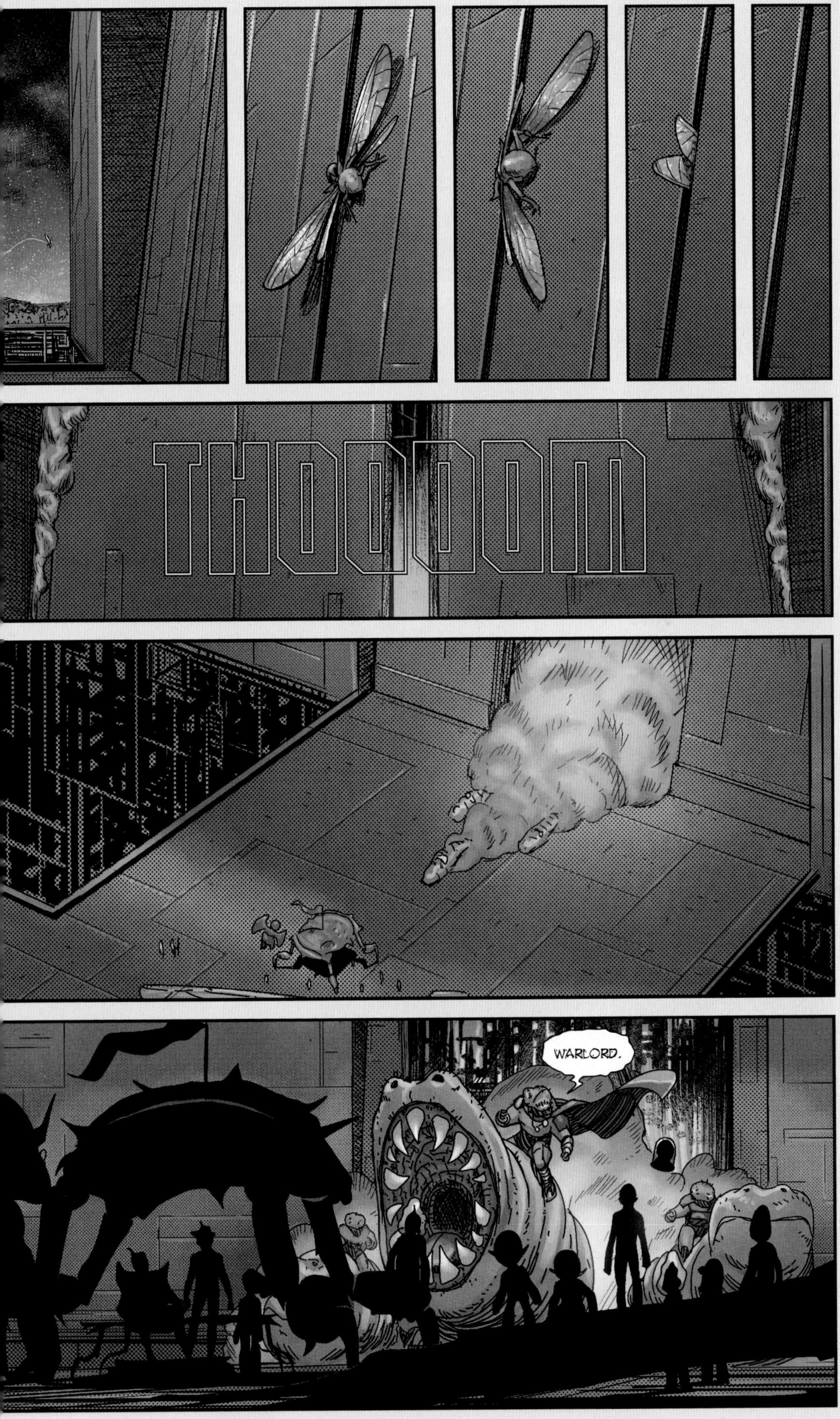
THOOOOM
WARLORD.

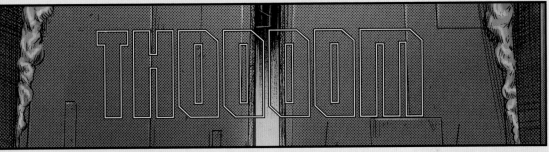

BOYS. HAVE A SEAT.

WELL...WHAT SEEMS TO BE THE PROBLEM?

I MEAN, WHAT POSSIBLE REASON COULD A BUNCH OF NIHILIST BUGS EVER HAVE FOR WANTING TO FIGHT AND THEN BLOW EACH OTHER UP?

DO YOU HAVE ANY IDEA HOW DISAPPOINTED I AM IN ALL OF YOU?

WE HAVE DEMANDSSSSSS.

A DEMAND. SSSSSSSINGULAR.

I CERTAINLY HOPE IT'S "PLEASE, WARLORD, DON'T WHIP OUT YOUR CONTROL ROD AND INCINERATE THE ENTIRE SUB-CITY."

BECAUSE BURNING YOU DOWN IS PRETTY HIGH ON MY LIST.

WELL, WHAT IS IT? LET'S HEAR YOUR DEMAND.

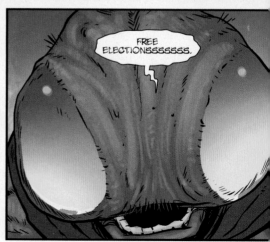

FREE ELECTIONSSSSSSSS.

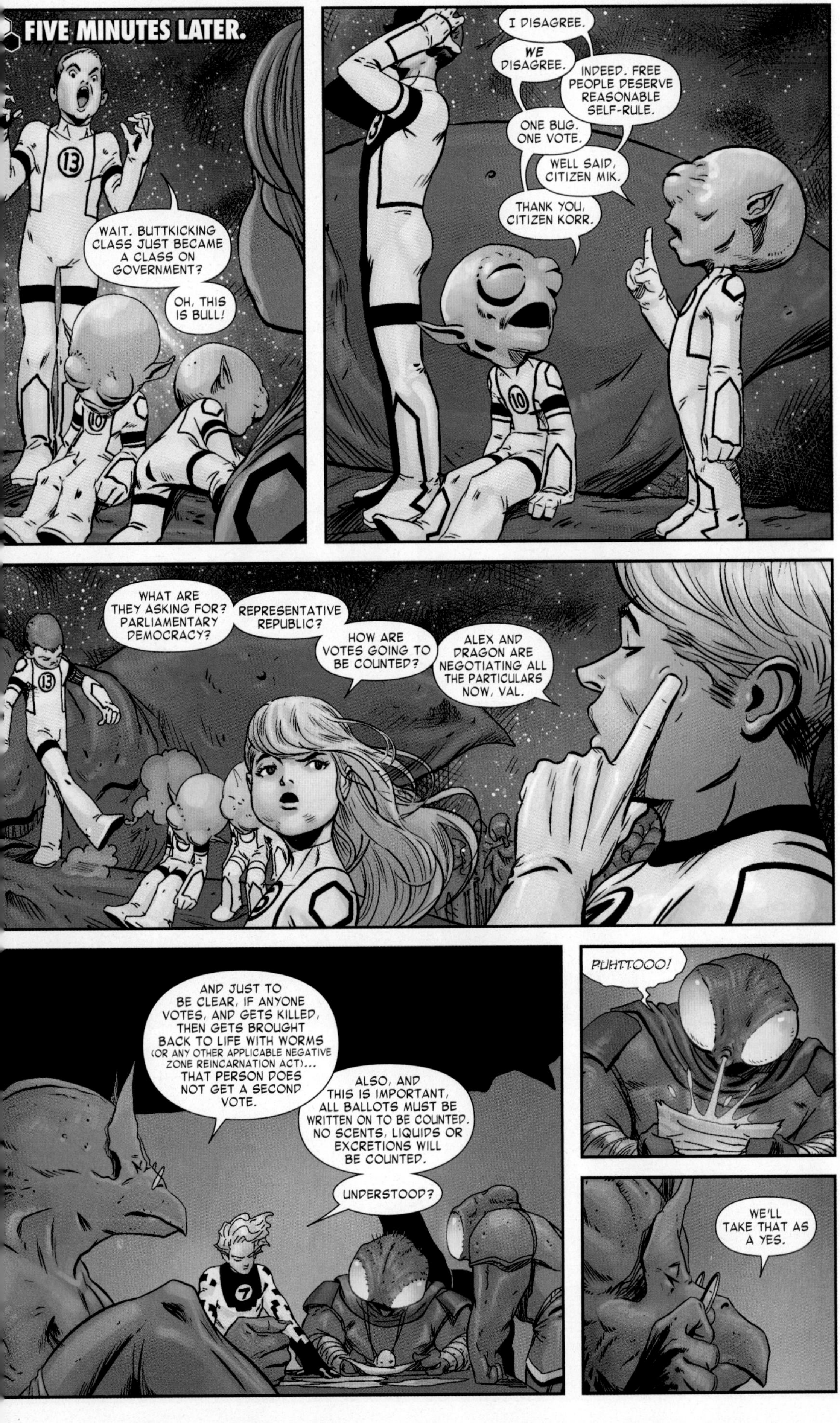
FIVE MINUTES LATER.
WAIT. BUTTKICKING CLASS JUST BECAME A CLASS ON GOVERNMENT?
OH, THIS IS BULL!
I DISAGREE.
WE DISAGREE.
INDEED. FREE PEOPLE DESERVE REASONABLE SELF-RULE.
ONE BUG. ONE VOTE.
WELL SAID, CITIZEN MIK.
THANK YOU, CITIZEN KORR.
WHAT ARE THEY ASKING FOR? PARLIAMENTARY DEMOCRACY?
REPRESENTATIVE REPUBLIC?
HOW ARE VOTES GOING TO BE COUNTED?
ALEX AND DRAGON ARE NEGOTIATING ALL THE PARTICULARS NOW, VAL.
AND JUST TO BE CLEAR, IF ANYONE VOTES, AND GETS KILLED, THEN GETS BROUGHT BACK TO LIFE WITH WORMS (OR ANY OTHER APPLICABLE NEGATIVE ZONE REINCARNATION ACT)... THAT PERSON DOES NOT GET A SECOND VOTE.
ALSO, AND THIS IS IMPORTANT, ALL BALLOTS MUST BE WRITTEN ON TO BE COUNTED. NO SCENTS, LIQUIDS OR EXCRETIONS WILL BE COUNTED.
UNDERSTOOD?
PUHTTOOO!
WE'LL TAKE THAT AS A YES.

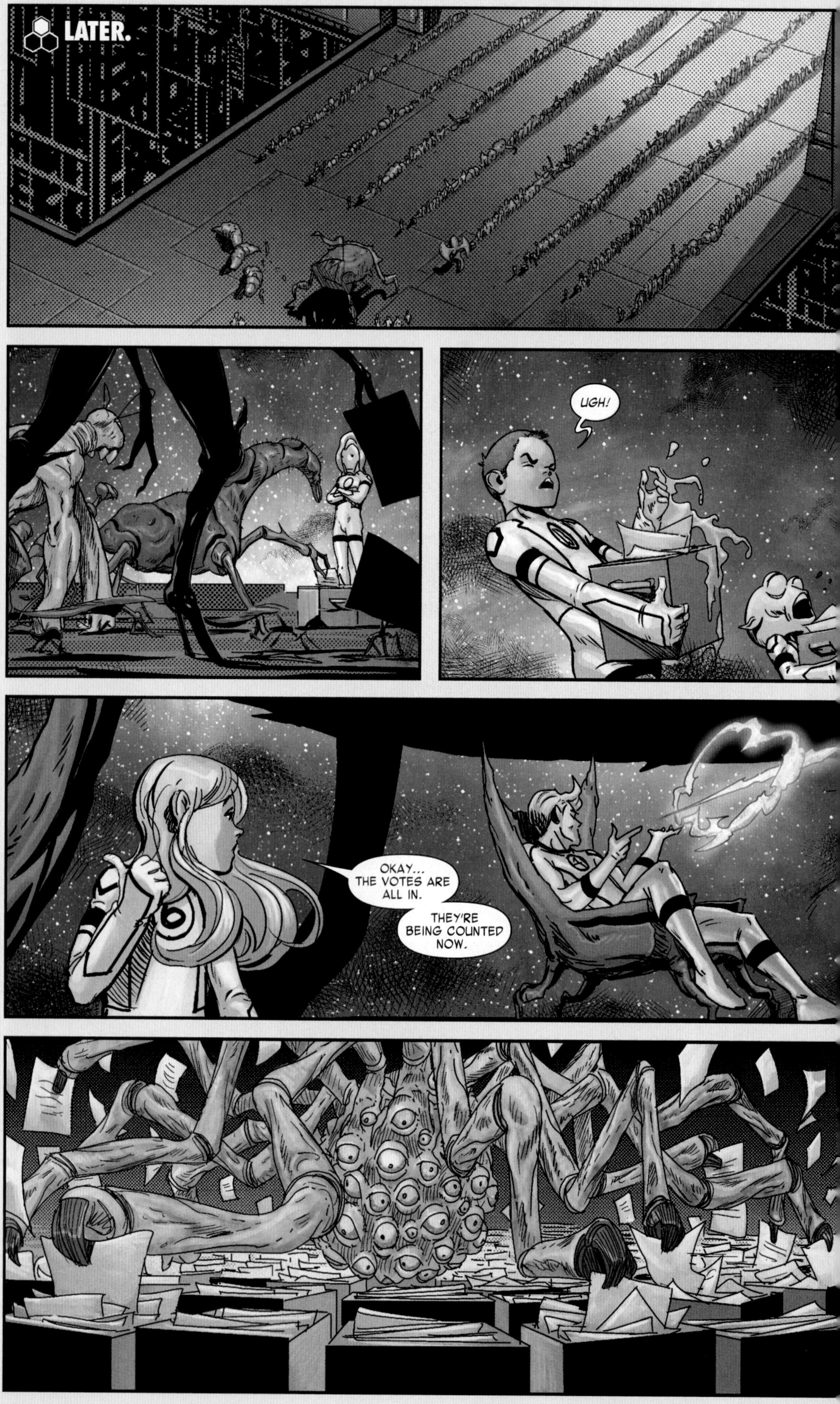
LATER.
UGH!
OKAY... THE VOTES ARE ALL IN.
THEY'RE BEING COUNTED NOW.

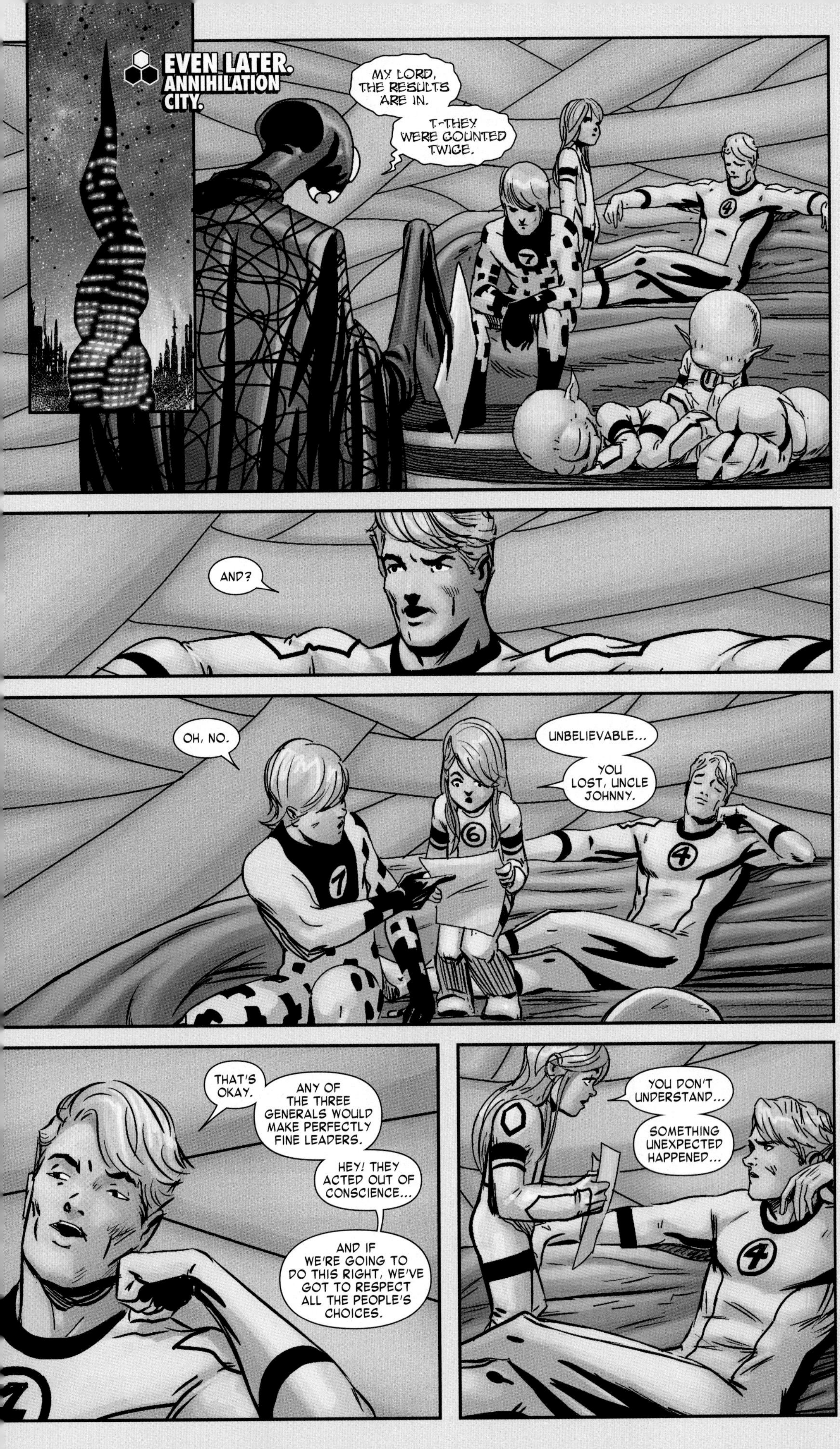
EVEN LATER. ANNIHILATION CITY.
MY LORD, THE RESULTS ARE IN.
T-THEY WERE COUNTED TWICE.
AND?
OH, NO.
UNBELIEVABLE...
YOU LOST, UNCLE JOHNNY.
THAT'S OKAY.
ANY OF THE THREE GENERALS WOULD MAKE PERFECTLY FINE LEADERS.
HEY! THEY ACTED OUT OF CONSCIENCE...
AND IF WE'RE GOING TO DO THIS RIGHT, WE'VE GOT TO RESPECT ALL THE PEOPLE'S CHOICES.
YOU DON'T UNDERSTAND...
SOMETHING UNEXPECTED HAPPENED...

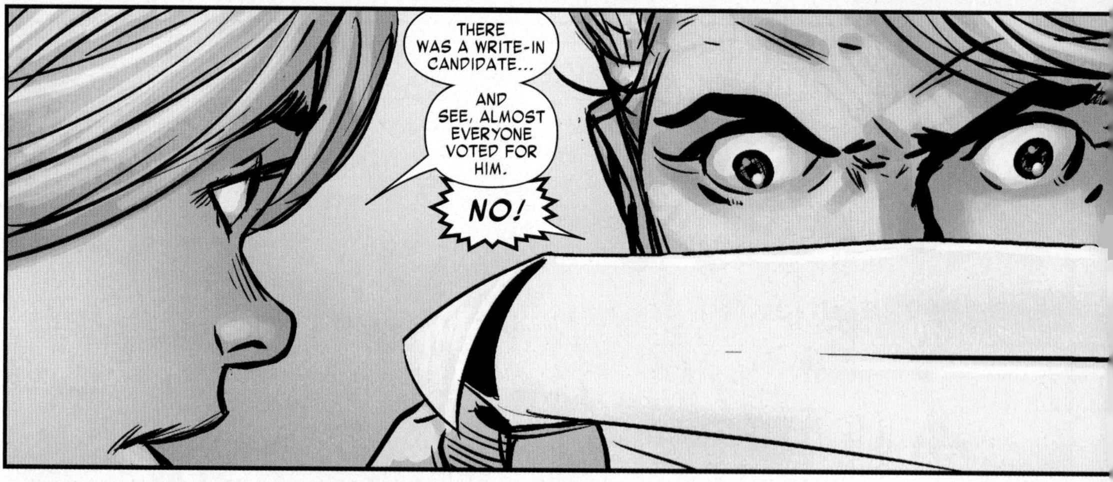
THERE WAS A WRITE-IN CANDIDATE...
AND SEE, ALMOST EVERYONE VOTED FOR HIM.
NO!

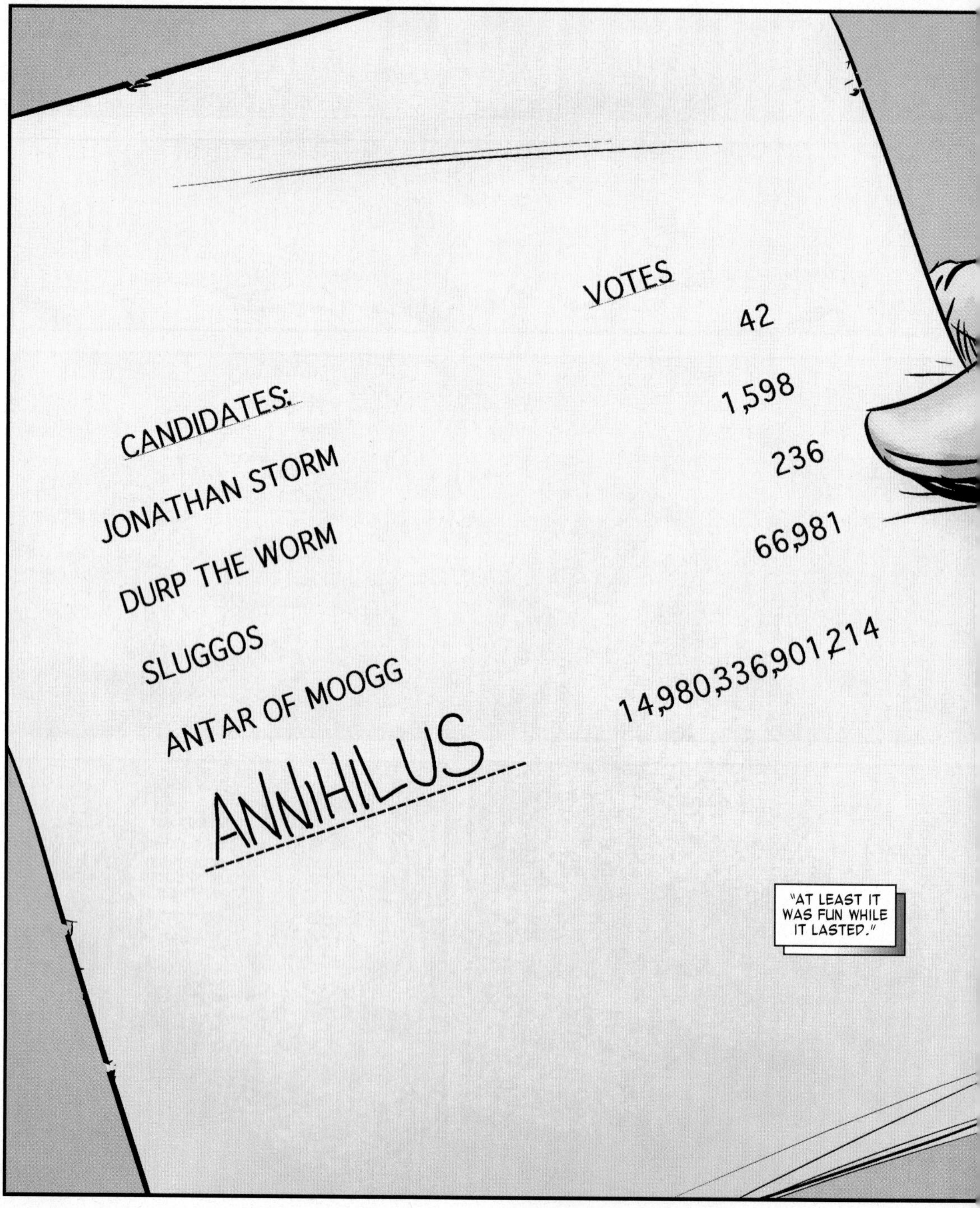
CANDIDATES:
VOTES
JONATHAN STORM
42
DURP THE WORM
1,598
SLUGGOS
236
ANTAR OF MOOGG
66,981
ANNIHILUS
14,980,336,901,214
"AT LEAST IT WAS FUN WHILE IT LASTED."

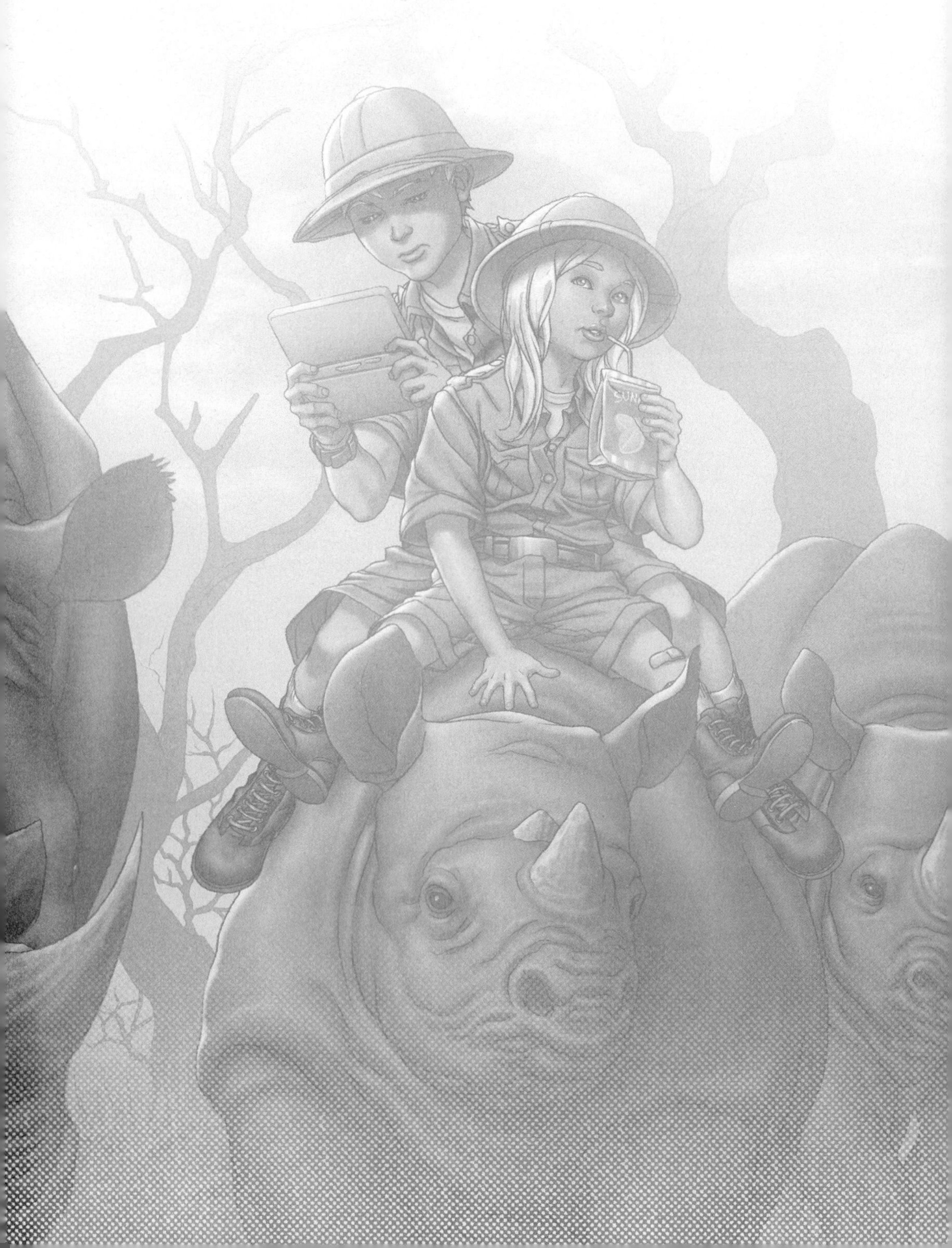

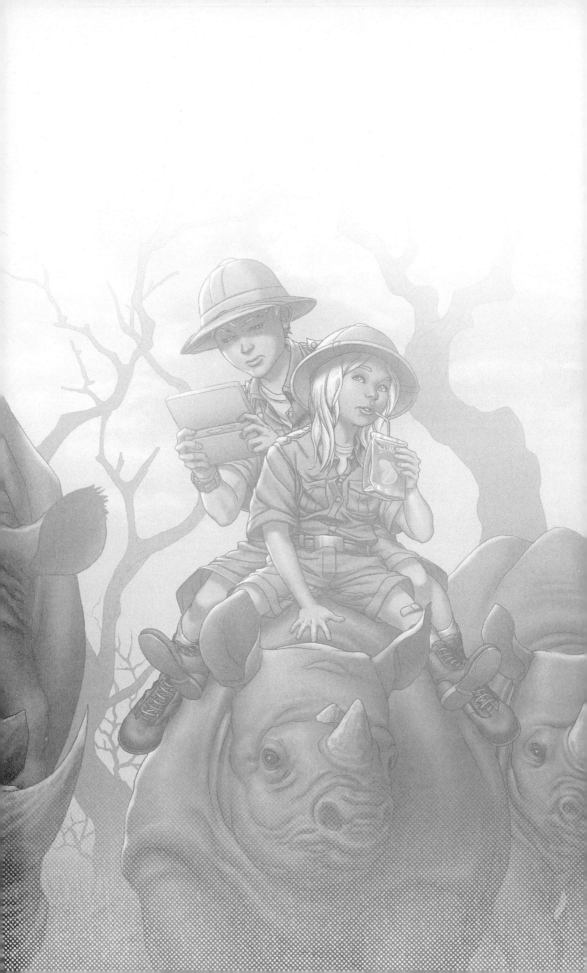

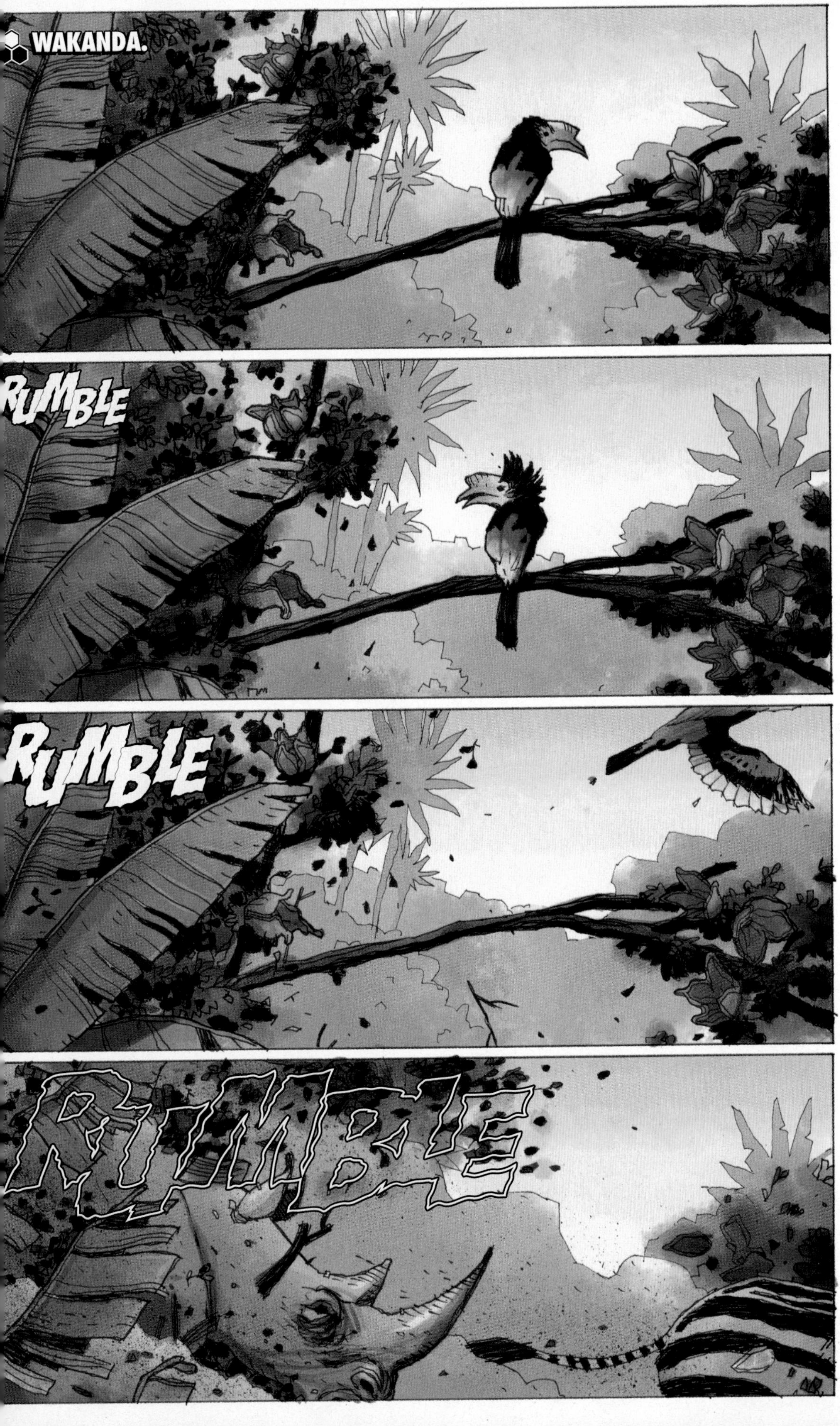
WAKANDA.
RUMBLE
RUMBLE
RUMBLE

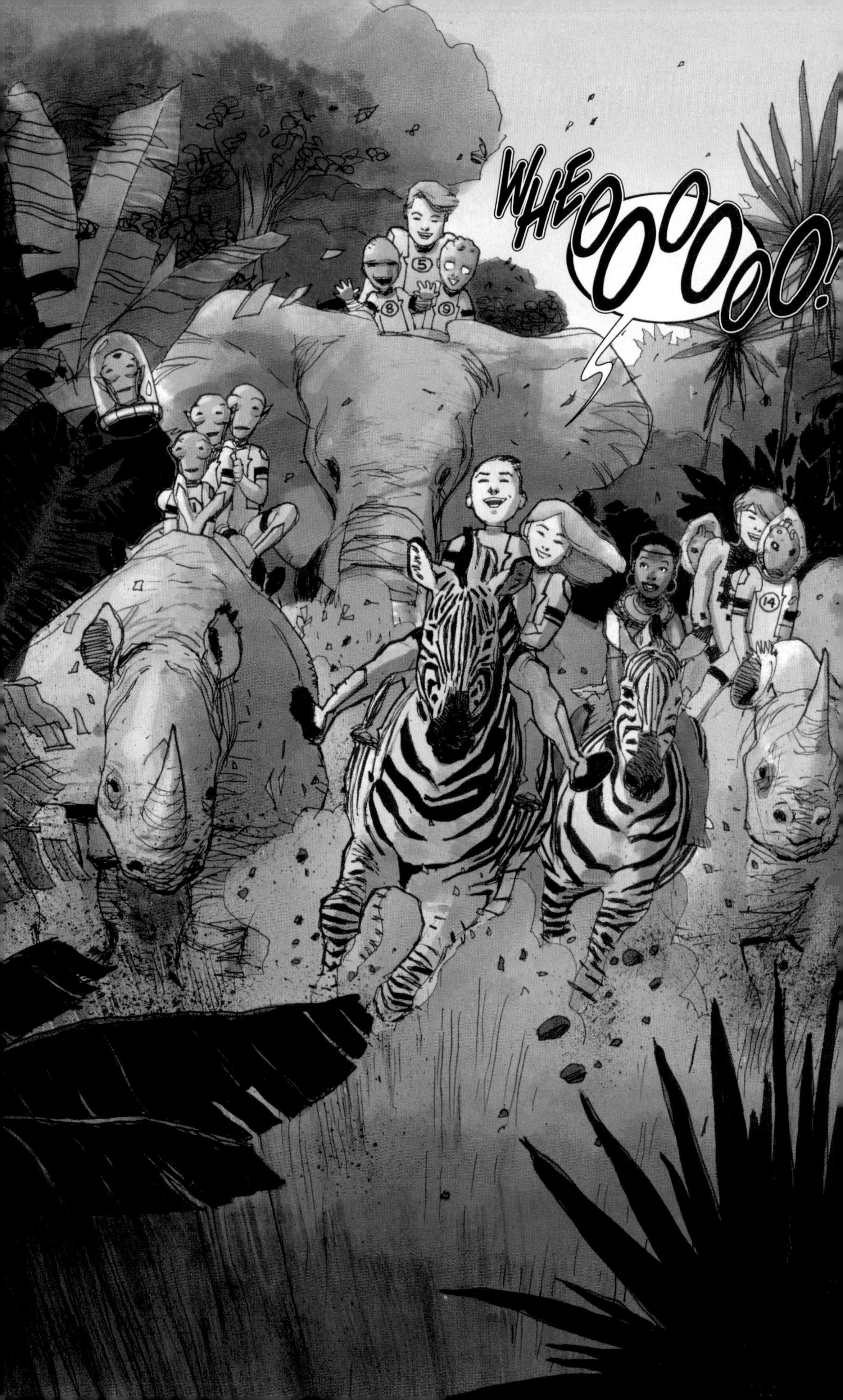
WHEOOOOOOO!

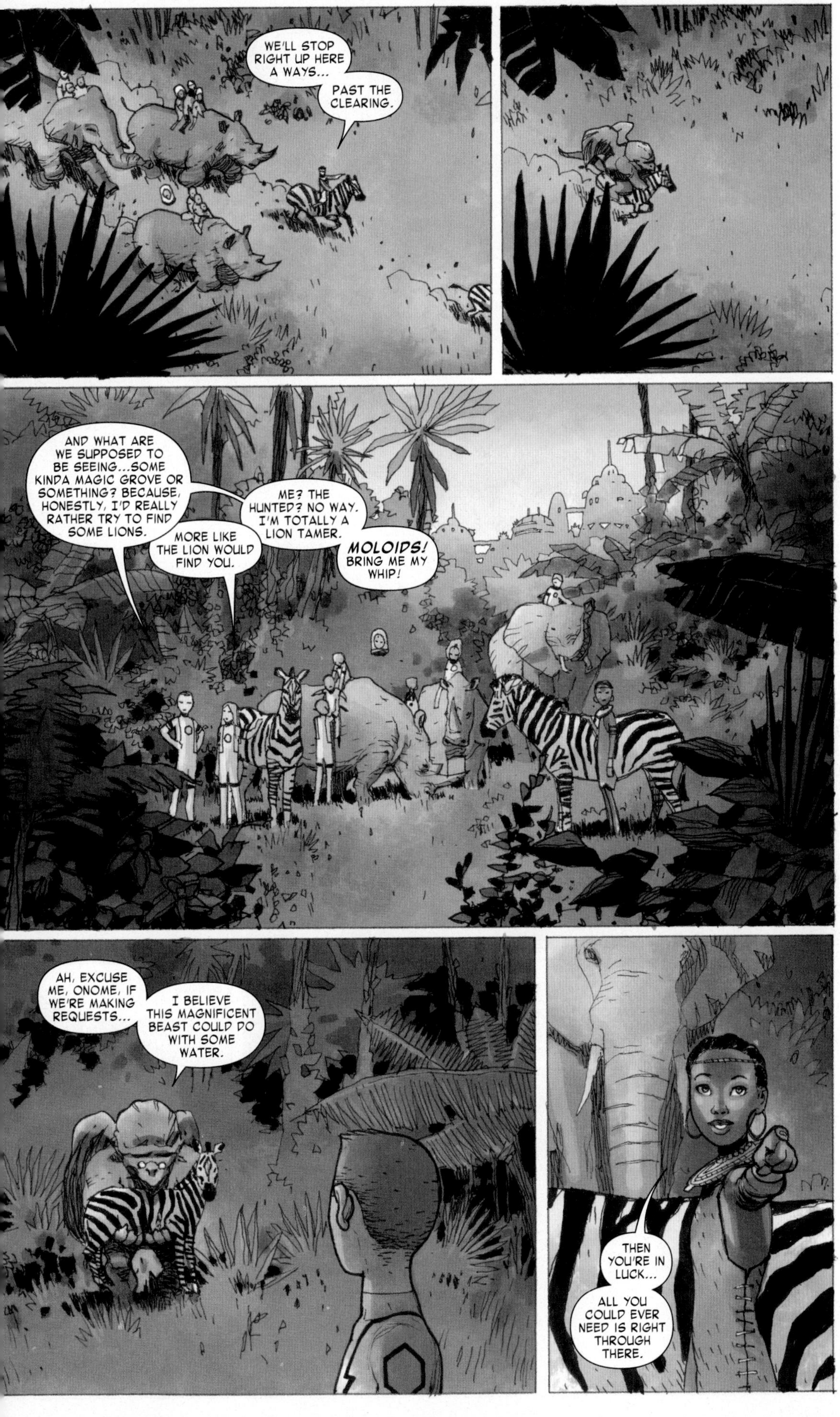
WE'LL STOP RIGHT UP HERE A WAYS...
PAST THE CLEARING.
AND WHAT ARE WE SUPPOSED TO BE SEEING...SOME KINDA MAGIC GROVE OR SOMETHING? BECAUSE, HONESTLY, I'D REALLY RATHER TRY TO FIND SOME LIONS.
MORE LIKE THE LION WOULD FIND YOU.
ME? THE HUNTED? NO WAY. I'M TOTALLY A LION TAMER.
MOLOIDS! BRING ME MY WHIP!
AH, EXCUSE ME, ONOME, IF WE'RE MAKING REQUESTS...
I BELIEVE THIS MAGNIFICENT BEAST COULD DO WITH SOME WATER.
THEN YOU'RE IN LUCK...
ALL YOU COULD EVER NEED IS RIGHT THROUGH THERE.

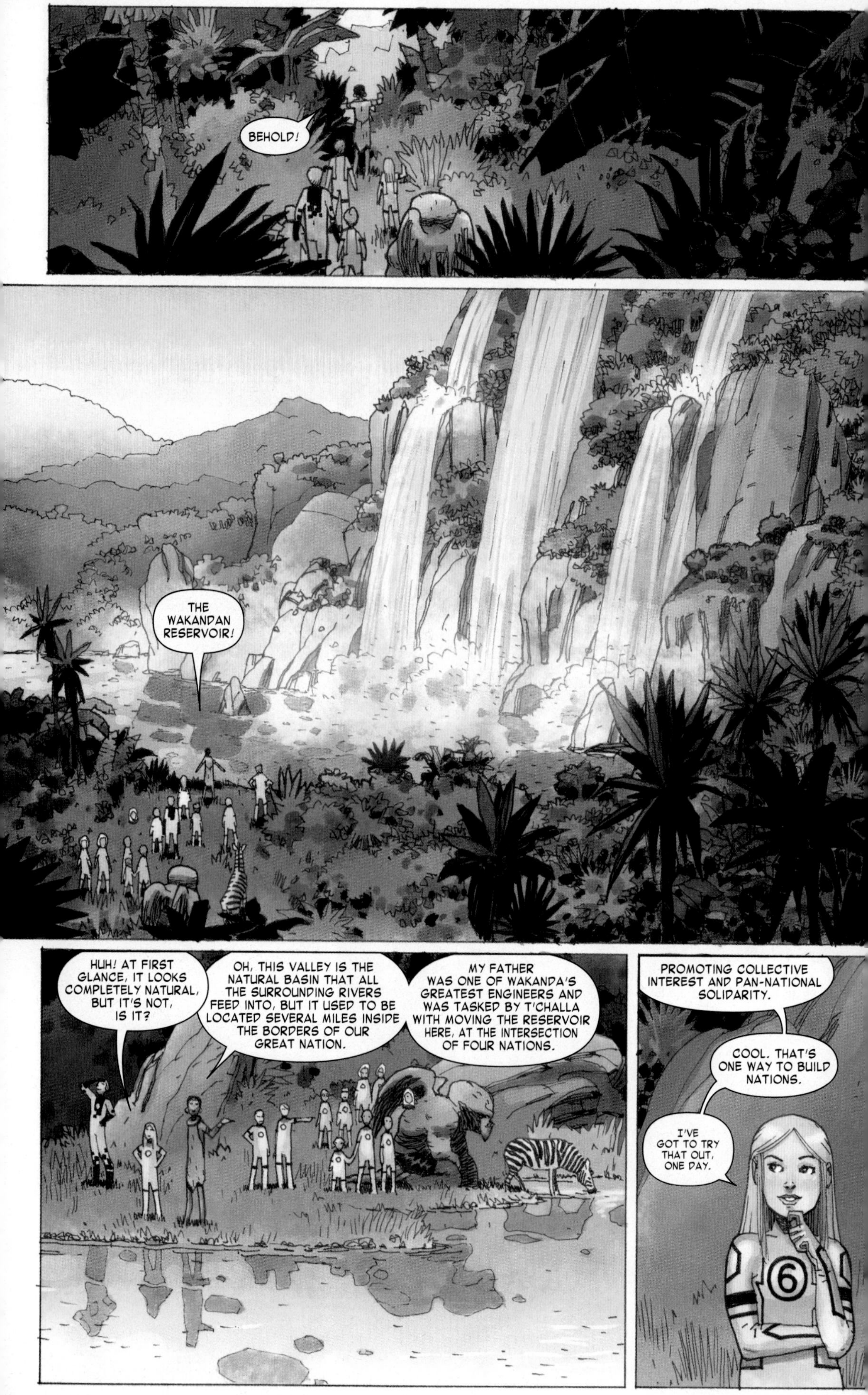

BEHOLD!
THE WAKANDAN RESERVOIR!
HUH! AT FIRST GLANCE, IT LOOKS COMPLETELY NATURAL, BUT IT'S NOT, IS IT?
OH, THIS VALLEY IS THE NATURAL BASIN THAT ALL THE SURROUNDING RIVERS FEED INTO, BUT IT USED TO BE LOCATED SEVERAL MILES INSIDE THE BORDERS OF OUR GREAT NATION.
MY FATHER WAS ONE OF WAKANDA'S GREATEST ENGINEERS AND WAS TASKED BY T'CHALLA WITH MOVING THE RESERVOIR HERE, AT THE INTERSECTION OF FOUR NATIONS.
PROMOTING COLLECTIVE INTEREST AND PAN-NATIONAL SOLIDARITY.
COOL. THAT'S ONE WAY TO BUILD NATIONS.
I'VE GOT TO TRY THAT OUT, ONE DAY.

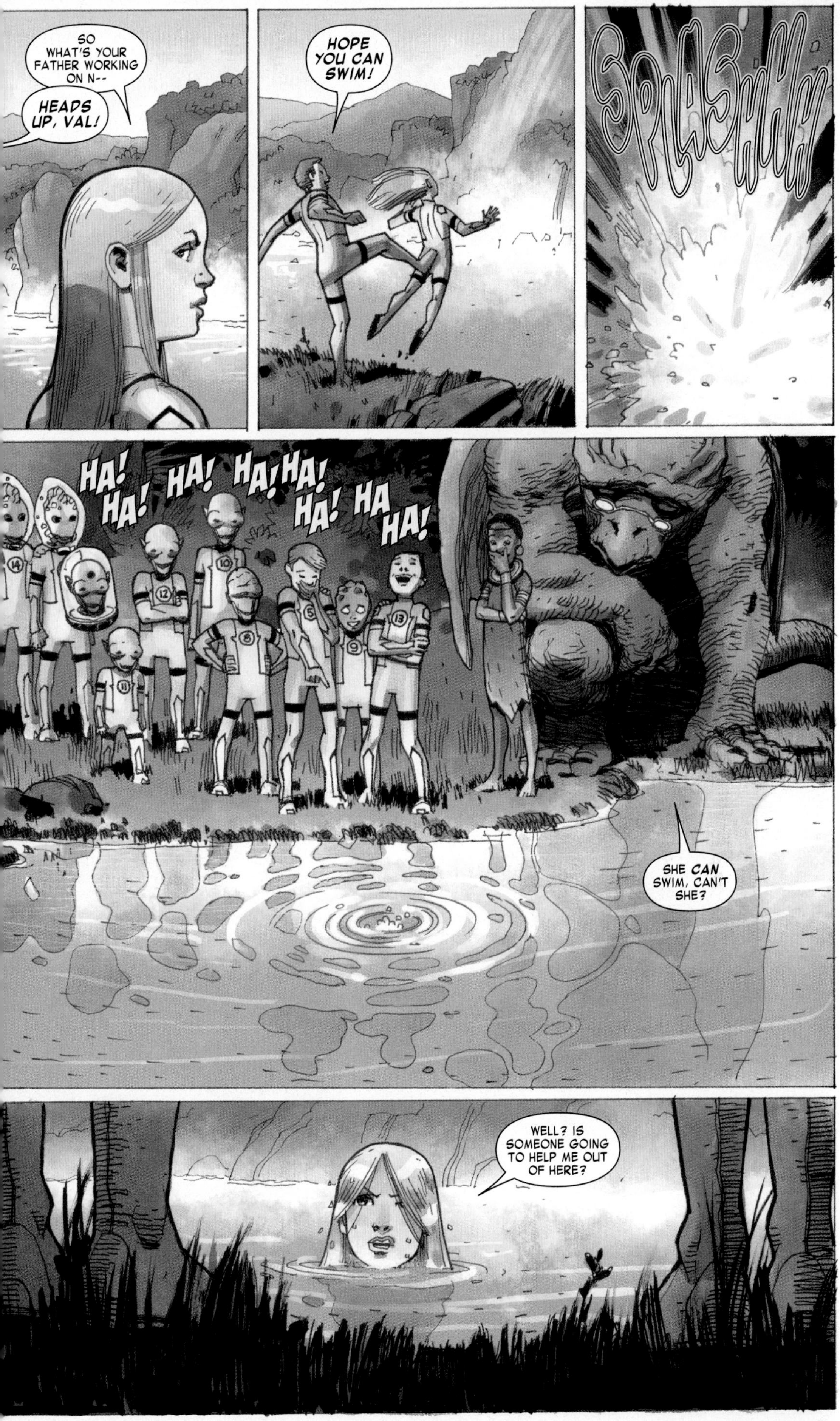
SO WHAT'S YOUR FATHER WORKING ON N--
HEADS UP, VAL!
HOPE YOU CAN SWIM!
HA! HA! HA! HA! HA! HA! HA HA!
SHE CAN SWIM, CAN'T SHE?
WELL? IS SOMEONE GOING TO HELP ME OUT OF HERE?

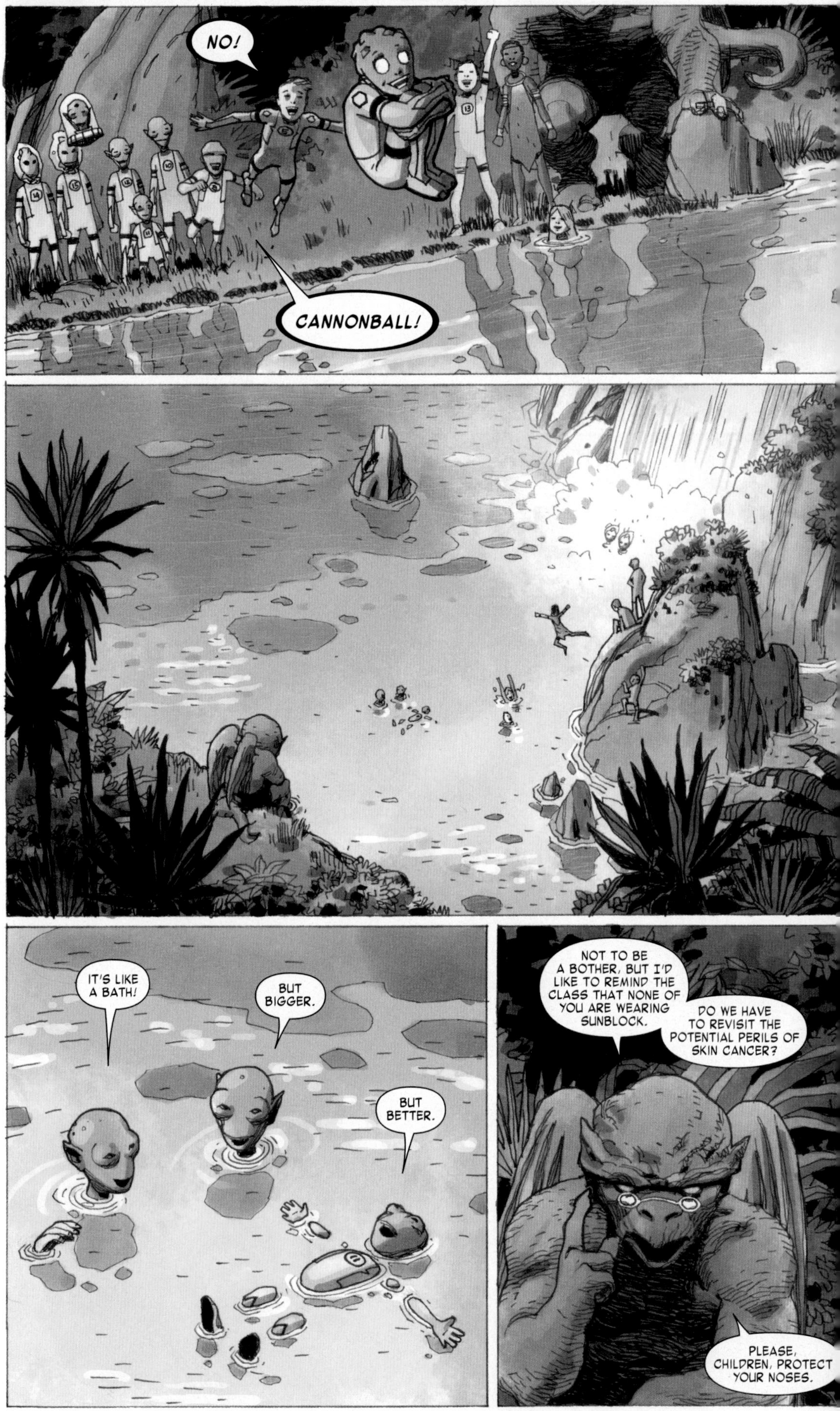
NO!
CANNONBALL!
IT'S LIKE A BATH!
BUT BIGGER.
BUT BETTER.
NOT TO BE A BOTHER, BUT I'D LIKE TO REMIND THE CLASS THAT NONE OF YOU ARE WEARING SUNBLOCK.
DO WE HAVE TO REVISIT THE POTENTIAL PERILS OF SKIN CANCER?
PLEASE, CHILDREN, PROTECT YOUR NOSES.

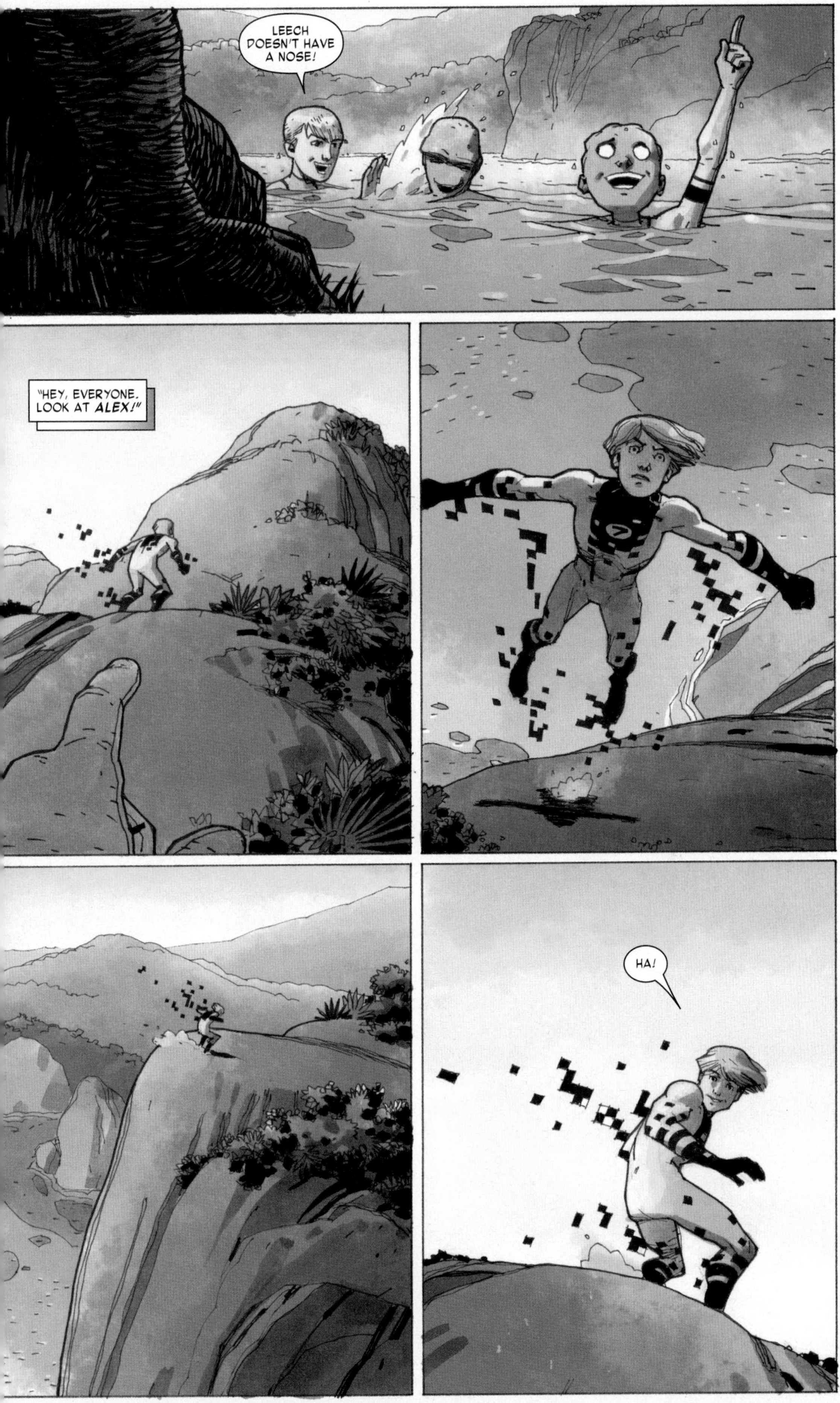
LEECH DOESN'T HAVE A NOSE!
"HEY, EVERYONE. LOOK AT ALEX!"
HA!

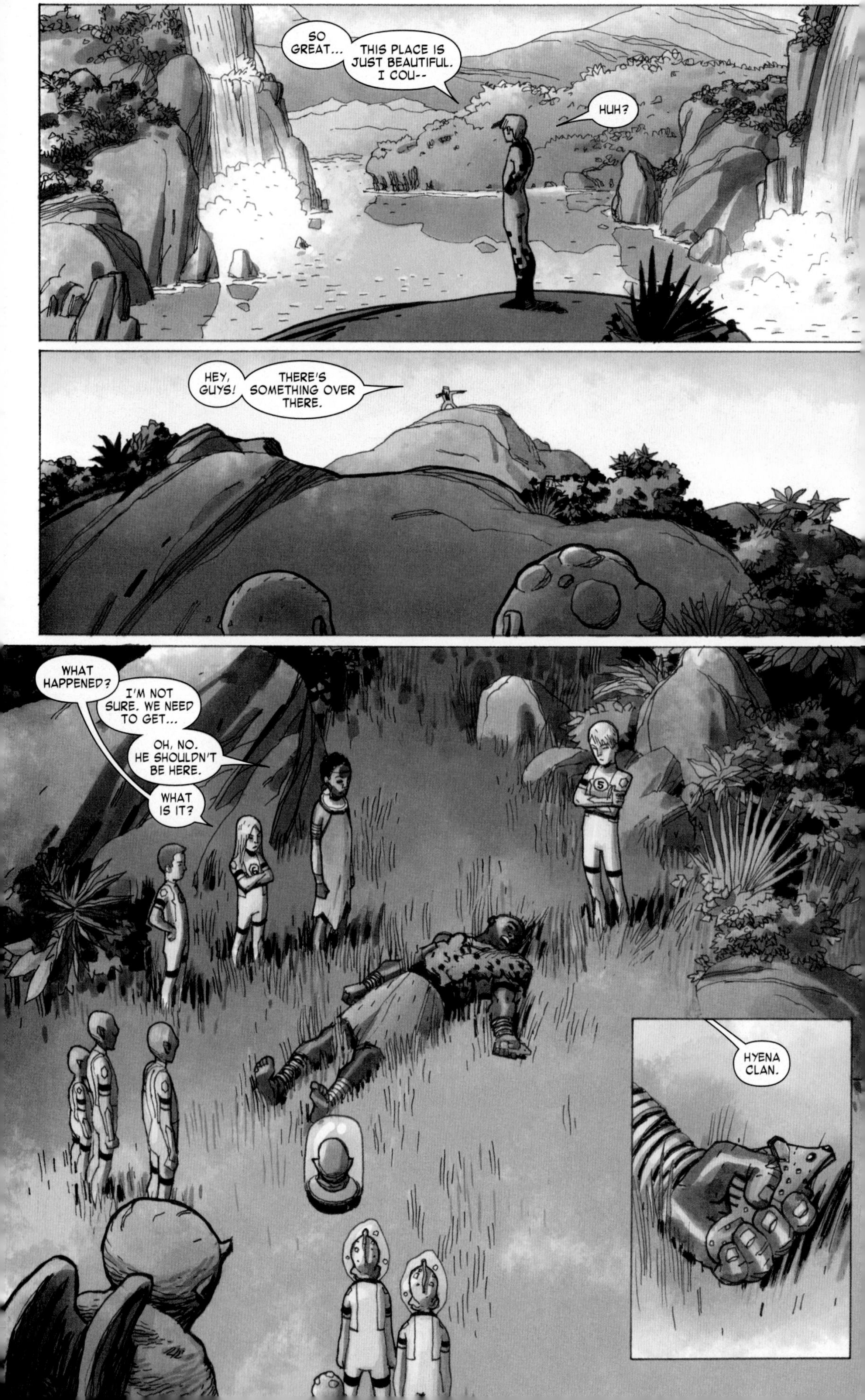

SO GREAT...
THIS PLACE IS JUST BEAUTIFUL. I COU--
HUH?
HEY, GUYS!
THERE'S SOMETHING OVER THERE.
WHAT HAPPENED?
I'M NOT SURE. WE NEED TO GET...
OH, NO. HE SHOULDN'T BE HERE.
WHAT IS IT?
HYENA CLAN.

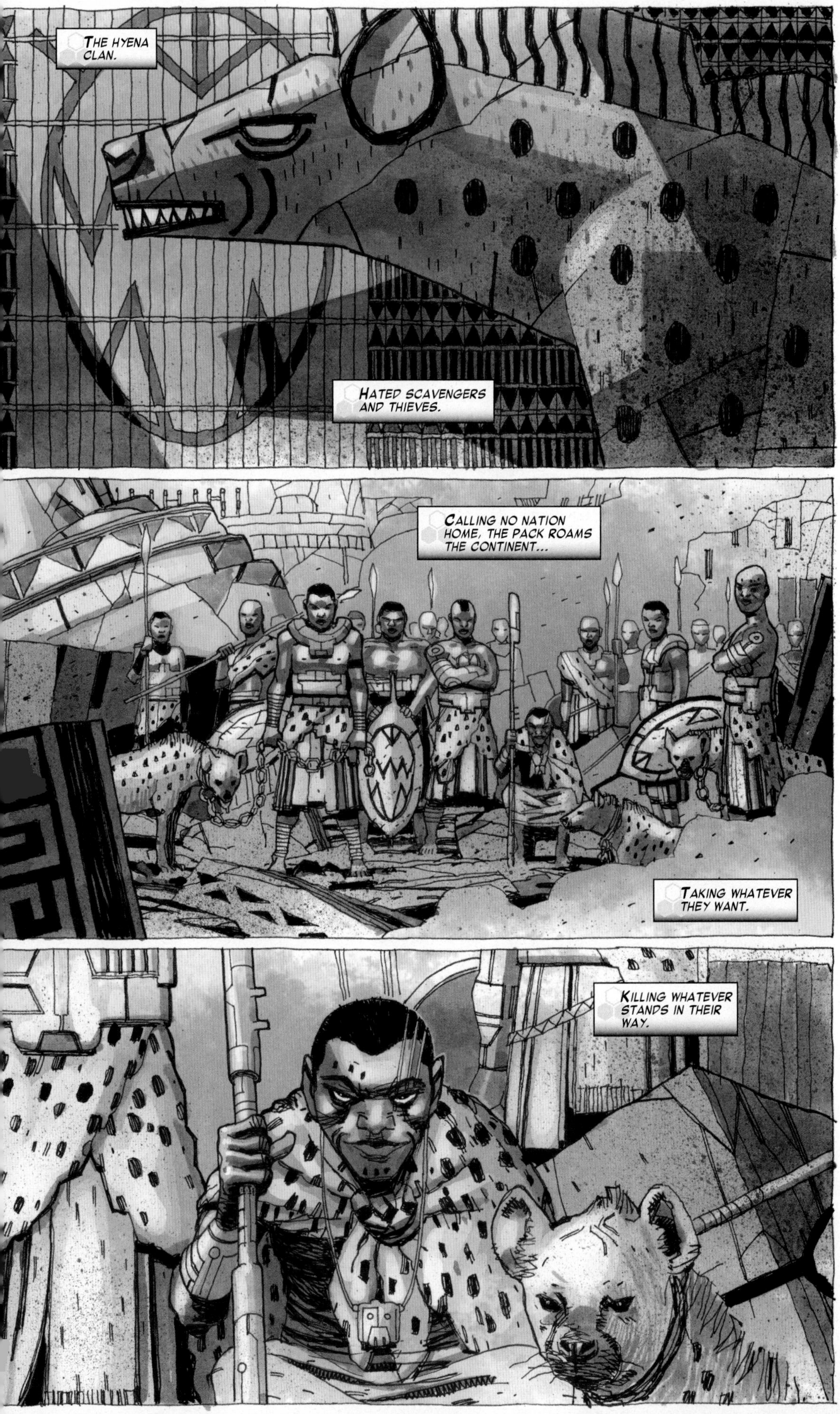
THE HYENA CLAN.
HATED SCAVENGERS AND THIEVES.
CALLING NO NATION HOME, THE PACK ROAMS THE CONTINENT...
TAKING WHATEVER THEY WANT.
KILLING WHATEVER STANDS IN THEIR WAY.

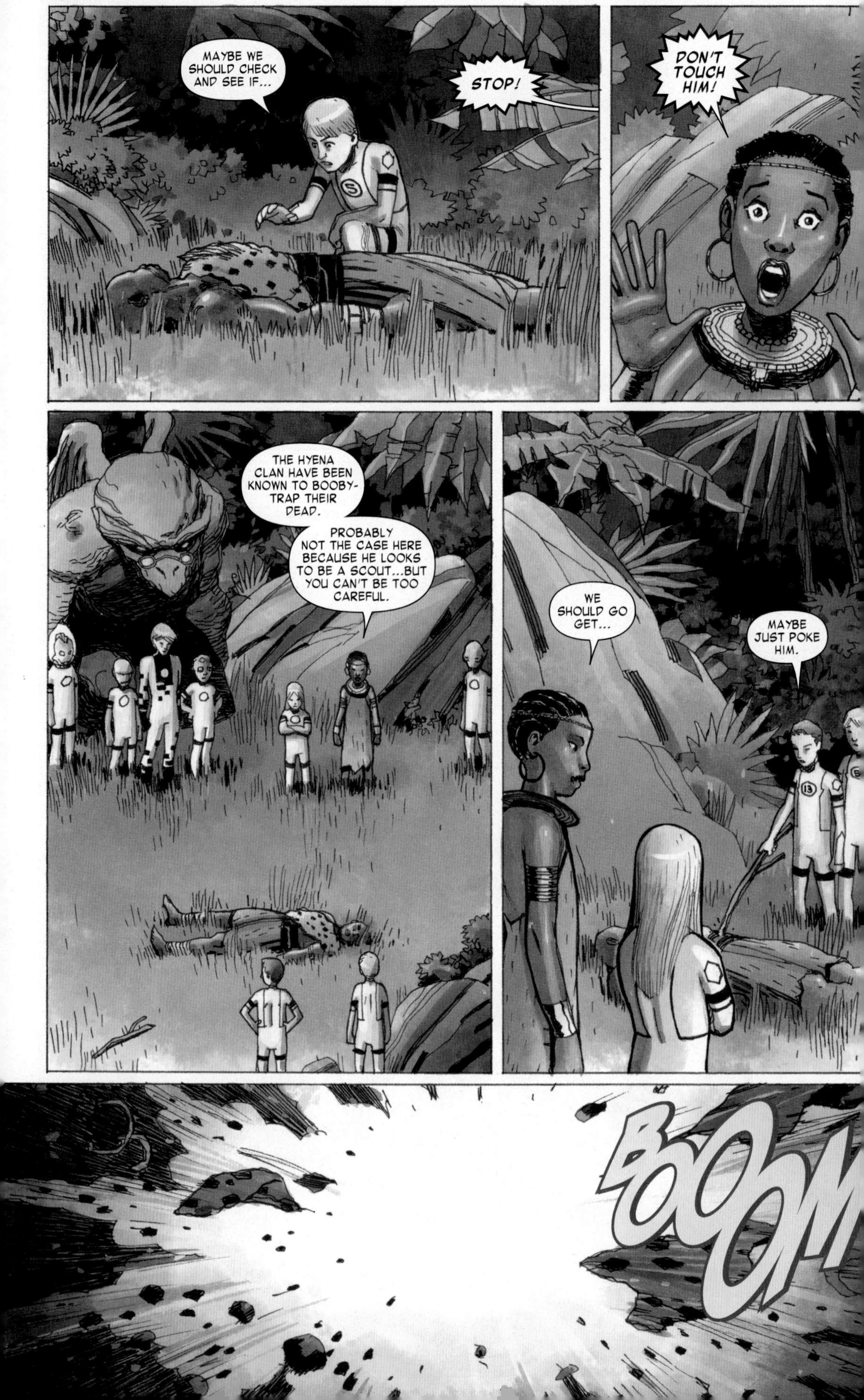
MAYBE WE SHOULD CHECK AND SEE IF...
STOP!
DON'T TOUCH HIM!
THE HYENA CLAN HAVE BEEN KNOWN TO BOOBY-TRAP THEIR DEAD.
PROBABLY NOT THE CASE HERE BECAUSE HE LOOKS TO BE A SCOUT...BUT YOU CAN'T BE TOO CAREFUL.
WE SHOULD GO GET...
MAYBE JUST POKE HIM.
BOOOM

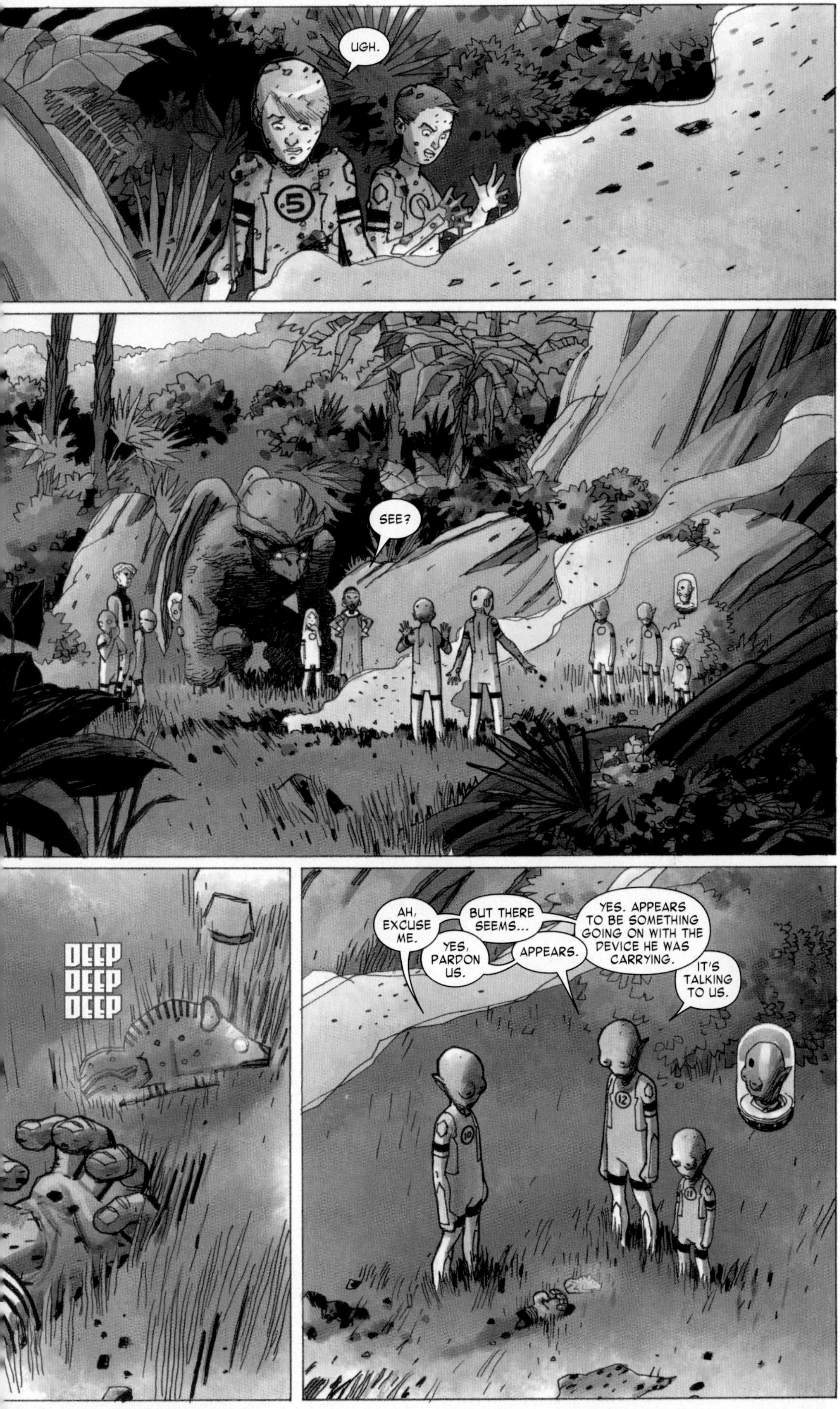
UGH.
SEE?
DEEP
DEEP
DEEP
AH, EXCUSE ME.
BUT THERE SEEMS...
YES, PARDON US.
APPEARS.
YES. APPEARS TO BE SOMETHING GOING ON WITH THE DEVICE HE WAS CARRYING.
IT'S TALKING TO US.

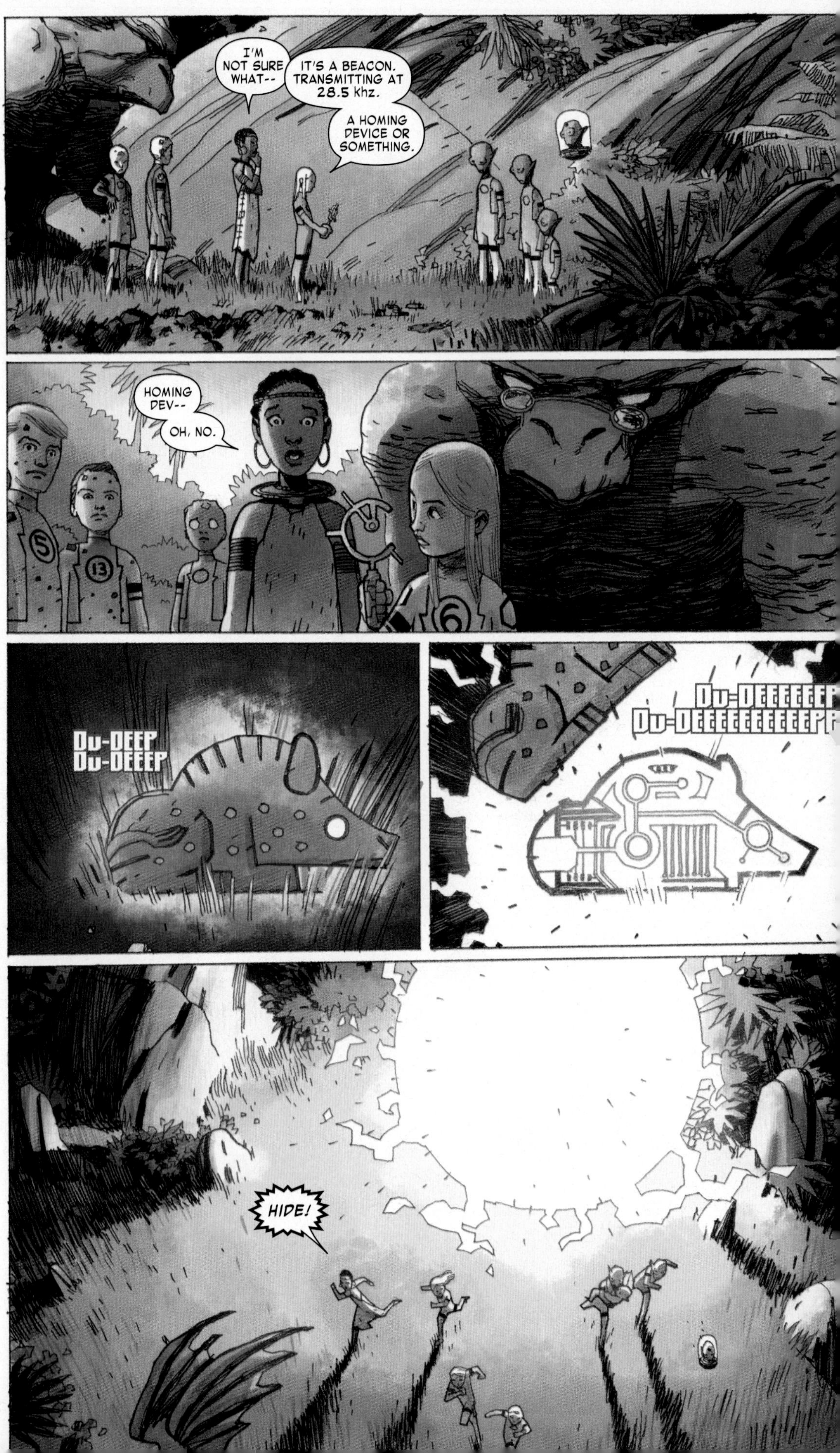
I'M NOT SURE WHAT--
IT'S A BEACON. TRANSMITTING AT 28.5 khz.
A HOMING DEVICE OR SOMETHING.
HOMING DEV--
OH, NO.
Du-DEEP
Du-DEEEP
Du-DEEEEEEP
Du-DEEEEEEEEEEP
HIDE!

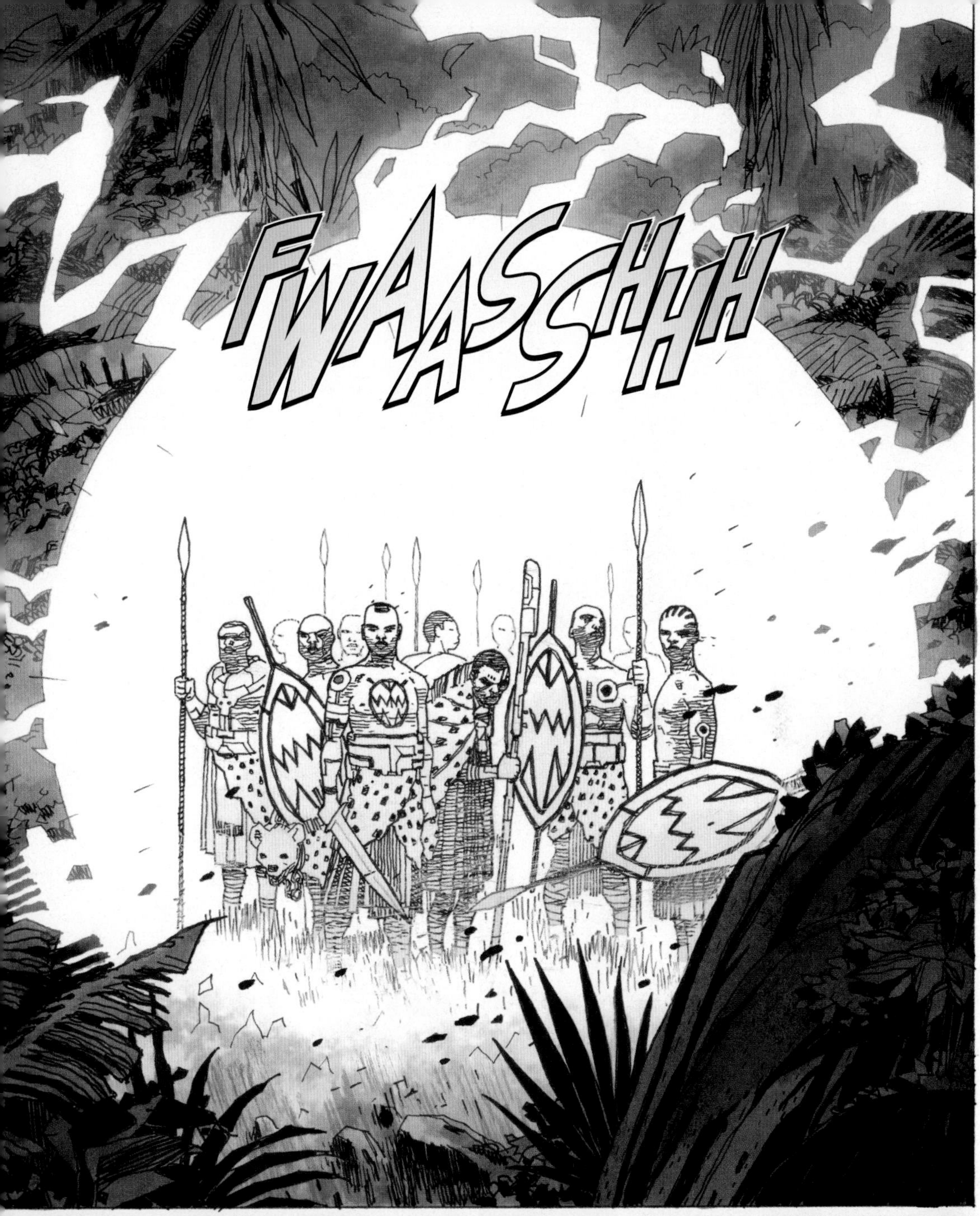
FWAASSHHH

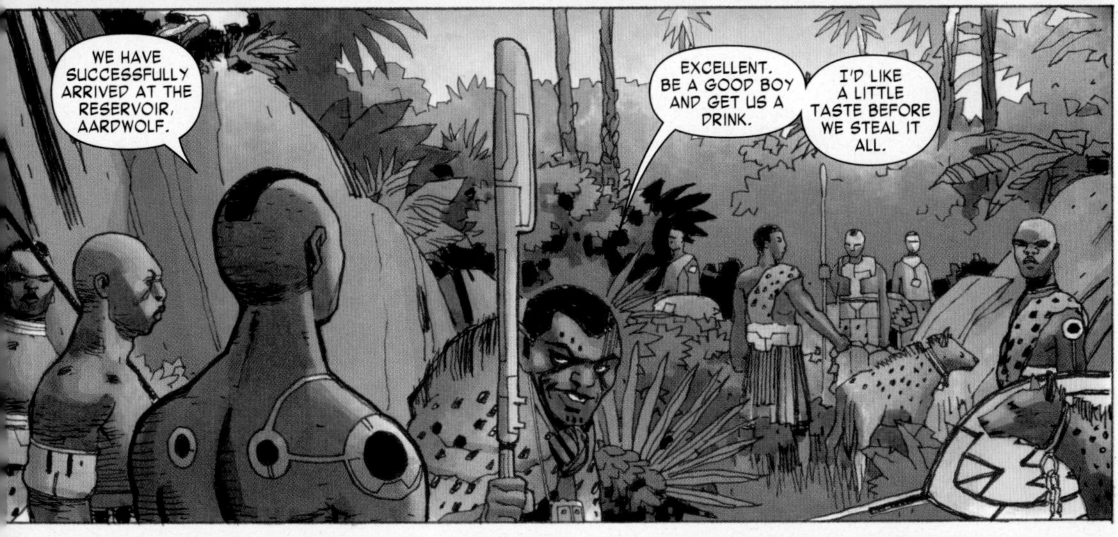
WE HAVE SUCCESSFULLY ARRIVED AT THE RESERVOIR, AARDWOLF.
EXCELLENT. BE A GOOD BOY AND GET US A DRINK.
I'D LIKE A LITTLE TASTE BEFORE WE STEAL IT ALL.

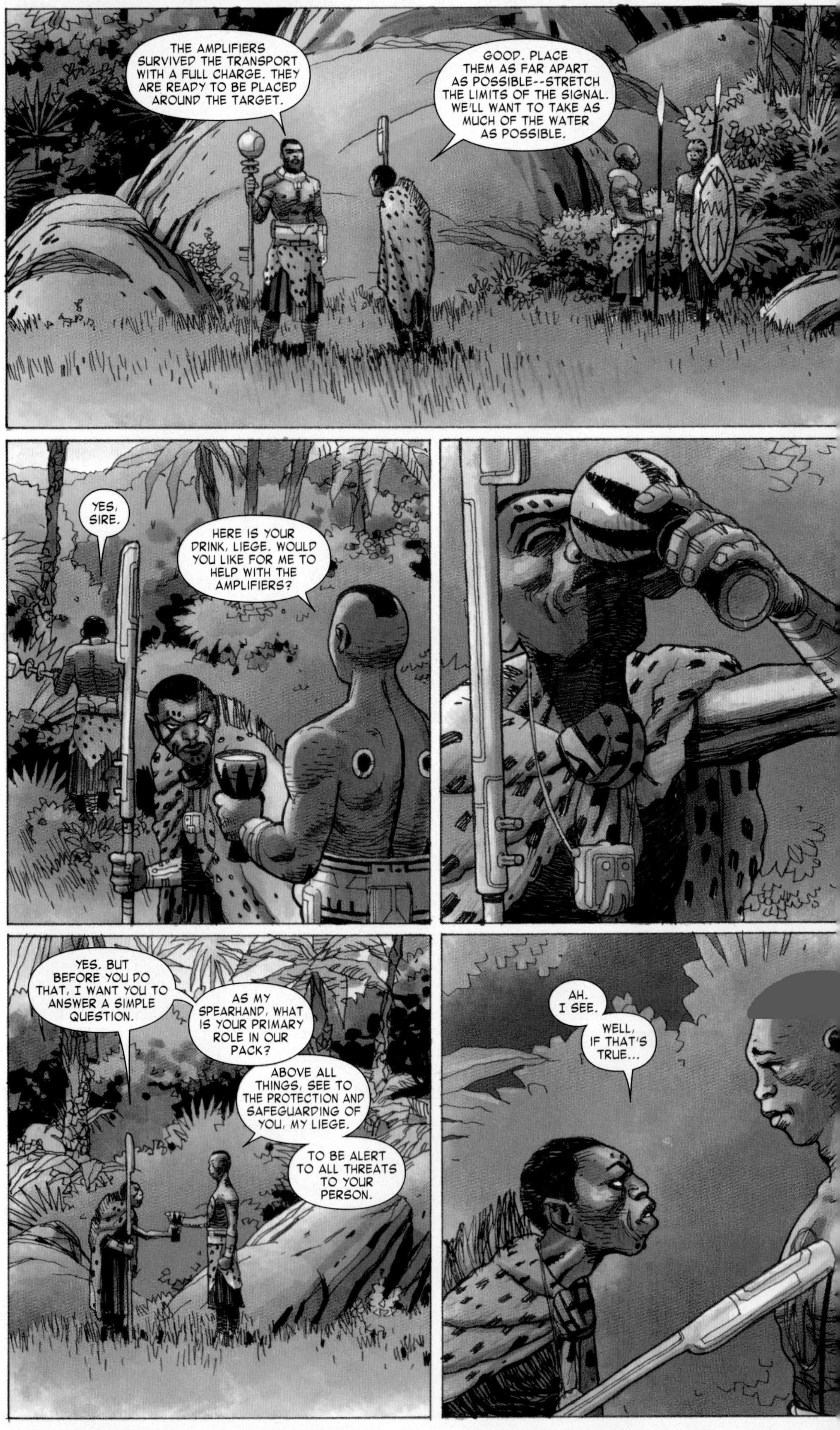
THE AMPLIFIERS SURVIVED THE TRANSPORT WITH A FULL CHARGE. THEY ARE READY TO BE PLACED AROUND THE TARGET.
GOOD. PLACE THEM AS FAR APART AS POSSIBLE--STRETCH THE LIMITS OF THE SIGNAL. WE'LL WANT TO TAKE AS MUCH OF THE WATER AS POSSIBLE.
YES, SIRE.
HERE IS YOUR DRINK, LIEGE. WOULD YOU LIKE FOR ME TO HELP WITH THE AMPLIFIERS?
YES. BUT BEFORE YOU DO THAT, I WANT YOU TO ANSWER A SIMPLE QUESTION.
AS MY SPEARHAND, WHAT IS YOUR PRIMARY ROLE IN OUR PACK?
ABOVE ALL THINGS, SEE TO THE PROTECTION AND SAFEGUARDING OF YOU, MY LIEGE.
TO BE ALERT TO ALL THREATS TO YOUR PERSON.
AH. I SEE.
WELL, IF THAT'S TRUE...

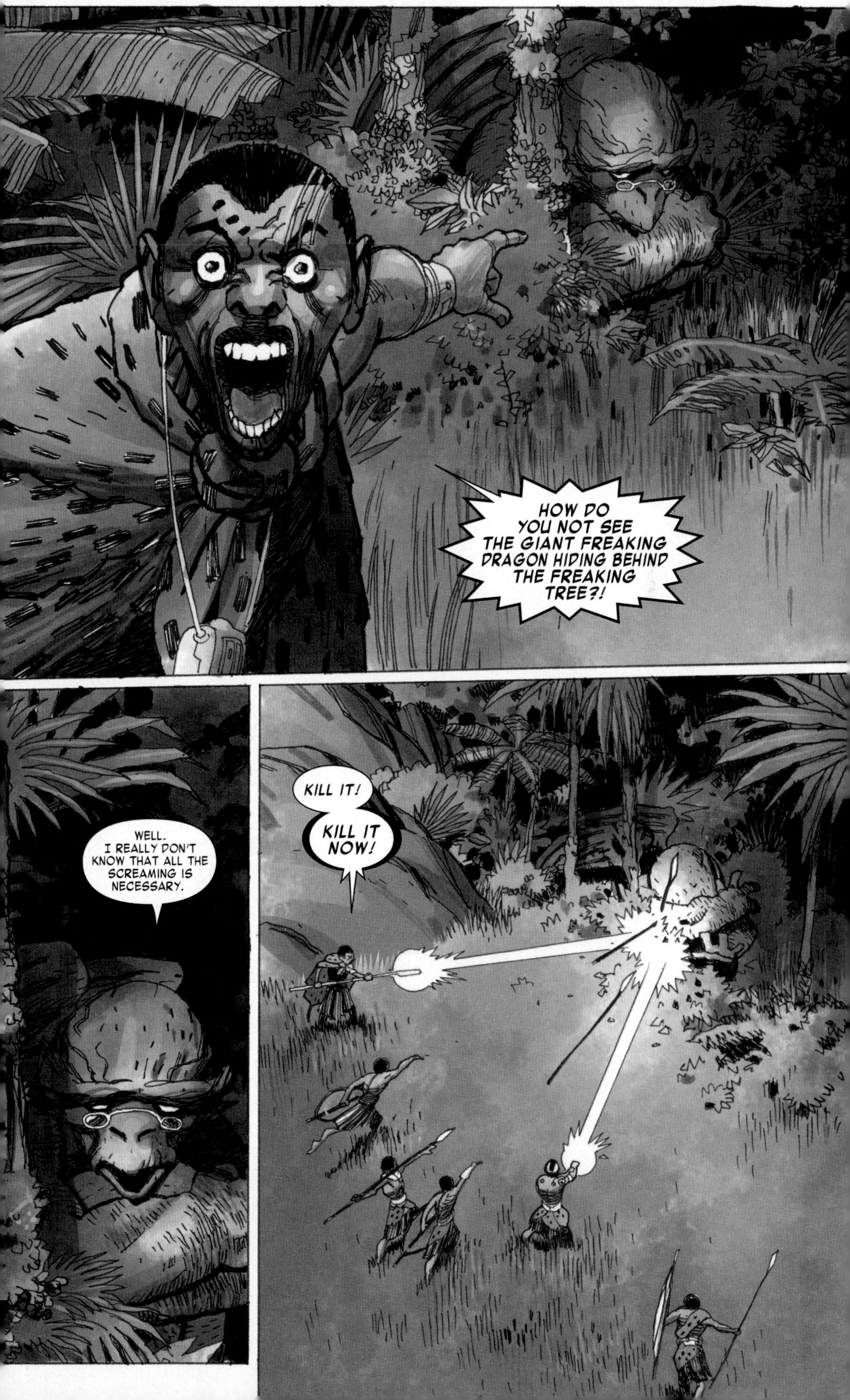
HOW DO YOU NOT SEE THE GIANT FREAKING DRAGON HIDING BEHIND THE FREAKING TREE?!
WELL. I REALLY DON'T KNOW THAT ALL THE SCREAMING IS NECESSARY.
KILL IT!
KILL IT NOW!

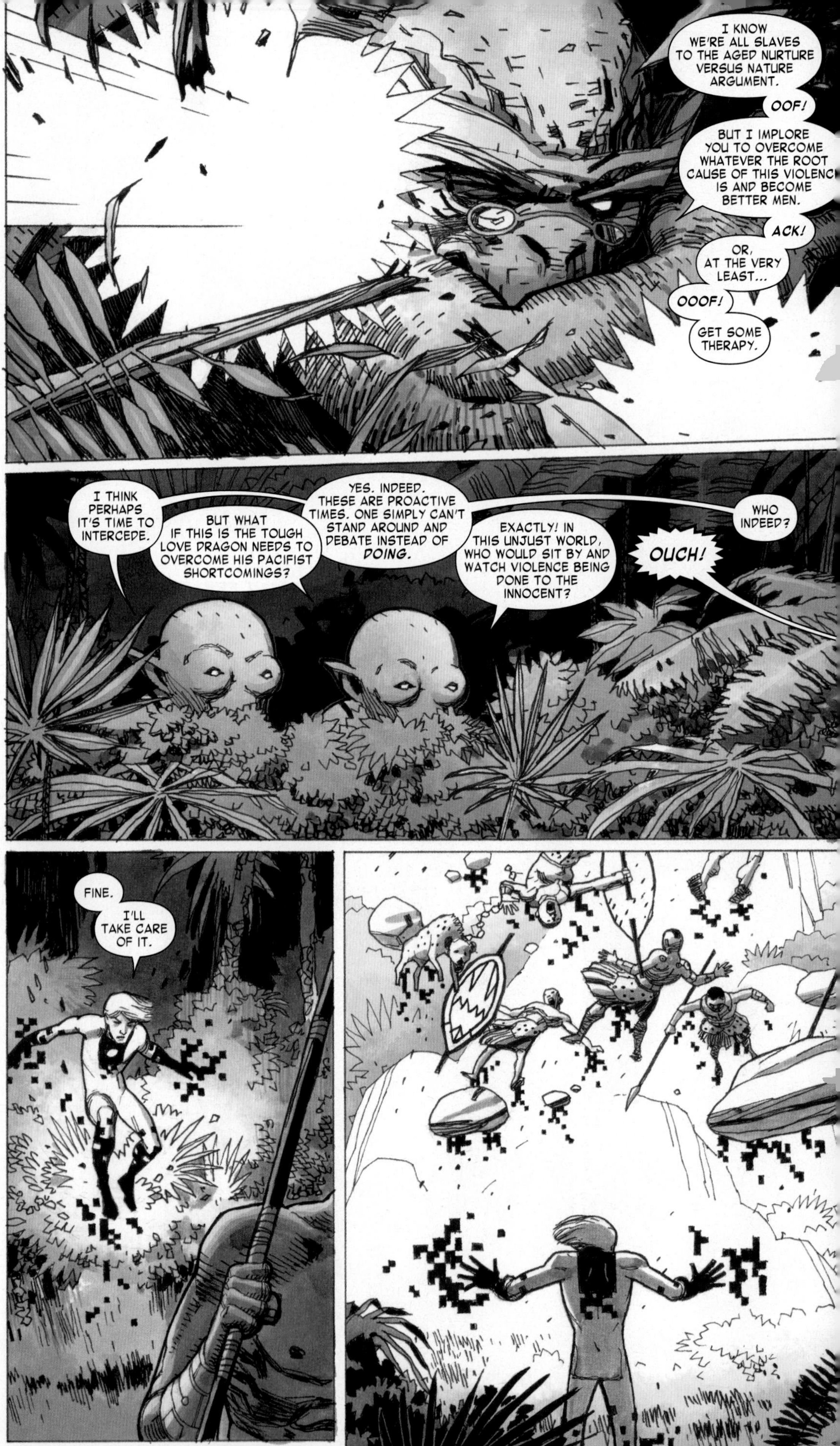

I KNOW WE'RE ALL SLAVES TO THE AGED NURTURE VERSUS NATURE ARGUMENT.
OOF!
BUT I IMPLORE YOU TO OVERCOME WHATEVER THE ROOT CAUSE OF THIS VIOLENC IS AND BECOME BETTER MEN.
ACK!
OR, AT THE VERY LEAST...
OOOF!
GET SOME THERAPY.
I THINK PERHAPS IT'S TIME TO INTERCEDE.
BUT WHAT IF THIS IS THE TOUGH LOVE DRAGON NEEDS TO OVERCOME HIS PACIFIST SHORTCOMINGS?
YES. INDEED. THESE ARE PROACTIVE TIMES. ONE SIMPLY CAN'T STAND AROUND AND DEBATE INSTEAD OF DOING.
EXACTLY! IN THIS UNJUST WORLD, WHO WOULD SIT BY AND WATCH VIOLENCE BEING DONE TO THE INNOCENT?
WHO INDEED?
OUCH!
FINE.
I'LL TAKE CARE OF IT.

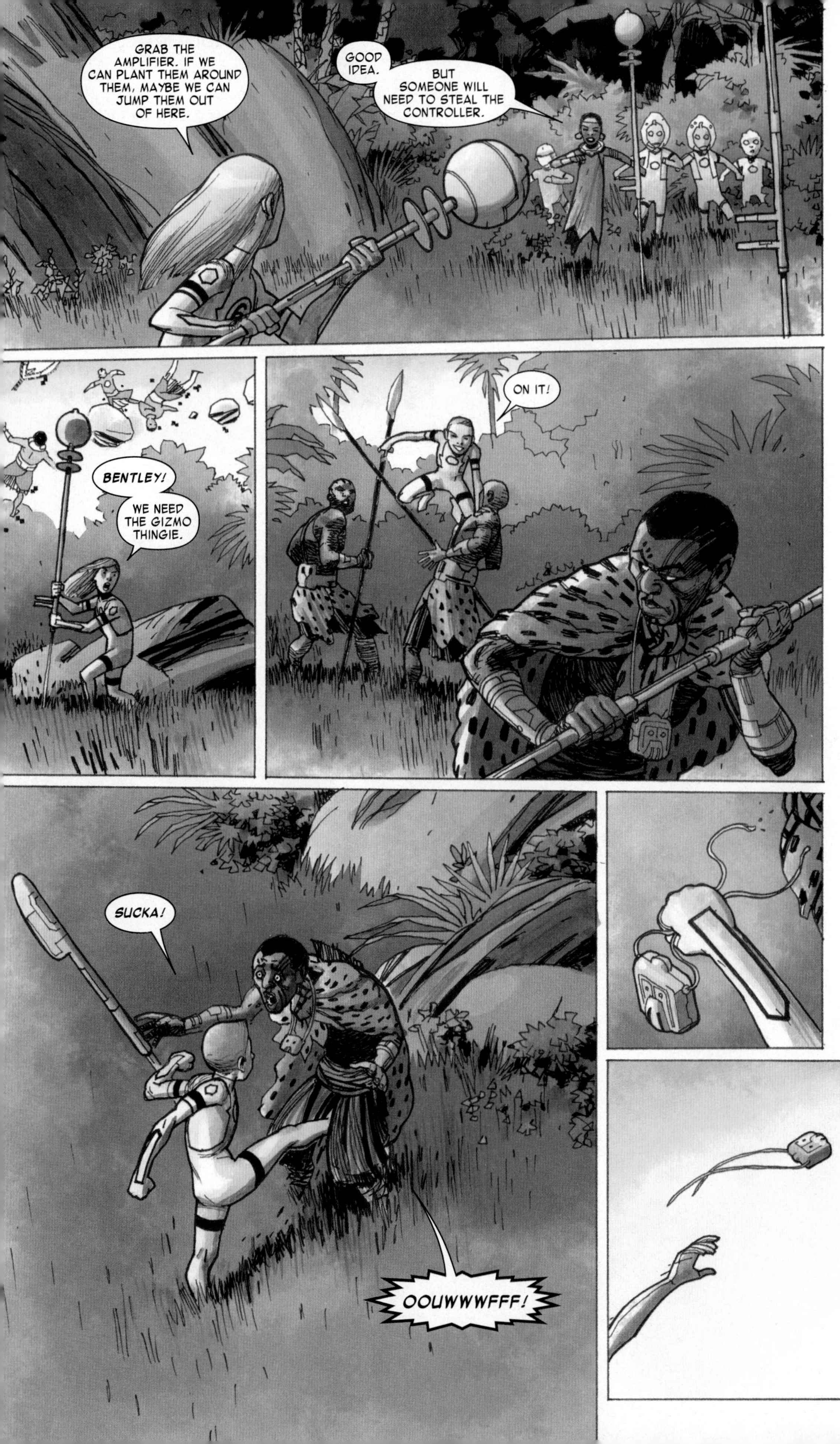
GRAB THE AMPLIFIER. IF WE CAN PLANT THEM AROUND THEM, MAYBE WE CAN JUMP THEM OUT OF HERE.
GOOD IDEA.
BUT SOMEONE WILL NEED TO STEAL THE CONTROLLER.
BENTLEY!
WE NEED THE GIZMO THINGIE.
ON IT!
SUCKA!
OOUWWWFFF!

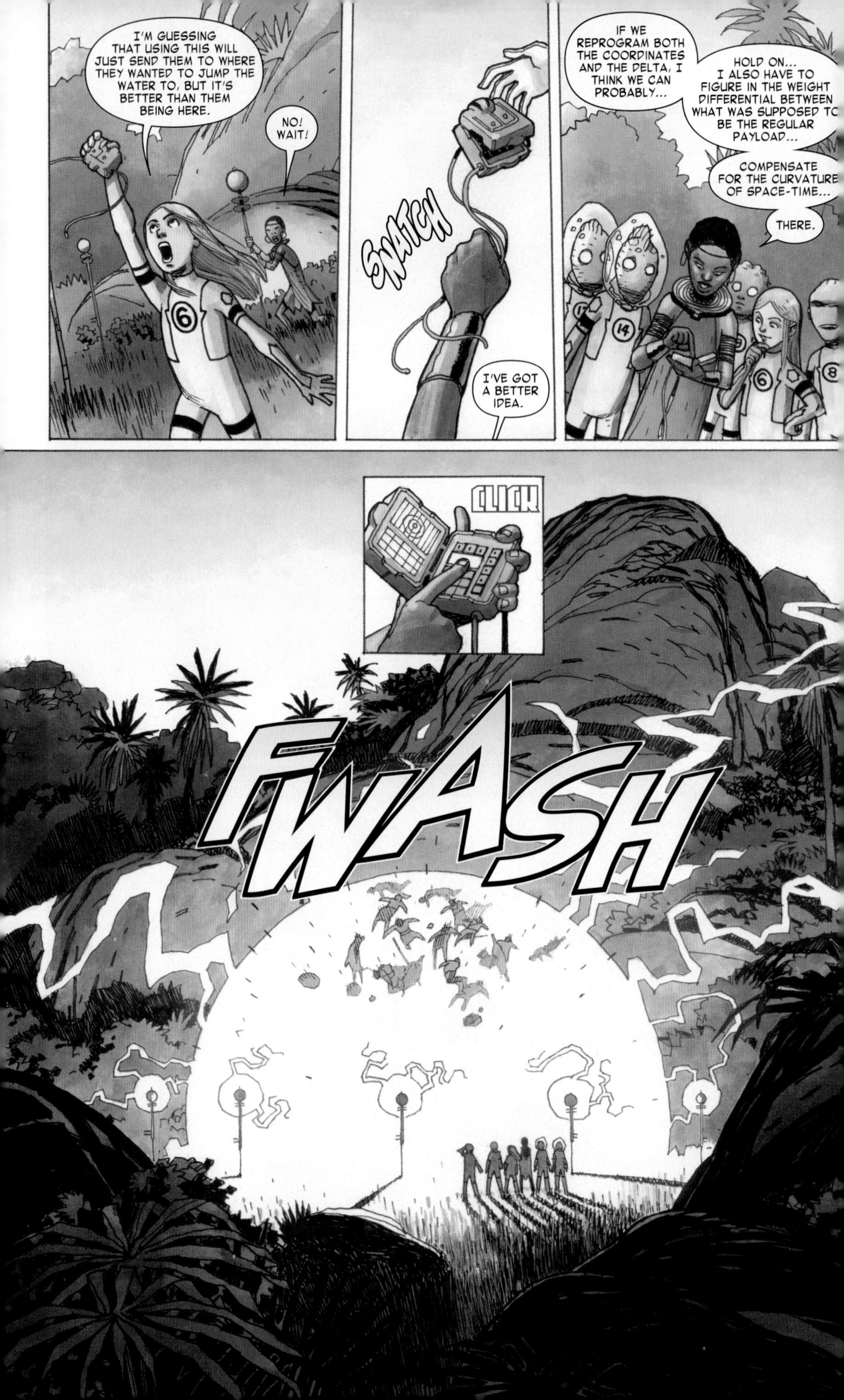
I'M GUESSING THAT USING THIS WILL JUST SEND THEM TO WHERE THEY WANTED TO JUMP THE WATER TO, BUT IT'S BETTER THAN THEM BEING HERE.
NO! WAIT!
SNATCH
I'VE GOT A BETTER IDEA.
IF WE REPROGRAM BOTH THE COORDINATES AND THE DELTA, I THINK WE CAN PROBABLY...
HOLD ON... I ALSO HAVE TO FIGURE IN THE WEIGHT DIFFERENTIAL BETWEEN WHAT WAS SUPPOSED TO BE THE REGULAR PAYLOAD...
COMPENSATE FOR THE CURVATURE OF SPACE-TIME...
THERE.
CLICK
FWASH

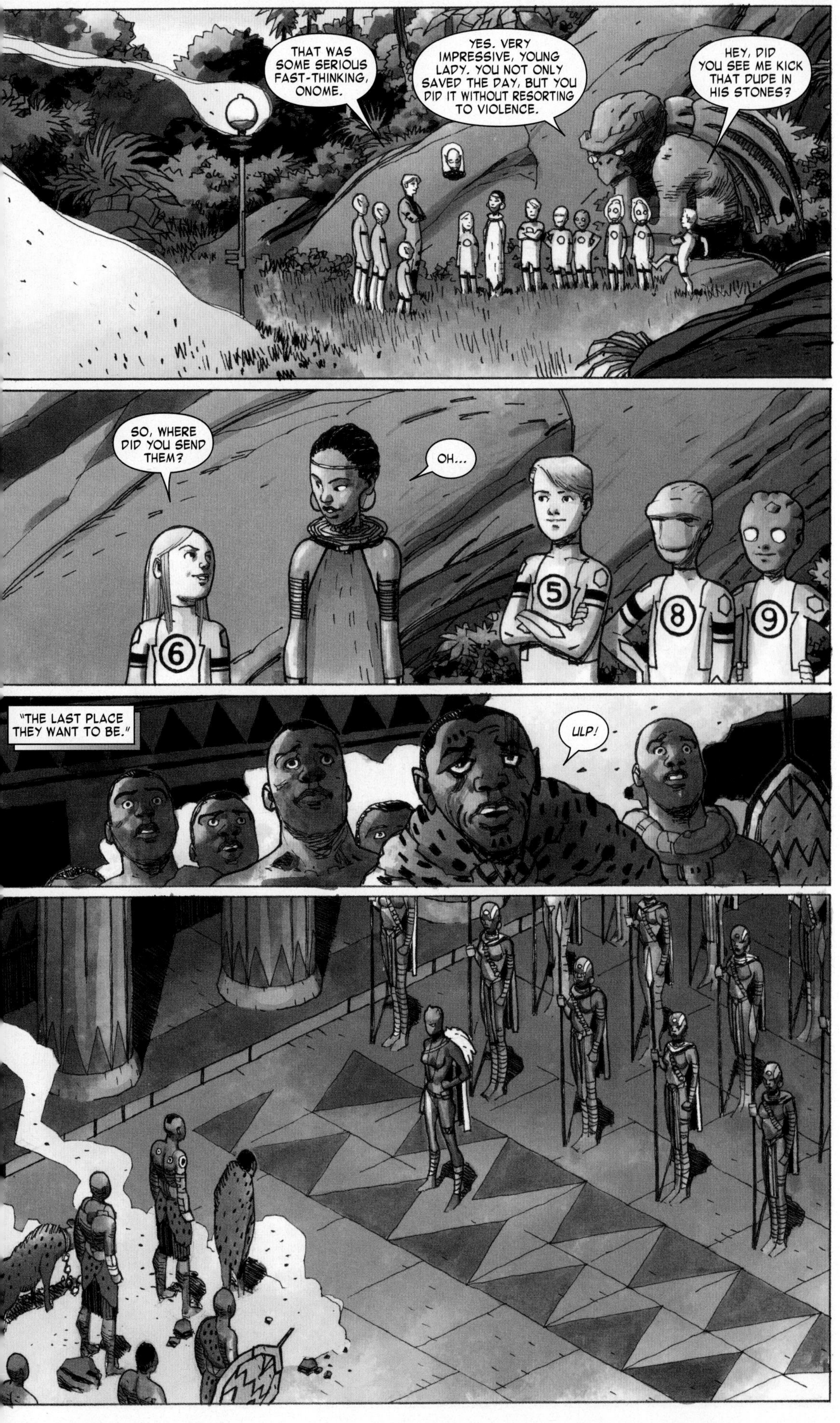
THAT WAS SOME SERIOUS FAST-THINKING, ONOME.
YES. VERY IMPRESSIVE, YOUNG LADY. YOU NOT ONLY SAVED THE DAY, BUT YOU DID IT WITHOUT RESORTING TO VIOLENCE.
HEY, DID YOU SEE ME KICK THAT DUDE IN HIS STONES?
SO, WHERE DID YOU SEND THEM?
OH...
"THE LAST PLACE THEY WANT TO BE."
ULP!

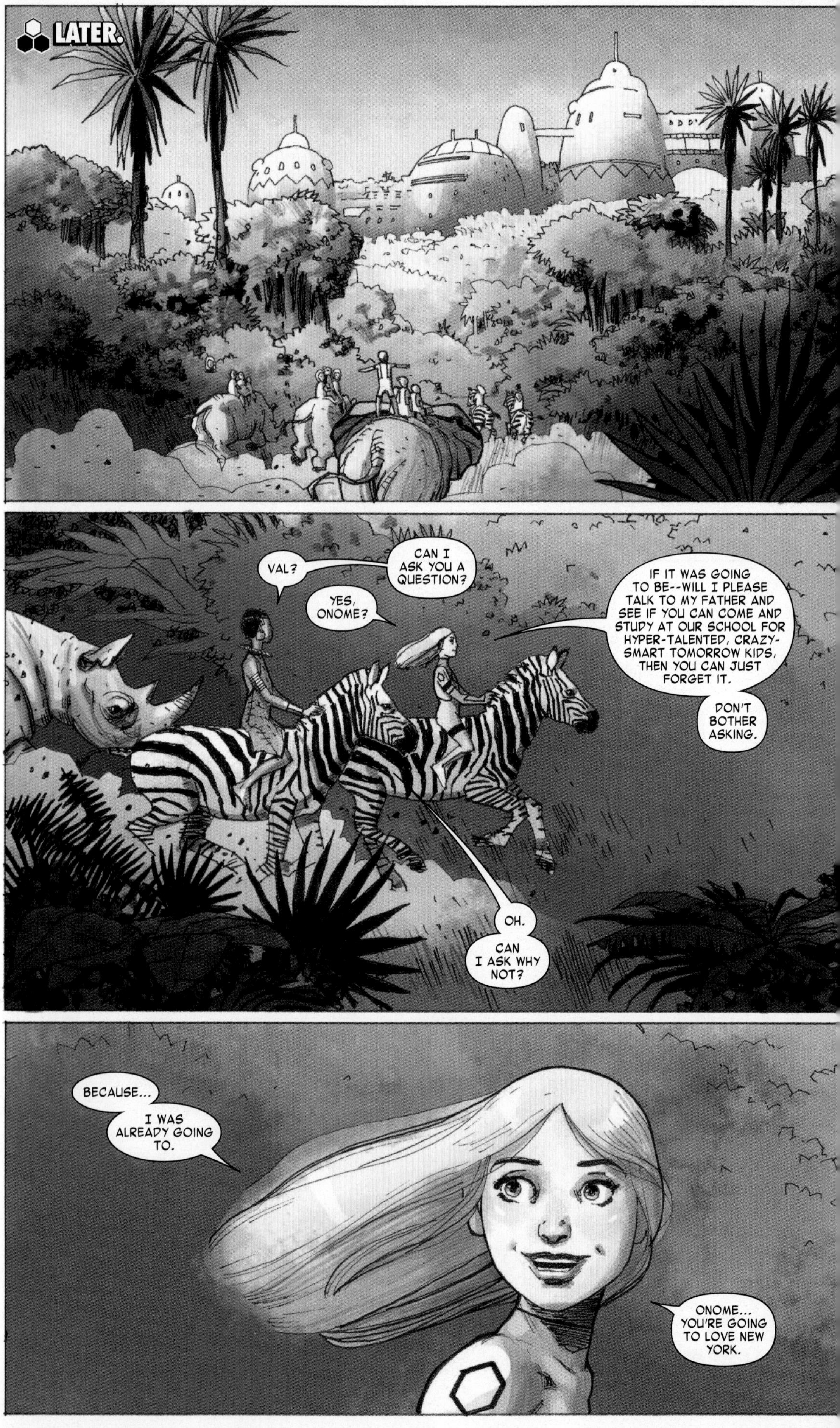
LATER.
VAL?
CAN I ASK YOU A QUESTION?
YES, ONOME?
IF IT WAS GOING TO BE--WILL I PLEASE TALK TO MY FATHER AND SEE IF YOU CAN COME AND STUDY AT OUR SCHOOL FOR HYPER-TALENTED, CRAZY-SMART TOMORROW KIDS, THEN YOU CAN JUST FORGET IT.
DON'T BOTHER ASKING.
OH.
CAN I ASK WHY NOT?
BECAUSE...
I WAS ALREADY GOING TO.
ONOME... YOU'RE GOING TO LOVE NEW YORK.

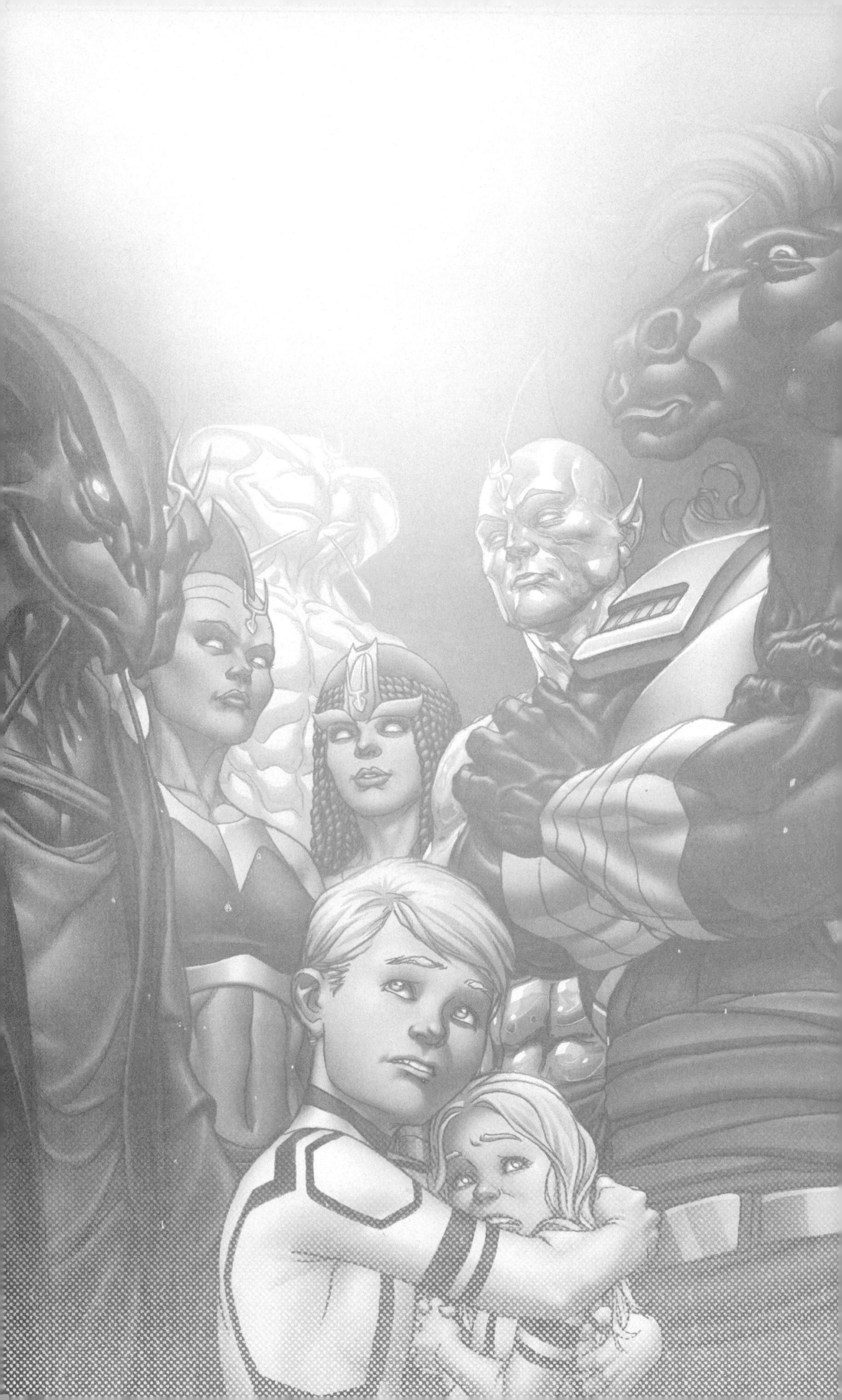

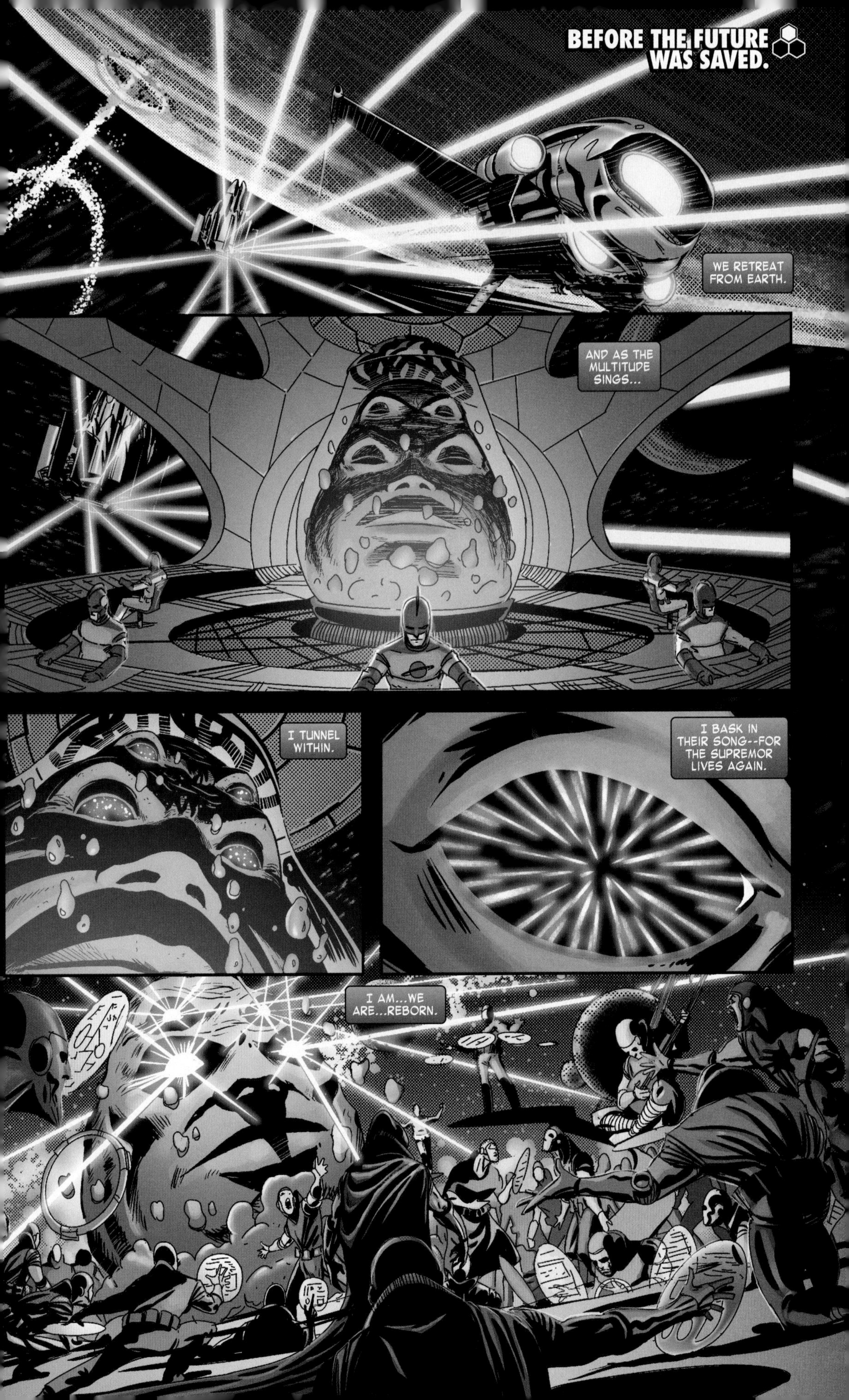
BEFORE THE FUTURE WAS SAVED.
WE RETREAT FROM EARTH.
AND AS THE MULTITUDE SINGS...
I TUNNEL WITHIN.
I BASK IN THEIR SONG--FOR THE SUPREMOR LIVES AGAIN.
I AM...WE ARE...REBORN.

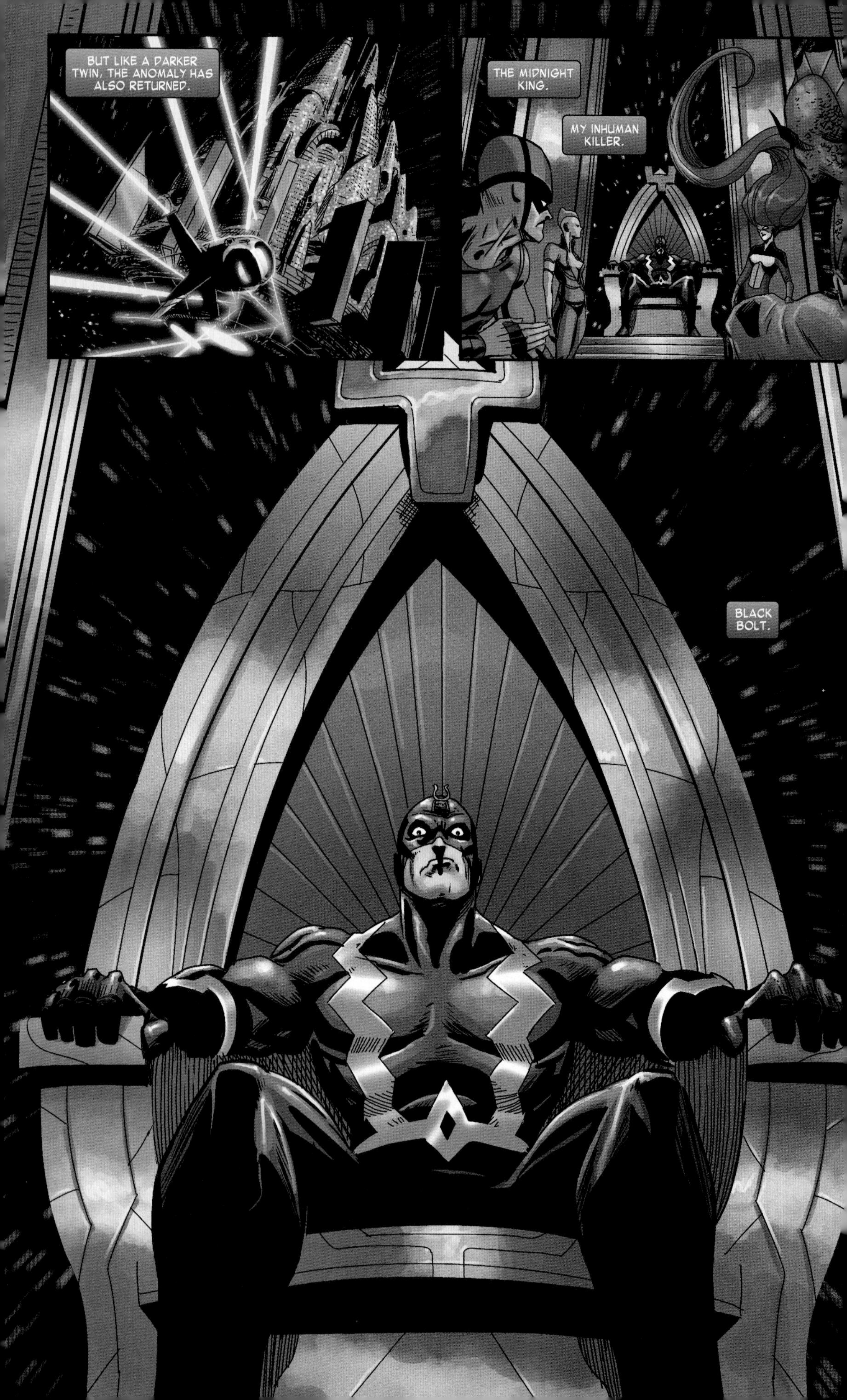
BUT LIKE A DARKER TWIN, THE ANOMALY HAS ALSO RETURNED.
THE MIDNIGHT KING.
MY INHUMAN KILLER.
BLACK BOLT.

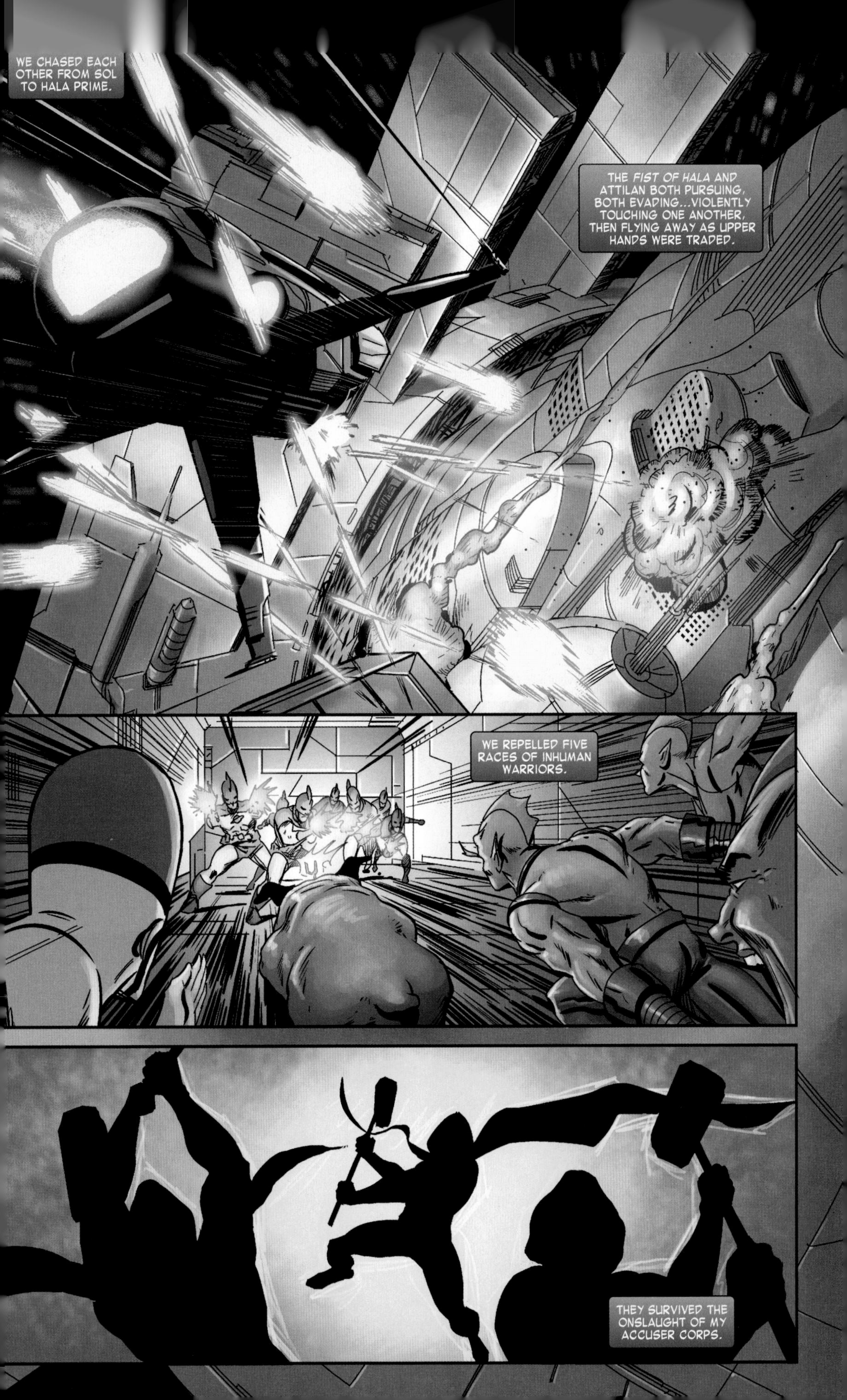
WE CHASED EACH OTHER FROM SOL TO HALA PRIME.
THE FIST OF HALA AND ATTILAN BOTH PURSUING, BOTH EVADING...VIOLENTLY TOUCHING ONE ANOTHER, THEN FLYING AWAY AS UPPER HANDS WERE TRADED.
WE REPELLED FIVE RACES OF INHUMAN WARRIORS.
THEY SURVIVED THE ONSLAUGHT OF MY ACCUSER CORPS.

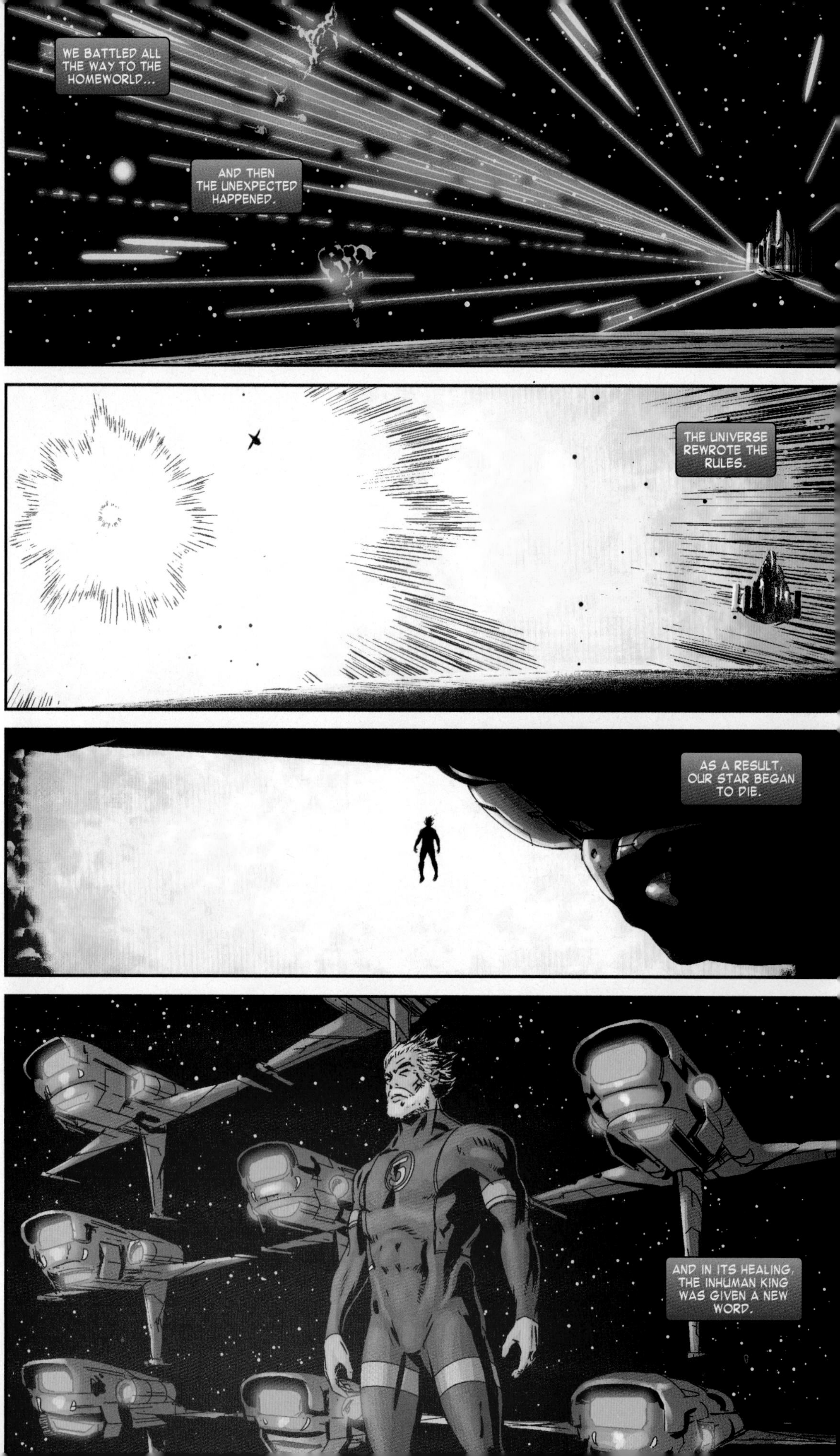
WE BATTLED ALL THE WAY TO THE HOMEWORLD...
AND THEN THE UNEXPECTED HAPPENED.
THE UNIVERSE REWROTE THE RULES.
AS A RESULT, OUR STAR BEGAN TO DIE.
AND IN ITS HEALING, THE INHUMAN KING WAS GIVEN A NEW WORD.

YOU MUST RETURN TO EARTH.

YOU HAVE TO BE THERE.

EVERYTHING DIES.

SO NOW HE RETURNS TO HOME.

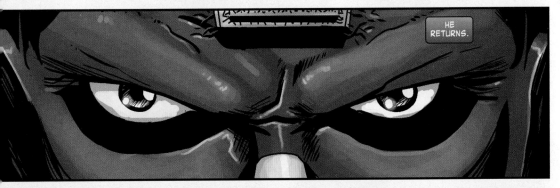

HE RETURNS.

HE RETURNS.

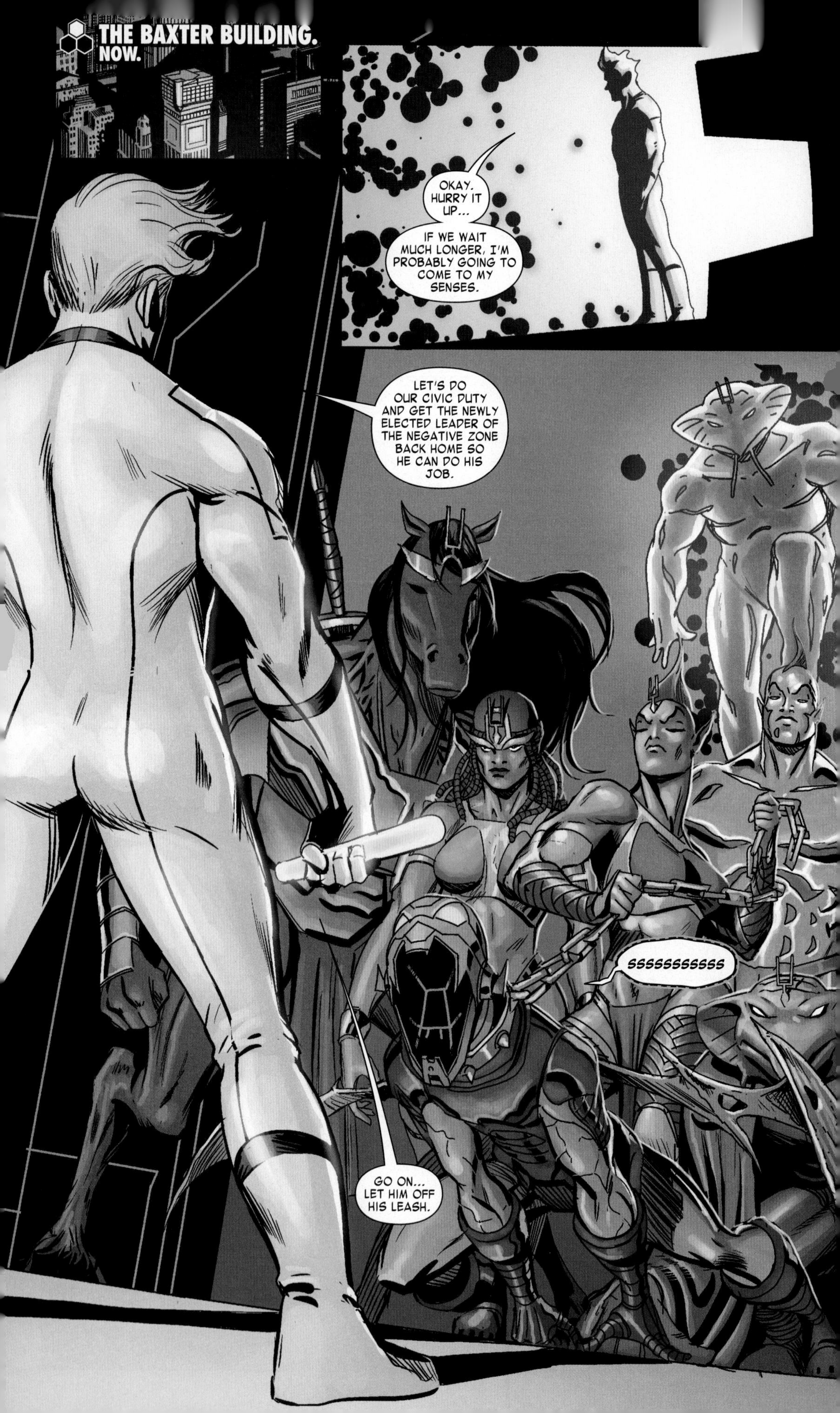
THE BAXTER BUILDING.
NOW.
OKAY. HURRY IT UP...
IF WE WAIT MUCH LONGER, I'M PROBABLY GOING TO COME TO MY SENSES.
LET'S DO OUR CIVIC DUTY AND GET THE NEWLY ELECTED LEADER OF THE NEGATIVE ZONE BACK HOME SO HE CAN DO HIS JOB.
SSSSSSSSSSS
GO ON... LET HIM OFF HIS LEASH.

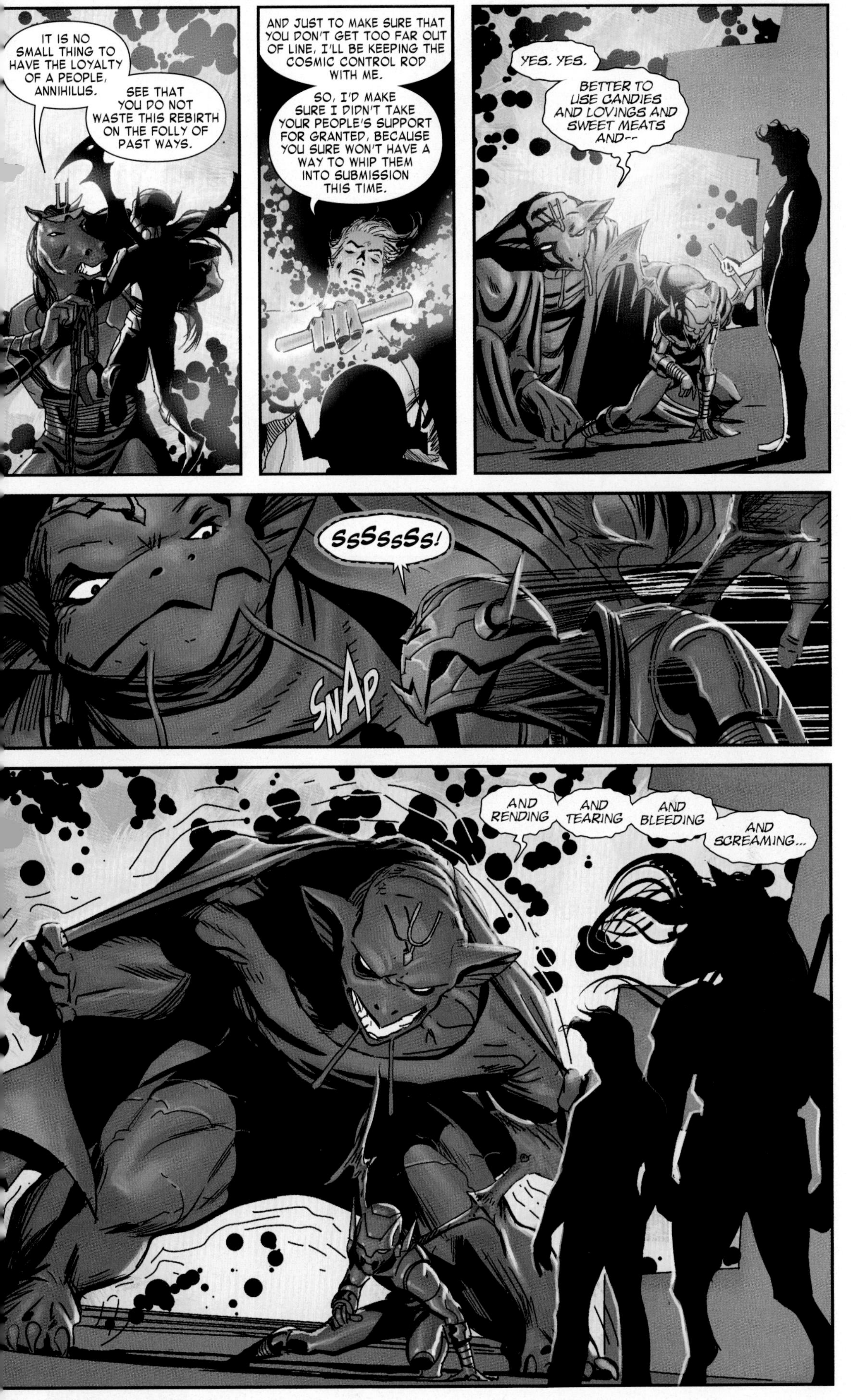
IT IS NO SMALL THING TO HAVE THE LOYALTY OF A PEOPLE, ANNIHILUS.
SEE THAT YOU DO NOT WASTE THIS REBIRTH ON THE FOLLY OF PAST WAYS.
AND JUST TO MAKE SURE THAT YOU DON'T GET TOO FAR OUT OF LINE, I'LL BE KEEPING THE COSMIC CONTROL ROD WITH ME.
SO, I'D MAKE SURE I DIDN'T TAKE YOUR PEOPLE'S SUPPORT FOR GRANTED, BECAUSE YOU SURE WON'T HAVE A WAY TO WHIP THEM INTO SUBMISSION THIS TIME.
YES. YES.
BETTER TO USE CANDIES AND LOVINGS AND SWEET MEATS AND--
SsSssSs!
SNAP
AND RENDING
AND TEARING
AND BLEEDING
AND SCREAMING...

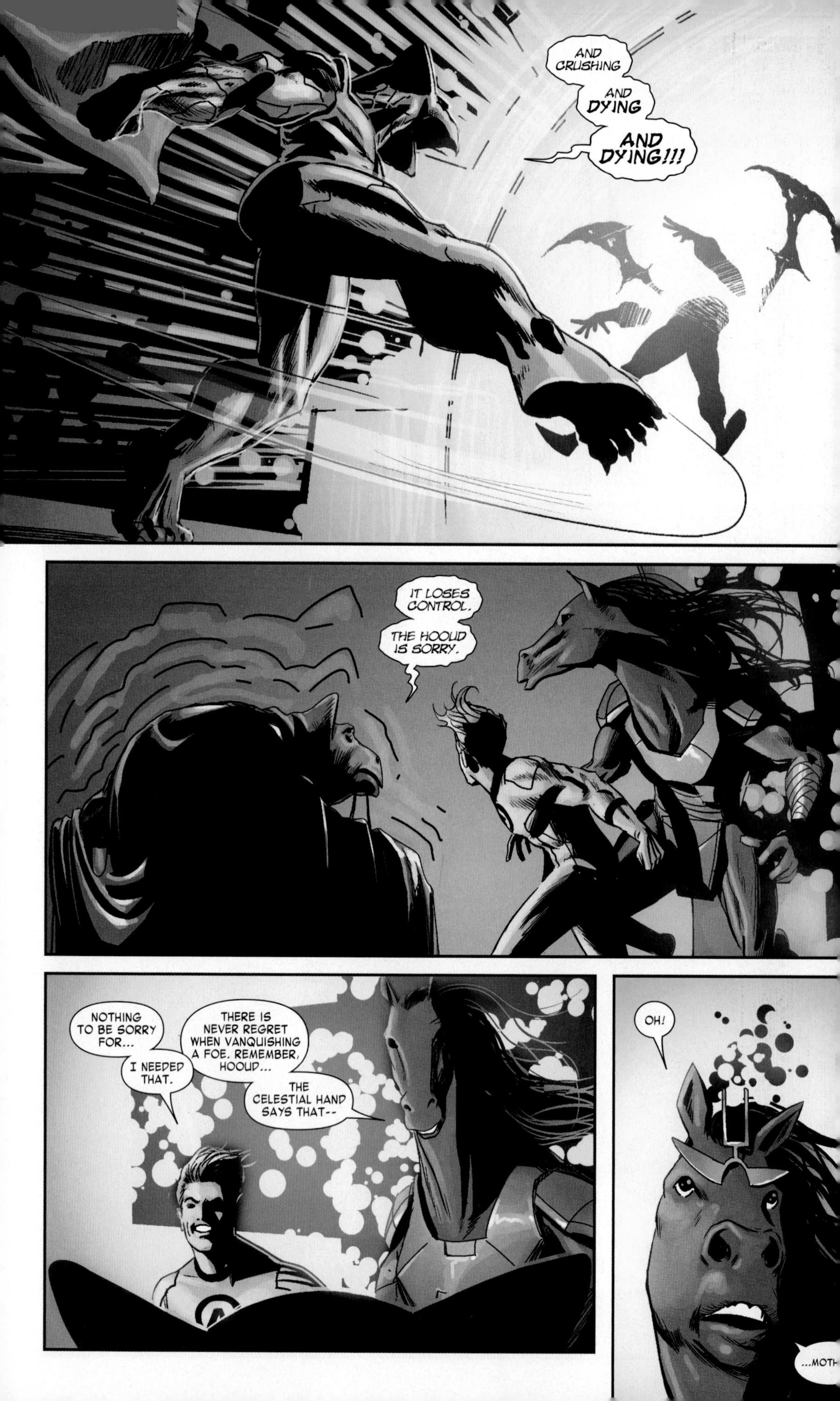

AND CRUSHING
AND DYING
AND DYING!!!
IT LOSES CONTROL.
THE HOOUD IS SORRY.
NOTHING TO BE SORRY FOR...
I NEEDED THAT.
THERE IS NEVER REGRET WHEN VANQUISHING A FOE. REMEMBER, HOOUD...
THE CELESTIAL HAND SAYS THAT--
OH!

ZUNDAMITES — OVOIDS — FONABI — HERMS

DRUFFS

SM'GGANI — NAND — KOBAL

WOBBS — GRUNDS

XANTHA — ELAN

COTATI

PLEASE PAY ATTENTION, CLASS.

WHILE IT SEEMS THAT WE HAVE CURRENTLY ENTERED A PERIOD OF PEACE WITH OUR GALACTIC NEIGHBORS, WE CAN NEVER TAKE SUCH A FICKLE, FICKLE STATE FOR GRANTED.

OVOIDS

'GGANI

XANTHA

WOBBS

SO...

WITH THAT IN MIND, TODAY WE WILL COVER THE TYPE II CIVILIZATIONS THAT WE KNOW EXIST WITHIN OUR MILKY WAY GALAXY, AND THEN EXPAND OUTWARD FROM THERE.

BE-DOOP

ZUNDAMITES — OVOIDS — FONABI — HERMS

SM'GGANI — DRUFFS — KOBADAKS

NANDA

COTATI — WOBBS — XANTHA

GRUNDS

WE'LL START WITH THE BADOON.

BADOON

ELAN

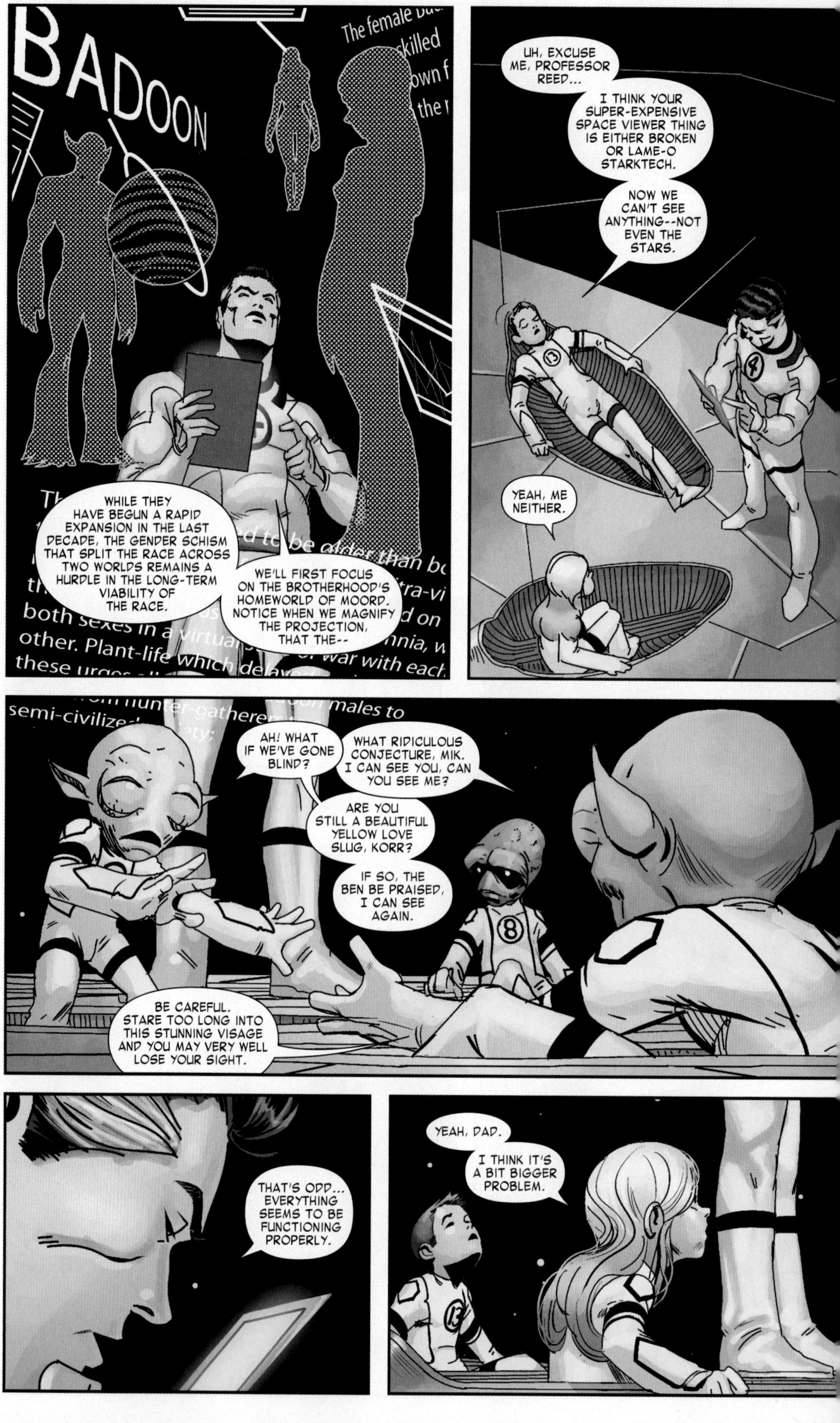
BADOON
WHILE THEY HAVE BEGUN A RAPID EXPANSION IN THE LAST DECADE, THE GENDER SCHISM THAT SPLIT THE RACE ACROSS TWO WORLDS REMAINS A HURDLE IN THE LONG-TERM VIABILITY OF THE RACE.
WE'LL FIRST FOCUS ON THE BROTHERHOOD'S HOMEWORLD OF MOORD. NOTICE WHEN WE MAGNIFY THE PROJECTION, THAT THE--
UH, EXCUSE ME, PROFESSOR REED...
I THINK YOUR SUPER-EXPENSIVE SPACE VIEWER THING IS EITHER BROKEN OR LAME-O STARKTECH.
NOW WE CAN'T SEE ANYTHING--NOT EVEN THE STARS.
YEAH, ME NEITHER.
AH! WHAT IF WE'VE GONE BLIND?
WHAT RIDICULOUS CONJECTURE, MIK. I CAN SEE YOU, CAN YOU SEE ME?
ARE YOU STILL A BEAUTIFUL YELLOW LOVE SLUG, KORR?
IF SO, THE BEN BE PRAISED, I CAN SEE AGAIN.
BE CAREFUL. STARE TOO LONG INTO THIS STUNNING VISAGE AND YOU MAY VERY WELL LOSE YOUR SIGHT.
THAT'S ODD... EVERYTHING SEEMS TO BE FUNCTIONING PROPERLY.
YEAH, DAD.
I THINK IT'S A BIT BIGGER PROBLEM.

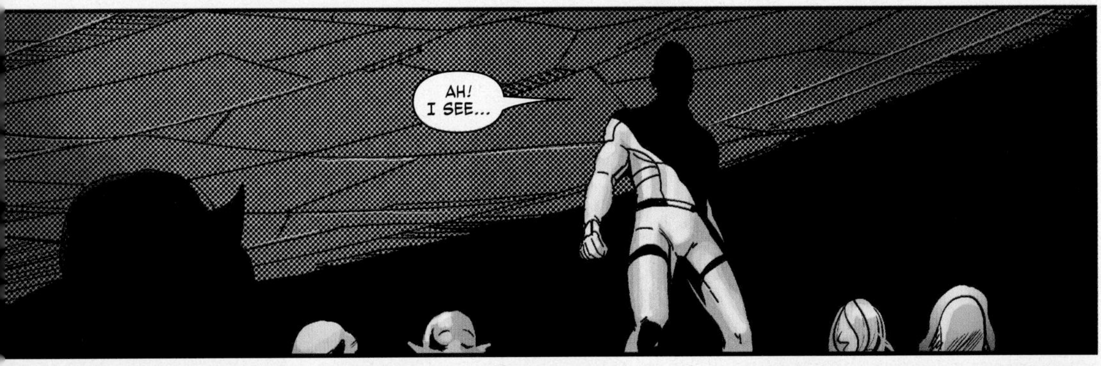
AH!
I SEE...
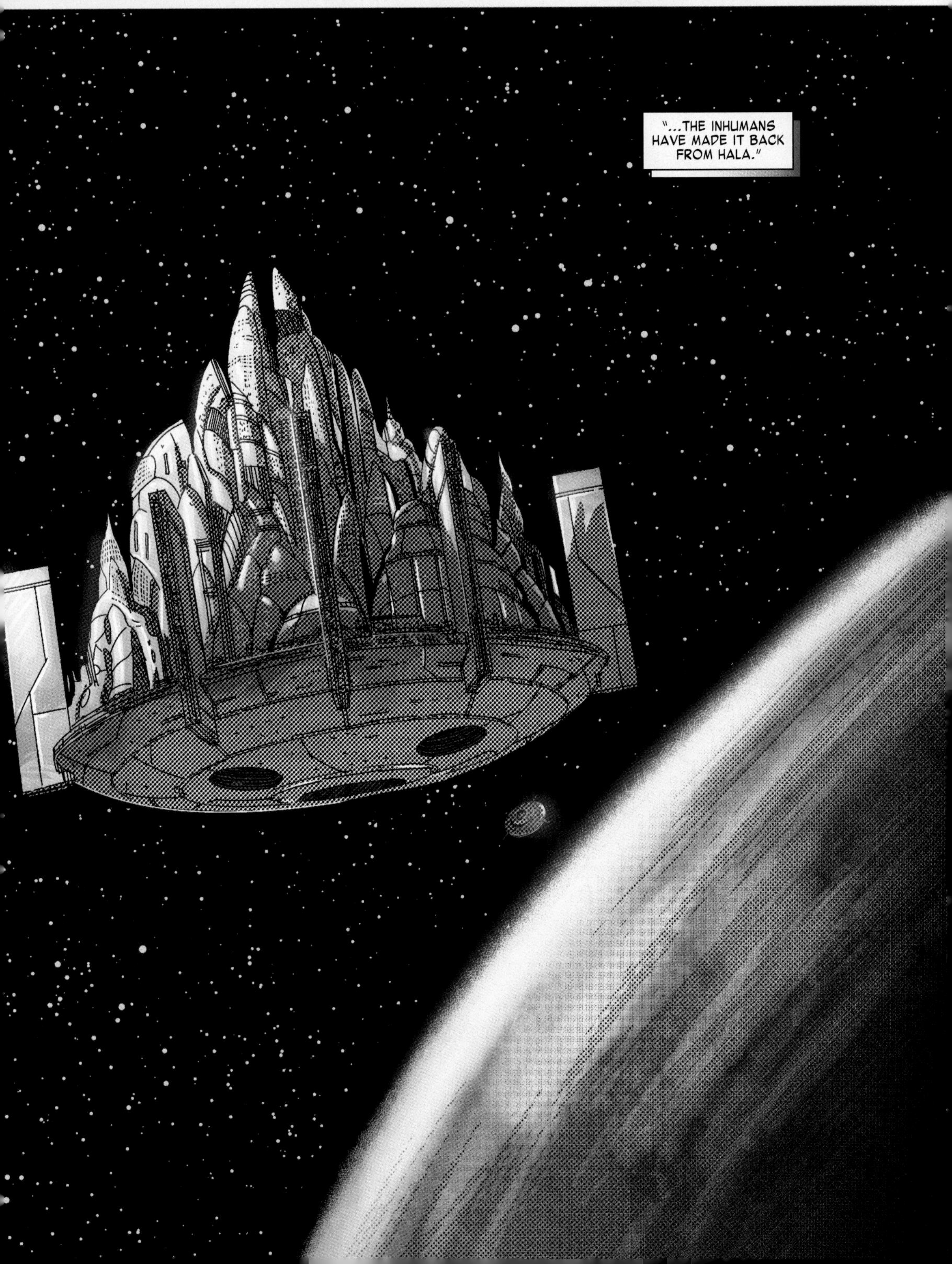
"...THE INHUMANS HAVE MADE IT BACK FROM HALA."

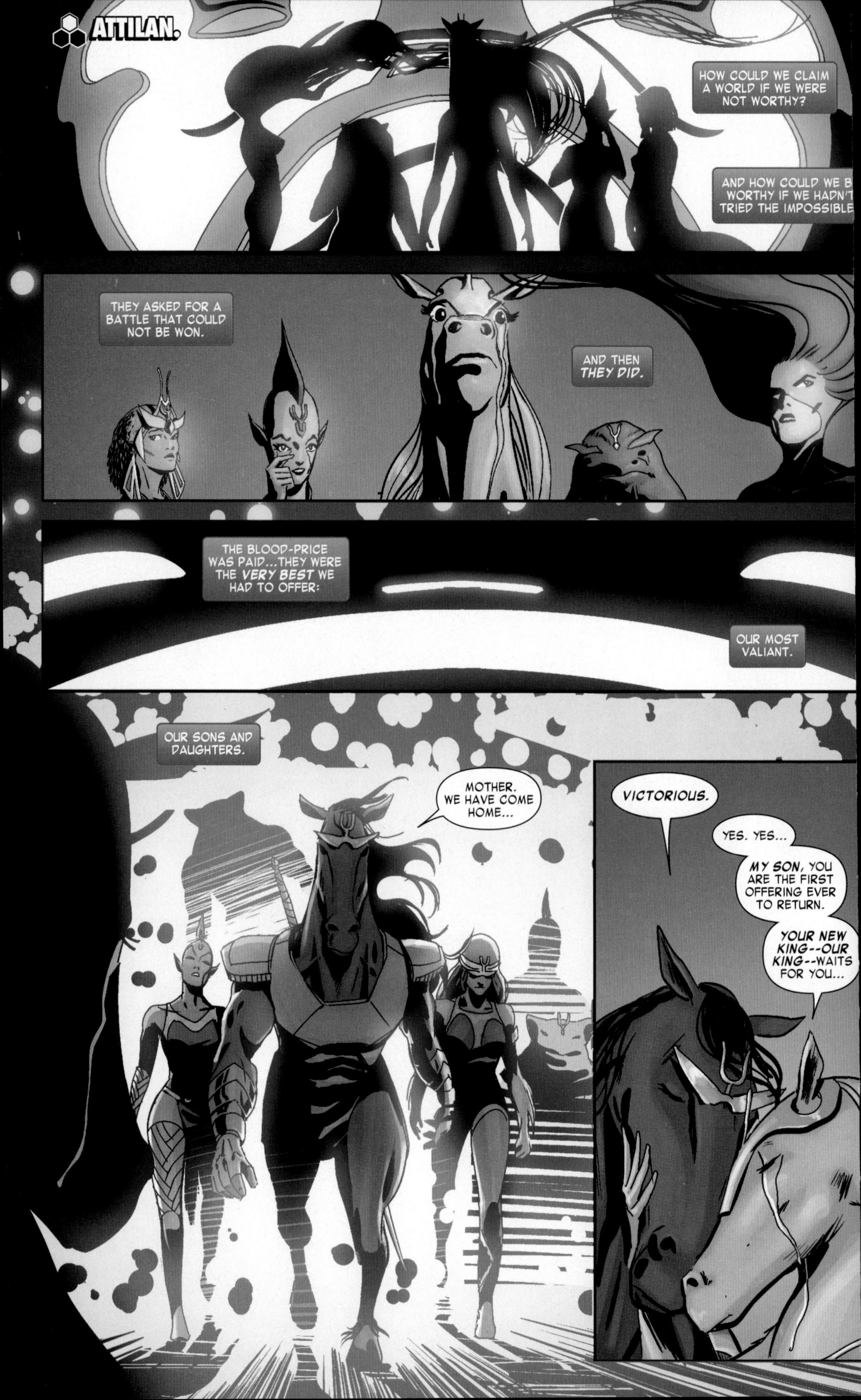
ATTILAN.
HOW COULD WE CLAIM A WORLD IF WE WERE NOT WORTHY?
AND HOW COULD WE BE WORTHY IF WE HADN'T TRIED THE IMPOSSIBLE?
THEY ASKED FOR A BATTLE THAT COULD NOT BE WON.
AND THEN THEY DID.
THE BLOOD-PRICE WAS PAID...THEY WERE THE VERY BEST WE HAD TO OFFER:
OUR MOST VALIANT.
OUR SONS AND DAUGHTERS.
MOTHER. WE HAVE COME HOME...
VICTORIOUS.
YES. YES...
MY SON, YOU ARE THE FIRST OFFERING EVER TO RETURN.
YOUR NEW KING--OUR KING--WAITS FOR YOU...

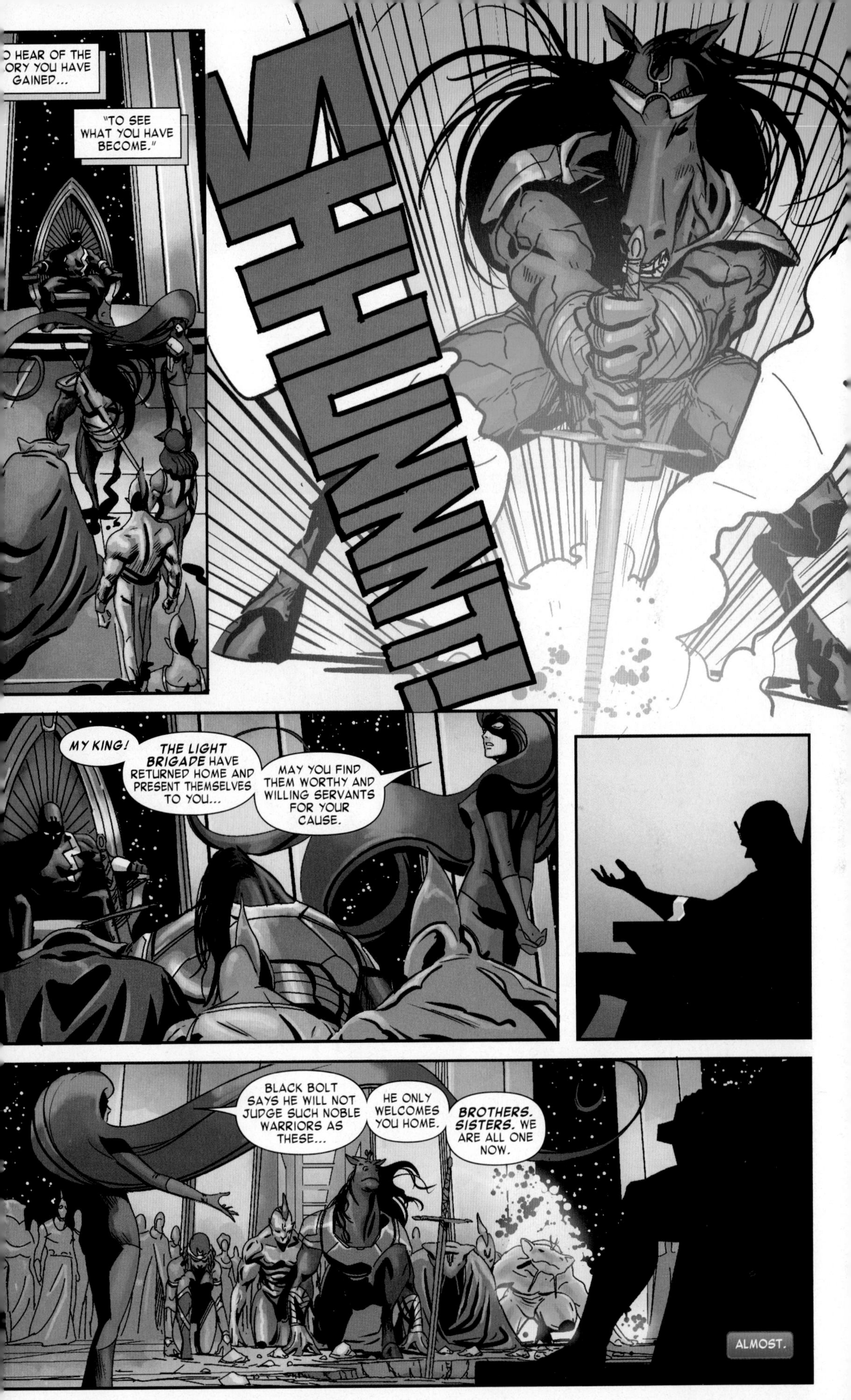

O HEAR OF THE
ORY YOU HAVE
GAINED...
"TO SEE WHAT YOU HAVE BECOME."
SHHUNNT!
MY KING!
THE LIGHT BRIGADE HAVE RETURNED HOME AND PRESENT THEMSELVES TO YOU...
MAY YOU FIND THEM WORTHY AND WILLING SERVANTS FOR YOUR CAUSE.
BLACK BOLT SAYS HE WILL NOT JUDGE SUCH NOBLE WARRIORS AS THESE...
HE ONLY WELCOMES YOU HOME.
BROTHERS. SISTERS. WE ARE ALL ONE NOW.
ALMOST.

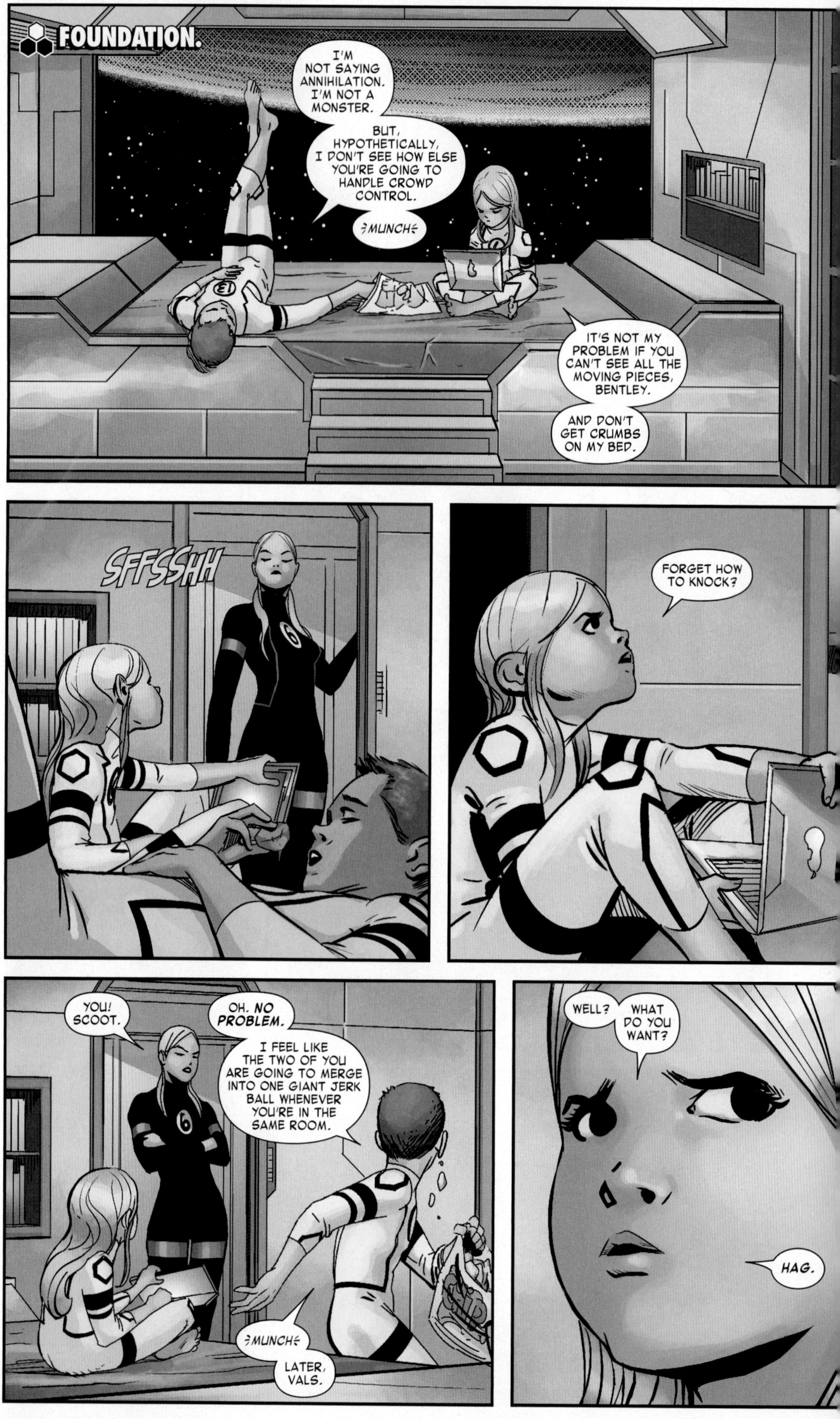
FOUNDATION.
I'M NOT SAYING ANNIHILATION. I'M NOT A MONSTER.
BUT, HYPOTHETICALLY, I DON'T SEE HOW ELSE YOU'RE GOING TO HANDLE CROWD CONTROL.
MUNCH
IT'S NOT MY PROBLEM IF YOU CAN'T SEE ALL THE MOVING PIECES, BENTLEY.
AND DON'T GET CRUMBS ON MY BED.
SFFSSHH
FORGET HOW TO KNOCK?
YOU! SCOOT.
OH. NO PROBLEM.
I FEEL LIKE THE TWO OF YOU ARE GOING TO MERGE INTO ONE GIANT JERK BALL WHENEVER YOU'RE IN THE SAME ROOM.
MUNCH
LATER, VALS.
WELL?
WHAT DO YOU WANT?
HAG.

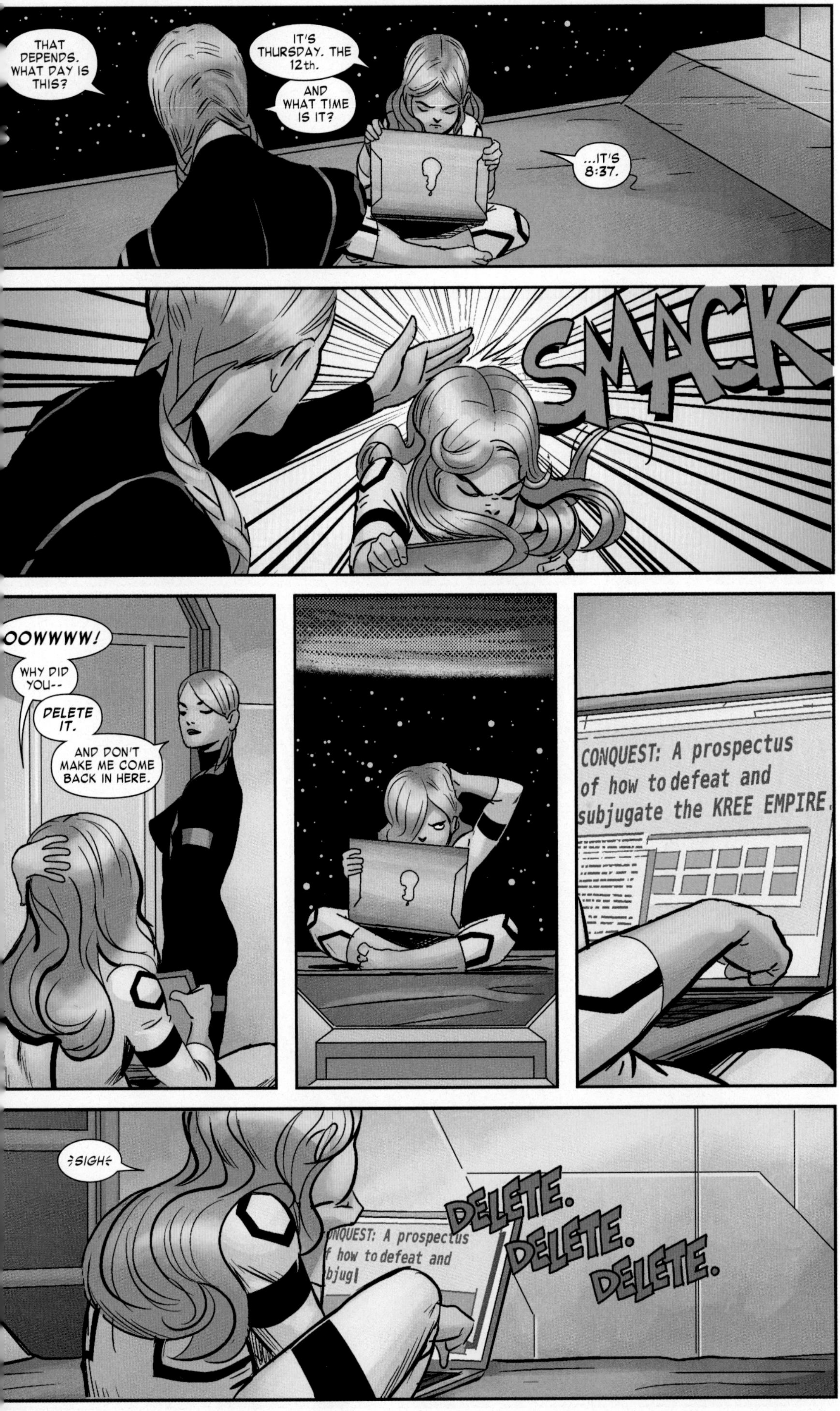

THAT DEPENDS. WHAT DAY IS THIS?
IT'S THURSDAY. THE 12th.
AND WHAT TIME IS IT?
...IT'S 8:37.
SMACK
OOWWWW!
WHY DID YOU--
DELETE IT.
AND DON'T MAKE ME COME BACK IN HERE.
CONQUEST: A prospectus of how to defeat and subjugate the KREE EMPIRE.
⸗SIGH⸗
CONQUEST: A prospectus
f how to defeat and
bjug
DELETE.
DELETE.
DELETE.

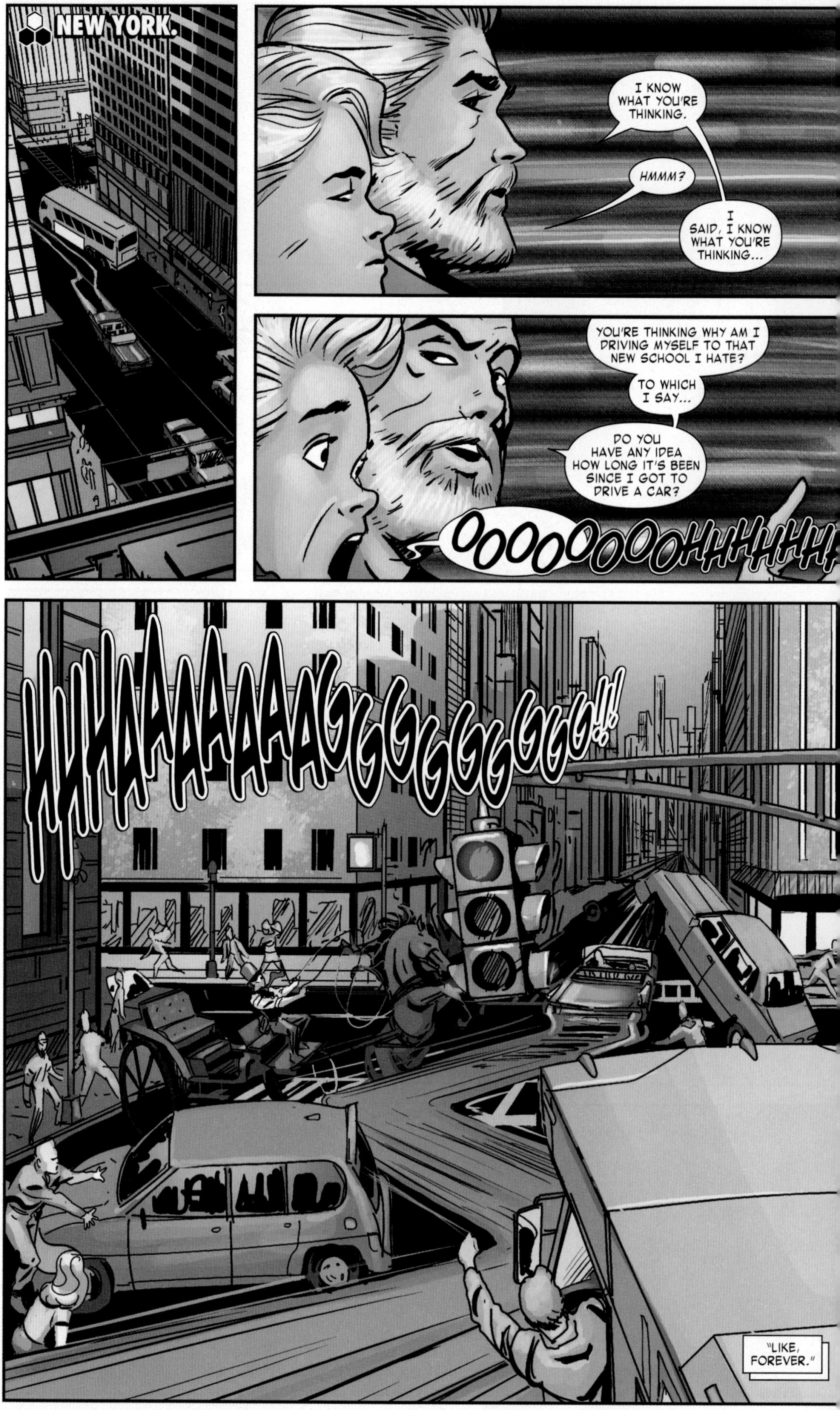
NEW YORK.
I KNOW WHAT YOU'RE THINKING.
HMMM?
I SAID, I KNOW WHAT YOU'RE THINKING...
YOU'RE THINKING WHY AM I DRIVING MYSELF TO THAT NEW SCHOOL I HATE?
TO WHICH I SAY...
DO YOU HAVE ANY IDEA HOW LONG IT'S BEEN SINCE I GOT TO DRIVE A CAR?
OOOOOOOOHHHHHH
HHHAAAAAAAGGGGGGGGG!!!
"LIKE, FOREVER."

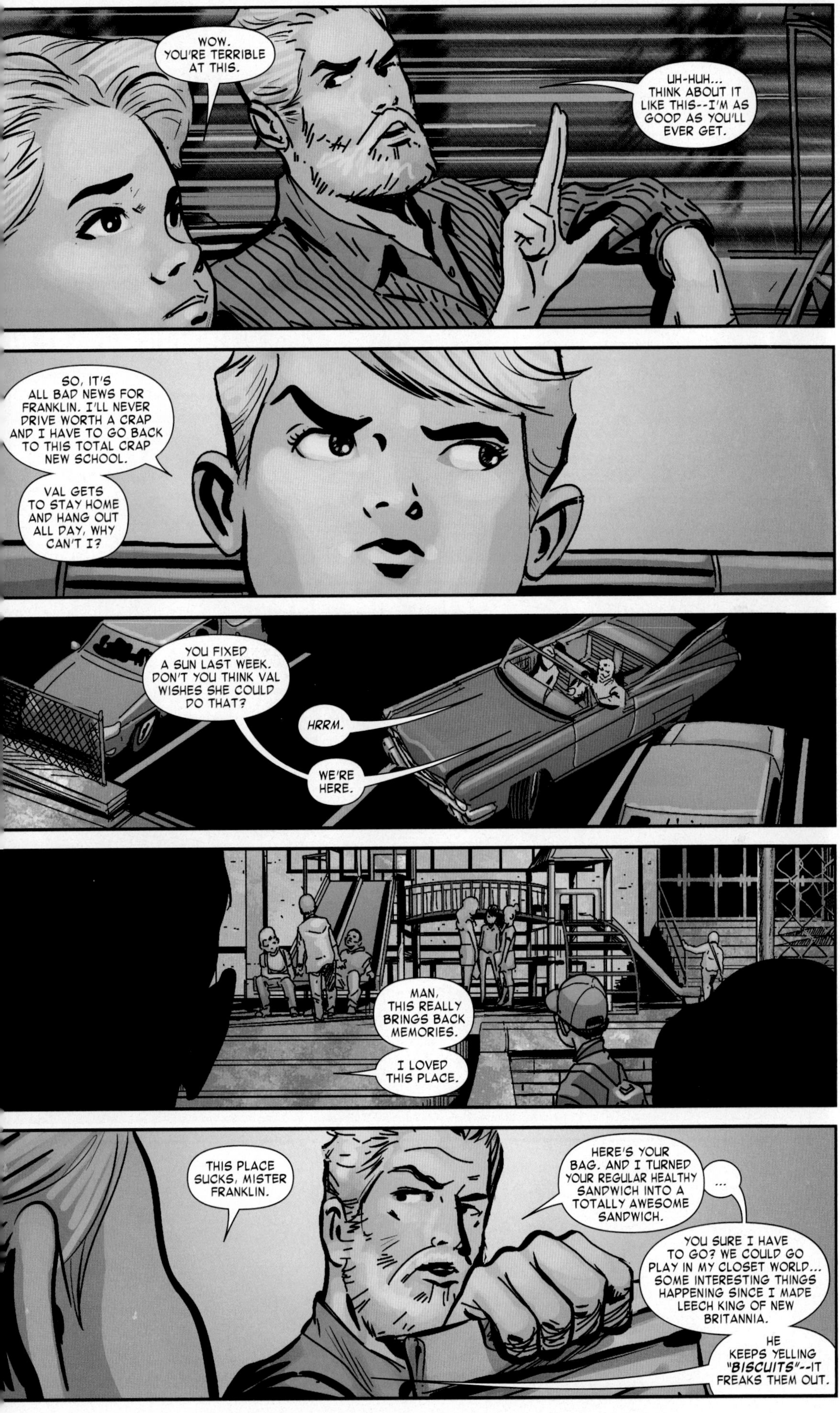
WOW. YOU'RE TERRIBLE AT THIS.
UH-HUH... THINK ABOUT IT LIKE THIS--I'M AS GOOD AS YOU'LL EVER GET.
SO, IT'S ALL BAD NEWS FOR FRANKLIN. I'LL NEVER DRIVE WORTH A CRAP AND I HAVE TO GO BACK TO THIS TOTAL CRAP NEW SCHOOL.
VAL GETS TO STAY HOME AND HANG OUT ALL DAY, WHY CAN'T I?
YOU FIXED A SUN LAST WEEK. DON'T YOU THINK VAL WISHES SHE COULD DO THAT?
HRRM.
WE'RE HERE.
MAN, THIS REALLY BRINGS BACK MEMORIES.
I LOVED THIS PLACE.
THIS PLACE SUCKS, MISTER FRANKLIN.
HERE'S YOUR BAG. AND I TURNED YOUR REGULAR HEALTHY SANDWICH INTO A TOTALLY AWESOME SANDWICH.
...
YOU SURE I HAVE TO GO? WE COULD GO PLAY IN MY CLOSET WORLD... SOME INTERESTING THINGS HAPPENING SINCE I MADE LEECH KING OF NEW BRITANNIA.
HE KEEPS YELLING "BISCUITS"--IT FREAKS THEM OUT.

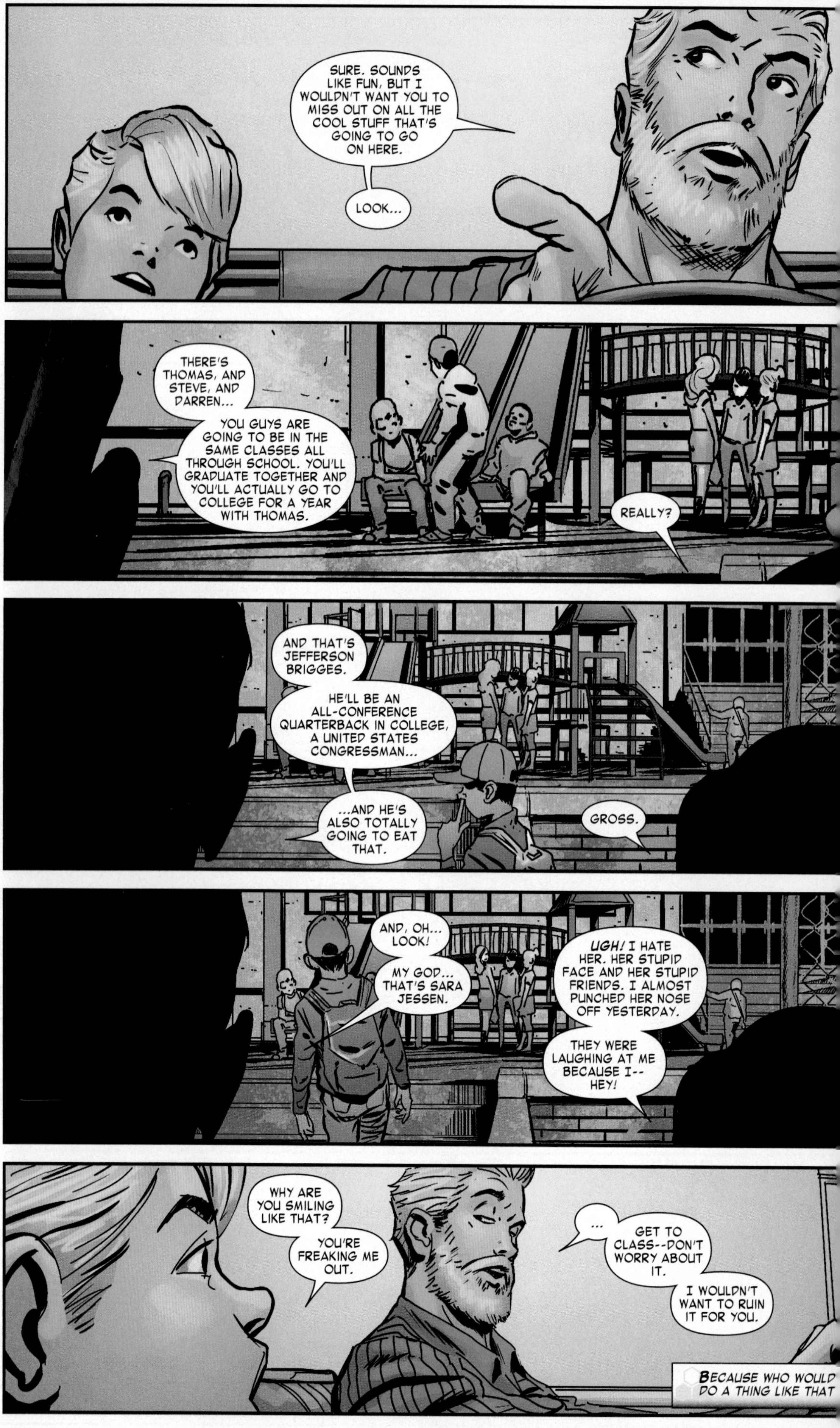
SURE. SOUNDS LIKE FUN, BUT I WOULDN'T WANT YOU TO MISS OUT ON ALL THE COOL STUFF THAT'S GOING TO GO ON HERE.
LOOK...
THERE'S THOMAS, AND STEVE, AND DARREN...
YOU GUYS ARE GOING TO BE IN THE SAME CLASSES ALL THROUGH SCHOOL. YOU'LL GRADUATE TOGETHER AND YOU'LL ACTUALLY GO TO COLLEGE FOR A YEAR WITH THOMAS.
REALLY?
AND THAT'S JEFFERSON BRIGGES.
HE'LL BE AN ALL-CONFERENCE QUARTERBACK IN COLLEGE, A UNITED STATES CONGRESSMAN...
...AND HE'S ALSO TOTALLY GOING TO EAT THAT.
GROSS.
AND, OH... LOOK!
MY GOD... THAT'S SARA JESSEN.
UGH! I HATE HER. HER STUPID FACE AND HER STUPID FRIENDS. I ALMOST PUNCHED HER NOSE OFF YESTERDAY.
THEY WERE LAUGHING AT ME BECAUSE I-- HEY!
WHY ARE YOU SMILING LIKE THAT?
YOU'RE FREAKING ME OUT.
...
GET TO CLASS--DON'T WORRY ABOUT IT.
I WOULDN'T WANT TO RUIN IT FOR YOU.
BECAUSE WHO WOULD DO A THING LIKE THAT

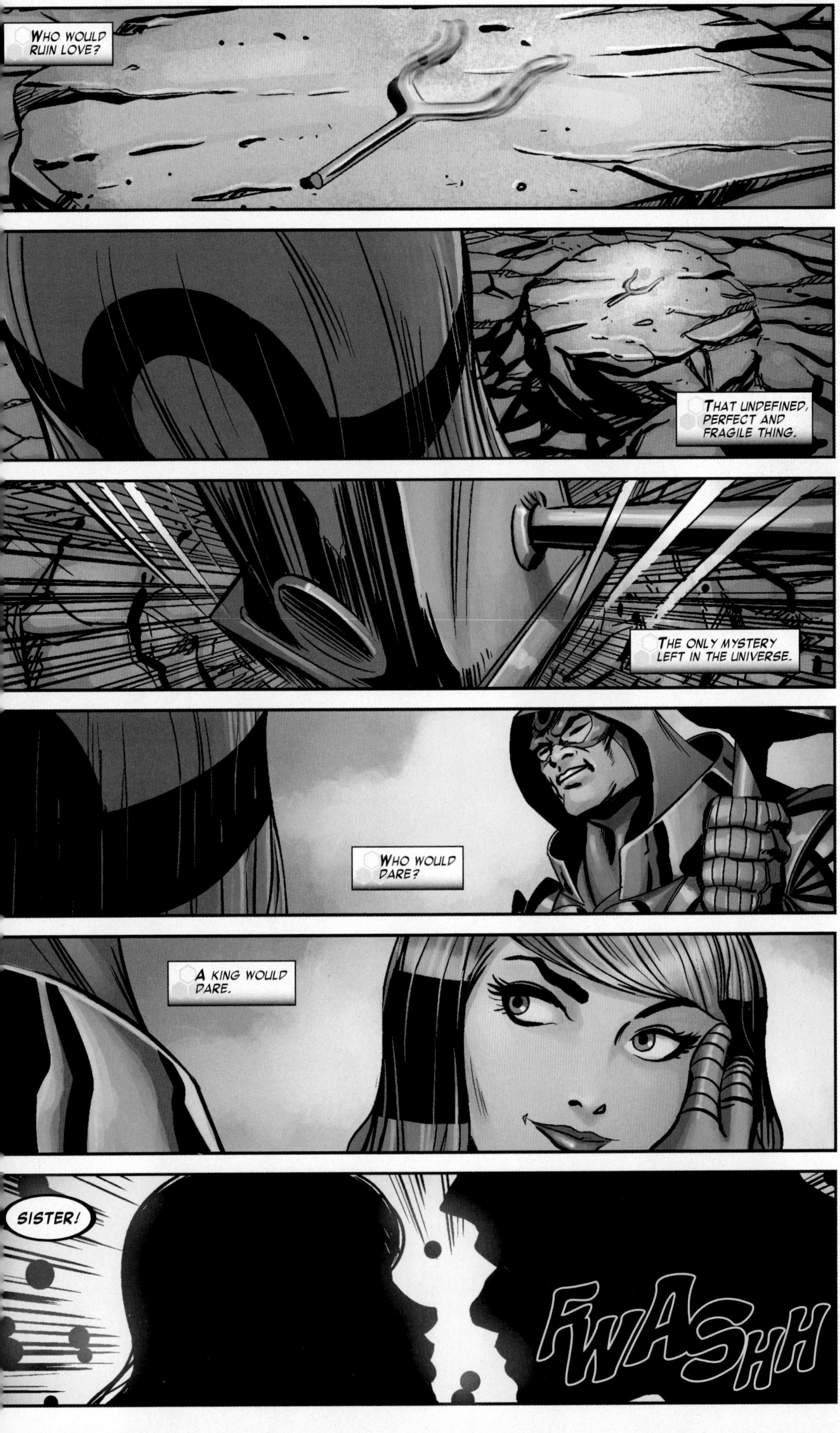
WHO WOULD RUIN LOVE?
THAT UNDEFINED, PERFECT AND FRAGILE THING.
THE ONLY MYSTERY LEFT IN THE UNIVERSE.
WHO WOULD DARE?
A KING WOULD DARE.
SISTER!
FWASHH

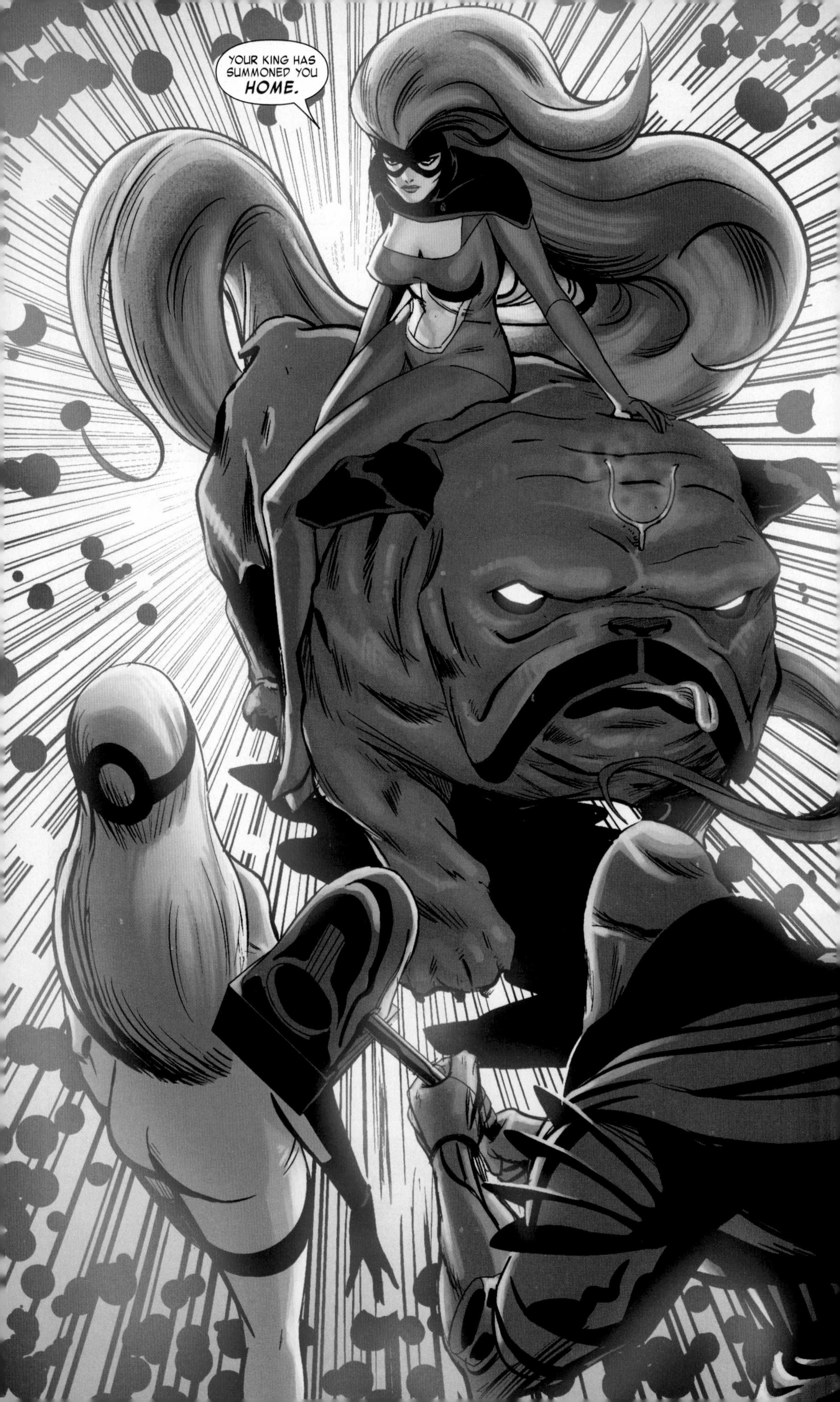
YOUR KING HAS SUMMONED YOU HOME.

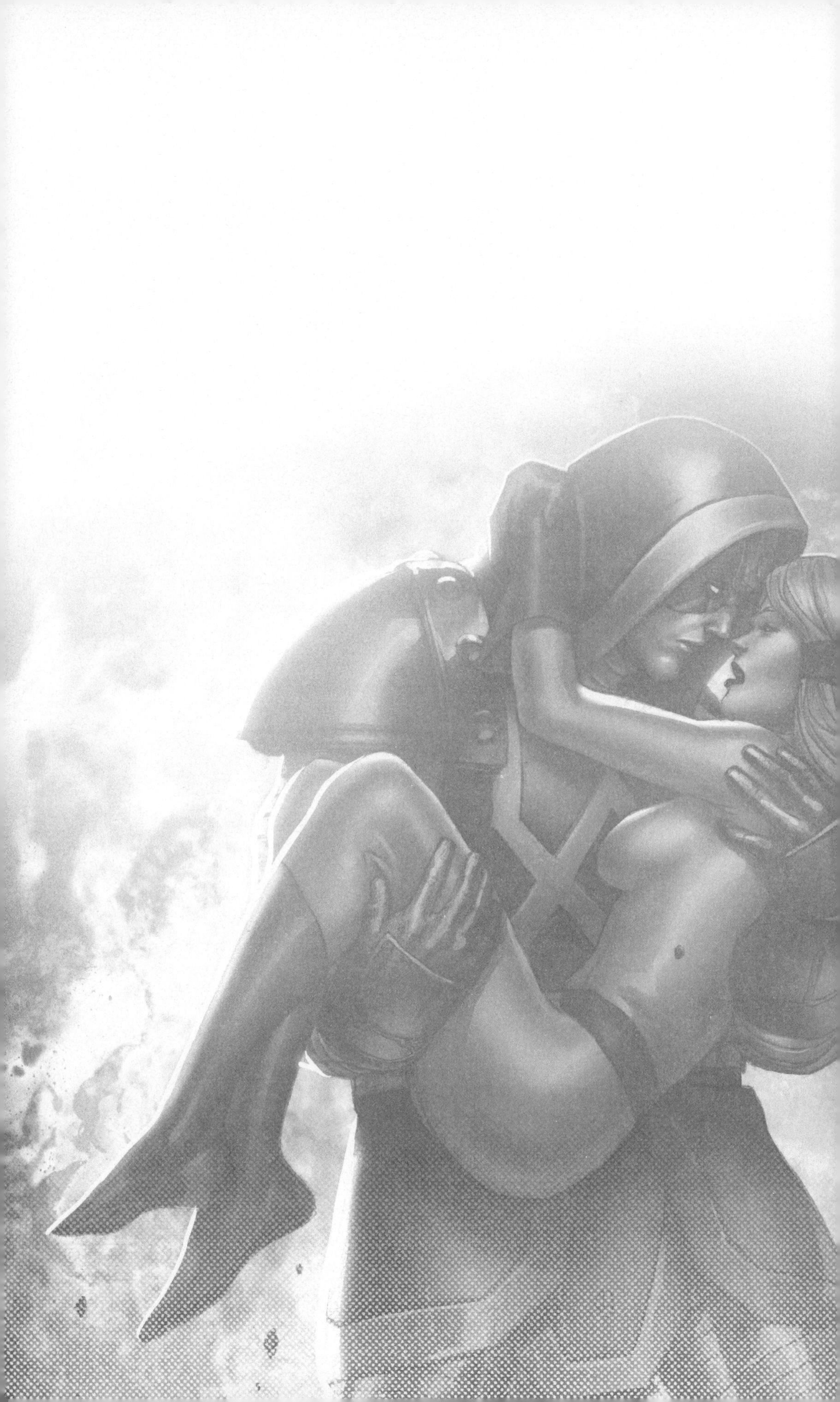

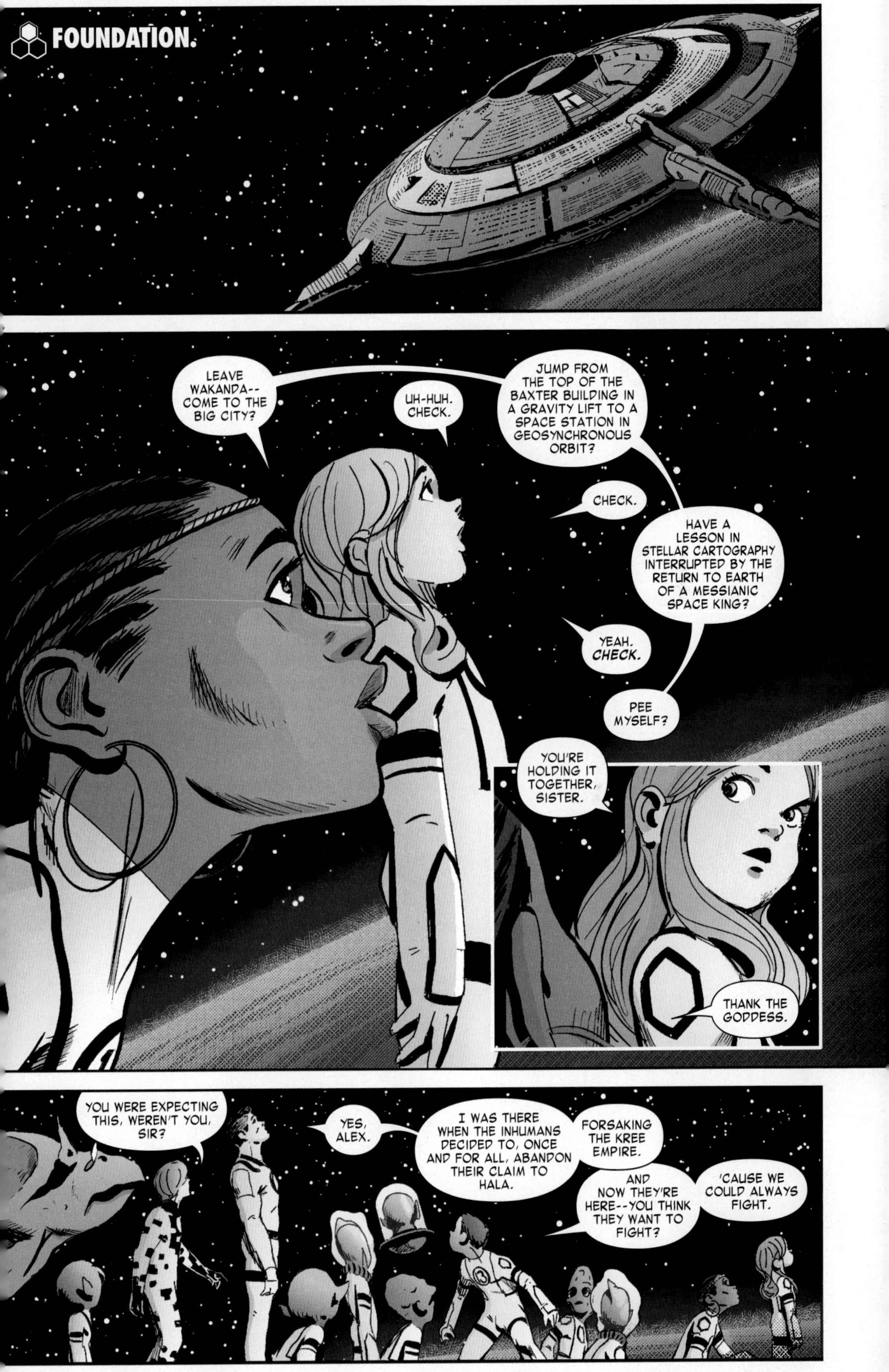
FOUNDATION.
LEAVE WAKANDA--COME TO THE BIG CITY?
UH-HUH. CHECK.
JUMP FROM THE TOP OF THE BAXTER BUILDING IN A GRAVITY LIFT TO A SPACE STATION IN GEOSYNCHRONOUS ORBIT?
CHECK.
HAVE A LESSON IN STELLAR CARTOGRAPHY INTERRUPTED BY THE RETURN TO EARTH OF A MESSIANIC SPACE KING?
YEAH. CHECK.
PEE MYSELF?
YOU'RE HOLDING IT TOGETHER, SISTER.
THANK THE GODDESS.
YOU WERE EXPECTING THIS, WEREN'T YOU, SIR?
YES, ALEX.
I WAS THERE WHEN THE INHUMANS DECIDED TO, ONCE AND FOR ALL, ABANDON THEIR CLAIM TO HALA.
FORSAKING THE KREE EMPIRE.
AND NOW THEY'RE HERE--YOU THINK THEY WANT TO FIGHT?
'CAUSE WE COULD ALWAYS FIGHT.

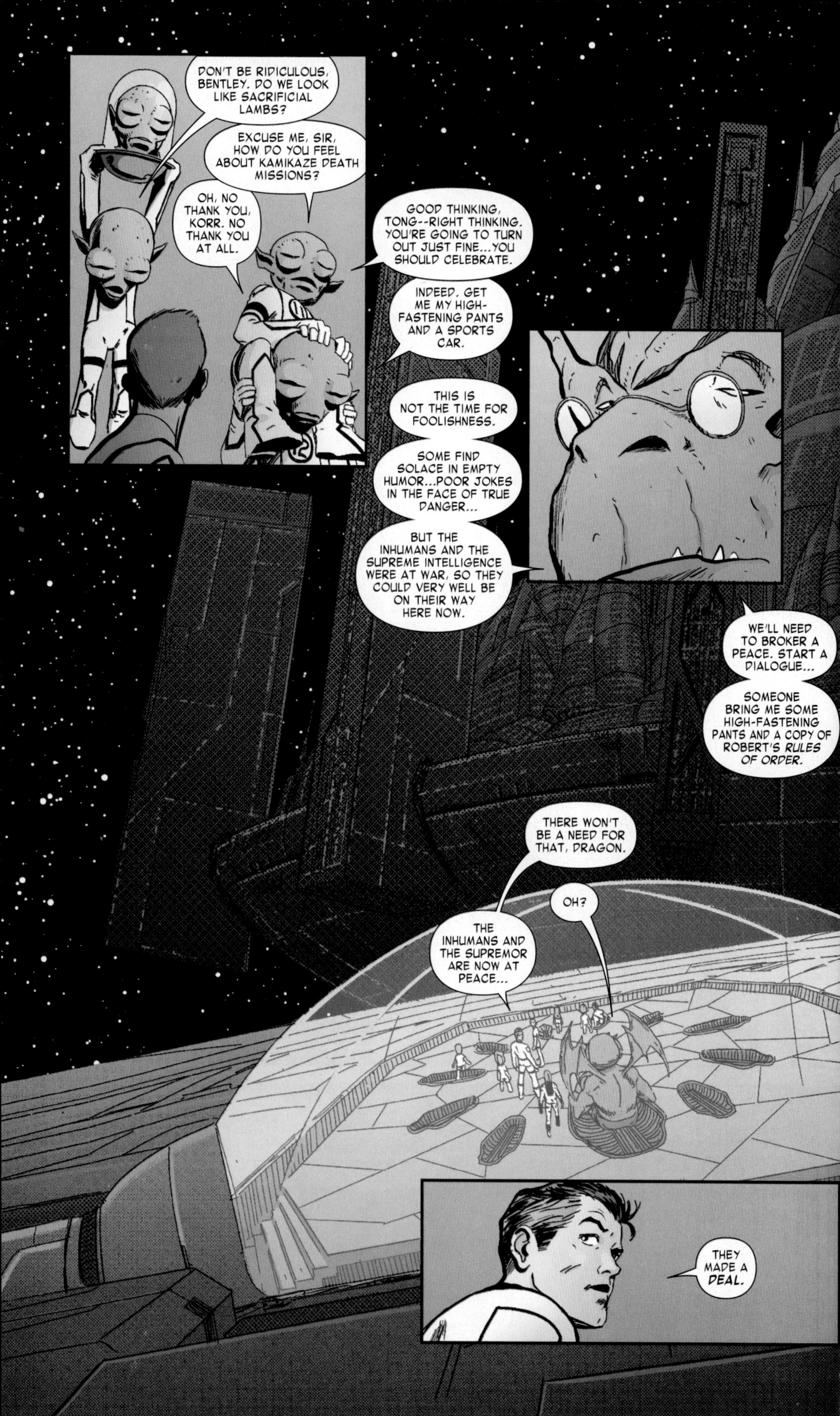
DON'T BE RIDICULOUS, BENTLEY. DO WE LOOK LIKE SACRIFICIAL LAMBS?
EXCUSE ME, SIR, HOW DO YOU FEEL ABOUT KAMIKAZE DEATH MISSIONS?
OH, NO THANK YOU, KORR. NO THANK YOU AT ALL.
GOOD THINKING, TONG--RIGHT THINKING. YOU'RE GOING TO TURN OUT JUST FINE...YOU SHOULD CELEBRATE.
INDEED. GET ME MY HIGH-FASTENING PANTS AND A SPORTS CAR.
THIS IS NOT THE TIME FOR FOOLISHNESS.
SOME FIND SOLACE IN EMPTY HUMOR...POOR JOKES IN THE FACE OF TRUE DANGER...
BUT THE INHUMANS AND THE SUPREME INTELLIGENCE WERE AT WAR, SO THEY COULD VERY WELL BE ON THEIR WAY HERE NOW.
WE'LL NEED TO BROKER A PEACE. START A DIALOGUE...
SOMEONE BRING ME SOME HIGH-FASTENING PANTS AND A COPY OF ROBERT'S *RULES OF ORDER.*
THERE WON'T BE A NEED FOR THAT, DRAGON.
OH?
THE INHUMANS AND THE SUPREMOR ARE NOW AT PEACE...
THEY MADE A *DEAL.*

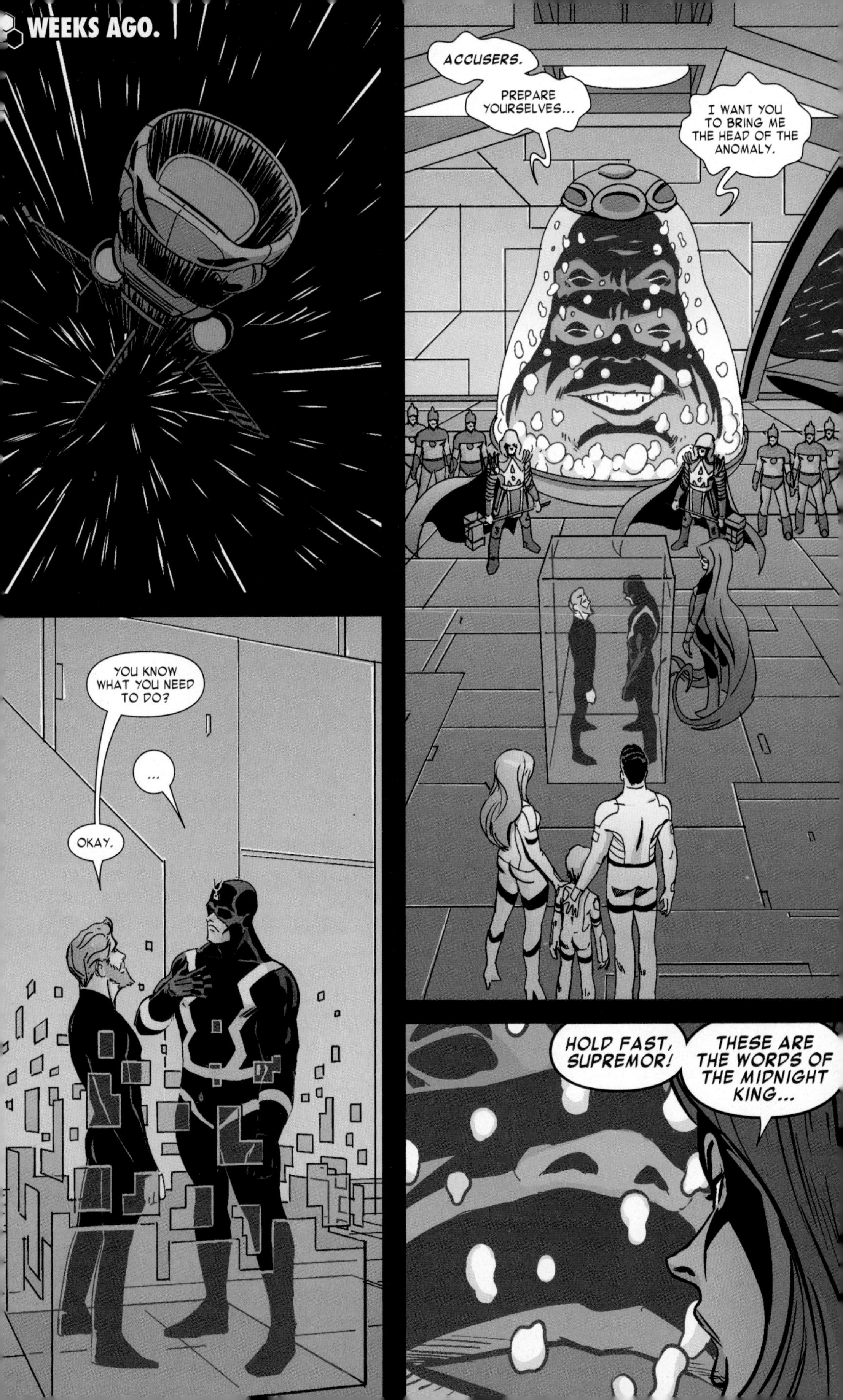
WEEKS AGO.
ACCUSERS.
PREPARE YOURSELVES...
I WANT YOU TO BRING ME THE HEAD OF THE ANOMALY.
YOU KNOW WHAT YOU NEED TO DO?
...
OKAY.
HOLD FAST, SUPREMOR!
THESE ARE THE WORDS OF THE MIDNIGHT KING...

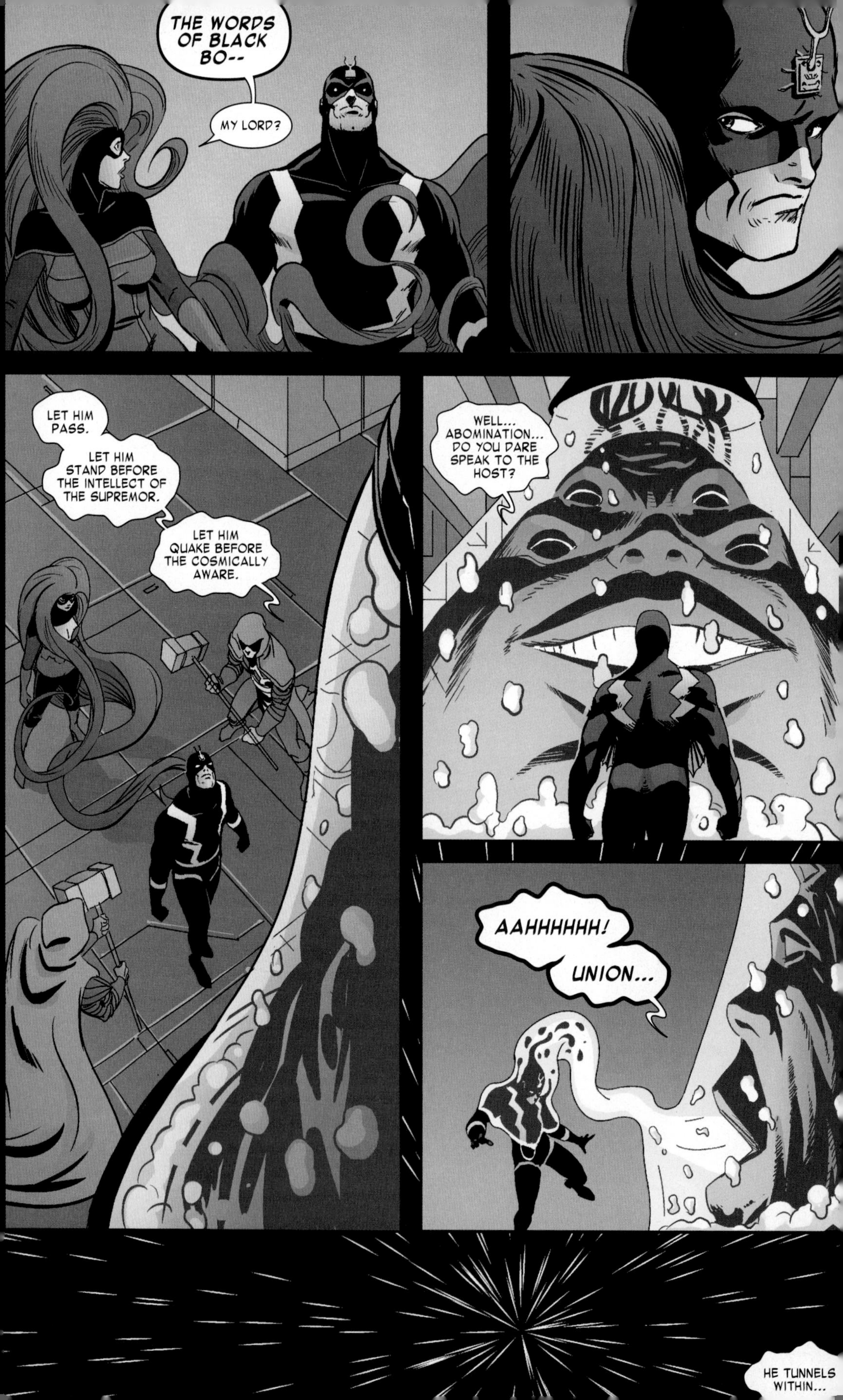
THE WORDS OF BLACK BO--
MY LORD?
LET HIM PASS.
LET HIM STAND BEFORE THE INTELLECT OF THE SUPREMOR.
LET HIM QUAKE BEFORE THE COSMICALLY AWARE.
WELL... ABOMINATION... DO YOU DARE SPEAK TO THE HOST?
AAHHHHHH!
UNION...
HE TUNNELS WITHIN...

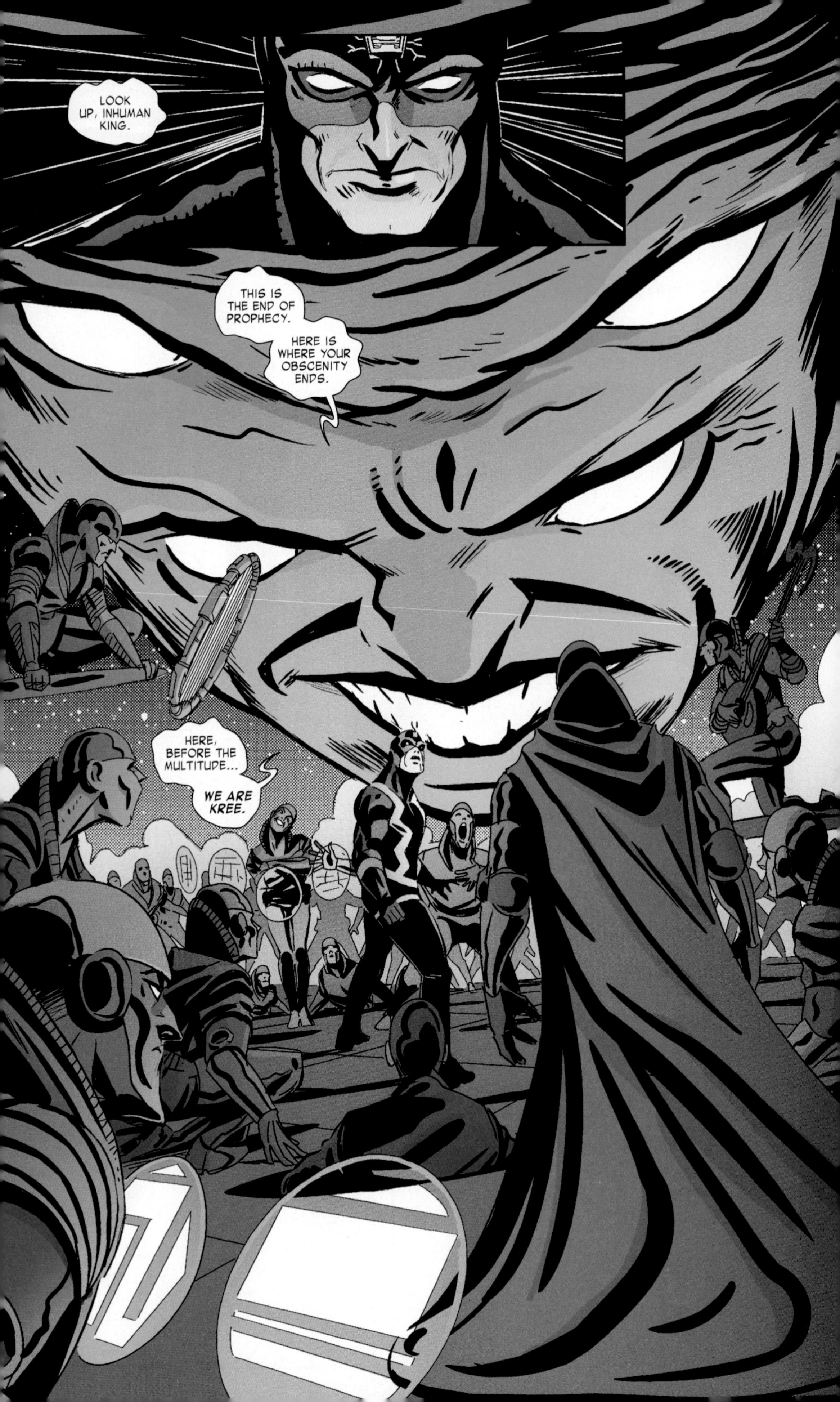
LOOK UP, INHUMAN KING.
THIS IS THE END OF PROPHECY.
HERE IS WHERE YOUR OBSCENITY ENDS.
HERE, BEFORE THE MULTITUDE...
WE ARE KREE.

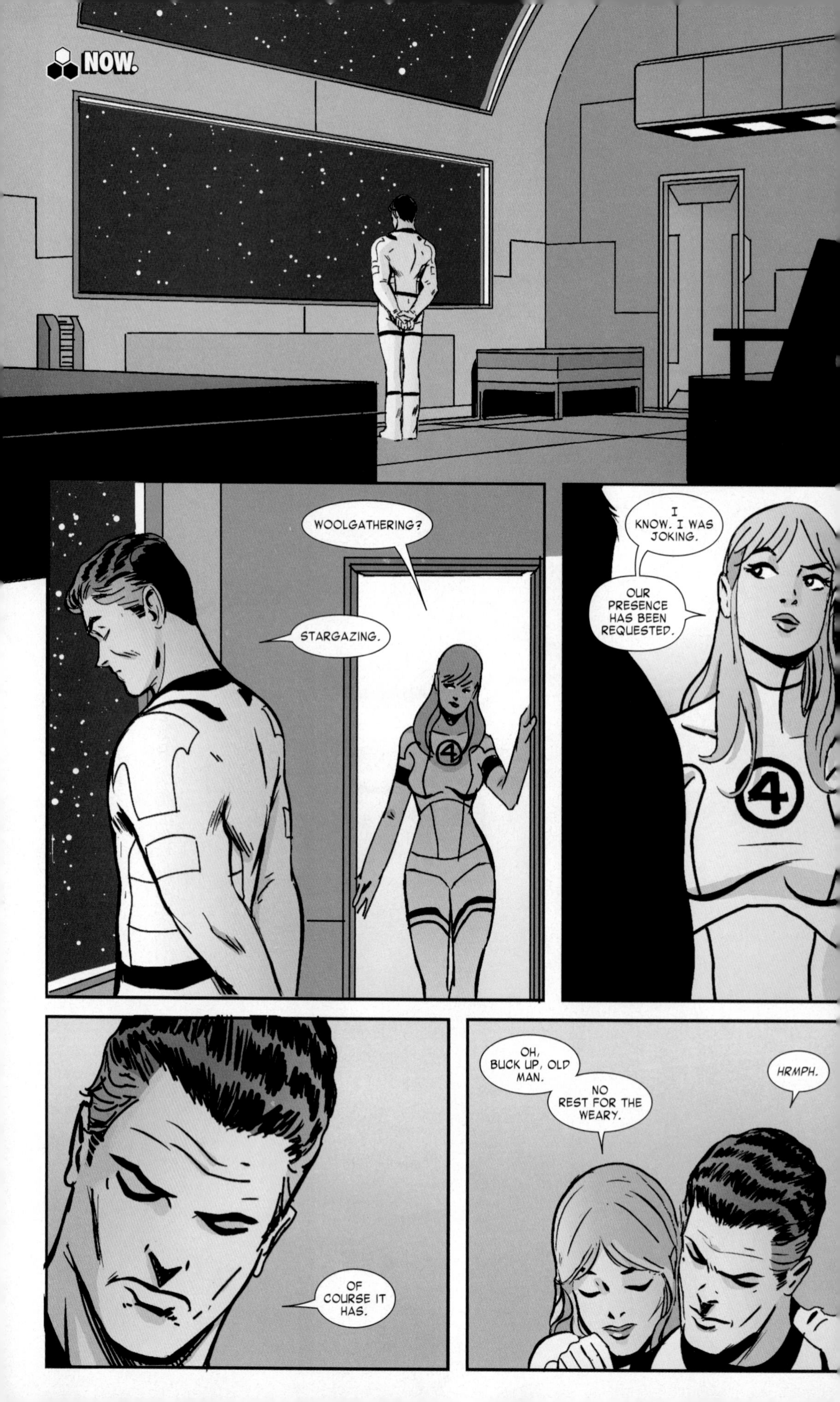
NOW.
WOOLGATHERING?
STARGAZING.
I KNOW. I WAS JOKING.
OUR PRESENCE HAS BEEN REQUESTED.
OF COURSE IT HAS.
OH, BUCK UP, OLD MAN.
NO REST FOR THE WEARY.
HRMPH.

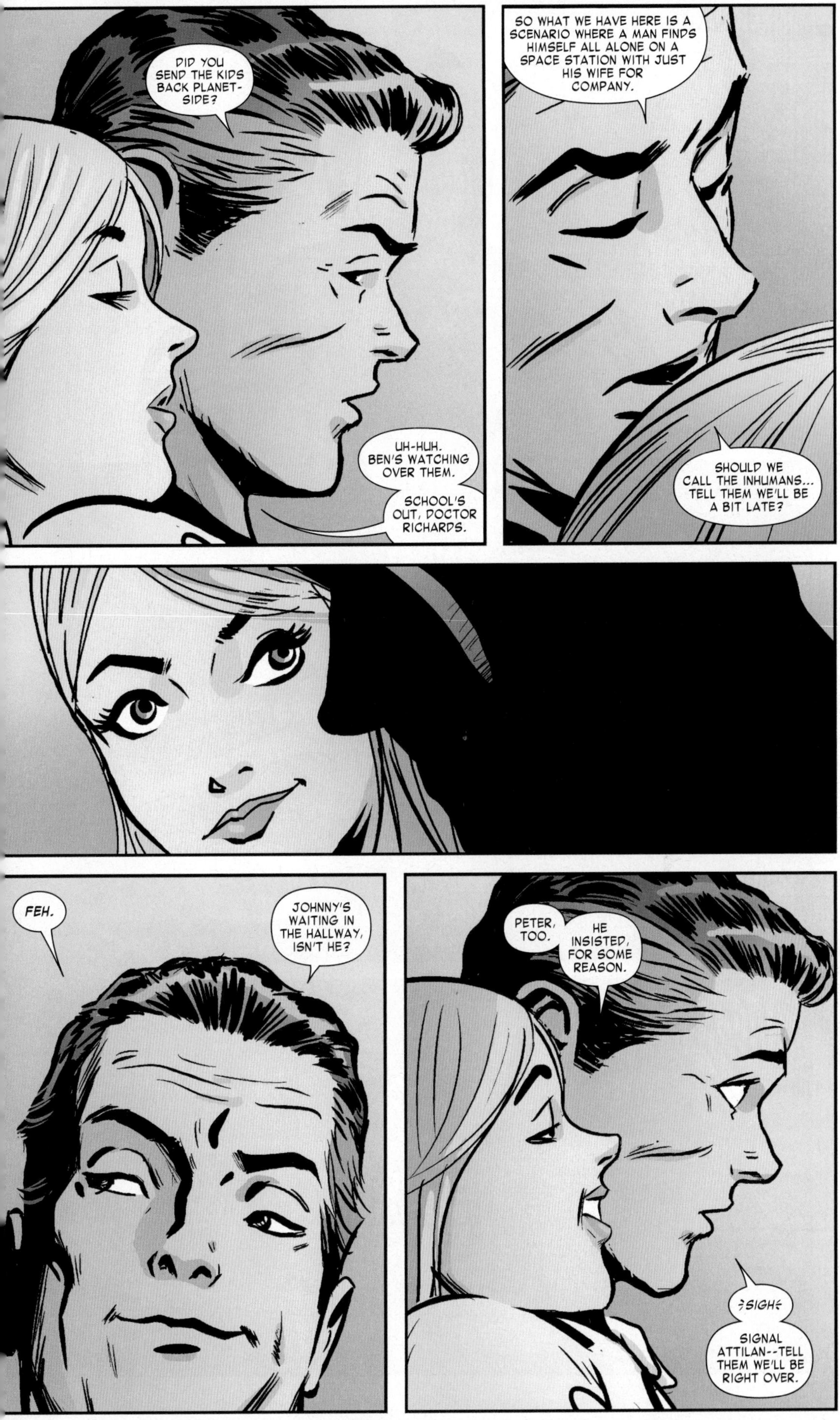
DID YOU SEND THE KIDS BACK PLANET-SIDE?
UH-HUH. BEN'S WATCHING OVER THEM.
SCHOOL'S OUT, DOCTOR RICHARDS.
SO WHAT WE HAVE HERE IS A SCENARIO WHERE A MAN FINDS HIMSELF ALL ALONE ON A SPACE STATION WITH JUST HIS WIFE FOR COMPANY.
SHOULD WE CALL THE INHUMANS... TELL THEM WE'LL BE A BIT LATE?
FEH.
JOHNNY'S WAITING IN THE HALLWAY, ISN'T HE?
PETER, TOO.
HE INSISTED, FOR SOME REASON.
SIGH
SIGNAL ATTILAN--TELL THEM WE'LL BE RIGHT OVER.

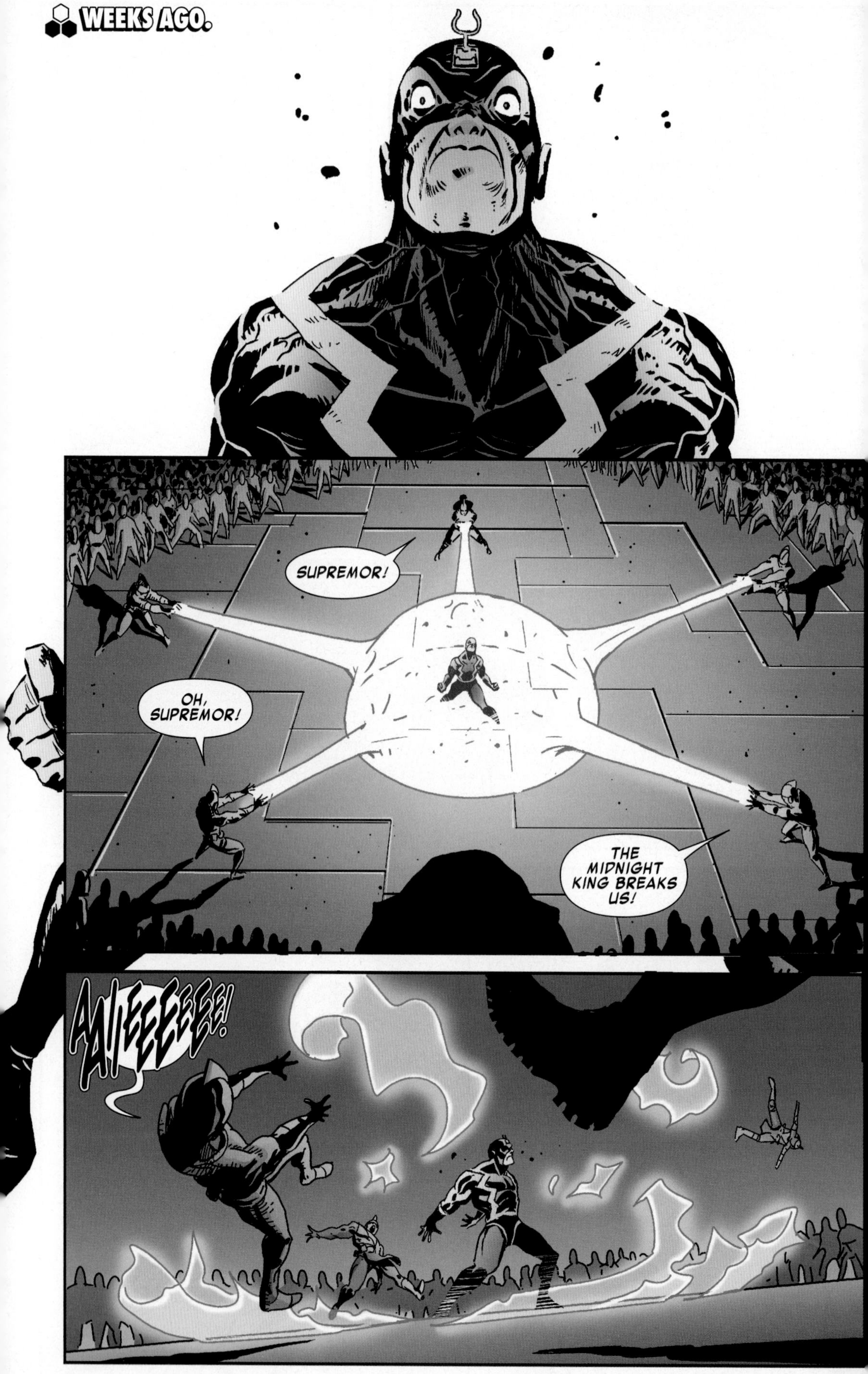
WEEKS AGO.
SUPREMOR!
OH, SUPREMOR!
THE MIDNIGHT KING BREAKS US!
AAIIEEEEEE!

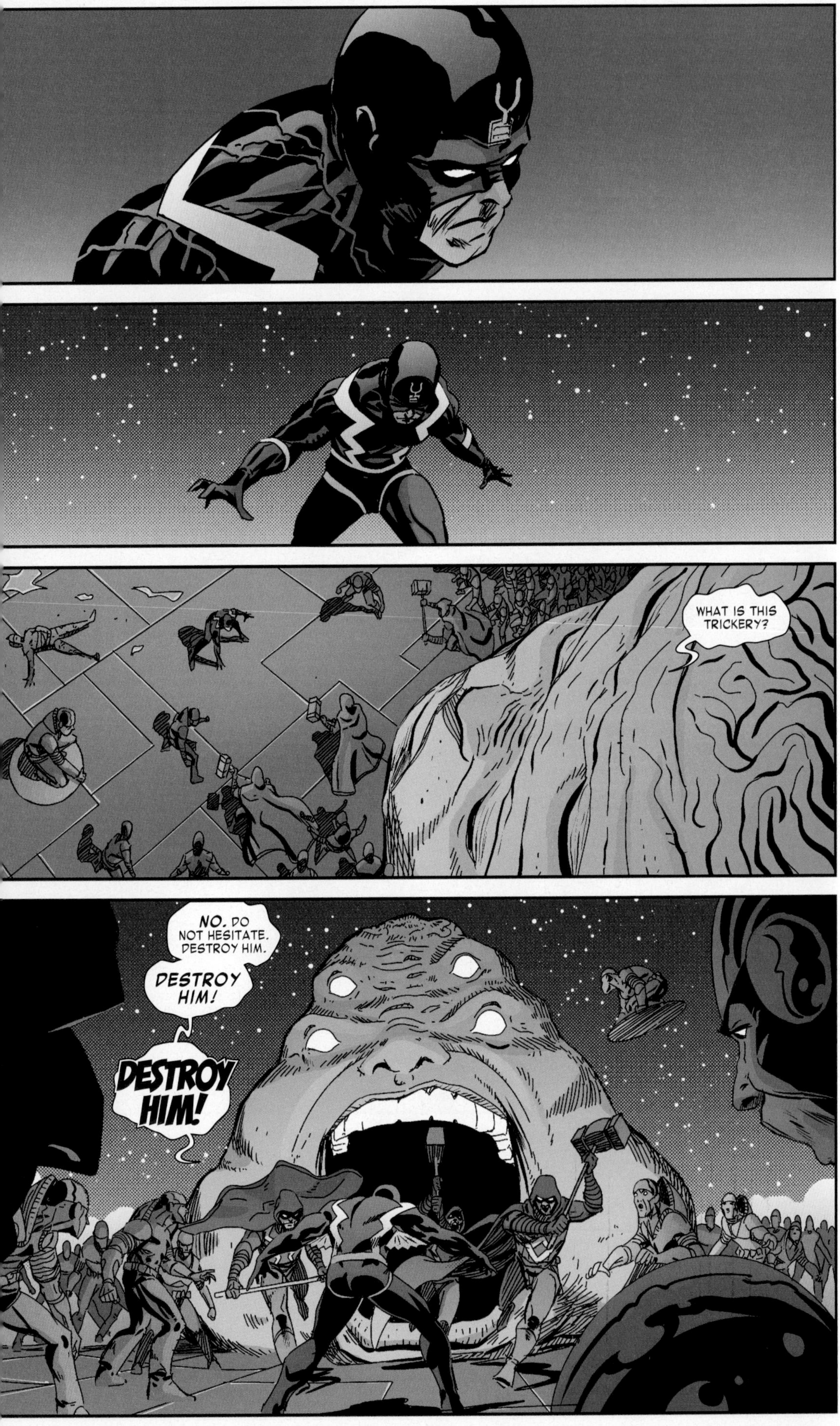
WHAT IS THIS TRICKERY?
NO. DO NOT HESITATE. DESTROY HIM.
DESTROY HIM!
DESTROY HIM!

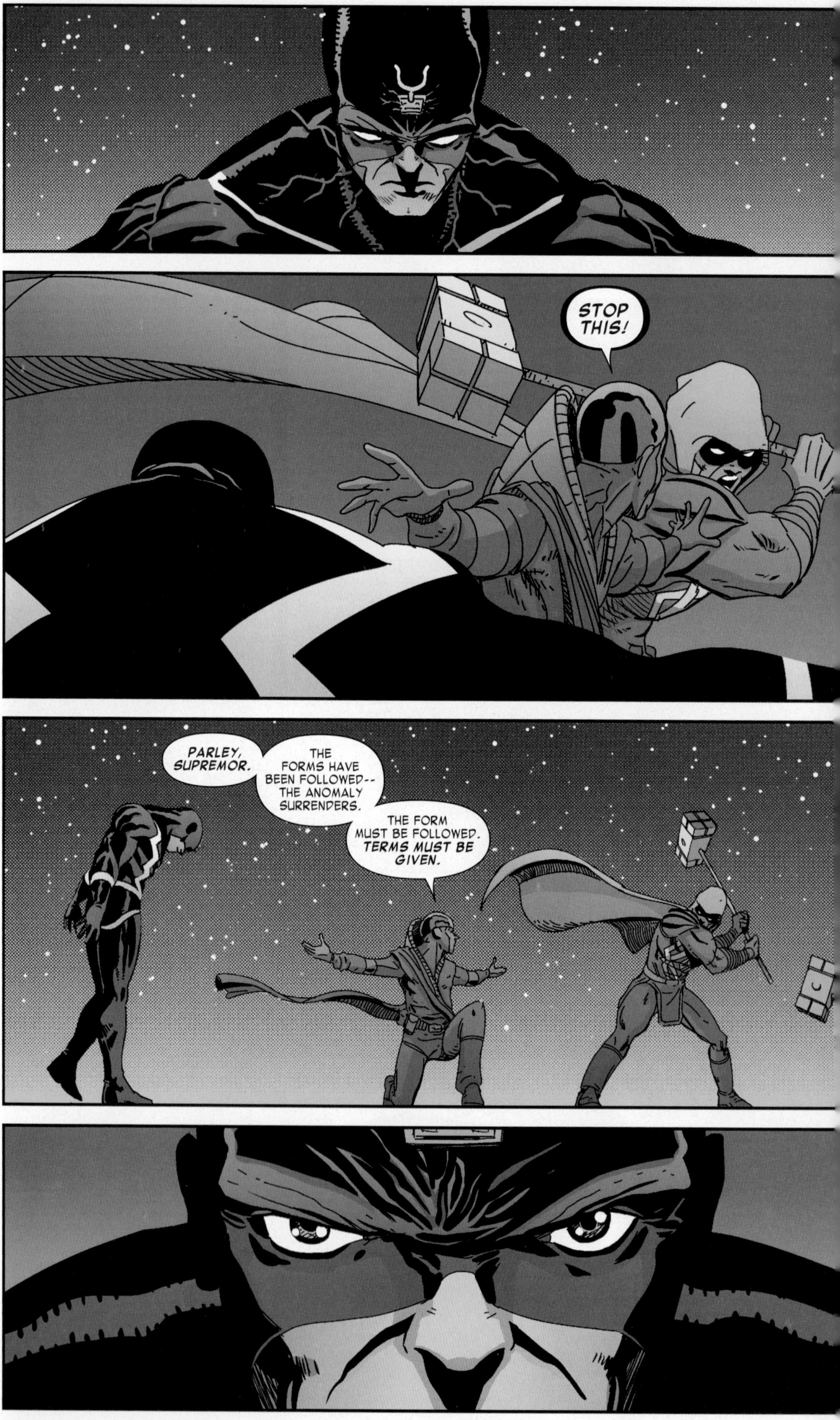
STOP THIS!
PARLEY, SUPREMOR.
THE FORMS HAVE BEEN FOLLOWED-- THE ANOMALY SURRENDERS.
THE FORM MUST BE FOLLOWED. TERMS MUST BE GIVEN.

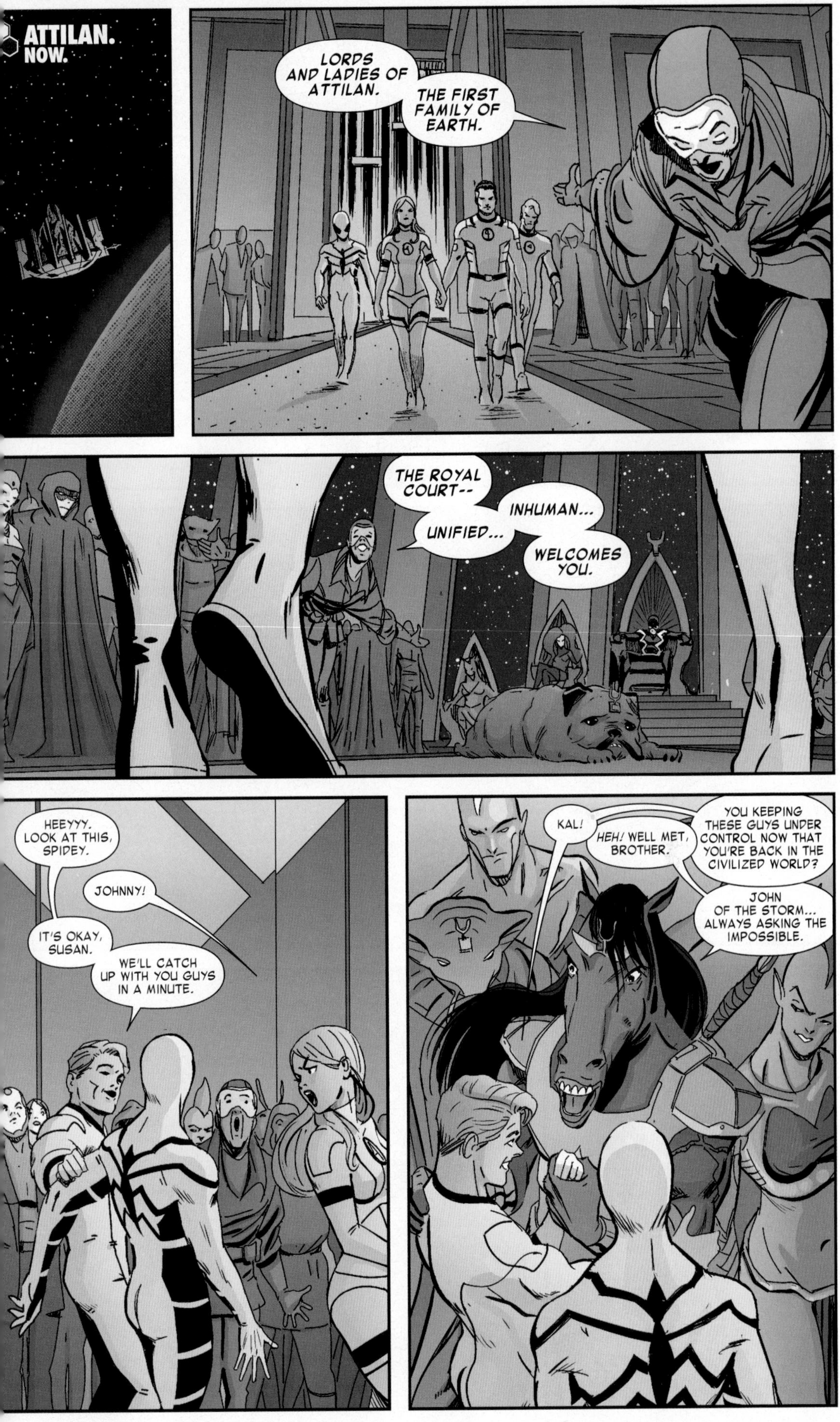
ATTILAN. NOW.
LORDS AND LADIES OF ATTILAN.
THE FIRST FAMILY OF EARTH.
THE ROYAL COURT--
UNIFIED...
INHUMAN...
WELCOMES YOU.
HEEYYY. LOOK AT THIS, SPIDEY.
JOHNNY!
IT'S OKAY, SUSAN.
WE'LL CATCH UP WITH YOU GUYS IN A MINUTE.
KAL!
HEH! WELL MET, BROTHER.
YOU KEEPING THESE GUYS UNDER CONTROL NOW THAT YOU'RE BACK IN THE CIVILIZED WORLD?
JOHN OF THE STORM... ALWAYS ASKING THE IMPOSSIBLE.

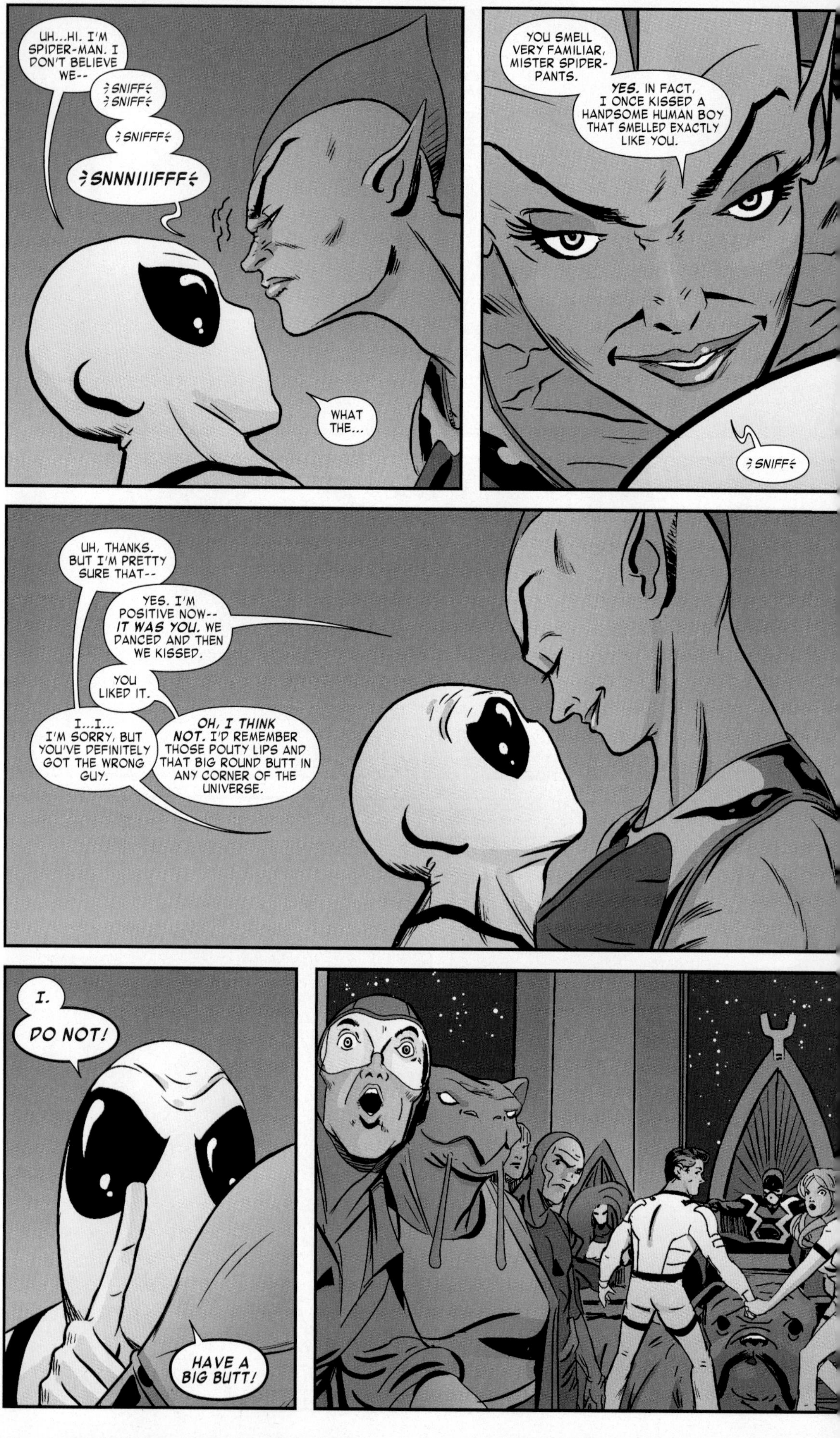
UH...HI. I'M SPIDER-MAN. I DON'T BELIEVE WE--
SNIFF SNIFF
SNIFFF
SNNNIIIFFF
WHAT THE...
YOU SMELL VERY FAMILIAR, MISTER SPIDER-PANTS.
YES. IN FACT, I ONCE KISSED A HANDSOME HUMAN BOY THAT SMELLED EXACTLY LIKE YOU.
SNIFF
UH, THANKS. BUT I'M PRETTY SURE THAT--
YES. I'M POSITIVE NOW-- IT WAS YOU. WE DANCED AND THEN WE KISSED.
YOU LIKED IT.
I...I... I'M SORRY, BUT YOU'VE DEFINITELY GOT THE WRONG GUY.
OH, I THINK NOT. I'D REMEMBER THOSE POUTY LIPS AND THAT BIG ROUND BUTT IN ANY CORNER OF THE UNIVERSE.
I.
DO NOT!
HAVE A BIG BUTT!

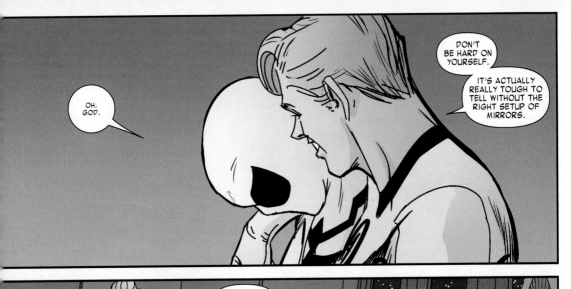

OH, GOD.

DON'T BE HARD ON YOURSELF.

IT'S ACTUALLY REALLY TOUGH TO TELL WITHOUT THE RIGHT SETUP OF MIRRORS.

WELL...WE'RE HERE.

WHAT CAN WE HELP YOU WITH, BLACK BOLT?

IT'S THE BARGAIN, REED RICHARDS.

WE HAVE ENCOUNTERED COMPLICATIONS...

AND NOW THAT TENUOUS PEACE IS IN PERIL.

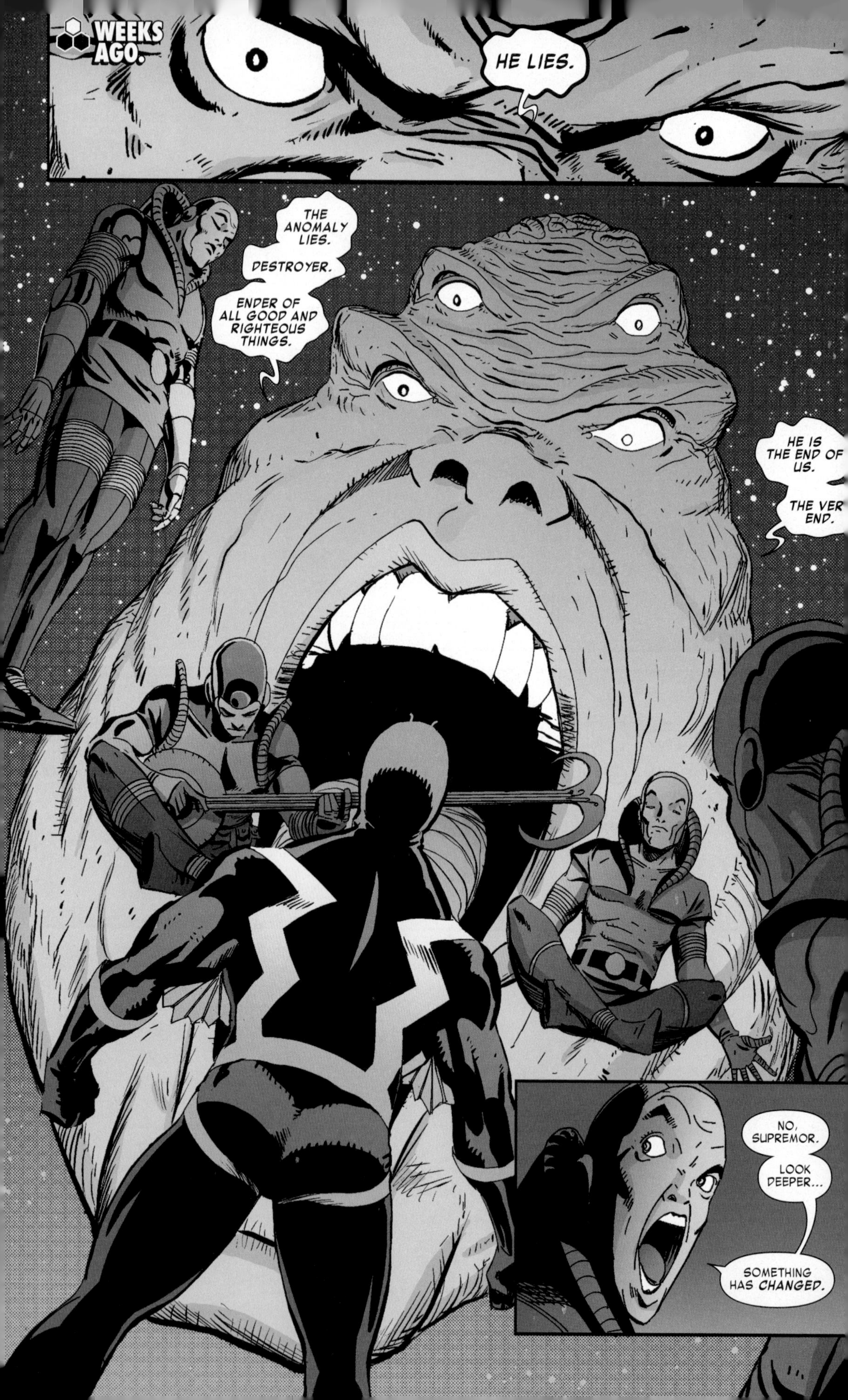
WEEKS AGO.
HE LIES.
THE ANOMALY LIES.
DESTROYER.
ENDER OF ALL GOOD AND RIGHTEOUS THINGS.
HE IS THE END OF US.
THE VER END.
NO, SUPREMOR.
LOOK DEEPER...
SOMETHING HAS CHANGED.

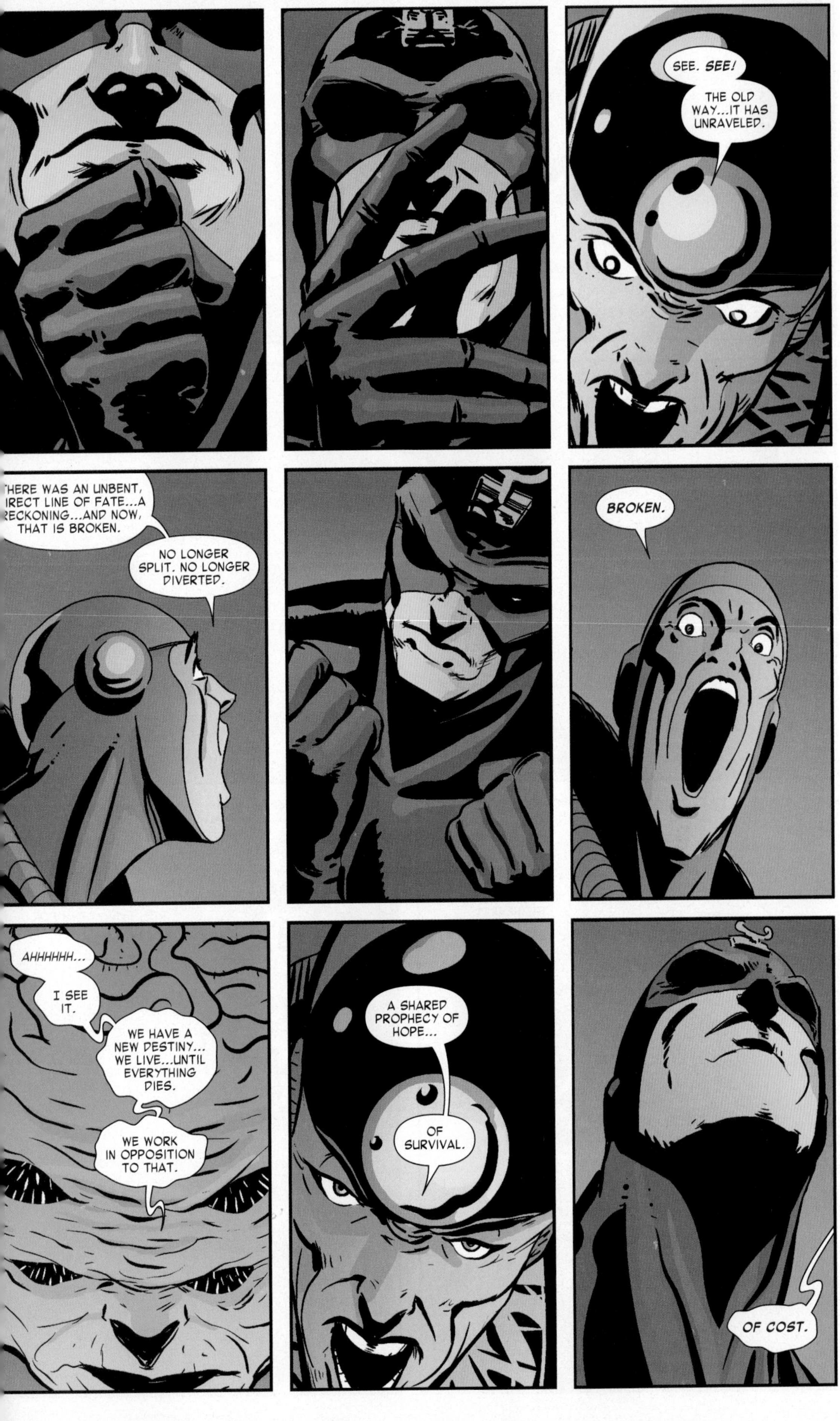
SEE. SEE!
THE OLD WAY...IT HAS UNRAVELED.
THERE WAS AN UNBENT, DIRECT LINE OF FATE...A RECKONING...AND NOW, THAT IS BROKEN.
NO LONGER SPLIT. NO LONGER DIVERTED.
BROKEN.
AHHHHHH...
I SEE IT.
WE HAVE A NEW DESTINY... WE LIVE...UNTIL EVERYTHING DIES.
WE WORK IN OPPOSITION TO THAT.
A SHARED PROPHECY OF HOPE...
OF SURVIVAL.
OF COST.

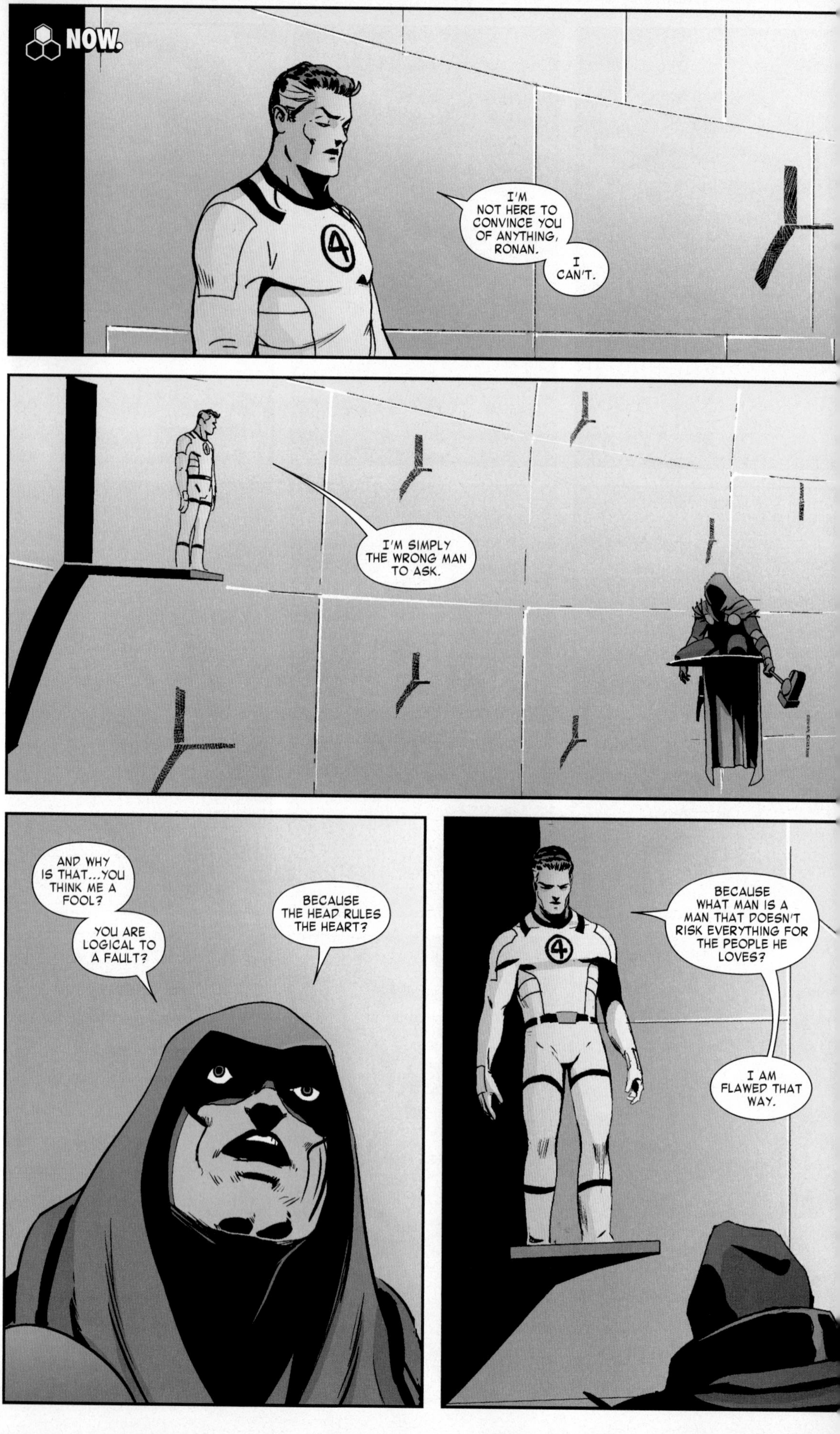
NOW.
I'M NOT HERE TO CONVINCE YOU OF ANYTHING, RONAN.
I CAN'T.
I'M SIMPLY THE WRONG MAN TO ASK.
AND WHY IS THAT...YOU THINK ME A FOOL?
YOU ARE LOGICAL TO A FAULT?
BECAUSE THE HEAD RULES THE HEART?
BECAUSE WHAT MAN IS A MAN THAT DOESN'T RISK EVERYTHING FOR THE PEOPLE HE LOVES?
I AM FLAWED THAT WAY.

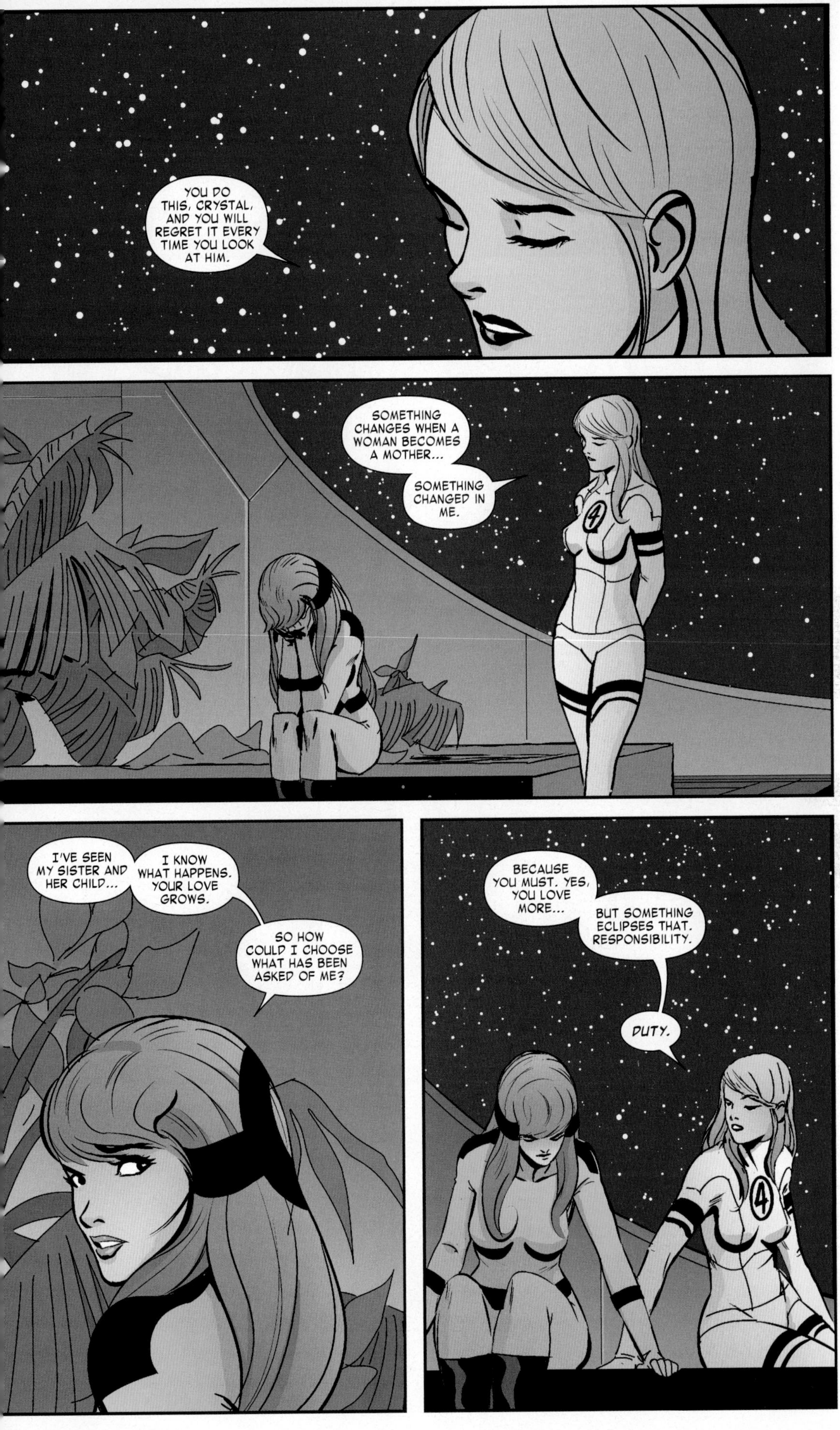
YOU DO THIS, CRYSTAL, AND YOU WILL REGRET IT EVERY TIME YOU LOOK AT HIM.
SOMETHING CHANGES WHEN A WOMAN BECOMES A MOTHER...
SOMETHING CHANGED IN ME.
I'VE SEEN MY SISTER AND HER CHILD...
I KNOW WHAT HAPPENS. YOUR LOVE GROWS.
SO HOW COULD I CHOOSE WHAT HAS BEEN ASKED OF ME?
BECAUSE YOU MUST. YES, YOU LOVE MORE...
BUT SOMETHING ECLIPSES THAT. RESPONSIBILITY.
DUTY.

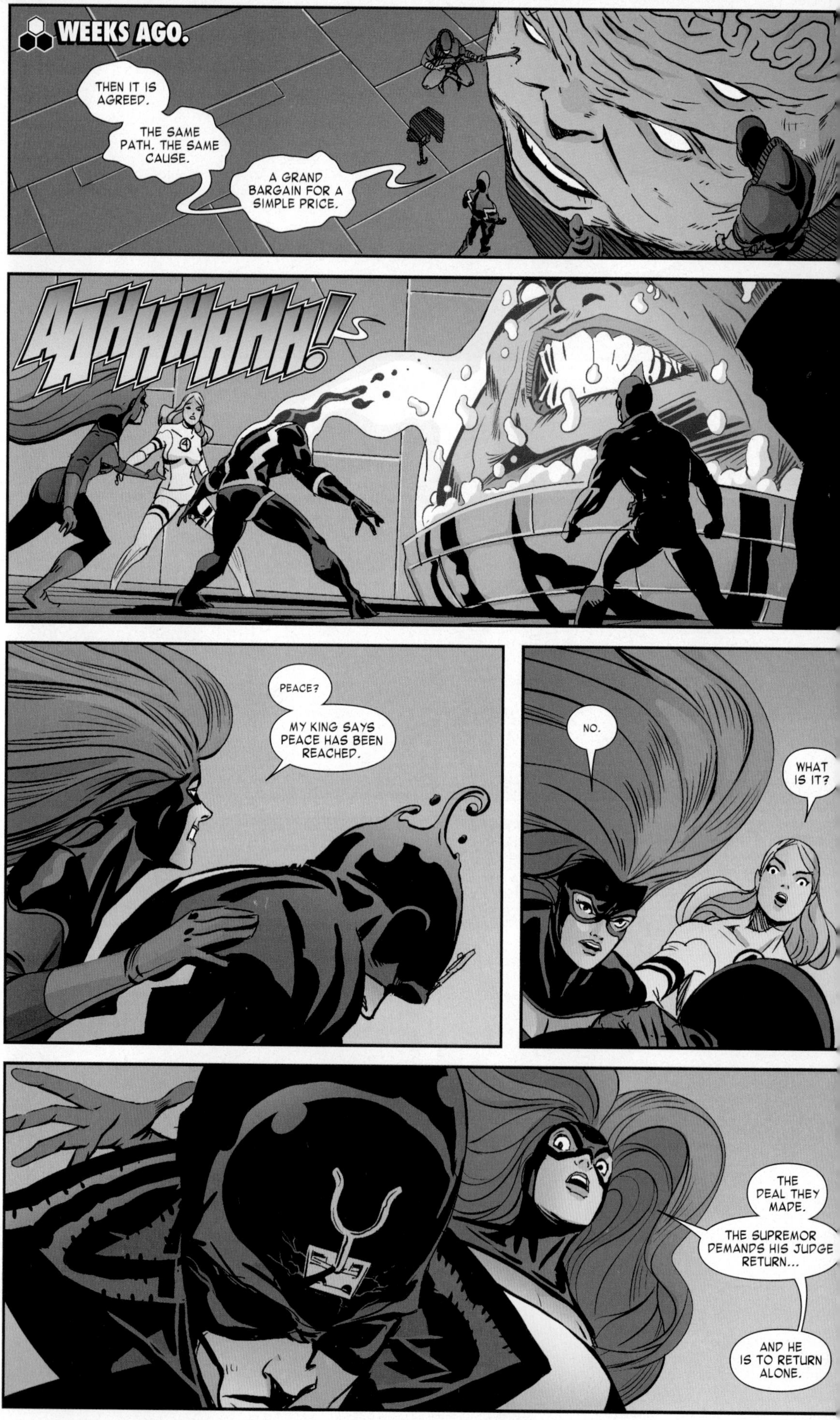
WEEKS AGO.
THEN IT IS AGREED.
THE SAME PATH. THE SAME CAUSE.
A GRAND BARGAIN FOR A SIMPLE PRICE.
AAHHHHHHH!
PEACE?
MY KING SAYS PEACE HAS BEEN REACHED.
NO.
WHAT IS IT?
THE DEAL THEY MADE.
THE SUPREMOR DEMANDS HIS JUDGE RETURN...
AND HE IS TO RETURN ALONE.

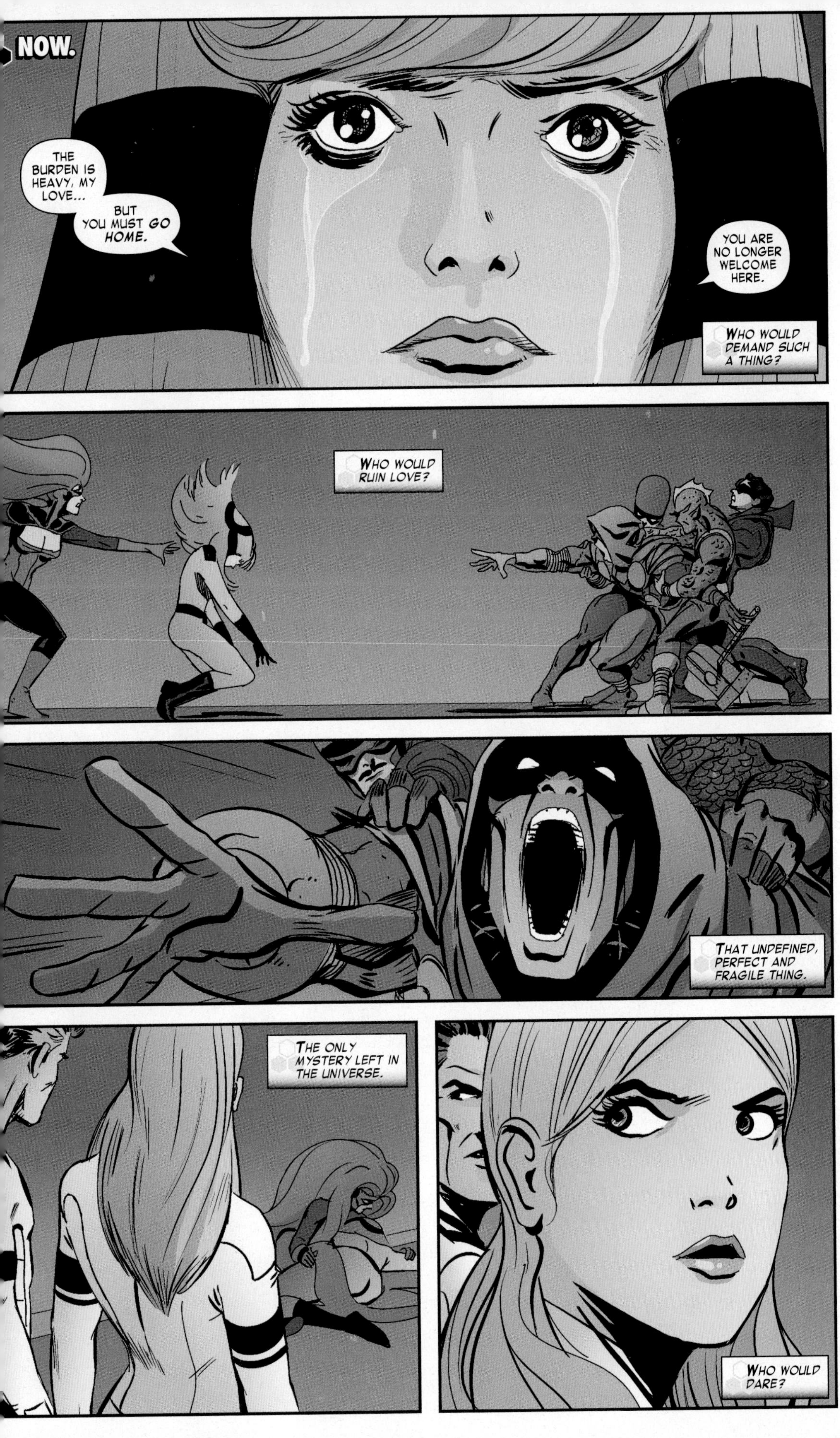
NOW.
THE BURDEN IS HEAVY, MY LOVE...
BUT YOU MUST GO HOME.
YOU ARE NO LONGER WELCOME HERE.
WHO WOULD DEMAND SUCH A THING?
WHO WOULD RUIN LOVE?
THAT UNDEFINED, PERFECT AND FRAGILE THING.
THE ONLY MYSTERY LEFT IN THE UNIVERSE.
WHO WOULD DARE?

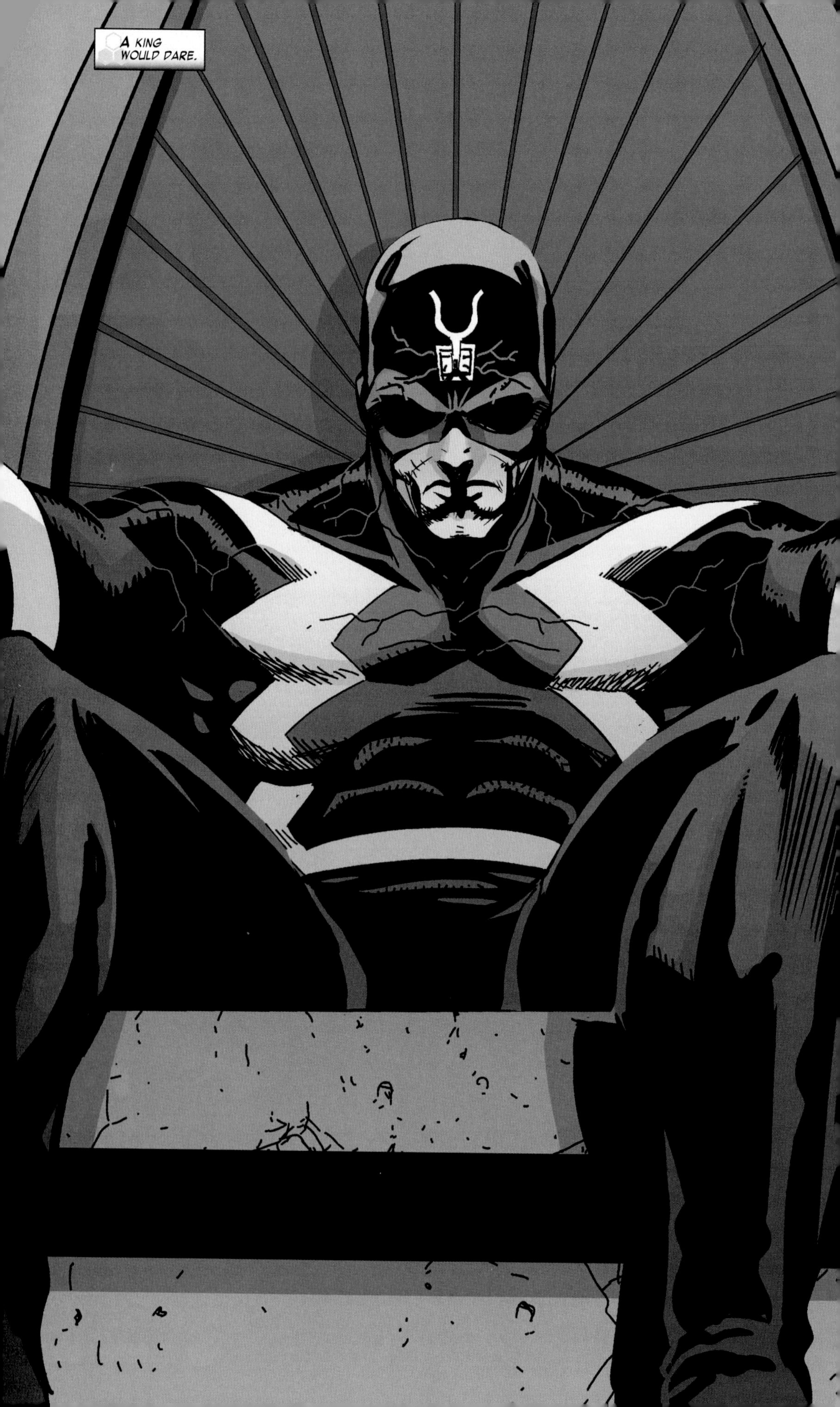
A KING
WOULD DARE.

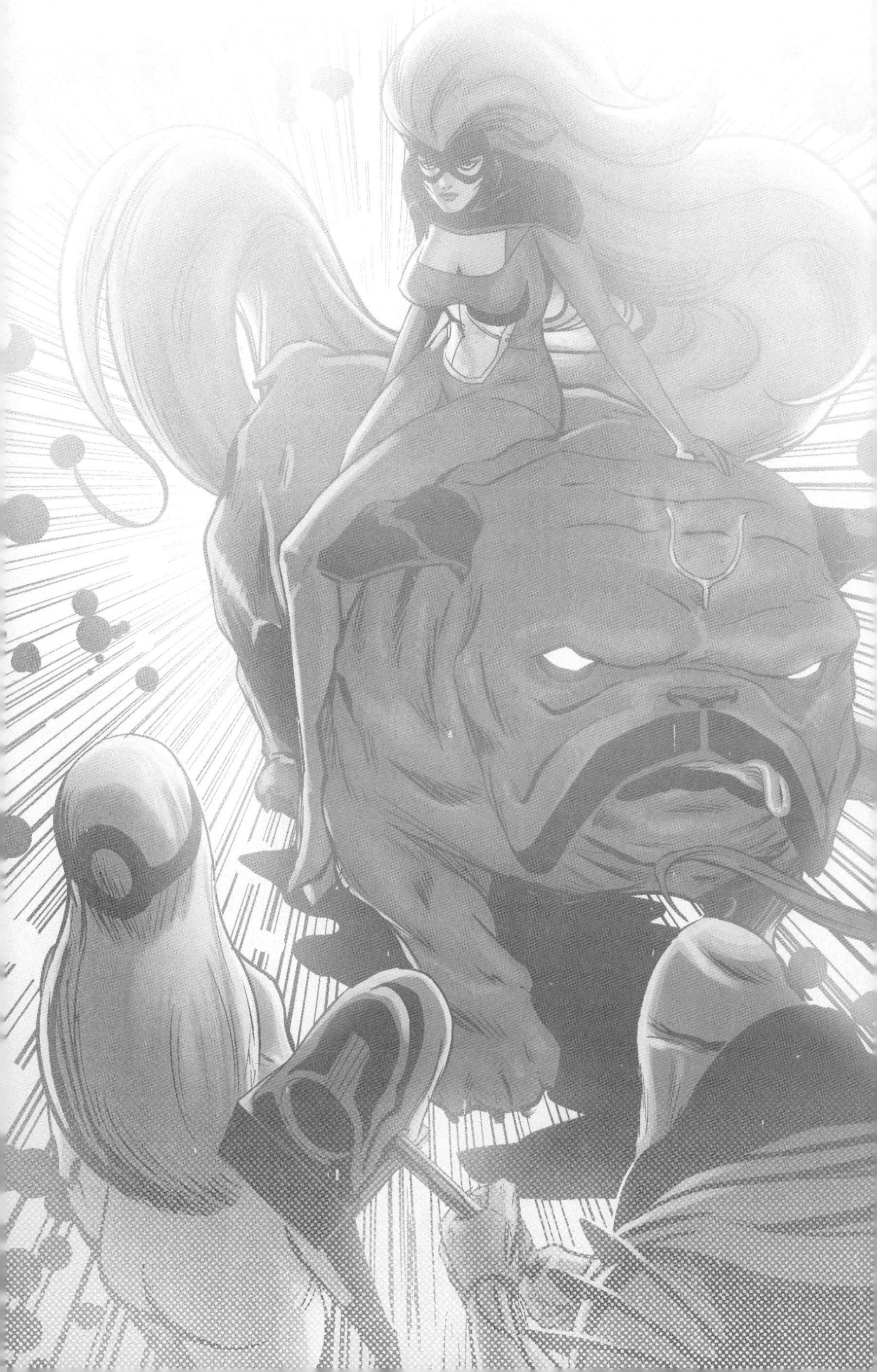

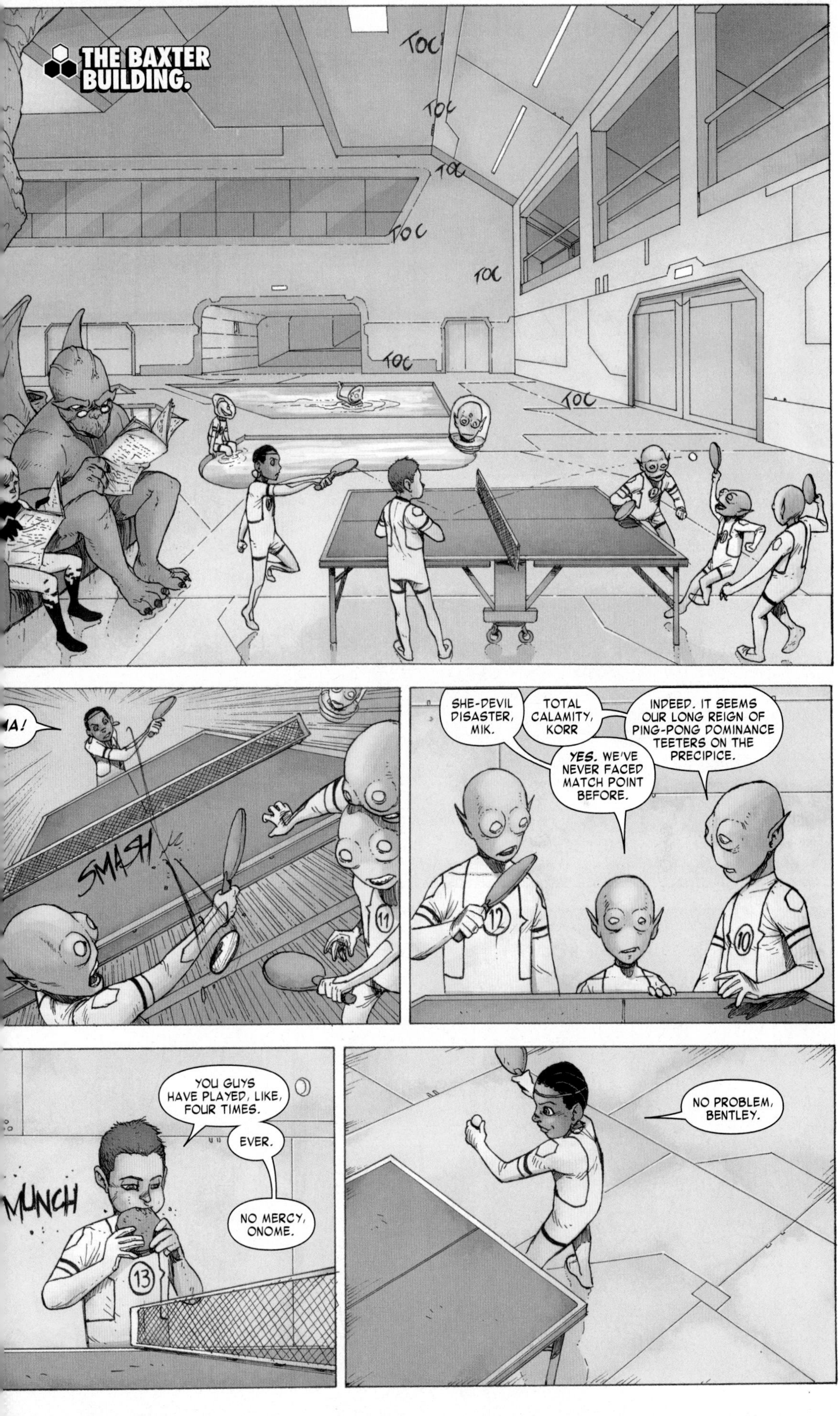

THE BAXTER BUILDING.
TOC
TOC
TOC
TOC
TOC
TOC
TOC
A!
SMASH
SHE-DEVIL DISASTER, MIK.
TOTAL CALAMITY, KORR
YES. WE'VE NEVER FACED MATCH POINT BEFORE.
INDEED. IT SEEMS OUR LONG REIGN OF PING-PONG DOMINANCE TEETERS ON THE PRECIPICE.
MUNCH
YOU GUYS HAVE PLAYED, LIKE, FOUR TIMES.
EVER.
NO MERCY, ONOME.
NO PROBLEM, BENTLEY.

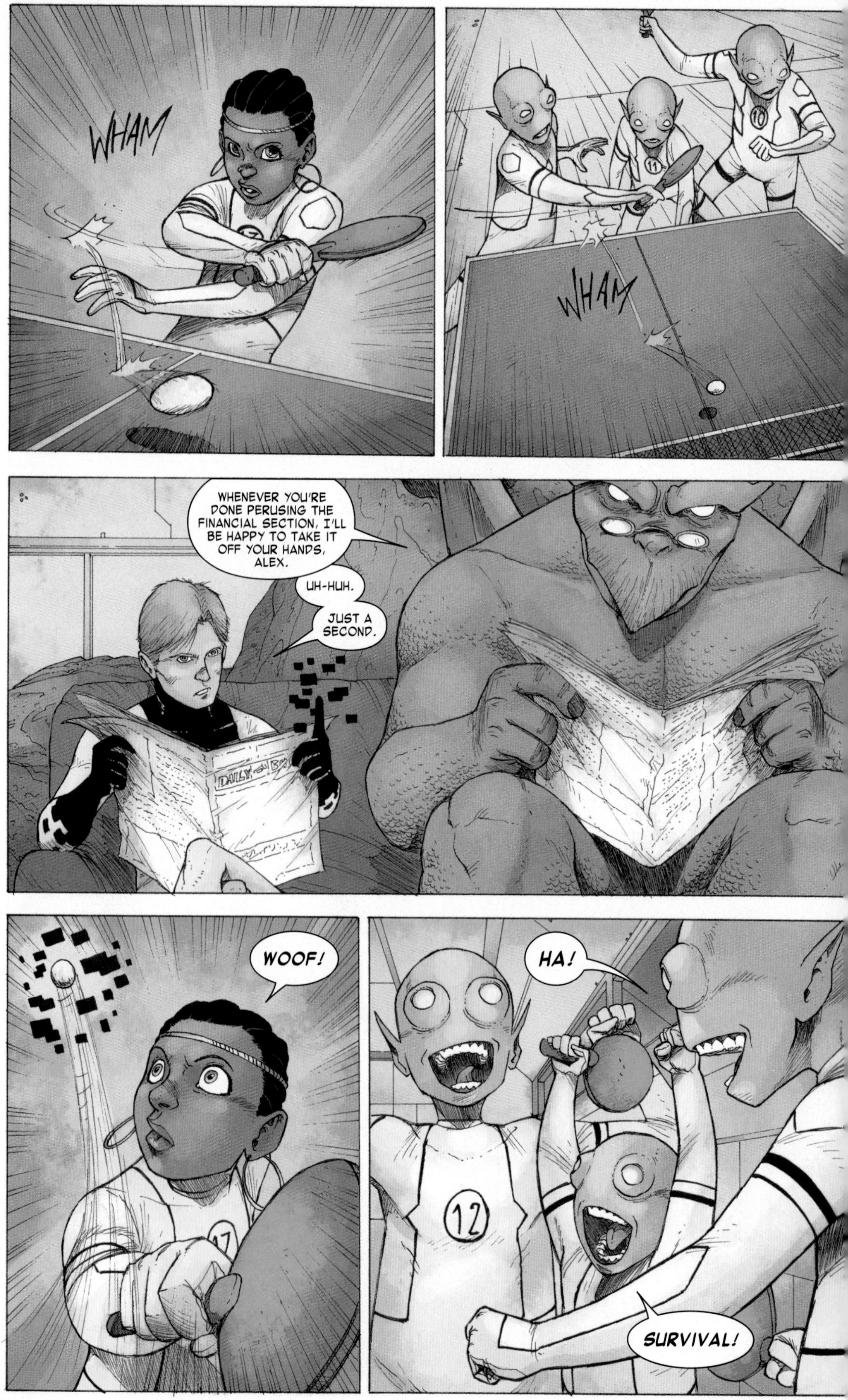
WHAM
WHAM
WHENEVER YOU'RE DONE PERUSING THE FINANCIAL SECTION, I'LL BE HAPPY TO TAKE IT OFF YOUR HANDS, ALEX.
UH-HUH.
JUST A SECOND.
WOOF!
HA!
SURVIVAL!

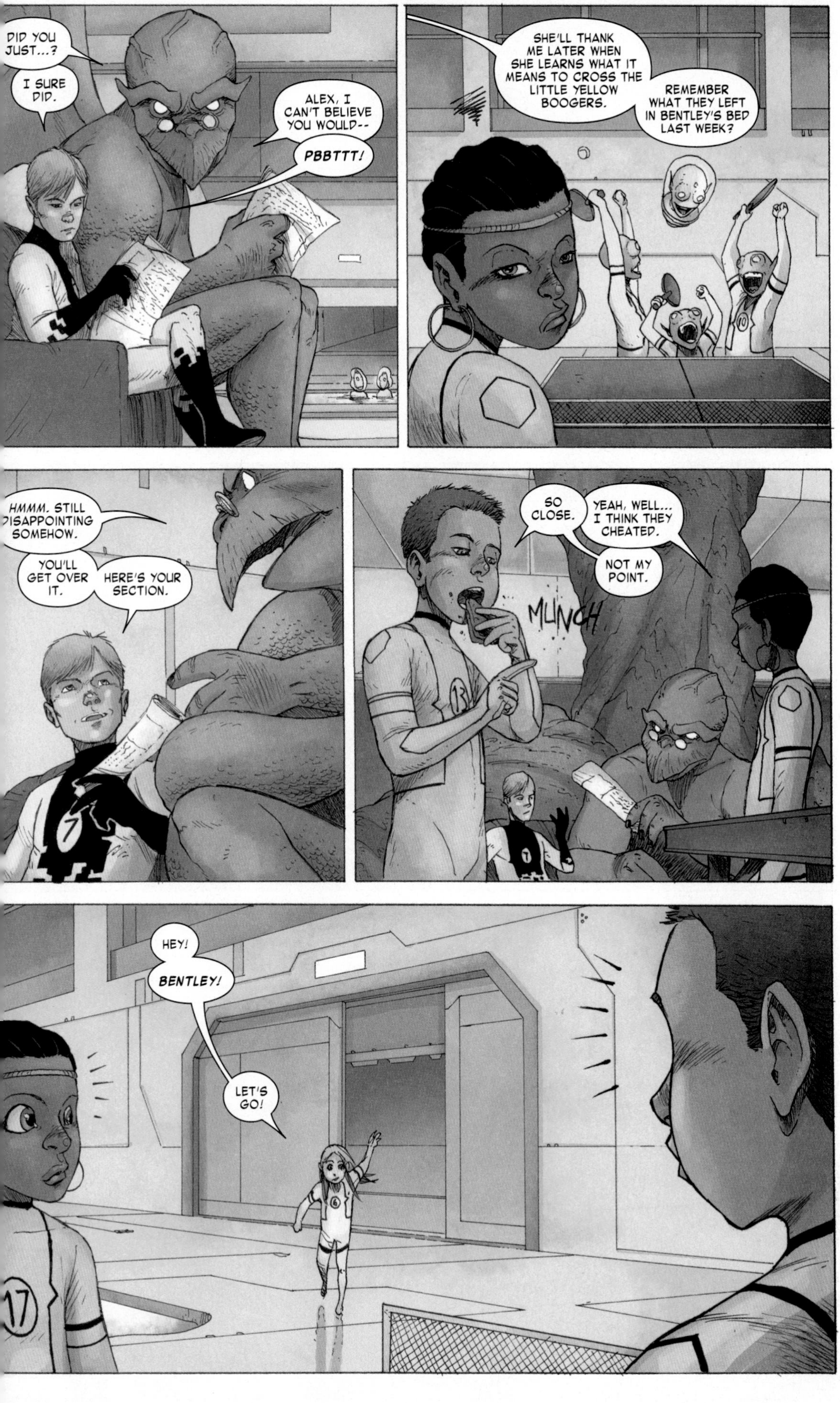

DID YOU JUST...?
I SURE DID.
ALEX, I CAN'T BELIEVE YOU WOULD--
PBBTTT!
SHE'LL THANK ME LATER WHEN SHE LEARNS WHAT IT MEANS TO CROSS THE LITTLE YELLOW BOOGERS.
REMEMBER WHAT THEY LEFT IN BENTLEY'S BED LAST WEEK?
HMMM. STILL DISAPPOINTING SOMEHOW.
YOU'LL GET OVER IT.
HERE'S YOUR SECTION.
SO CLOSE.
YEAH, WELL... I THINK THEY CHEATED.
NOT MY POINT.
MUNCH
HEY!
BENTLEY!
LET'S GO!

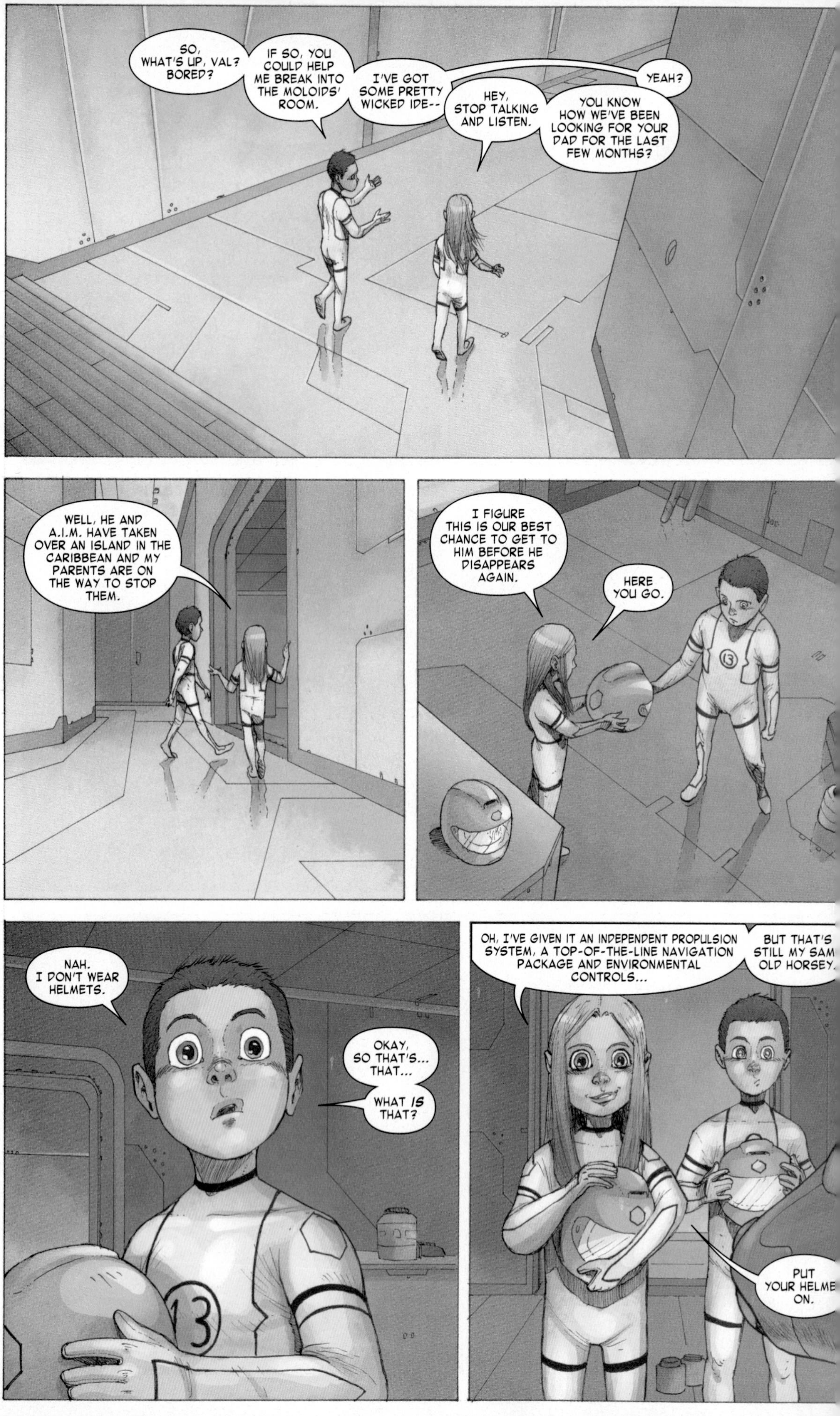

SO, WHAT'S UP, VAL? BORED?
IF SO, YOU COULD HELP ME BREAK INTO THE MOLOIDS' ROOM.
I'VE GOT SOME PRETTY WICKED IDE--
HEY, STOP TALKING AND LISTEN.
YEAH?
YOU KNOW HOW WE'VE BEEN LOOKING FOR YOUR DAD FOR THE LAST FEW MONTHS?
WELL, HE AND A.I.M. HAVE TAKEN OVER AN ISLAND IN THE CARIBBEAN AND MY PARENTS ARE ON THE WAY TO STOP THEM.
I FIGURE THIS IS OUR BEST CHANCE TO GET TO HIM BEFORE HE DISAPPEARS AGAIN.
HERE YOU GO.
NAH. I DON'T WEAR HELMETS.
OKAY, SO THAT'S... THAT...
WHAT IS THAT?
OH, I'VE GIVEN IT AN INDEPENDENT PROPULSION SYSTEM, A TOP-OF-THE-LINE NAVIGATION PACKAGE AND ENVIRONMENTAL CONTROLS...
BUT THAT'S STILL MY SAM OLD HORSEY.
PUT YOUR HELME ON.

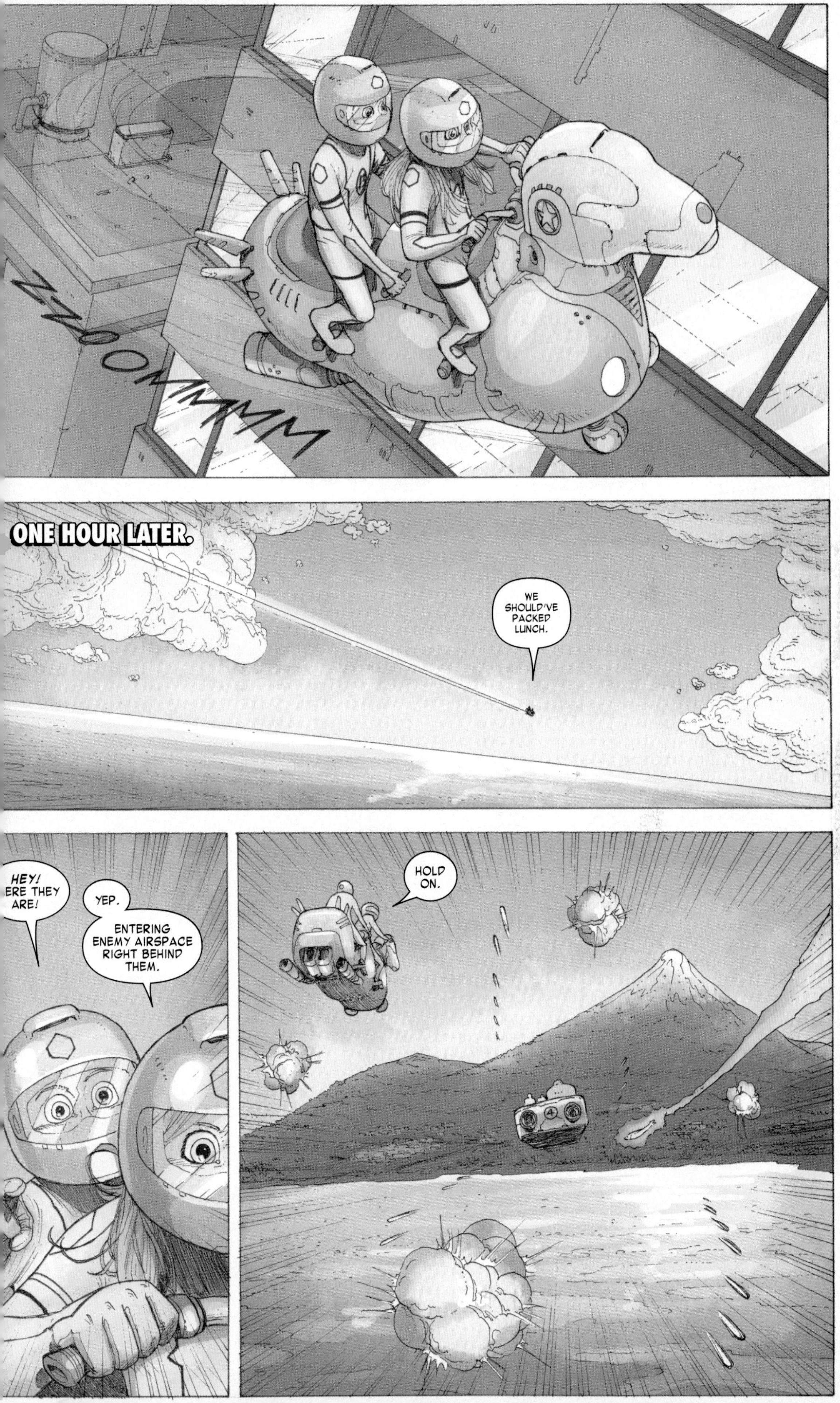

ZZZOOMMMMMM
ONE HOUR LATER.
WE SHOULD'VE PACKED LUNCH.
HEY! ERE THEY ARE!
YEP.
ENTERING ENEMY AIRSPACE RIGHT BEHIND THEM.
HOLD ON.

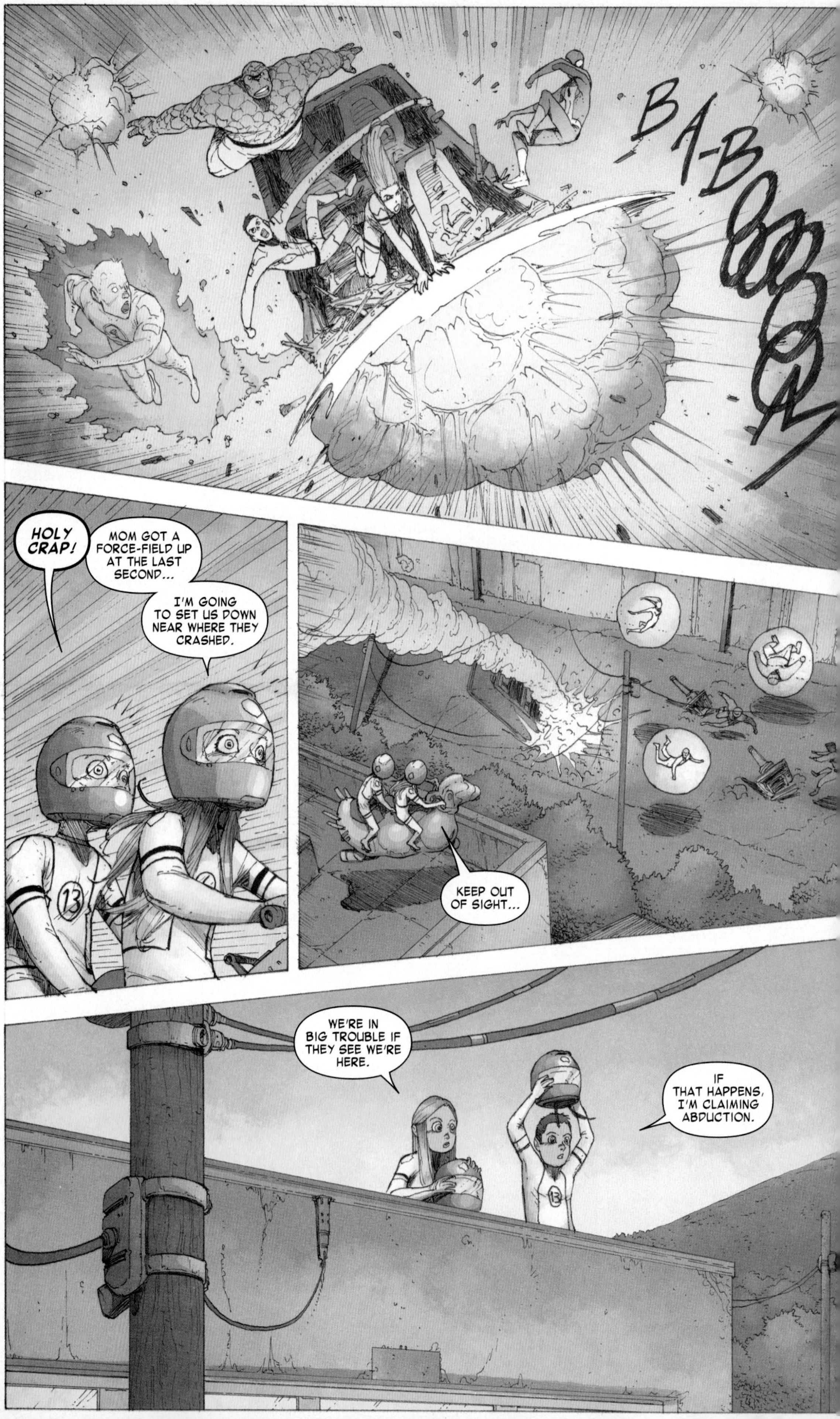
BA-BOOOOM
HOLY CRAP!
MOM GOT A FORCE-FIELD UP AT THE LAST SECOND...
I'M GOING TO SET US DOWN NEAR WHERE THEY CRASHED.
KEEP OUT OF SIGHT...
WE'RE IN BIG TROUBLE IF THEY SEE WE'RE HERE.
IF THAT HAPPENS, I'M CLAIMING ABDUCTION.

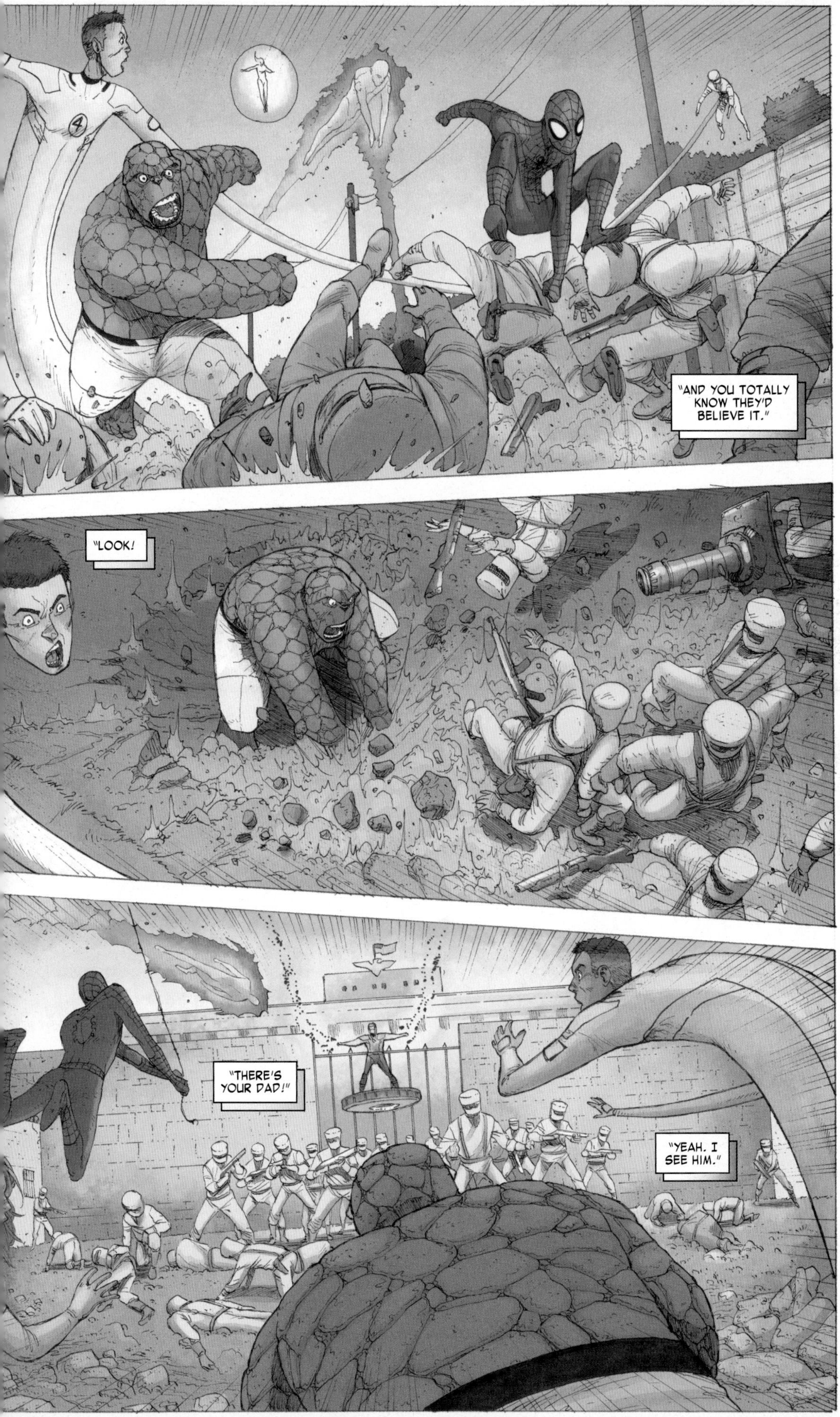
"AND YOU TOTALLY KNOW THEY'D BELIEVE IT."
"LOOK!
"THERE'S YOUR DAD!"
"YEAH. I SEE HIM."

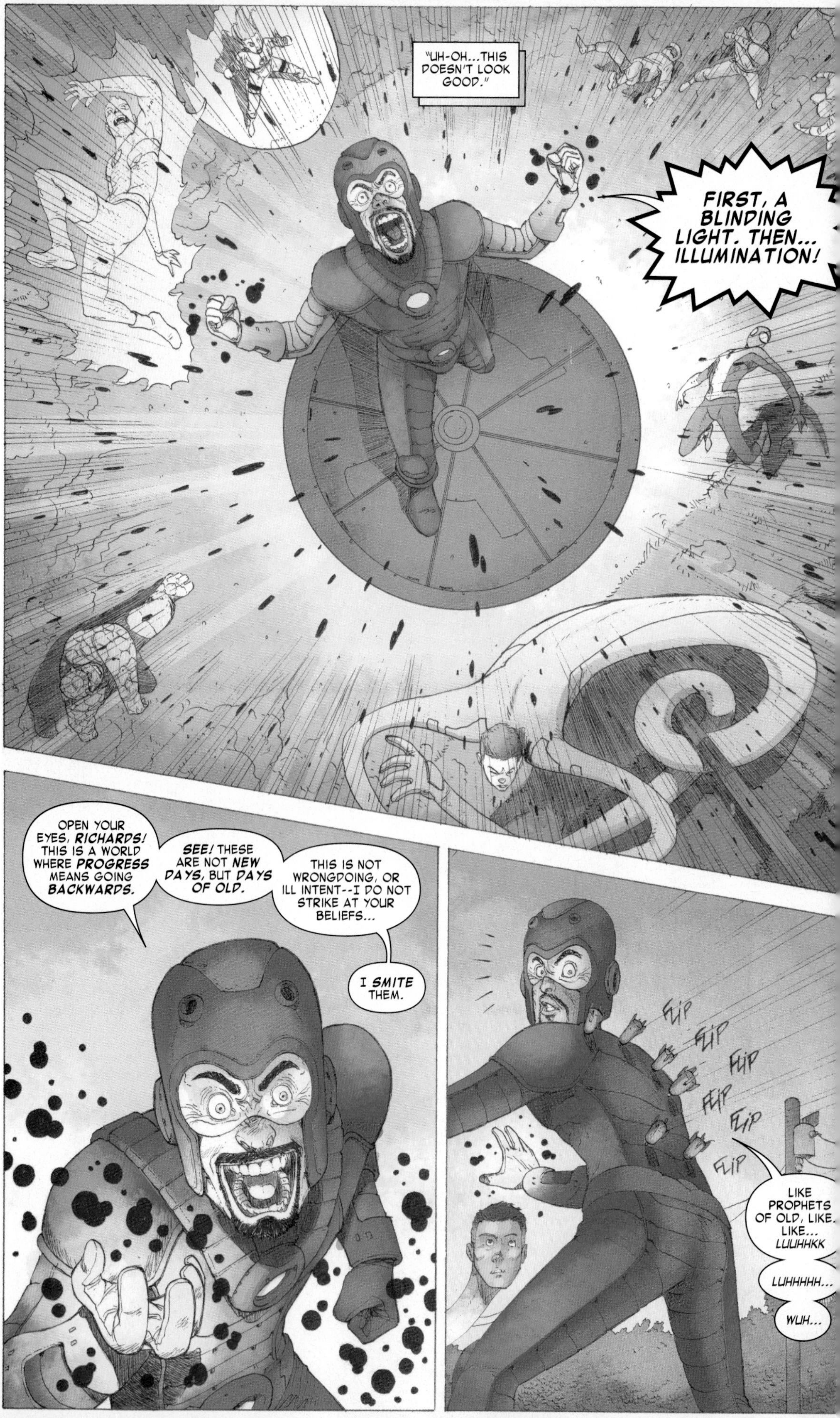
"UH-OH...THIS DOESN'T LOOK GOOD."
FIRST, A BLINDING LIGHT. THEN... ILLUMINATION!
OPEN YOUR EYES, RICHARDS! THIS IS A WORLD WHERE PROGRESS MEANS GOING BACKWARDS.
SEE! THESE ARE NOT NEW DAYS, BUT DAYS OF OLD.
THIS IS NOT WRONGDOING, OR ILL INTENT--I DO NOT STRIKE AT YOUR BELIEFS...
I SMITE THEM.
FLIP
FLIP
FLIP
FLIP
FLIP
FLIP
LIKE PROPHETS OF OLD, LIKE, LIKE... LUUHHKK
LUHHHHH...
WUH...

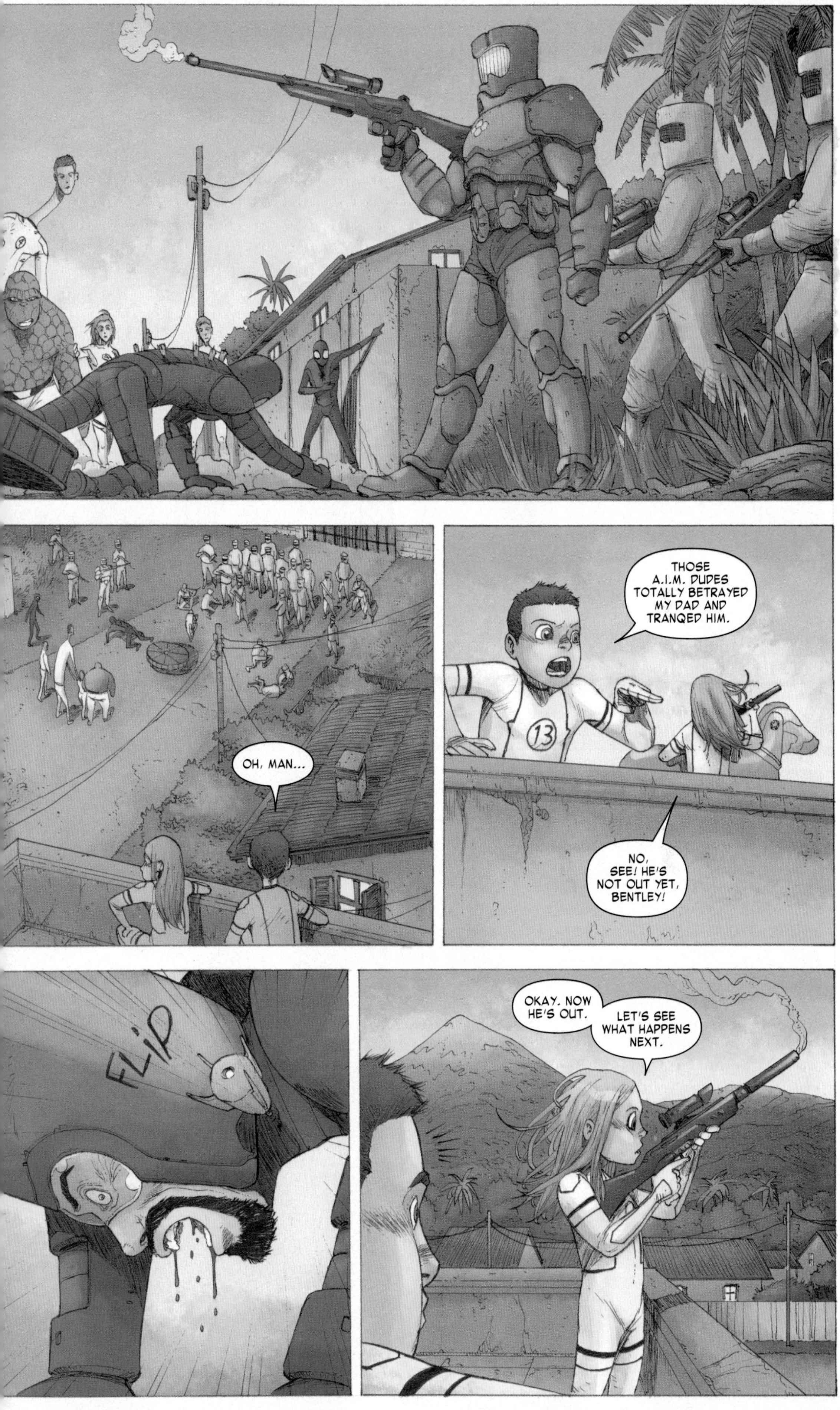
OH, MAN...
THOSE A.I.M. DUDES TOTALLY BETRAYED MY DAD AND TRANQED HIM.
NO, SEE! HE'S NOT OUT YET, BENTLEY!
FLIP
OKAY. NOW HE'S OUT.
LET'S SEE WHAT HAPPENS NEXT.

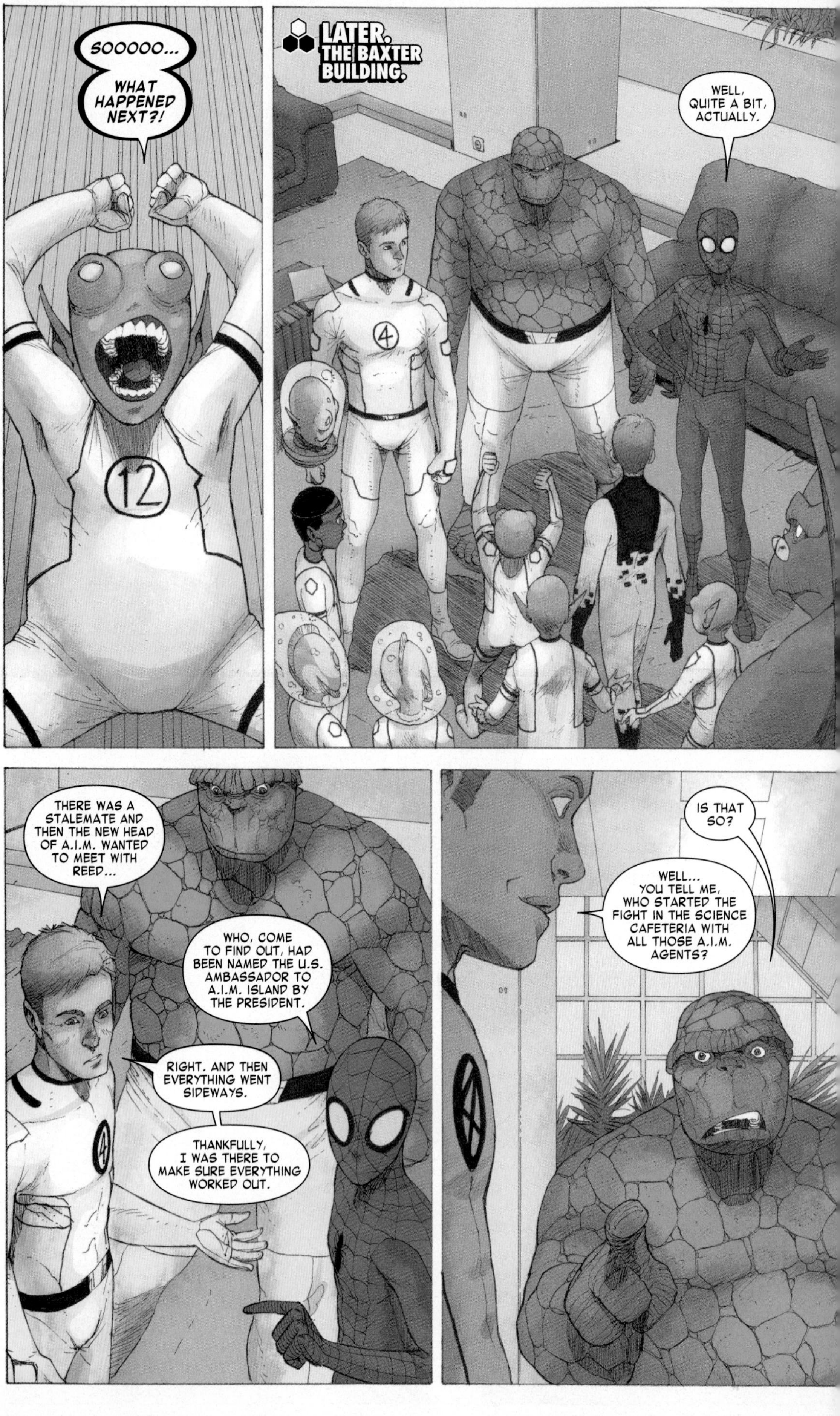
SOOOOO...
WHAT HAPPENED NEXT?!
LATER. THE BAXTER BUILDING.
WELL, QUITE A BIT, ACTUALLY.
THERE WAS A STALEMATE AND THEN THE NEW HEAD OF A.I.M. WANTED TO MEET WITH REED...
WHO, COME TO FIND OUT, HAD BEEN NAMED THE U.S. AMBASSADOR TO A.I.M. ISLAND BY THE PRESIDENT.
RIGHT. AND THEN EVERYTHING WENT SIDEWAYS.
THANKFULLY, I WAS THERE TO MAKE SURE EVERYTHING WORKED OUT.
IS THAT SO?
WELL... YOU TELL ME, WHO STARTED THE FIGHT IN THE SCIENCE CAFETERIA WITH ALL THOSE A.I.M. AGENTS?

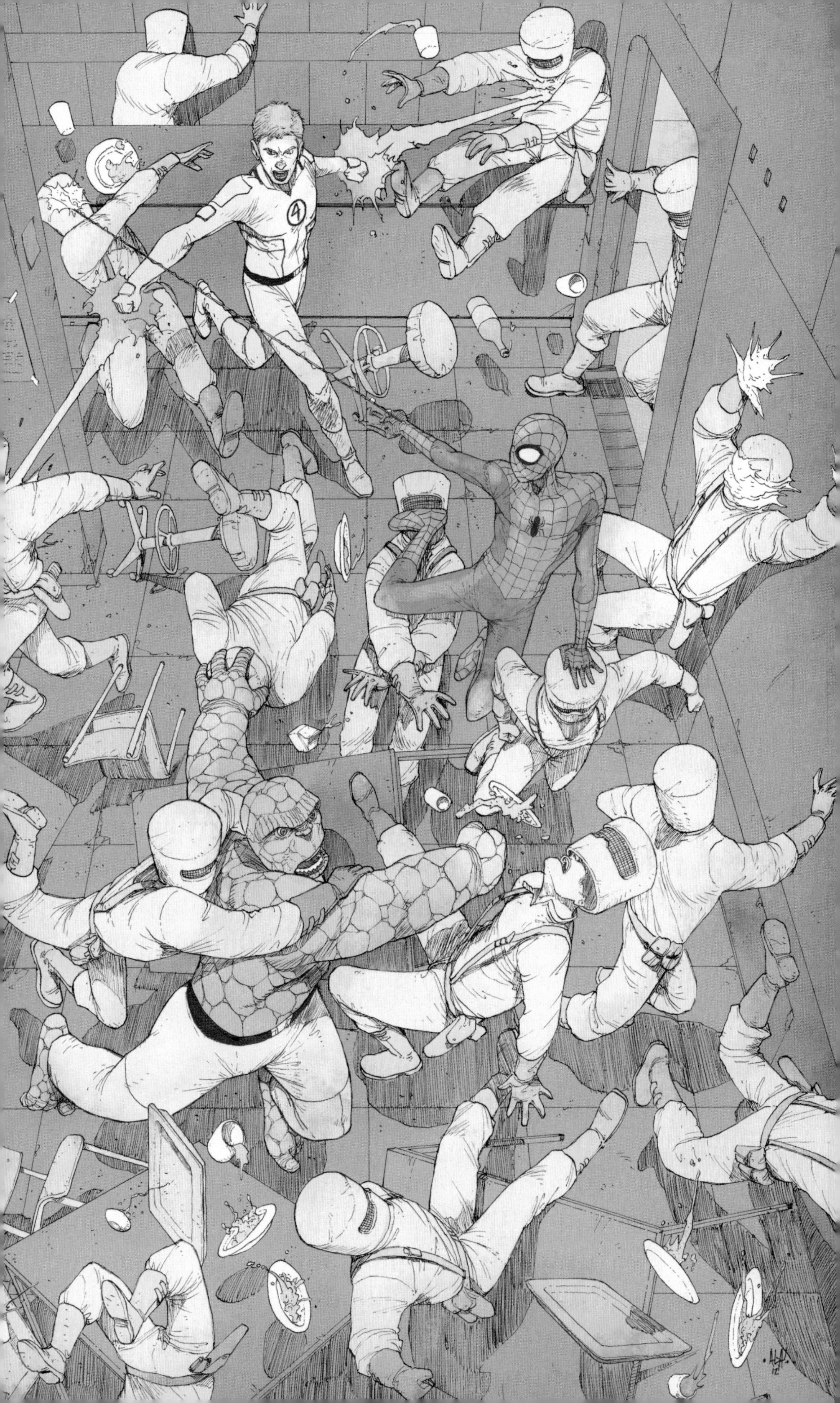

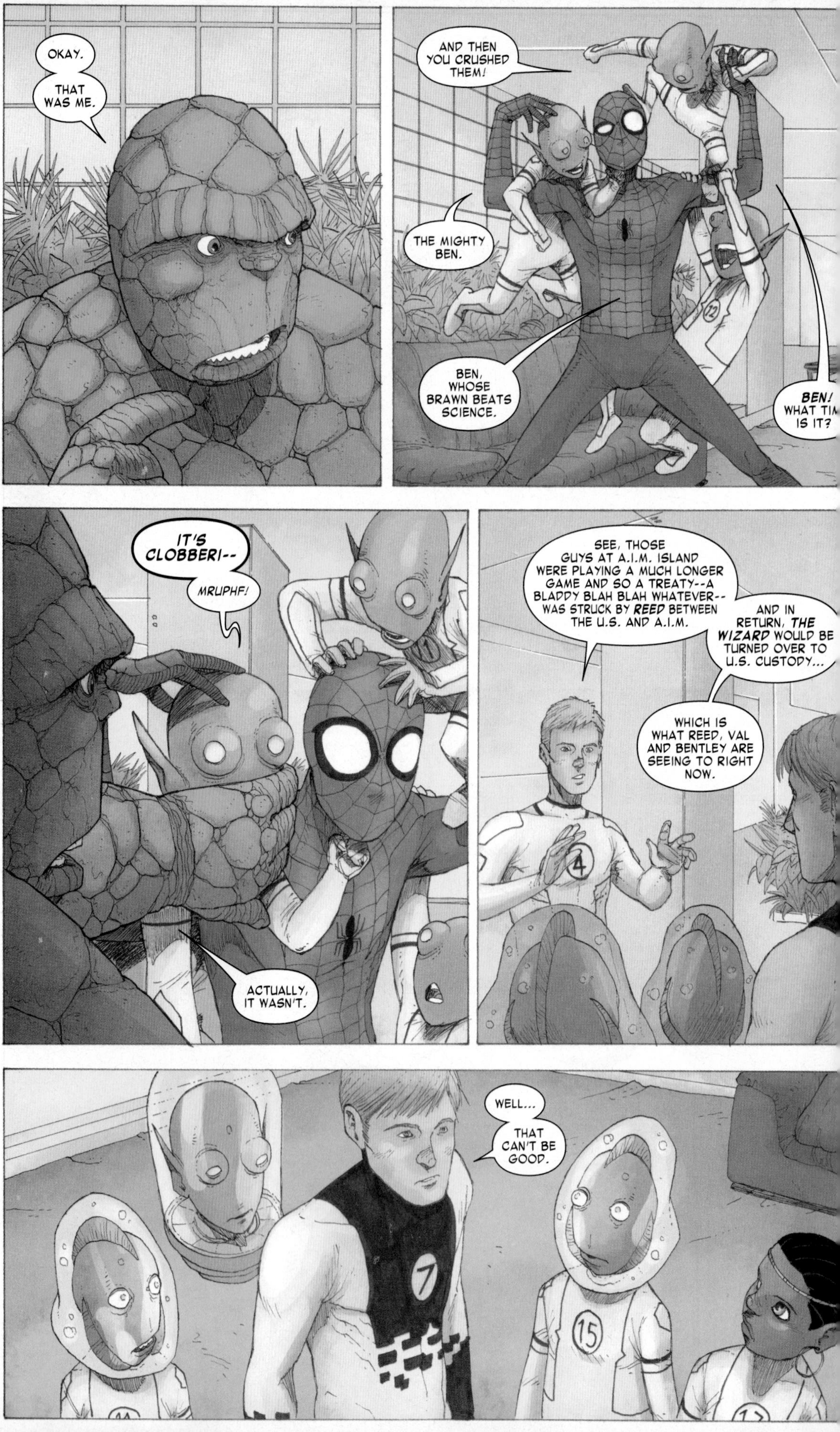
OKAY.
THAT WAS ME.
AND THEN YOU CRUSHED THEM!
THE MIGHTY BEN.
BEN, WHOSE BRAWN BEATS SCIENCE.
BEN! WHAT TIM IS IT?
IT'S CLOBBERI--
MRUPHF!
ACTUALLY, IT WASN'T.
SEE, THOSE GUYS AT A.I.M. ISLAND WERE PLAYING A MUCH LONGER GAME AND SO A TREATY--A BLADDY BLAH BLAH WHATEVER--WAS STRUCK BY REED BETWEEN THE U.S. AND A.I.M.
AND IN RETURN, THE WIZARD WOULD BE TURNED OVER TO U.S. CUSTODY...
WHICH IS WHAT REED, VAL AND BENTLEY ARE SEEING TO RIGHT NOW.
WELL...
THAT CAN'T BE GOOD.

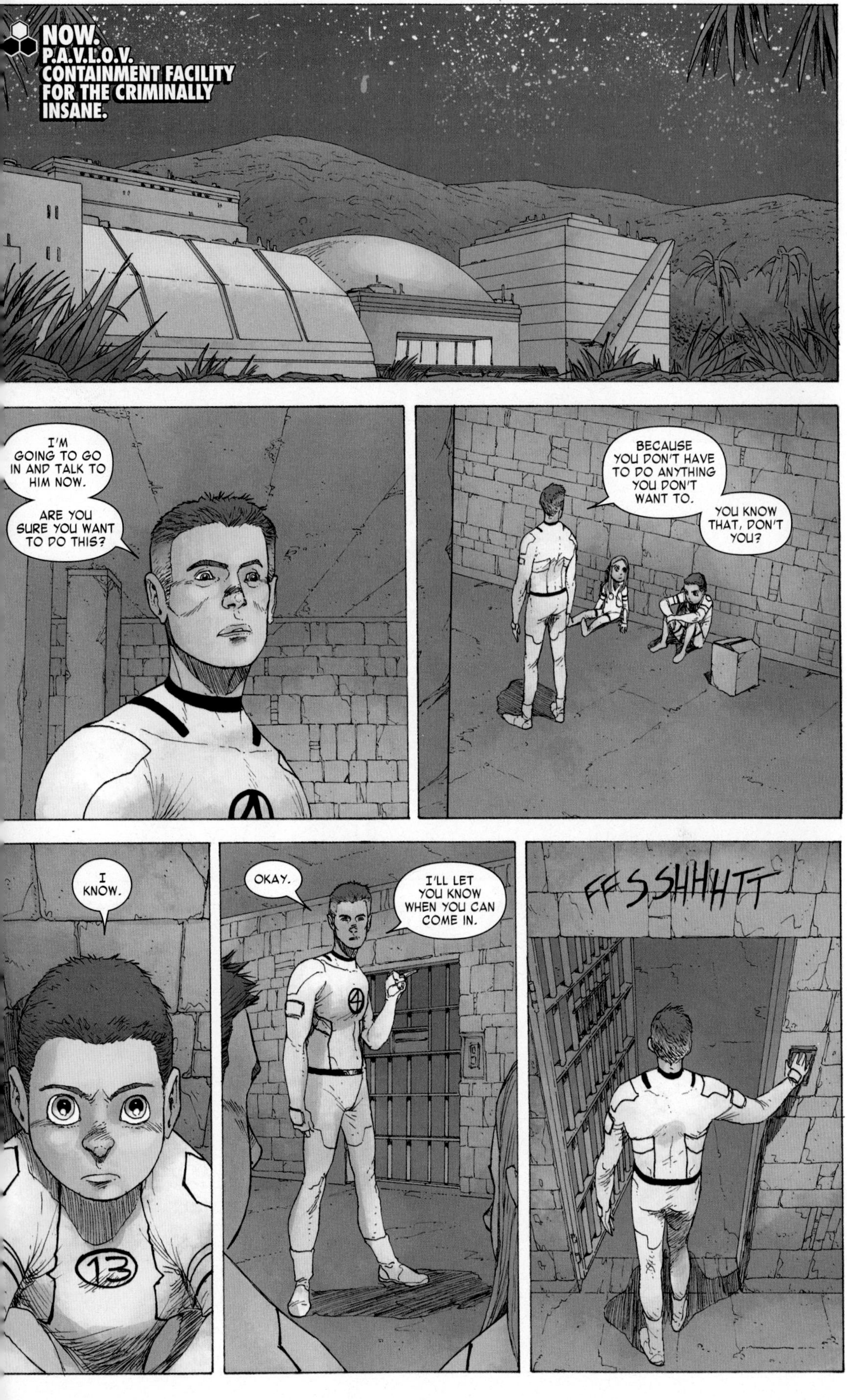
NOW.
P.A.V.L.O.V. CONTAINMENT FACILITY FOR THE CRIMINALLY INSANE.
I'M GOING TO GO IN AND TALK TO HIM NOW.
ARE YOU SURE YOU WANT TO DO THIS?
BECAUSE YOU DON'T HAVE TO DO ANYTHING YOU DON'T WANT TO.
YOU KNOW THAT, DON'T YOU?
I KNOW.
OKAY.
I'LL LET YOU KNOW WHEN YOU CAN COME IN.
FFSSHHHTT

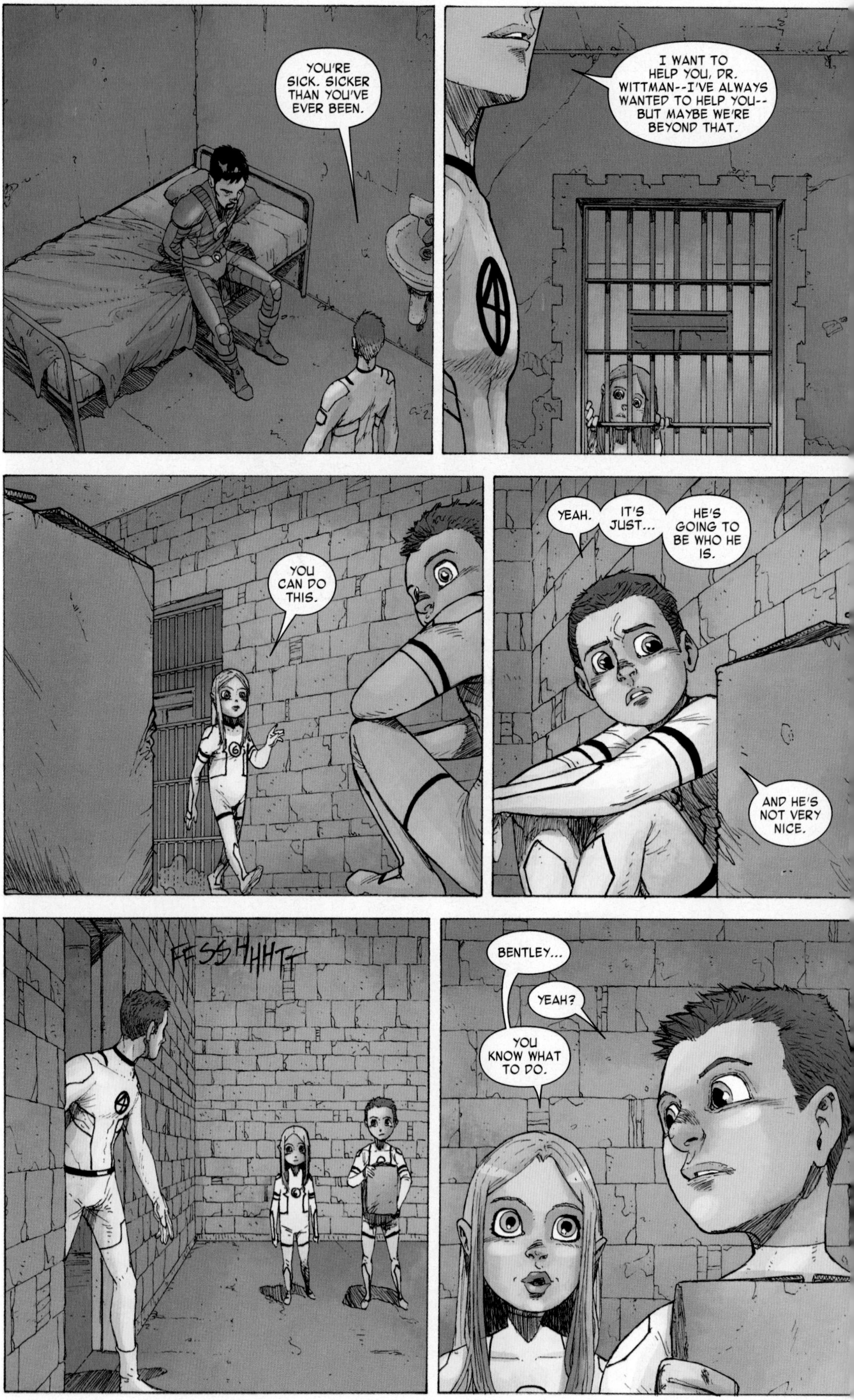
YOU'RE SICK. SICKER THAN YOU'VE EVER BEEN.
I WANT TO HELP YOU, DR. WITTMAN--I'VE ALWAYS WANTED TO HELP YOU--BUT MAYBE WE'RE BEYOND THAT.
YOU CAN DO THIS.
YEAH.
IT'S JUST...
HE'S GOING TO BE WHO HE IS.
AND HE'S NOT VERY NICE.
FFSSHHHTT
BENTLEY...
YEAH?
YOU KNOW WHAT TO DO.

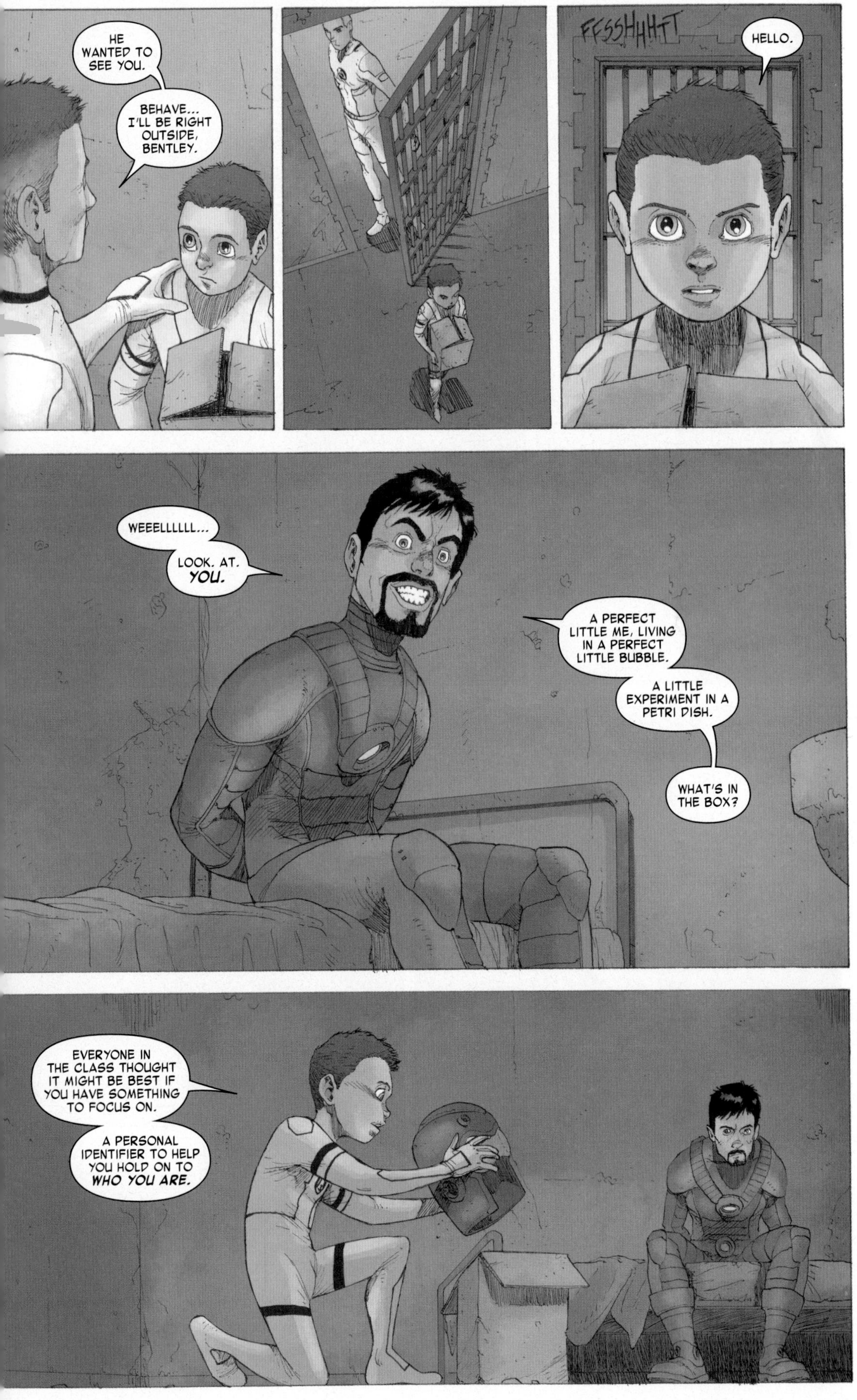
HE WANTED TO SEE YOU.
BEHAVE... I'LL BE RIGHT OUTSIDE, BENTLEY.
FFSSHHHT
HELLO.
WEEELLLLLL...
LOOK. AT. *YOU.*
A PERFECT LITTLE ME, LIVING IN A PERFECT LITTLE BUBBLE.
A LITTLE EXPERIMENT IN A PETRI DISH.
WHAT'S IN THE BOX?
EVERYONE IN THE CLASS THOUGHT IT MIGHT BE BEST IF YOU HAVE SOMETHING TO FOCUS ON.
A PERSONAL IDENTIFIER TO HELP YOU HOLD ON TO *WHO YOU ARE.*

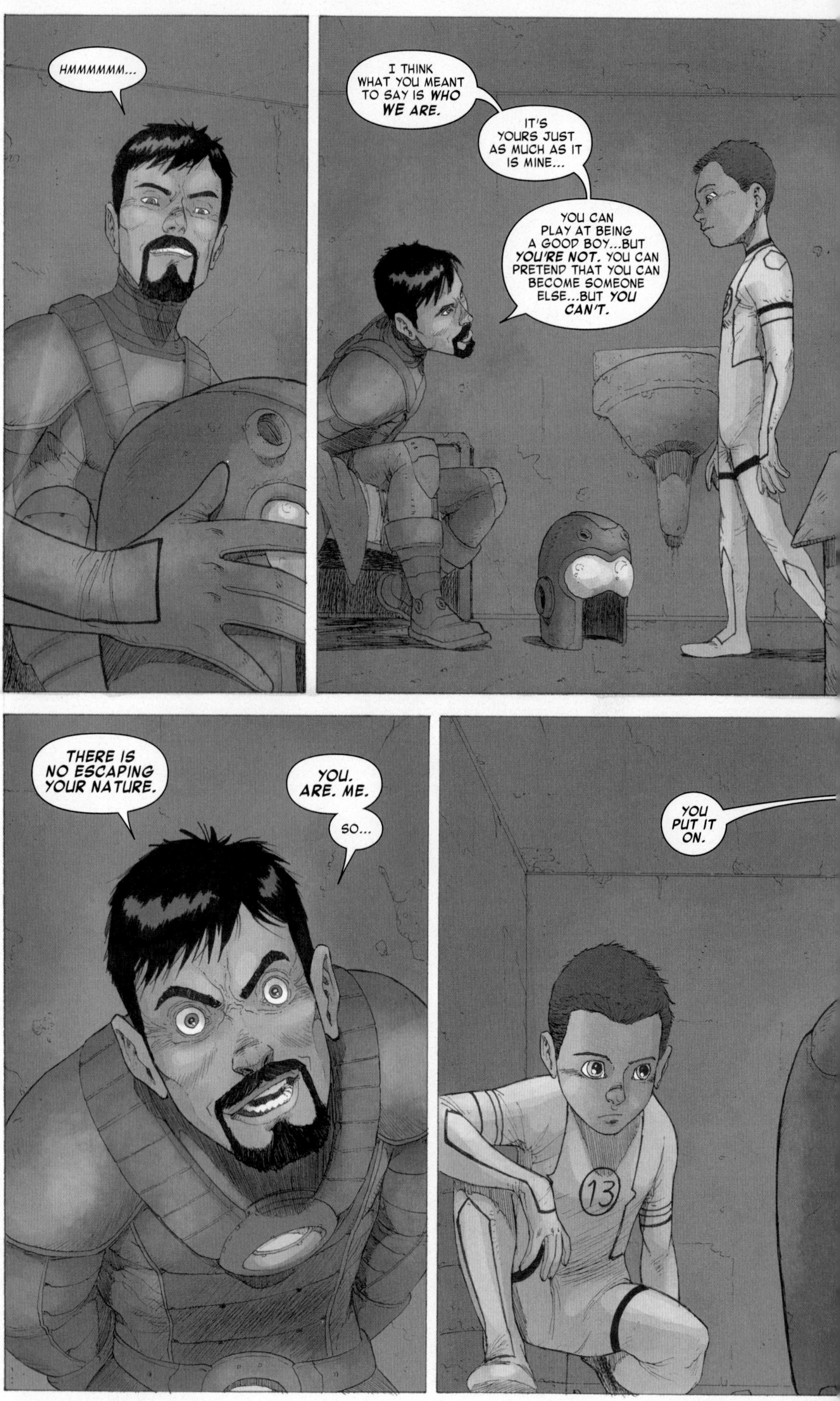
HMMMMMM...
I THINK WHAT YOU MEANT TO SAY IS WHO WE ARE.
IT'S YOURS JUST AS MUCH AS IT IS MINE...
YOU CAN PLAY AT BEING A GOOD BOY...BUT YOU'RE NOT. YOU CAN PRETEND THAT YOU CAN BECOME SOMEONE ELSE...BUT YOU CAN'T.
THERE IS NO ESCAPING YOUR NATURE.
YOU. ARE. ME.
SO...
YOU PUT IT ON.
13

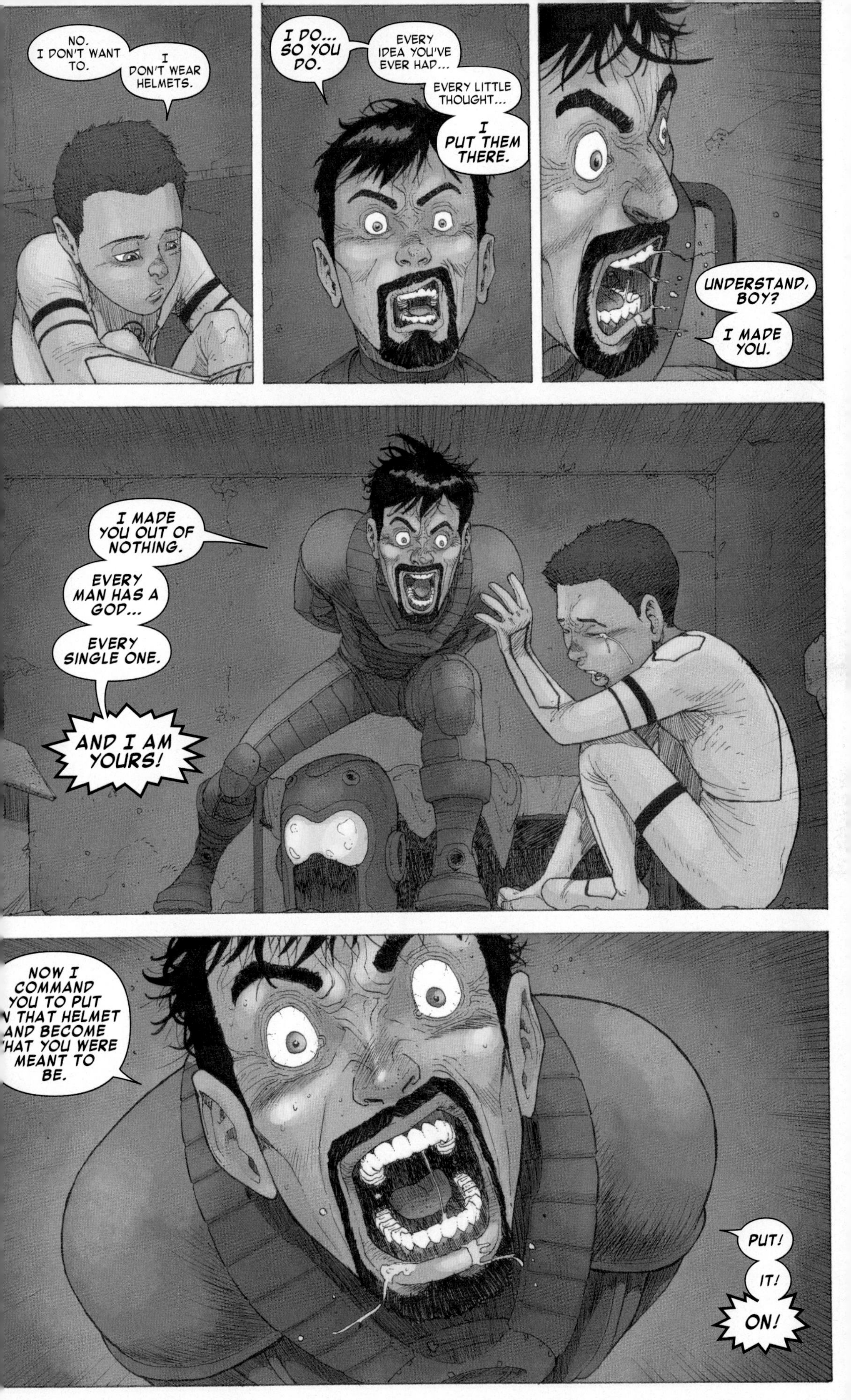

NO. I DON'T WANT TO.
I DON'T WEAR HELMETS.
I DO... SO YOU DO.
EVERY IDEA YOU'VE EVER HAD...
EVERY LITTLE THOUGHT...
I PUT THEM THERE.
UNDERSTAND, BOY?
I MADE YOU.
I MADE YOU OUT OF NOTHING.
EVERY MAN HAS A GOD...
EVERY SINGLE ONE.
AND I AM YOURS!
NOW I COMMAND YOU TO PUT N THAT HELMET AND BECOME HAT YOU WERE MEANT TO BE.
PUT!
IT!
ON!

GET BENT, DAD.

WHAM

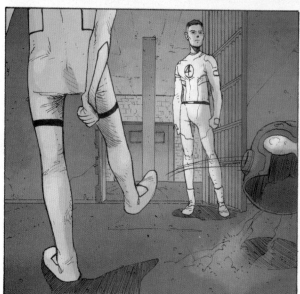

LOOK HERE, DOCTOR WITTMAN.

IF YOU REMEMBER, I MADE YOU A PROMISE.

THAT I WOULD RAISE BENTLEY AS MY OWN.

AND HE, WHILE BEING NO DIFFERENT FROM YOU, WOULD BECOME SOMETHING BETTER.

I MUST SAY... THE BOY HAS NOT DISAPPOINTED.

SO HERE'S MY WORD FROM ON HIGH--WE ARE NOT SLAVES TO O NATURE, DOCTOR WITTMAN...

YOU CAN BE WHATEVER YOU WANT TO BE.

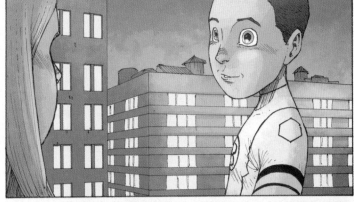

YOU WERE AWESOME IN THERE.

THANKS.

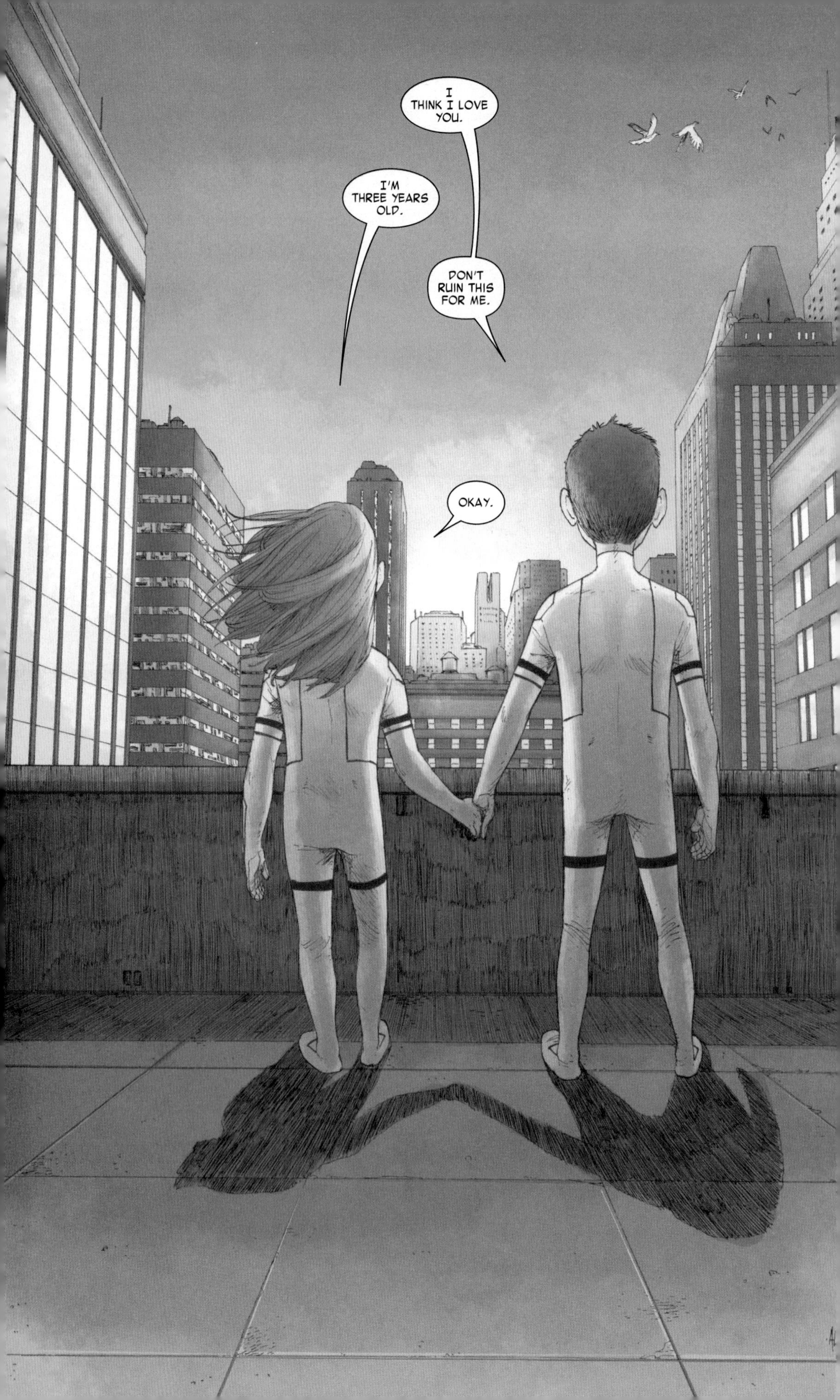
I THINK I LOVE YOU.
I'M THREE YEARS OLD.
DON'T RUIN THIS FOR ME.
OKAY.

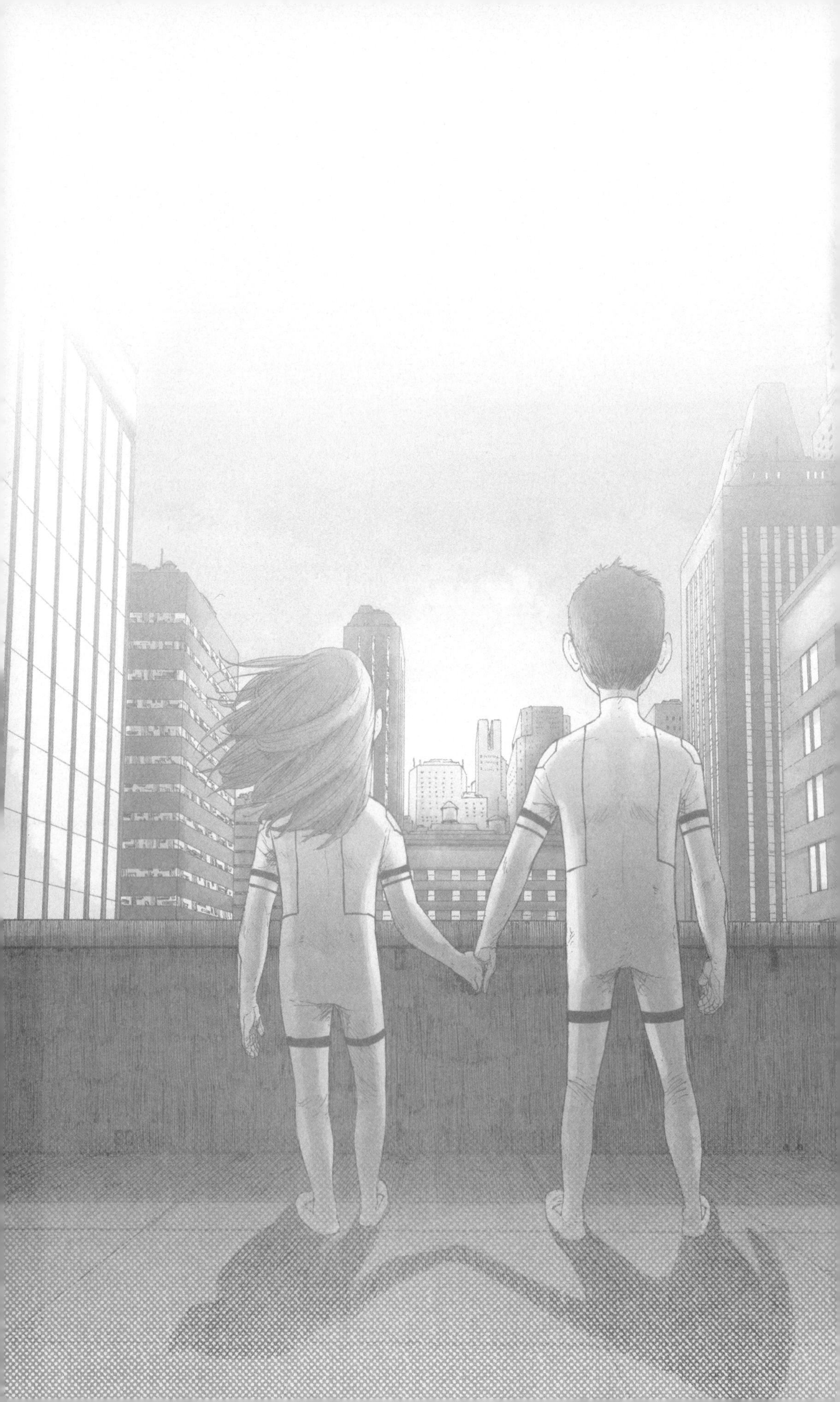

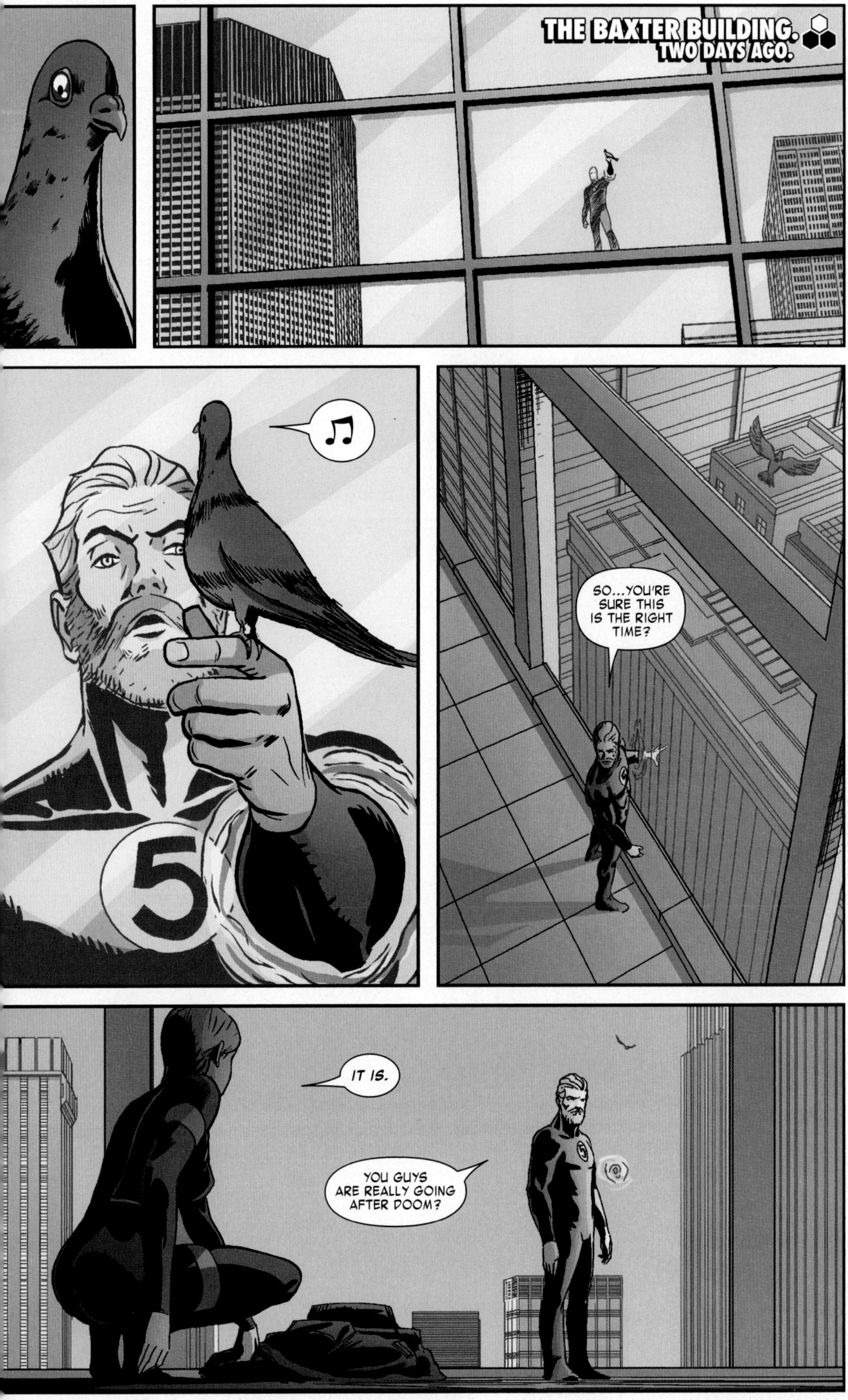
THE BAXTER BUILDING.
TWO DAYS AGO.
♫
SO...YOU'RE SURE THIS IS THE RIGHT TIME?
IT IS.
YOU GUYS ARE REALLY GOING AFTER DOOM?

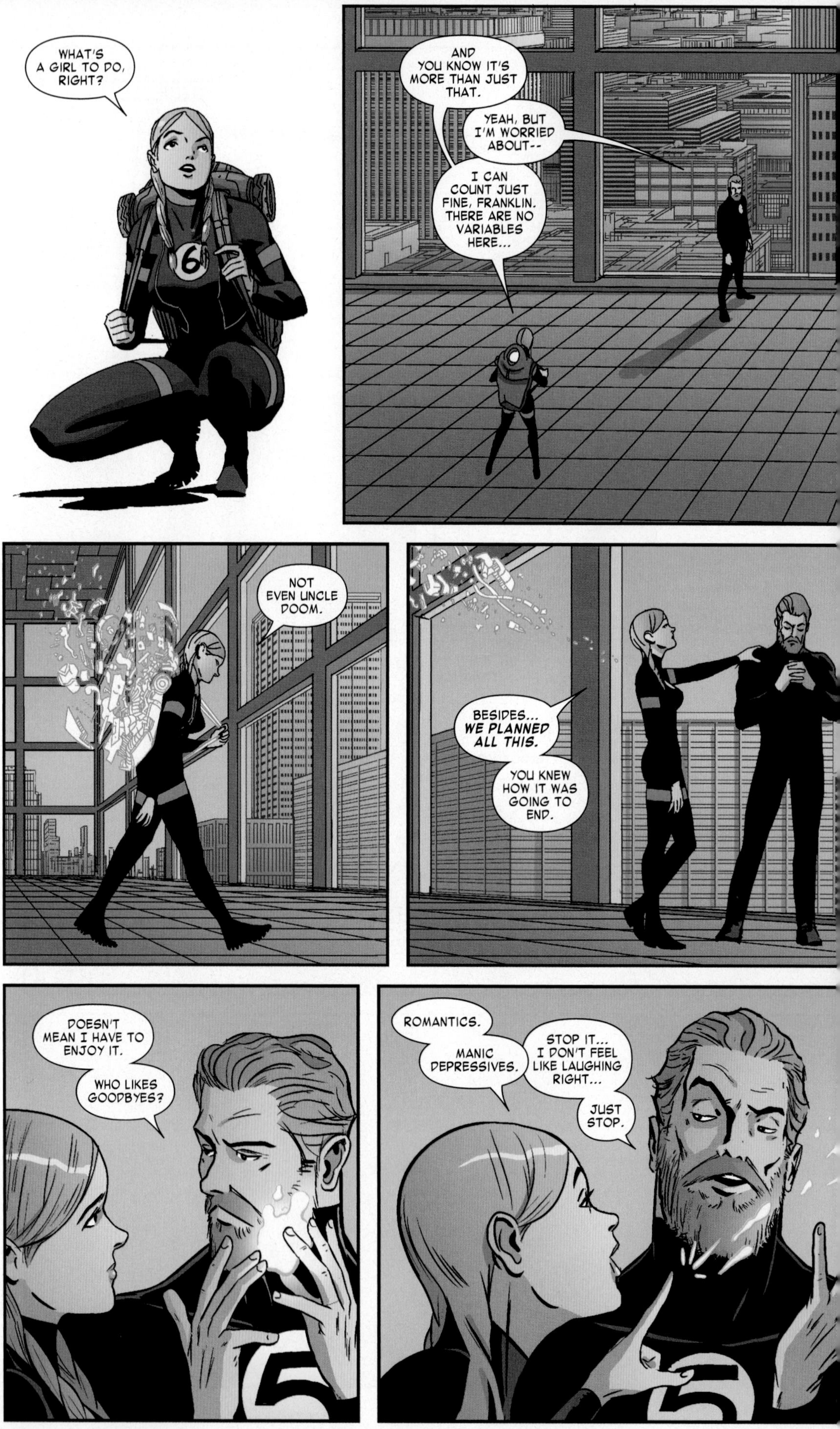
WHAT'S A GIRL TO DO, RIGHT?
AND YOU KNOW IT'S MORE THAN JUST THAT.
YEAH, BUT I'M WORRIED ABOUT--
I CAN COUNT JUST FINE, FRANKLIN. THERE ARE NO VARIABLES HERE...
NOT EVEN UNCLE DOOM.
BESIDES... WE PLANNED ALL THIS.
YOU KNEW HOW IT WAS GOING TO END.
DOESN'T MEAN I HAVE TO ENJOY IT.
WHO LIKES GOODBYES?
ROMANTICS.
MANIC DEPRESSIVES.
STOP IT... I DON'T FEEL LIKE LAUGHING RIGHT...
JUST STOP.

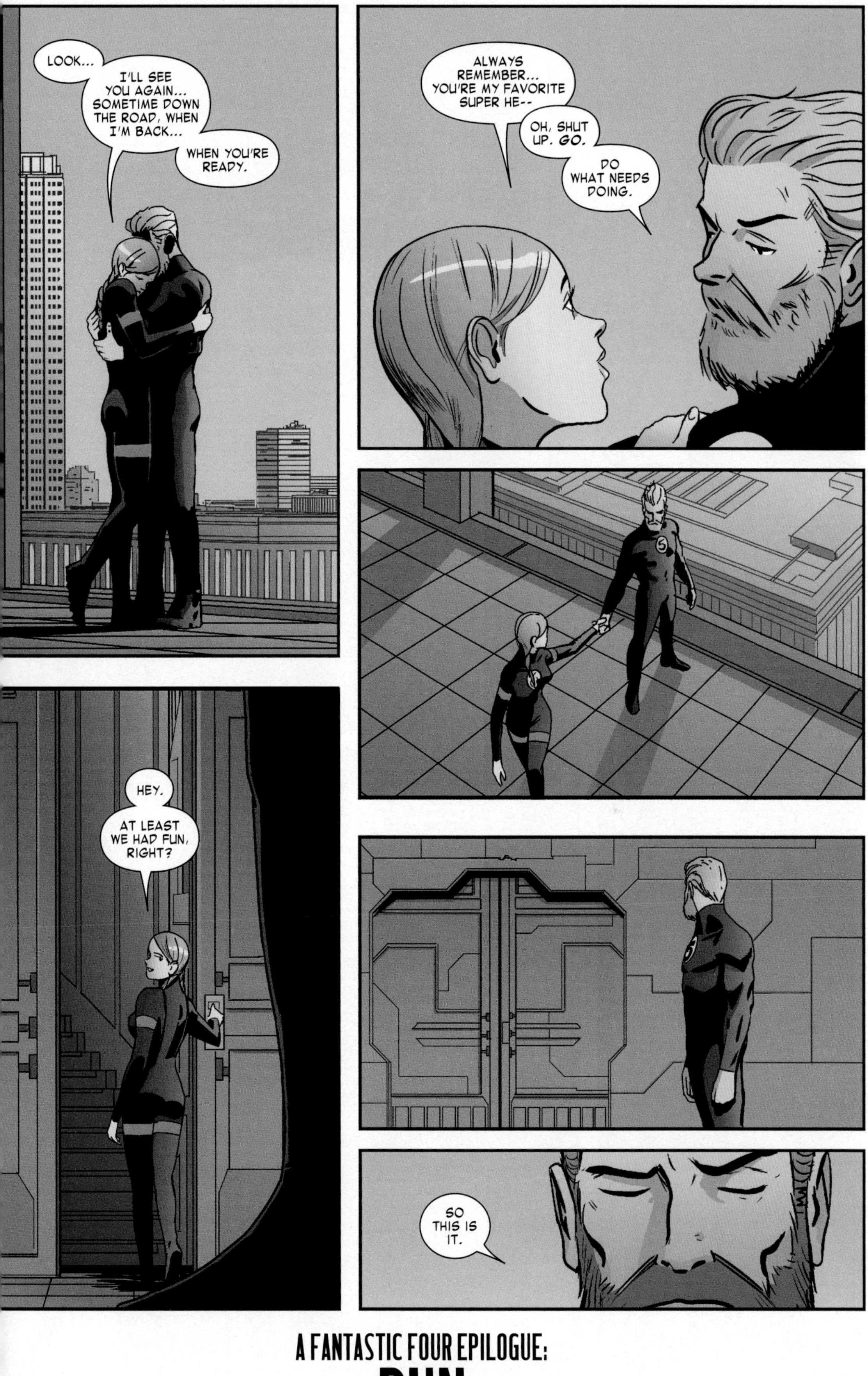
LOOK...
I'LL SEE YOU AGAIN... SOMETIME DOWN THE ROAD, WHEN I'M BACK...
WHEN YOU'RE READY.
ALWAYS REMEMBER... YOU'RE MY FAVORITE SUPER HE--
OH, SHUT UP. GO.
DO WHAT NEEDS DOING.
HEY.
AT LEAST WE HAD FUN, RIGHT?
SO THIS IS IT.

A FANTASTIC FOUR EPILOGUE:

RUN

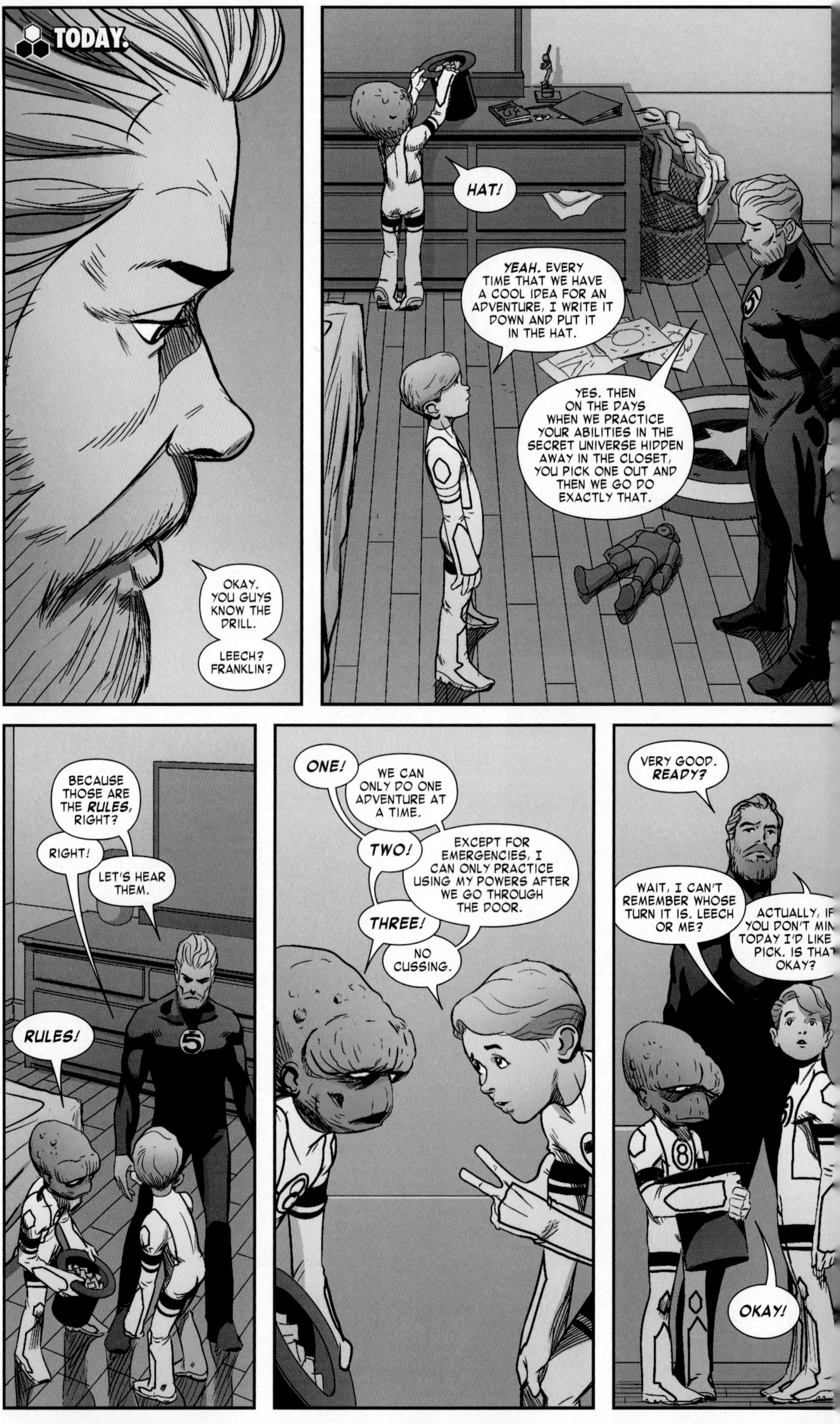

TODAY.
OKAY. YOU GUYS KNOW THE DRILL.
LEECH? FRANKLIN?
HAT!
YEAH. EVERY TIME THAT WE HAVE A COOL IDEA FOR AN ADVENTURE, I WRITE IT DOWN AND PUT IT IN THE HAT.
YES. THEN ON THE DAYS WHEN WE PRACTICE YOUR ABILITIES IN THE SECRET UNIVERSE HIDDEN AWAY IN THE CLOSET, YOU PICK ONE OUT AND THEN WE GO DO EXACTLY THAT.
BECAUSE THOSE ARE THE RULES, RIGHT?
RIGHT!
LET'S HEAR THEM.
RULES!
ONE!
WE CAN ONLY DO ONE ADVENTURE AT A TIME.
TWO!
EXCEPT FOR EMERGENCIES, I CAN ONLY PRACTICE USING MY POWERS AFTER WE GO THROUGH THE DOOR.
THREE!
NO CUSSING.
VERY GOOD. READY?
WAIT, I CAN'T REMEMBER WHOSE TURN IT IS. LEECH OR ME?
ACTUALLY, IF YOU DON'T MIN TODAY I'D LIKE PICK. IS THAT OKAY?
OKAY!

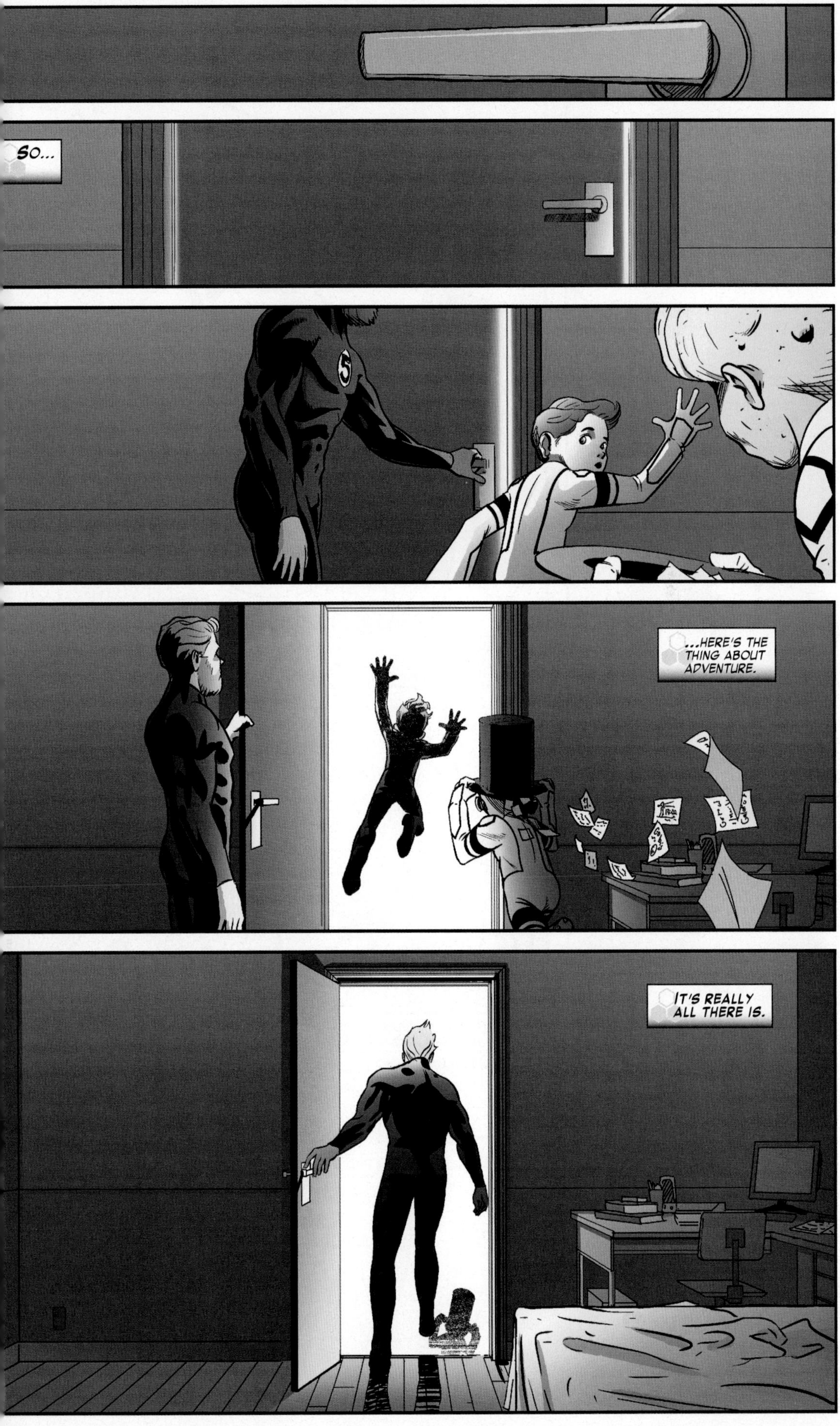
SO...
...HERE'S THE THING ABOUT ADVENTURE.
IT'S REALLY ALL THERE IS.

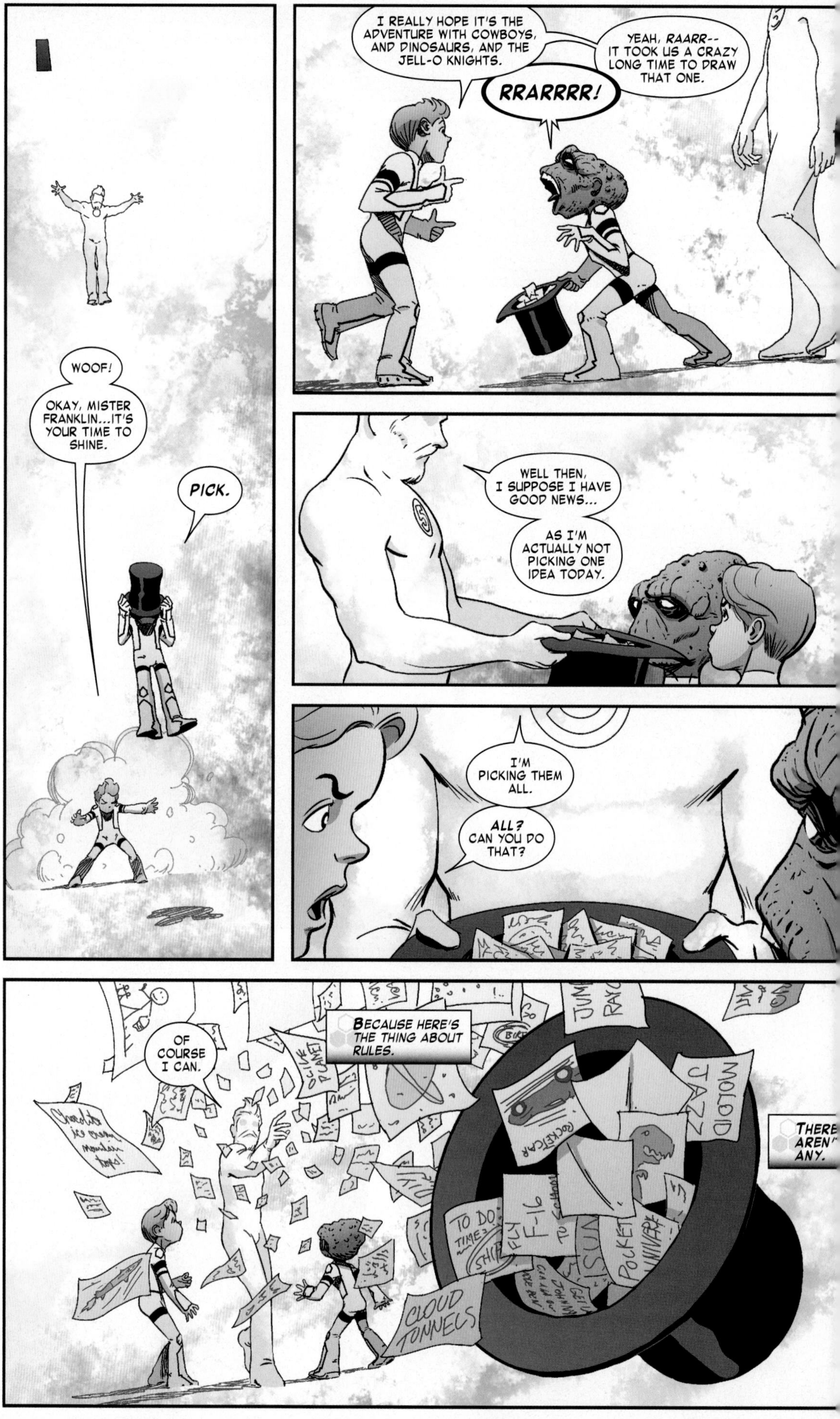
WOOF!
OKAY, MISTER FRANKLIN...IT'S YOUR TIME TO SHINE.
PICK.
I REALLY HOPE IT'S THE ADVENTURE WITH COWBOYS, AND DINOSAURS, AND THE JELL-O KNIGHTS.
RRARRRR!
YEAH, RAARR-- IT TOOK US A CRAZY LONG TIME TO DRAW THAT ONE.
WELL THEN, I SUPPOSE I HAVE GOOD NEWS...
AS I'M ACTUALLY NOT PICKING ONE IDEA TODAY.
I'M PICKING THEM ALL.
ALL? CAN YOU DO THAT?
OF COURSE I CAN.
BECAUSE HERE'S THE THING ABOUT RULES.
THERE AREN'T ANY.
CLOUD TUNNELS
JAZZ
MOLOID
ROCKET CAR

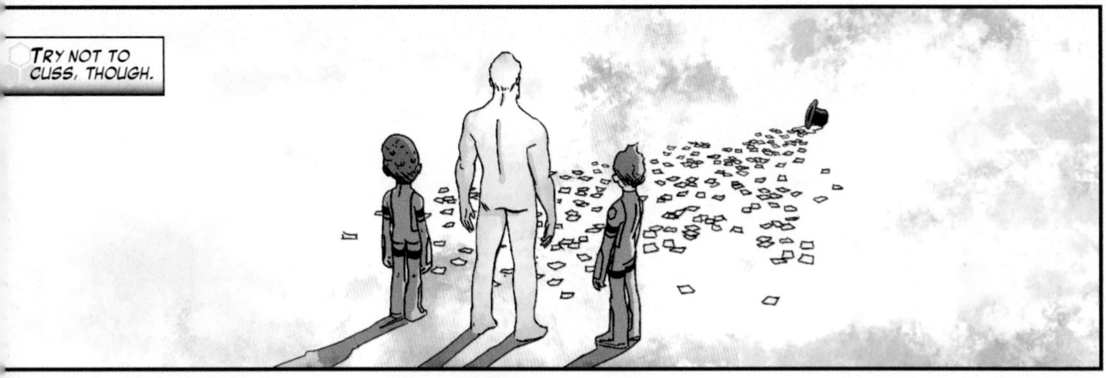
TRY NOT TO CUSS, THOUGH.

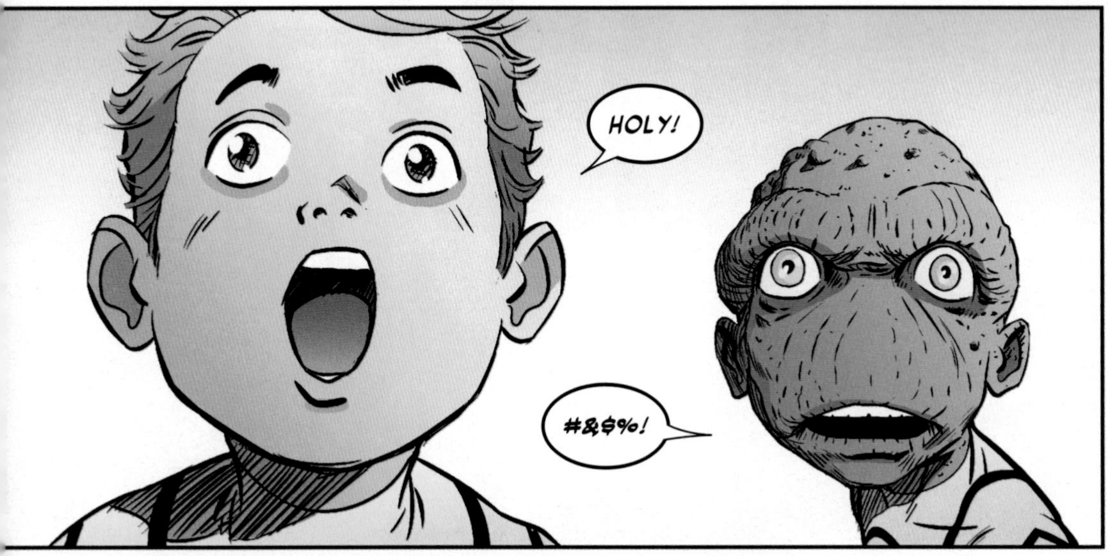
HOLY!
#&$%!

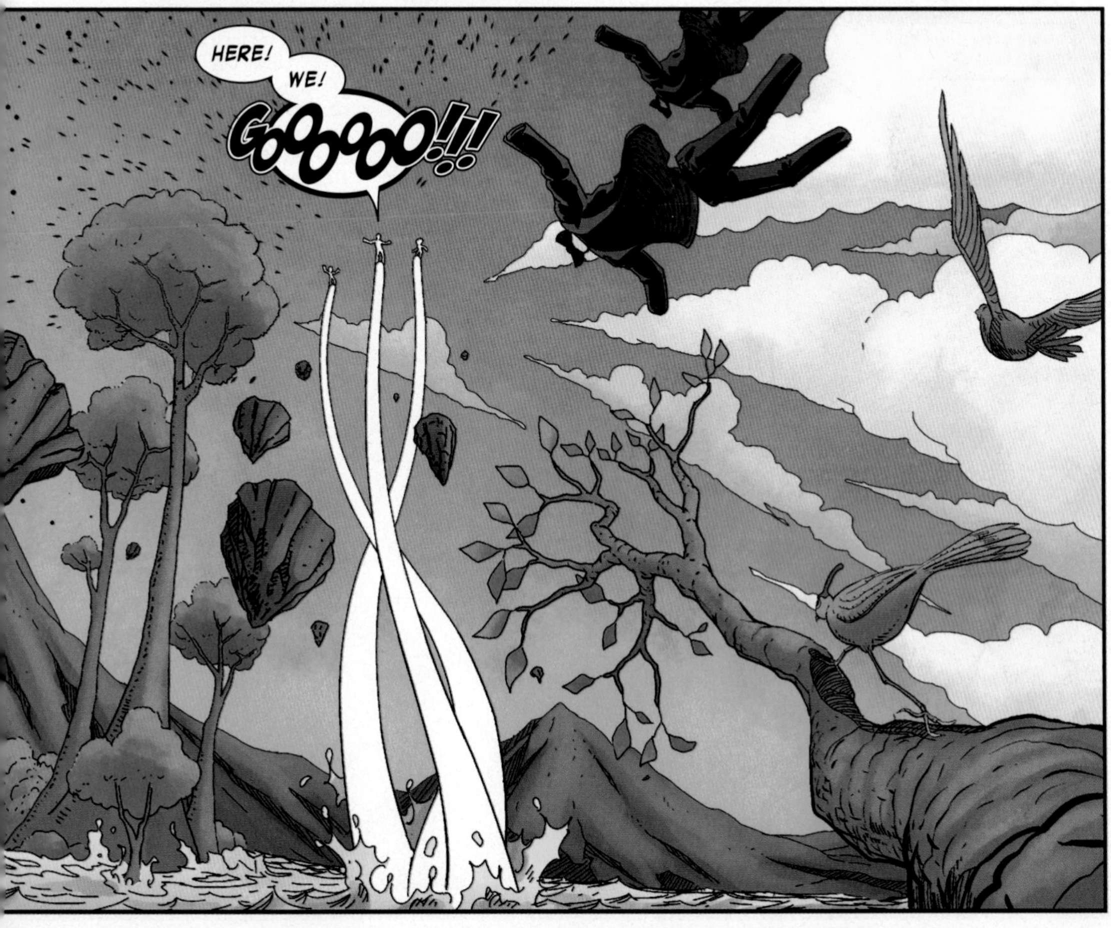
HERE!
WE!
GOOOOOO!!!

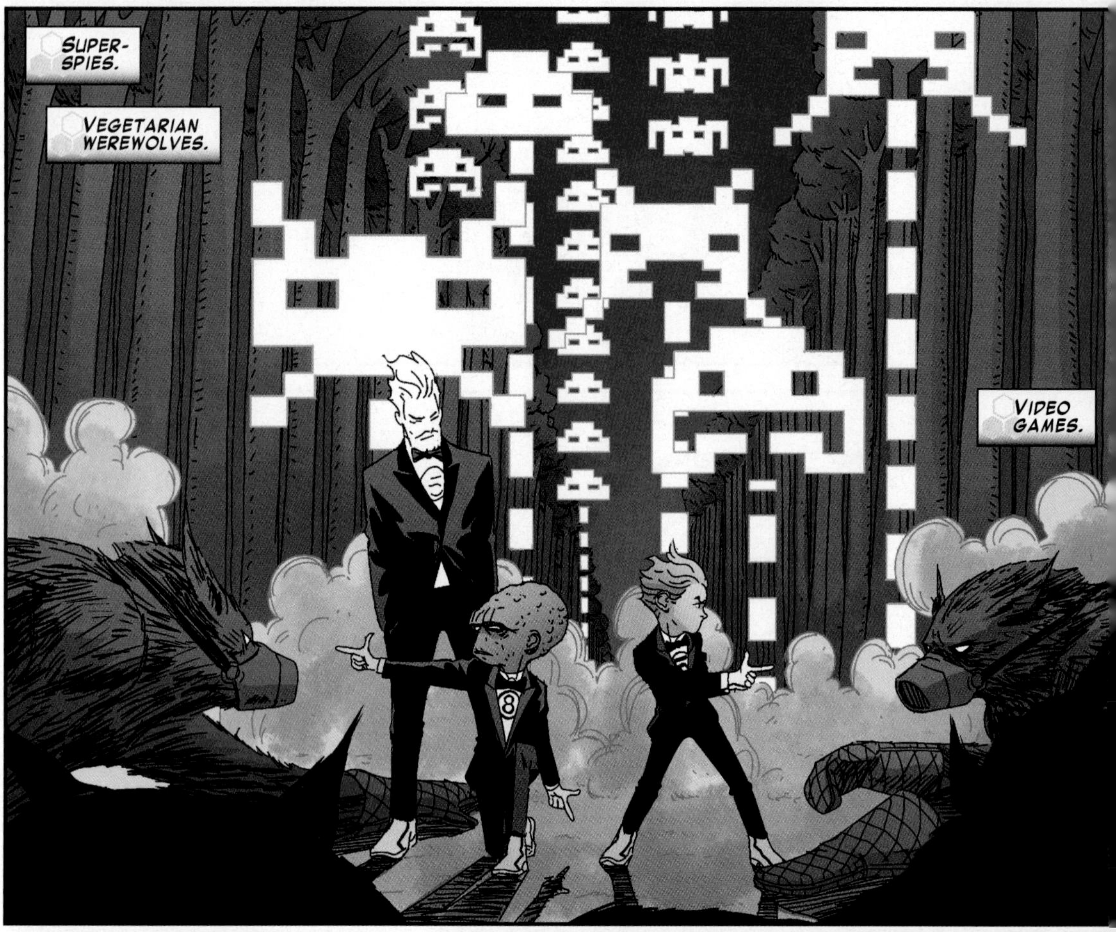
SUPER-SPIES.
VEGETARIAN WEREWOLVES.
VIDEO GAMES.

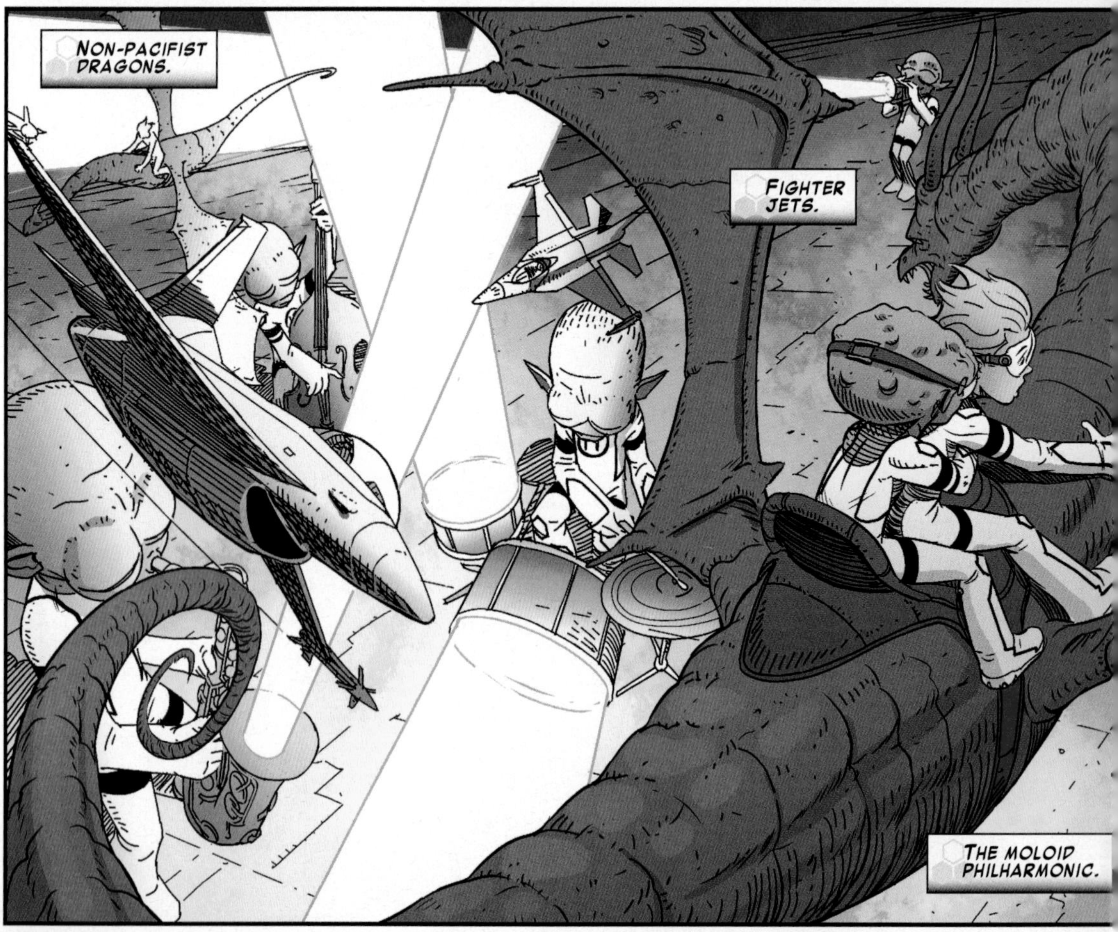
NON-PACIFIST DRAGONS.
FIGHTER JETS.
THE MOLOID PHILHARMONIC.

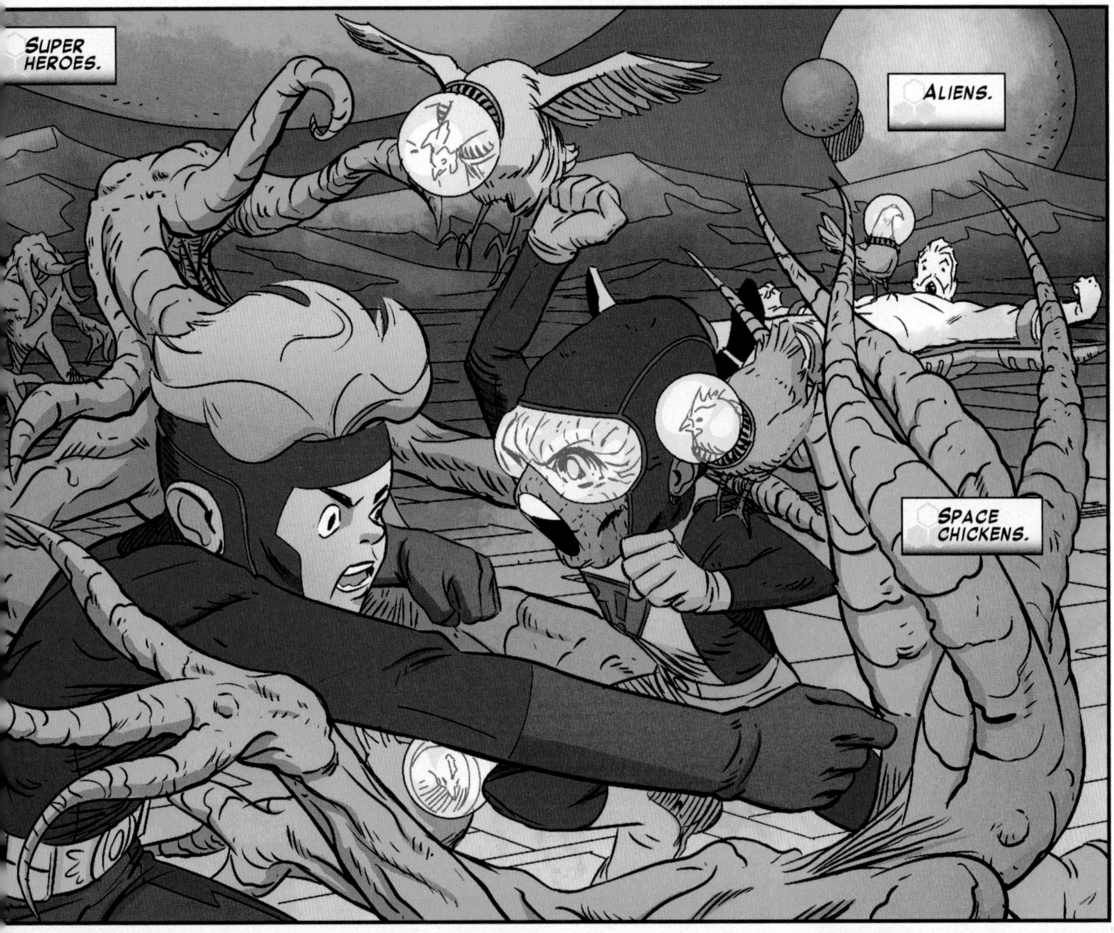
SUPER HEROES.
ALIENS.
SPACE CHICKENS.

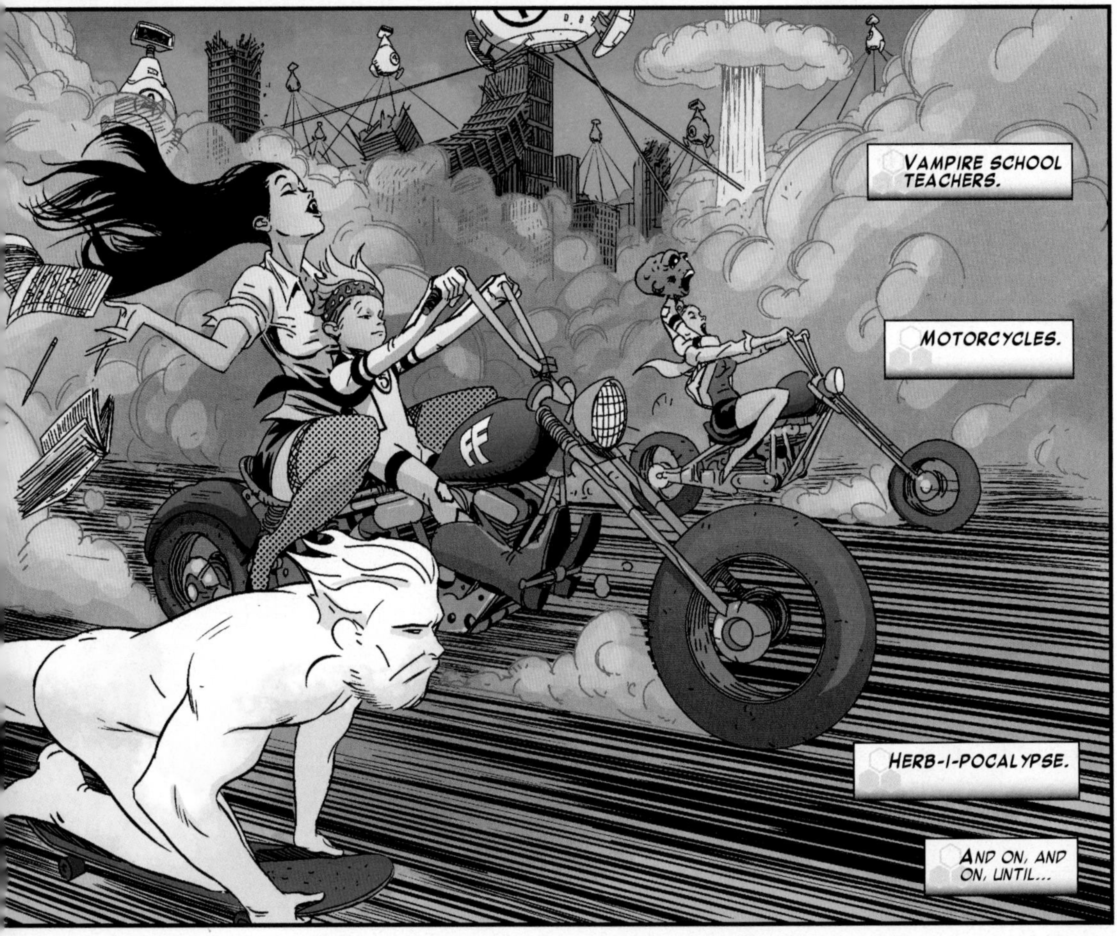
VAMPIRE SCHOOL TEACHERS.
MOTORCYCLES.
HERB-I-POCALYPSE.
AND ON, AND ON, UNTIL...

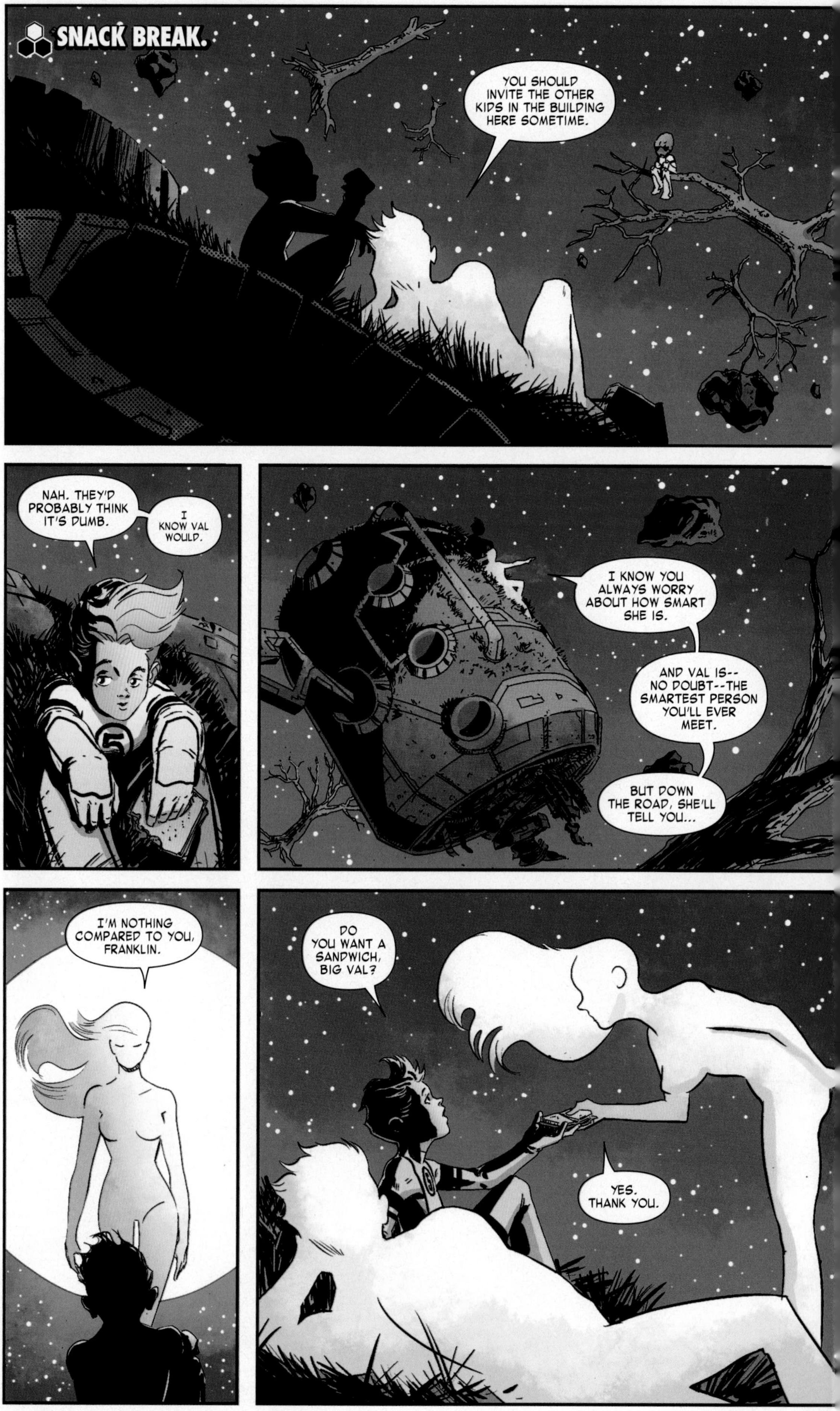
SNACK BREAK.
YOU SHOULD INVITE THE OTHER KIDS IN THE BUILDING HERE SOMETIME.
NAH. THEY'D PROBABLY THINK IT'S DUMB.
I KNOW VAL WOULD.
I KNOW YOU ALWAYS WORRY ABOUT HOW SMART SHE IS.
AND VAL IS-- NO DOUBT--THE SMARTEST PERSON YOU'LL EVER MEET.
BUT DOWN THE ROAD, SHE'LL TELL YOU...
I'M NOTHING COMPARED TO YOU, FRANKLIN.
DO YOU WANT A SANDWICH, BIG VAL?
YES. THANK YOU.

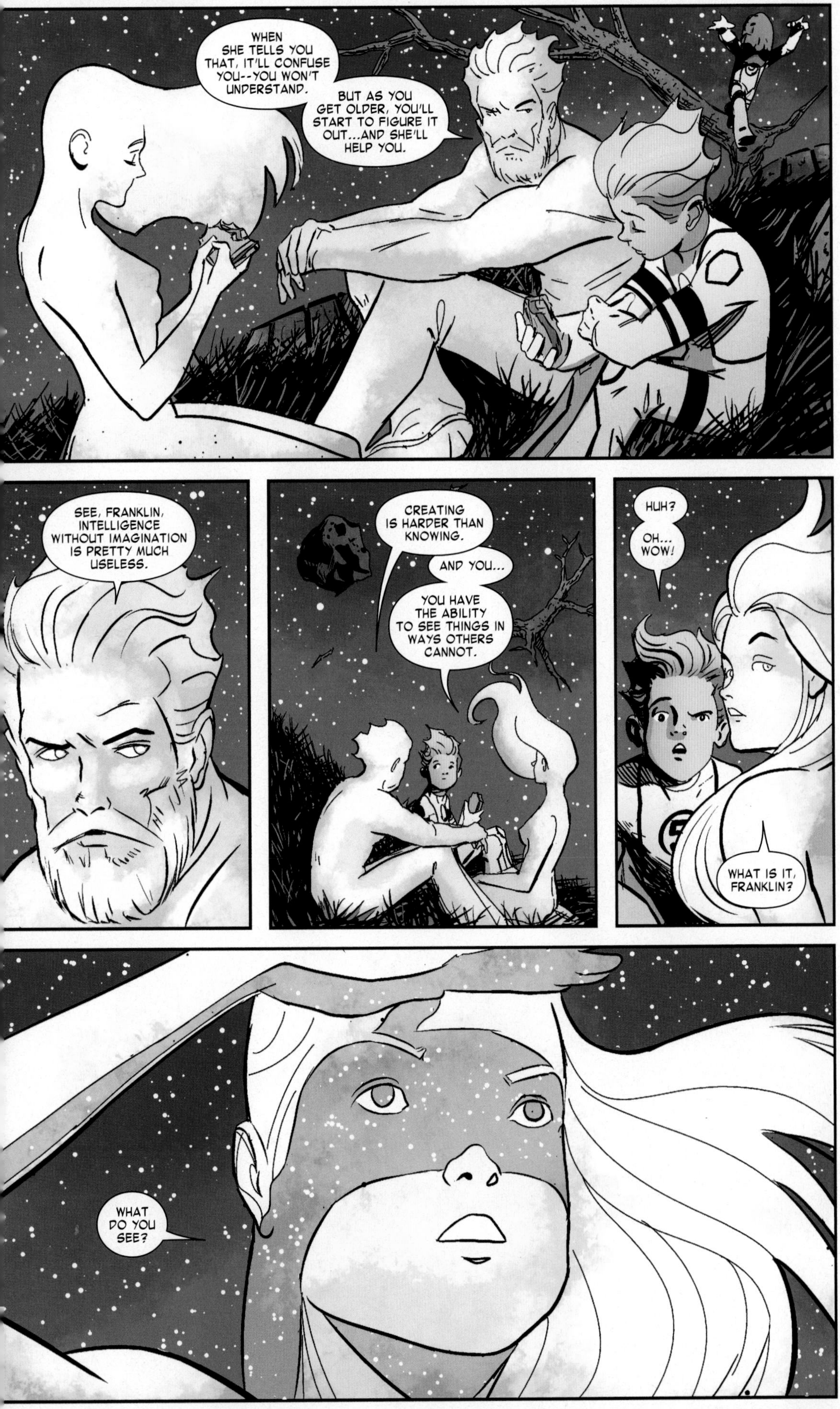
WHEN SHE TELLS YOU THAT, IT'LL CONFUSE YOU--YOU WON'T UNDERSTAND.
BUT AS YOU GET OLDER, YOU'LL START TO FIGURE IT OUT...AND SHE'LL HELP YOU.
SEE, FRANKLIN, INTELLIGENCE WITHOUT IMAGINATION IS PRETTY MUCH USELESS.
CREATING IS HARDER THAN KNOWING.
AND YOU...
YOU HAVE THE ABILITY TO SEE THINGS IN WAYS OTHERS CANNOT.
HUH?
OH... WOW!
WHAT IS IT, FRANKLIN?
WHAT DO YOU SEE?

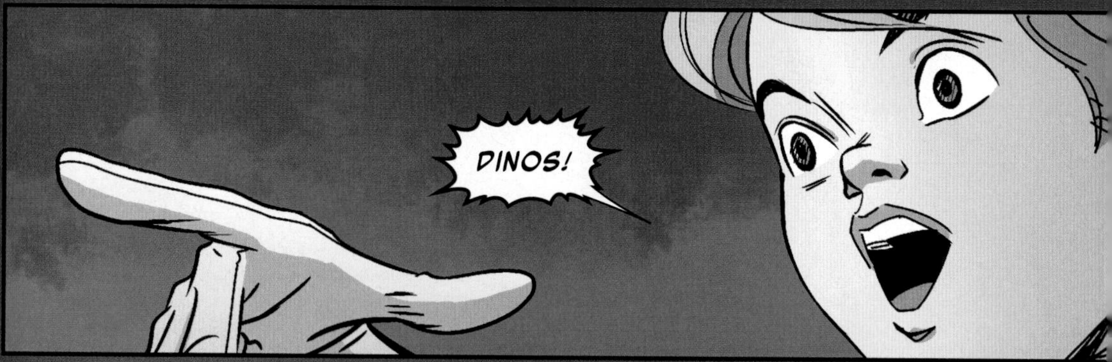
DINOS!

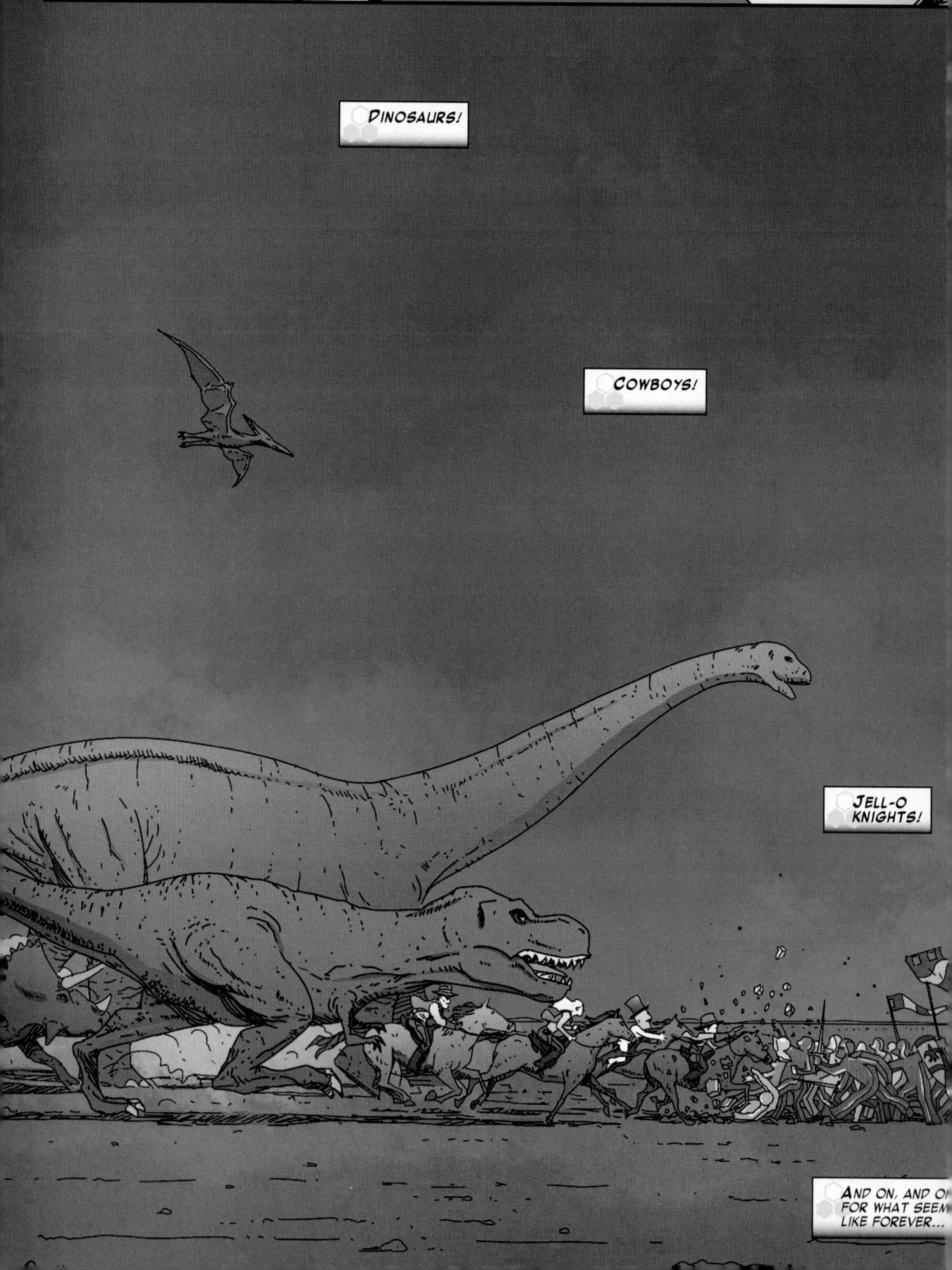
DINOSAURS!
COWBOYS!
JELL-O KNIGHTS!
AND ON, AND O
FOR WHAT SEEM
LIKE FOREVER...

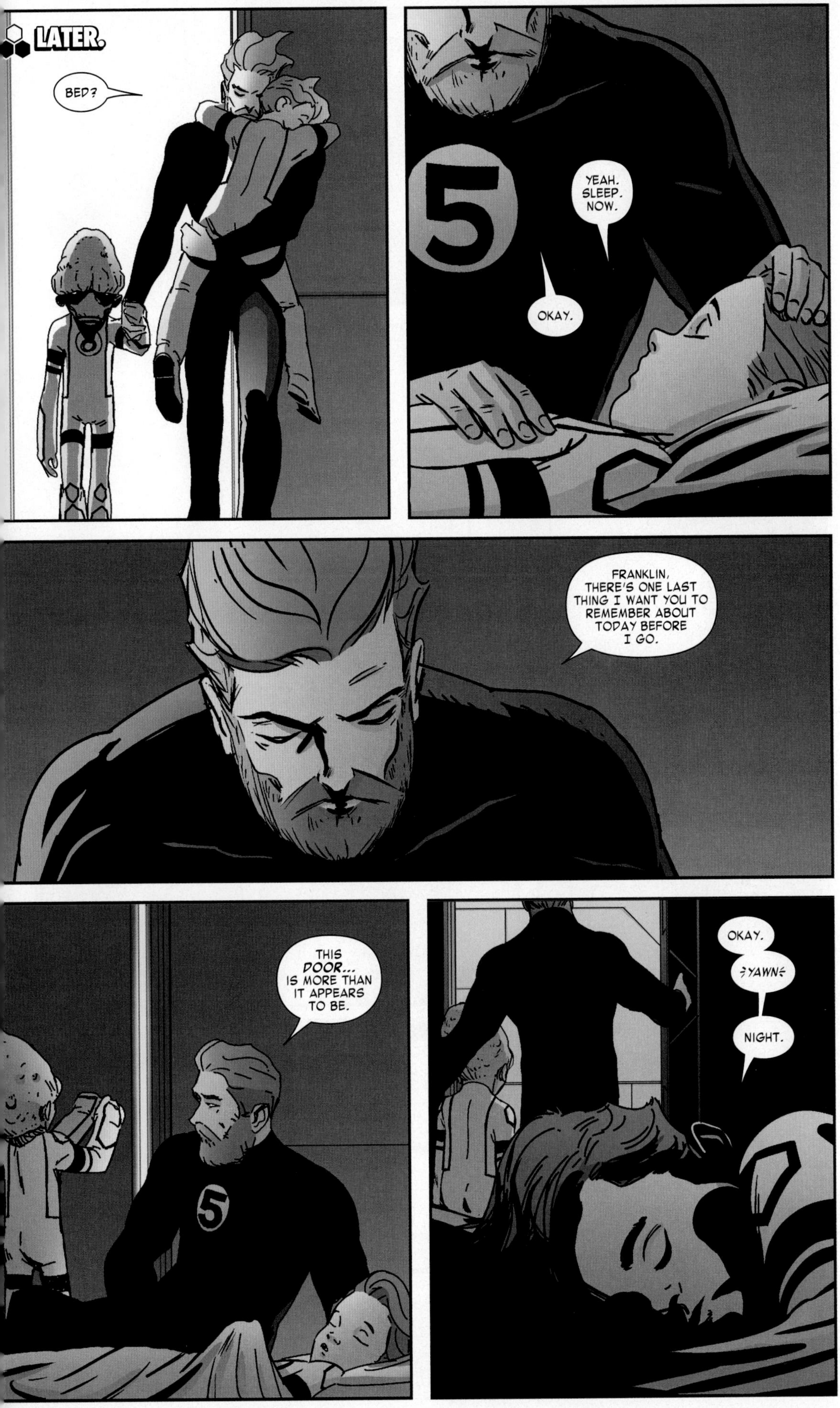
LATER.
BED?
YEAH. SLEEP. NOW.
OKAY.
FRANKLIN, THERE'S ONE LAST THING I WANT YOU TO REMEMBER ABOUT TODAY BEFORE I GO.
THIS *DOOR*... IS MORE THAN IT APPEARS TO BE.
OKAY.
⋞YAWN⋟
NIGHT.

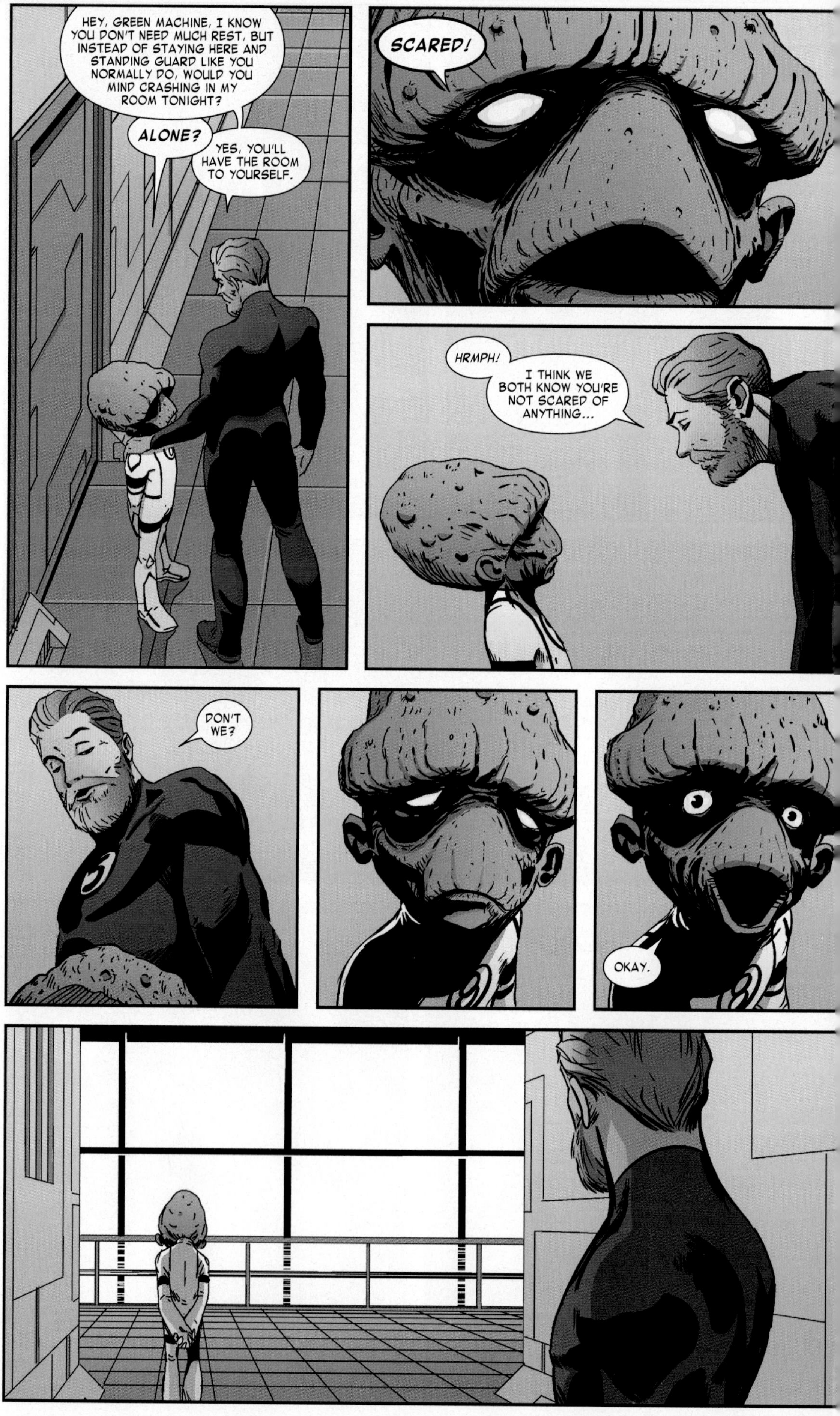
HEY, GREEN MACHINE, I KNOW YOU DON'T NEED MUCH REST, BUT INSTEAD OF STAYING HERE AND STANDING GUARD LIKE YOU NORMALLY DO, WOULD YOU MIND CRASHING IN MY ROOM TONIGHT?
ALONE?
YES, YOU'LL HAVE THE ROOM TO YOURSELF.
SCARED!
HRMPH!
I THINK WE BOTH KNOW YOU'RE NOT SCARED OF ANYTHING...
DON'T WE?
OKAY.

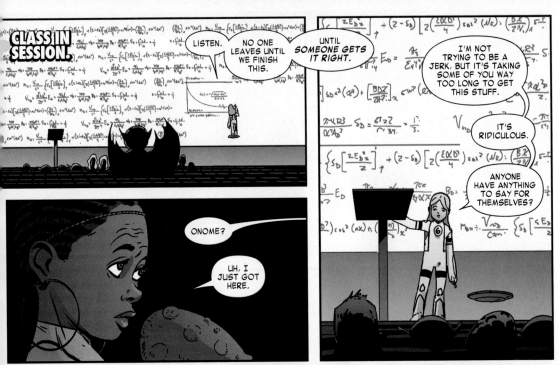

CLASS IN SESSION.

LISTEN. NO ONE LEAVES UNTIL WE FINISH THIS.

UNTIL SOMEONE GETS IT RIGHT.

I'M NOT TRYING TO BE A JERK, BUT IT'S TAKING SOME OF YOU WAY TOO LONG TO GET THIS STUFF.

IT'S RIDICULOUS.

ANYONE HAVE ANYTHING TO SAY FOR THEMSELVES?

ONOME?

UH, I JUST GOT HERE.

MOLOIDS?

SORRY. WE'RE ALL OUT OF JOKES, VAL.

WHO'S THERE?

KNOCK. KNOCK.

...

SEE? NOTHING.

DRAGON?

I DON'T WANT TO FIGHT ABOUT ME NOT FIGHTING ABOUT THIS.

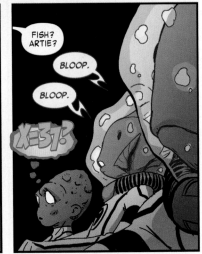

FISH? ARTIE?

BLOOP.

BLOOP.

XEST!?

NO, THE ANSWER ISN'T 37. ALEX?

I DUNNO.

YOU SHOULD ASK BENTLEY... HE'S SURE TO KNOW.

BENTLEY?

HUH?

WHAT'S YOUR ANSWER?

MY ANSWER? WE SHOULD MAKE COOKIES OR SOMETHING, RIGHT?

MAYBE RESCUE A DOG OR START A SMALL WAR?

ARRGGHHH!

I SWEAR! IF DAD ISN'T HERE YOU GU--

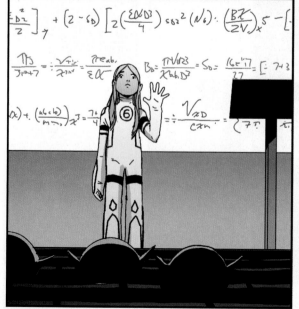

SO... SERIOUSLY!

IF I HAVE TO GO GET DAD, THEN DON'T THINK I WON'T BECAUSE...

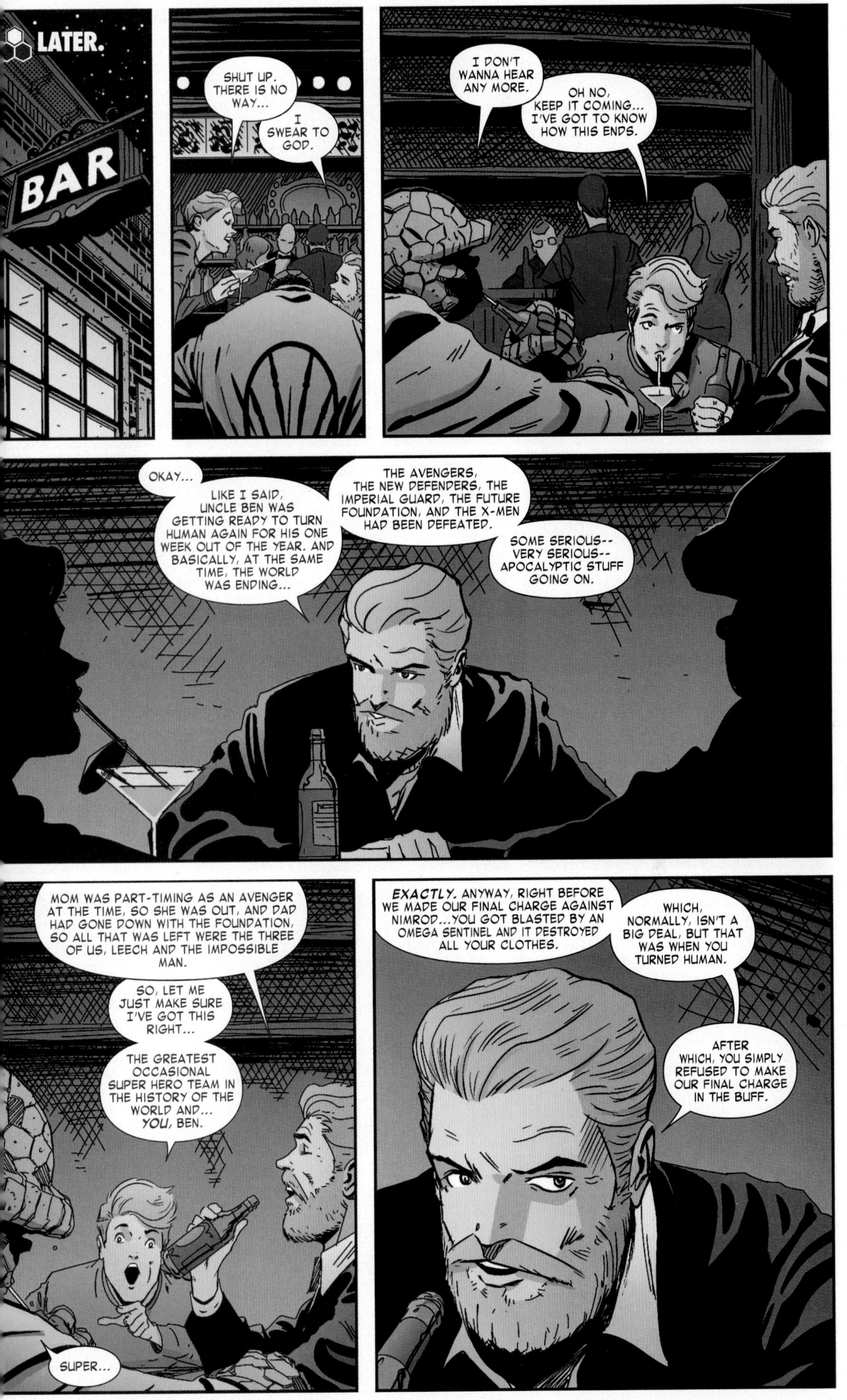

LATER.
BAR
SHUT UP. THERE IS NO WAY...
I SWEAR TO GOD.
I DON'T WANNA HEAR ANY MORE.
OH NO, KEEP IT COMING... I'VE GOT TO KNOW HOW THIS ENDS.
OKAY...
LIKE I SAID, UNCLE BEN WAS GETTING READY TO TURN HUMAN AGAIN FOR HIS ONE WEEK OUT OF THE YEAR. AND BASICALLY, AT THE SAME TIME, THE WORLD WAS ENDING...
THE AVENGERS, THE NEW DEFENDERS, THE IMPERIAL GUARD, THE FUTURE FOUNDATION, AND THE X-MEN HAD BEEN DEFEATED.
SOME SERIOUS-- VERY SERIOUS-- APOCALYPTIC STUFF GOING ON.
MOM WAS PART-TIMING AS AN AVENGER AT THE TIME, SO SHE WAS OUT, AND DAD HAD GONE DOWN WITH THE FOUNDATION, SO ALL THAT WAS LEFT WERE THE THREE OF US, LEECH AND THE IMPOSSIBLE MAN.
SO, LET ME JUST MAKE SURE I'VE GOT THIS RIGHT...
THE GREATEST OCCASIONAL SUPER HERO TEAM IN THE HISTORY OF THE WORLD AND... *YOU*, BEN.
SUPER...
EXACTLY. ANYWAY, RIGHT BEFORE WE MADE OUR FINAL CHARGE AGAINST NIMROD...YOU GOT BLASTED BY AN OMEGA SENTINEL AND IT DESTROYED ALL YOUR CLOTHES.
WHICH, NORMALLY, ISN'T A BIG DEAL, BUT THAT WAS WHEN YOU TURNED HUMAN.
AFTER WHICH, YOU SIMPLY REFUSED TO MAKE OUR FINAL CHARGE IN THE BUFF.

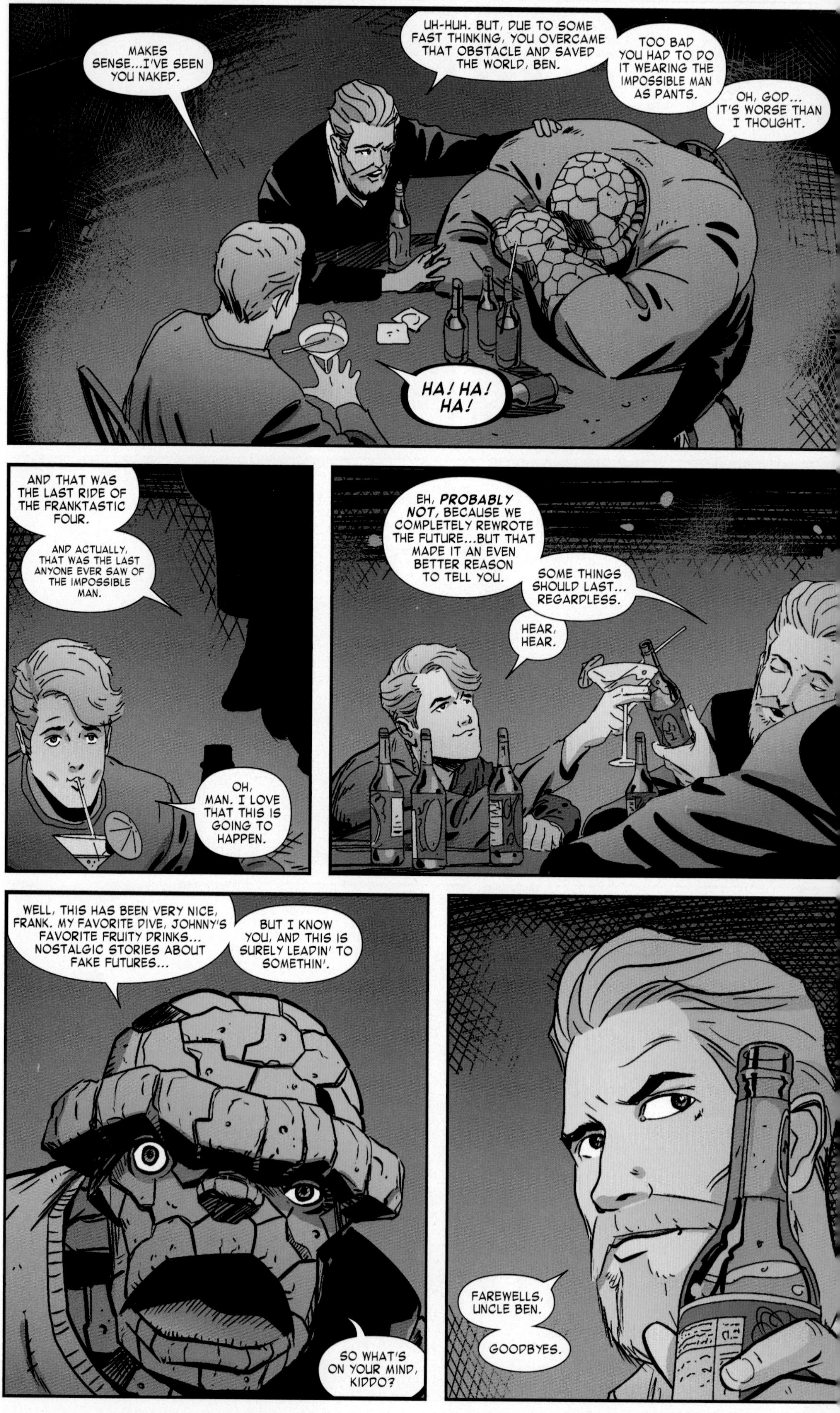
MAKES SENSE...I'VE SEEN YOU NAKED.
UH-HUH. BUT, DUE TO SOME FAST THINKING, YOU OVERCAME THAT OBSTACLE AND SAVED THE WORLD, BEN.
TOO BAD YOU HAD TO DO IT WEARING THE IMPOSSIBLE MAN AS PANTS.
OH, GOD... IT'S WORSE THAN I THOUGHT.
HA! HA! HA!
AND THAT WAS THE LAST RIDE OF THE FRANKTASTIC FOUR.
AND ACTUALLY, THAT WAS THE LAST ANYONE EVER SAW OF THE IMPOSSIBLE MAN.
OH, MAN. I LOVE THAT THIS IS GOING TO HAPPEN.
EH, PROBABLY NOT, BECAUSE WE COMPLETELY REWROTE THE FUTURE...BUT THAT MADE IT AN EVEN BETTER REASON TO TELL YOU.
SOME THINGS SHOULD LAST... REGARDLESS.
HEAR, HEAR.
WELL, THIS HAS BEEN VERY NICE, FRANK. MY FAVORITE DIVE, JOHNNY'S FAVORITE FRUITY DRINKS... NOSTALGIC STORIES ABOUT FAKE FUTURES...
BUT I KNOW YOU, AND THIS IS SURELY LEADIN' TO SOMETHIN'.
SO WHAT'S ON YOUR MIND, KIDDO?
FAREWELLS, UNCLE BEN.
GOODBYES.

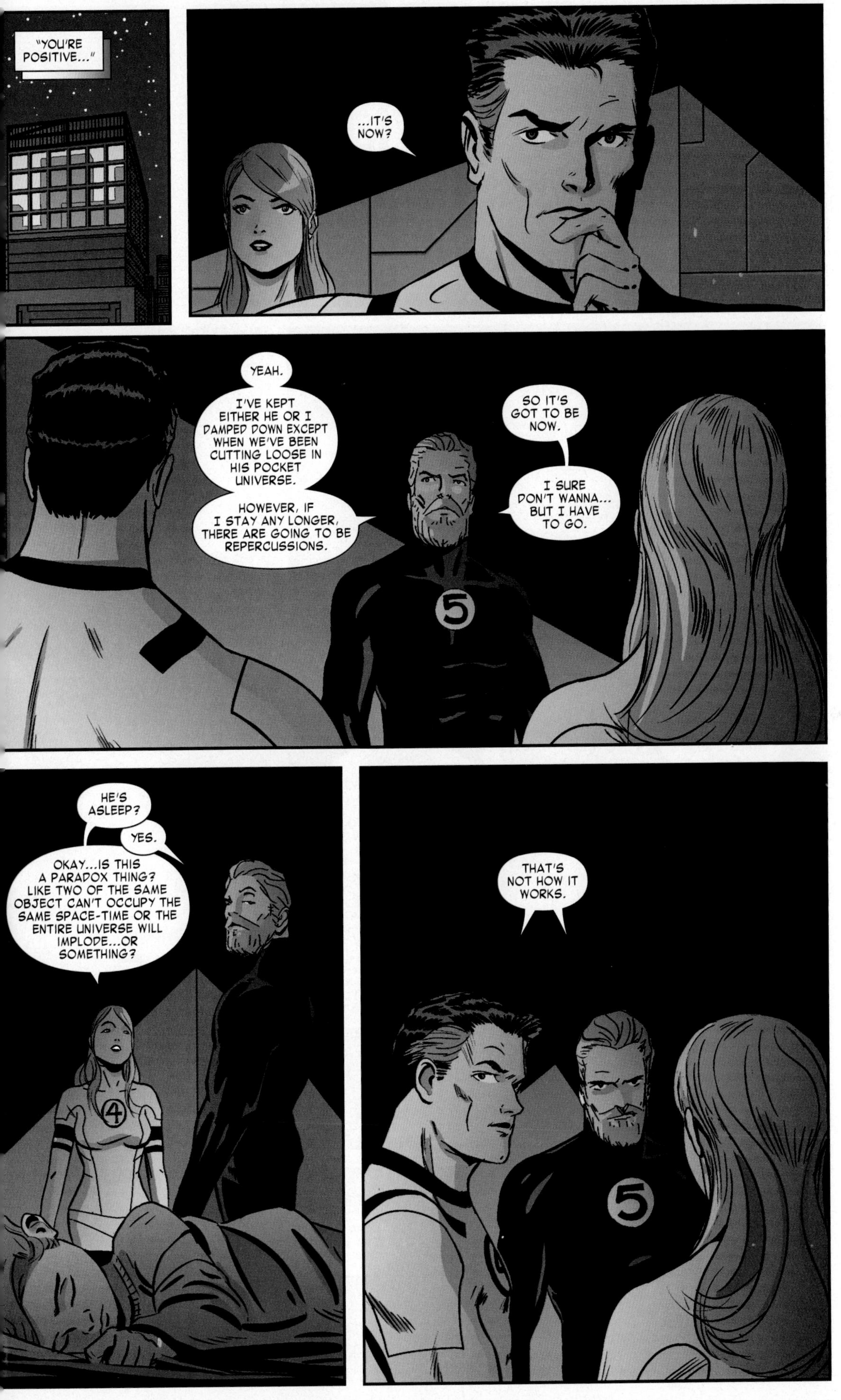
"YOU'RE POSITIVE..."
...IT'S NOW?
YEAH.
I'VE KEPT EITHER HE OR I DAMPED DOWN EXCEPT WHEN WE'VE BEEN CUTTING LOOSE IN HIS POCKET UNIVERSE.
HOWEVER, IF I STAY ANY LONGER, THERE ARE GOING TO BE REPERCUSSIONS.
SO IT'S GOT TO BE NOW.
I SURE DON'T WANNA... BUT I HAVE TO GO.
HE'S ASLEEP?
YES.
OKAY...IS THIS A PARADOX THING? LIKE TWO OF THE SAME OBJECT CAN'T OCCUPY THE SAME SPACE-TIME OR THE ENTIRE UNIVERSE WILL IMPLODE...OR SOMETHING?
THAT'S NOT HOW IT WORKS.

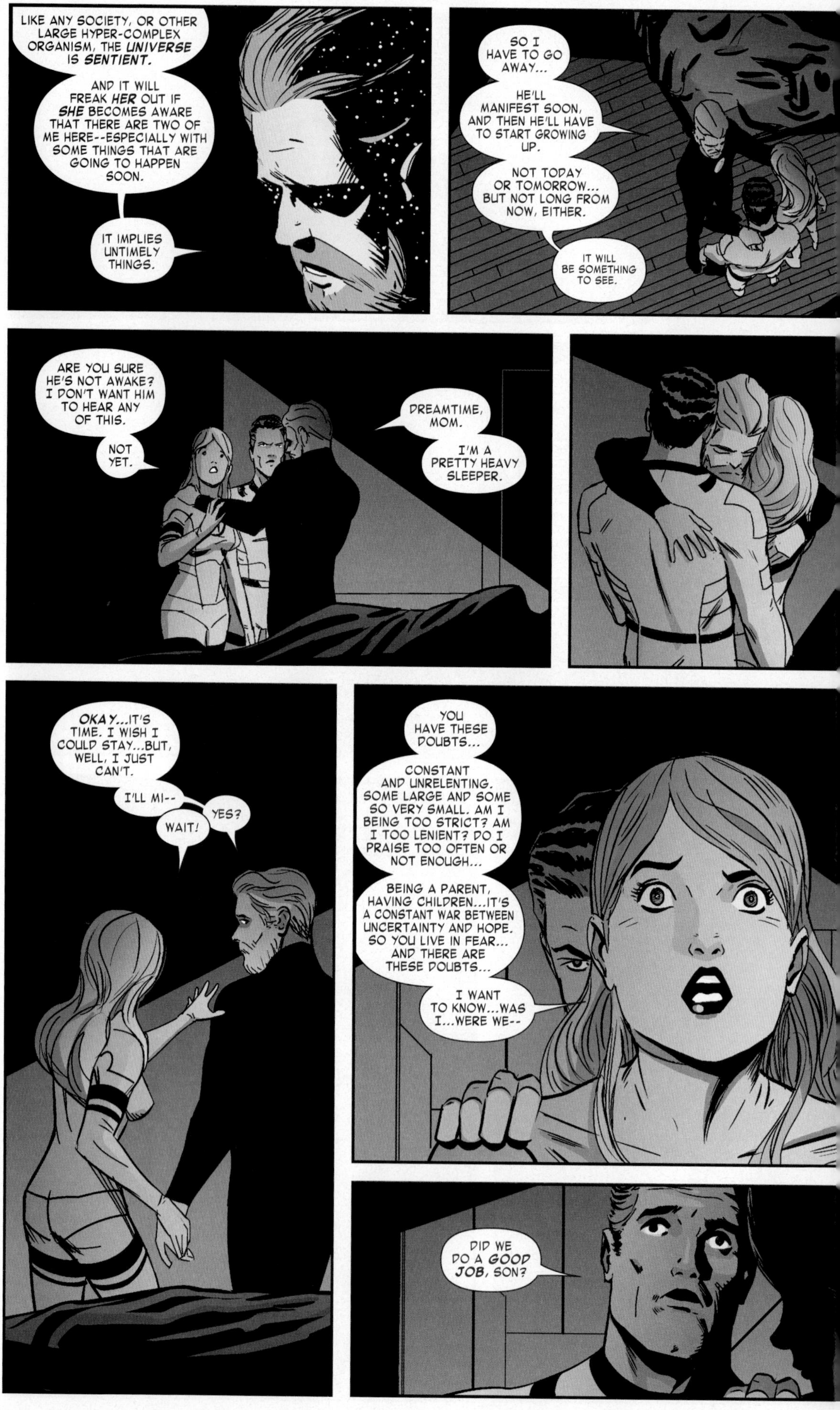
LIKE ANY SOCIETY, OR OTHER LARGE HYPER-COMPLEX ORGANISM, THE *UNIVERSE* IS *SENTIENT.*
AND IT WILL FREAK *HER* OUT IF *SHE* BECOMES AWARE THAT THERE ARE TWO OF ME HERE--ESPECIALLY WITH SOME THINGS THAT ARE GOING TO HAPPEN SOON.
IT IMPLIES UNTIMELY THINGS.
SO I HAVE TO GO AWAY...
HE'LL MANIFEST SOON, AND THEN HE'LL HAVE TO START GROWING UP.
NOT TODAY OR TOMORROW... BUT NOT LONG FROM NOW, EITHER.
IT WILL BE SOMETHING TO SEE.
ARE YOU SURE HE'S NOT AWAKE? I DON'T WANT HIM TO HEAR ANY OF THIS.
NOT YET.
DREAMTIME, MOM.
I'M A PRETTY HEAVY SLEEPER.
*OKAY...*IT'S TIME. I WISH I COULD STAY...BUT, WELL, I JUST CAN'T.
I'LL MI--
WAIT!
YES?
YOU HAVE THESE DOUBTS...
CONSTANT AND UNRELENTING. SOME LARGE AND SOME SO VERY SMALL. AM I BEING TOO STRICT? AM I TOO LENIENT? DO I PRAISE TOO OFTEN OR NOT ENOUGH...
BEING A PARENT, HAVING CHILDREN...IT'S A CONSTANT WAR BETWEEN UNCERTAINTY AND HOPE. SO YOU LIVE IN FEAR... AND THERE ARE THESE DOUBTS...
I WANT TO KNOW...WAS I...WERE WE--
DID WE DO A *GOOD JOB,* SON?

A PERFECT ONE.

I LOVE YOU GUYS.

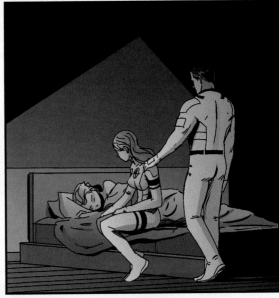

THIS DOOR...IS MORE THAN IT APPEARS TO BE.

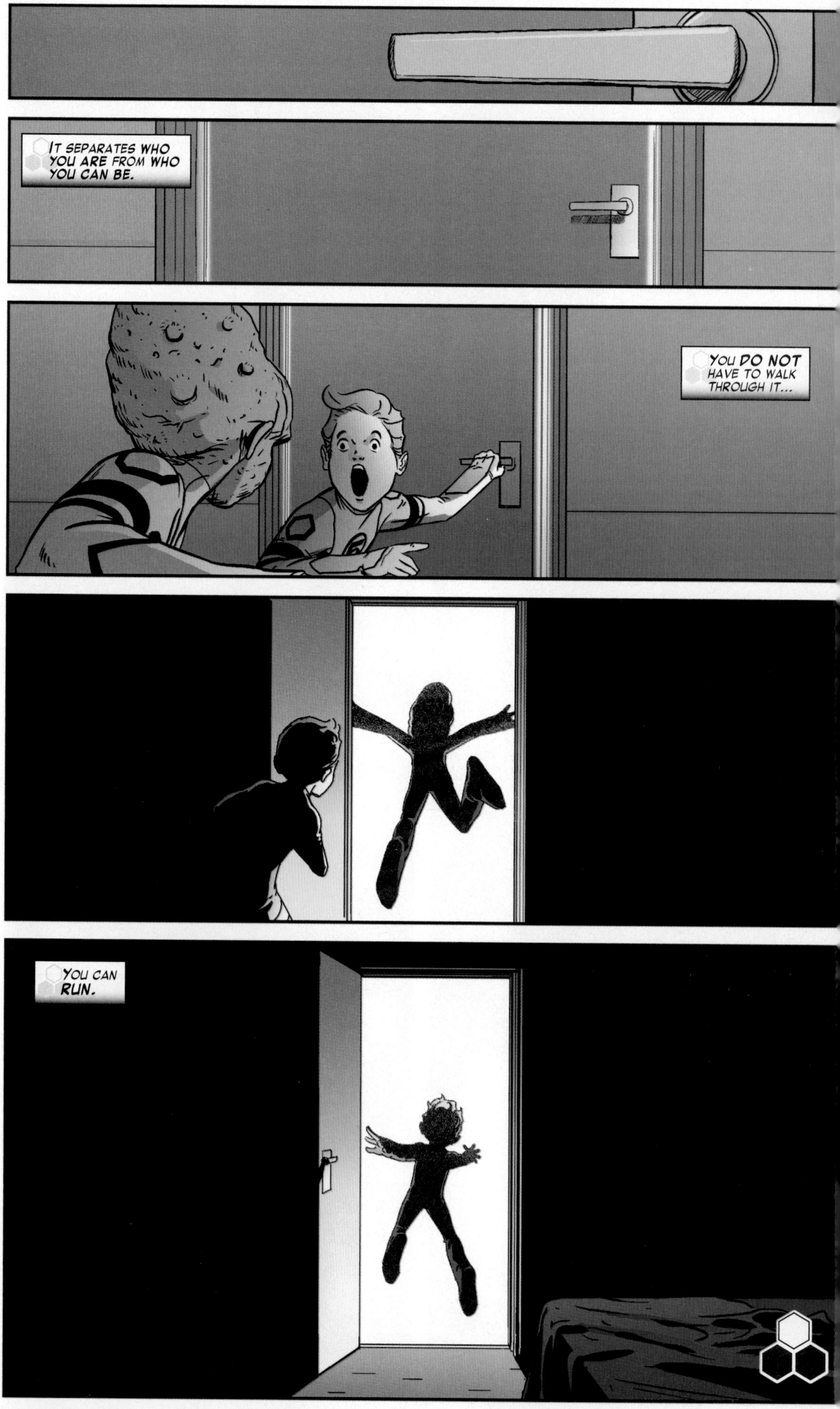
IT SEPARATES WHO YOU ARE FROM WHO YOU CAN BE.
YOU DO NOT HAVE TO WALK THROUGH IT...
YOU CAN RUN.

COVER GALLERY

#17 COVER: **MIKE CHOI & GURU-eFX**

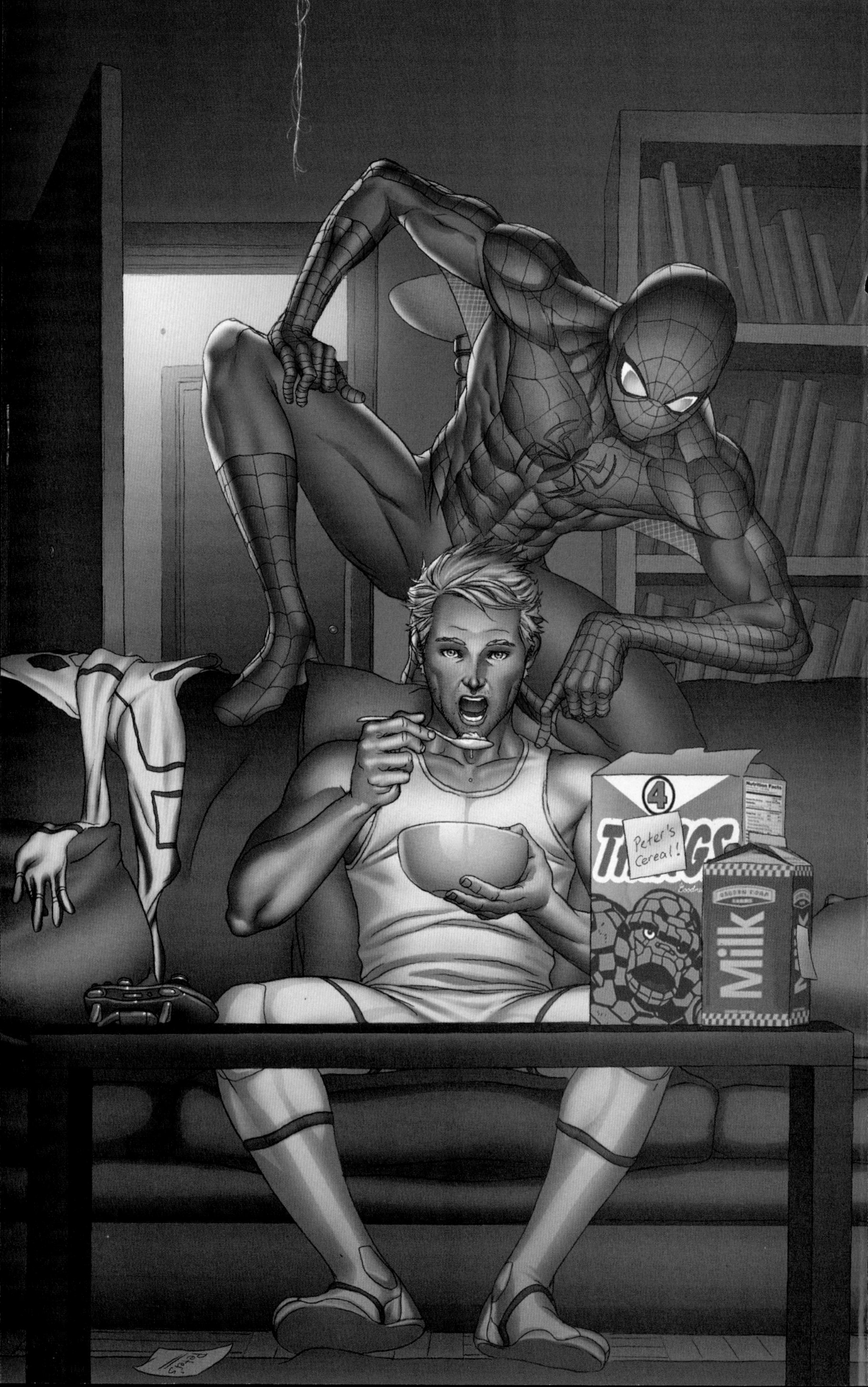

#18 COVER: **KALMAN ANDRASOFSZKY**

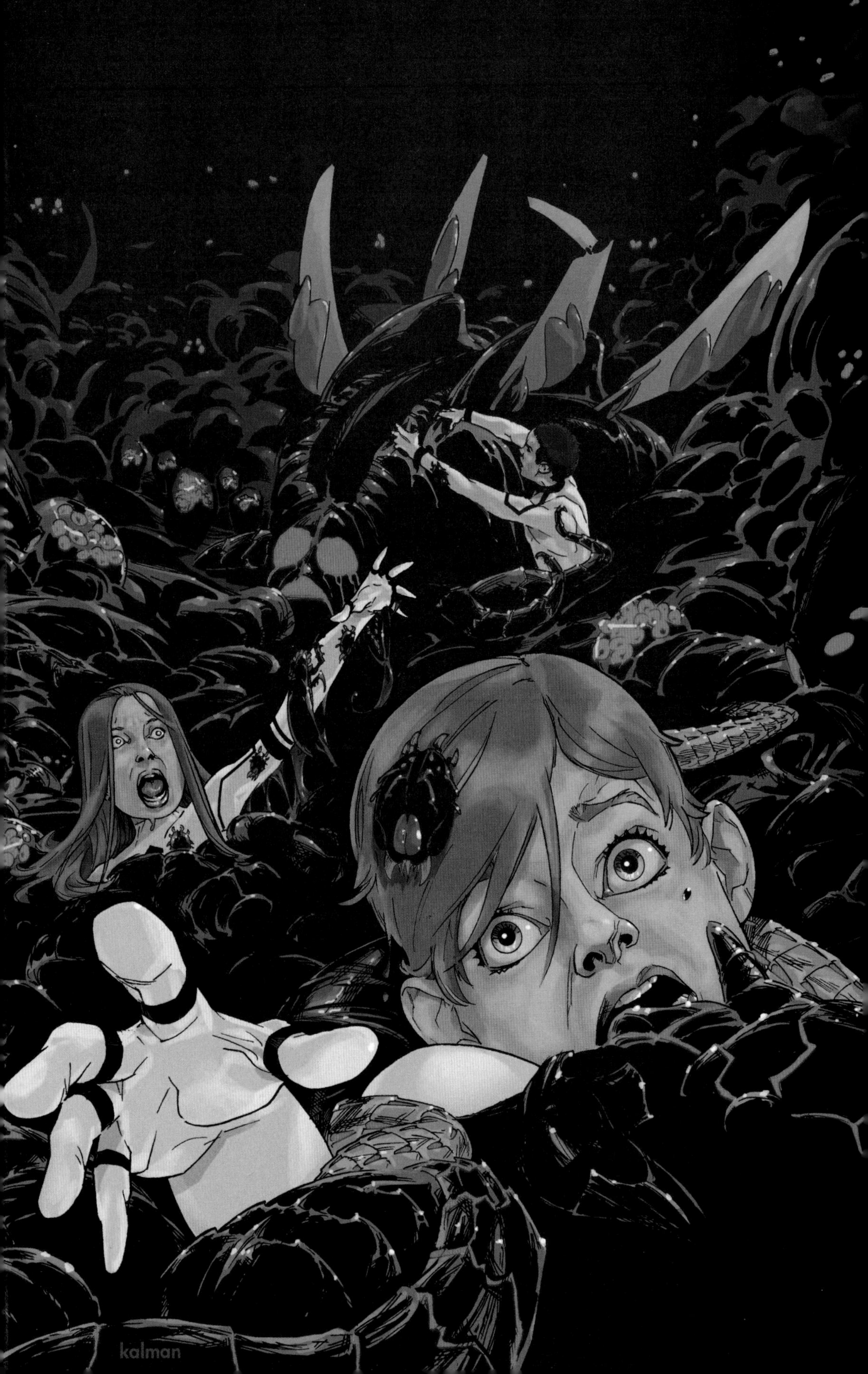
kalman

#19 COVER: MIKE CHOI & GURU-eFX

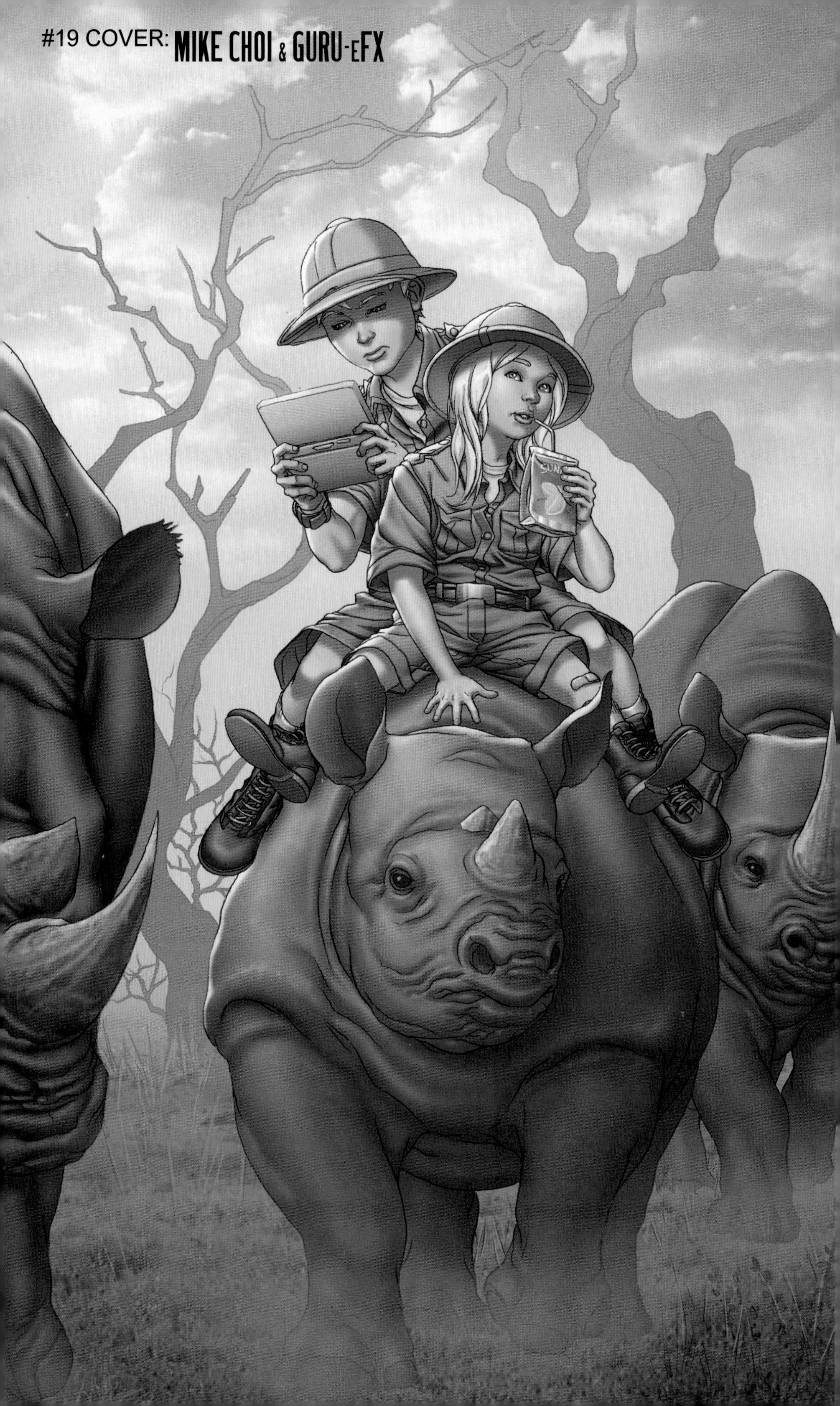

#20 COVER: **MIKE CHOI & GURU-eFX**

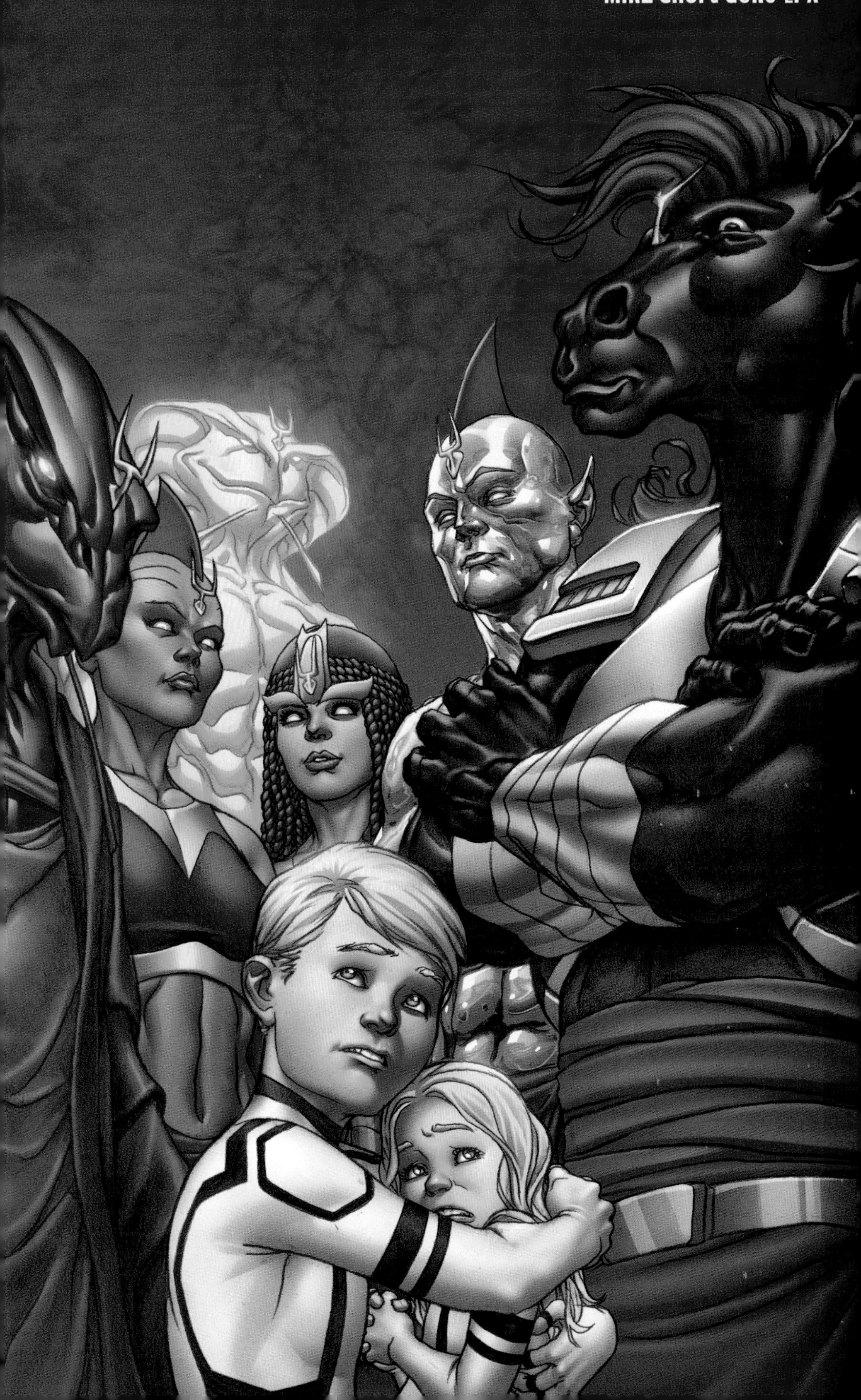

#21 COVER: **MIKE CHOI & GURU-eFX**

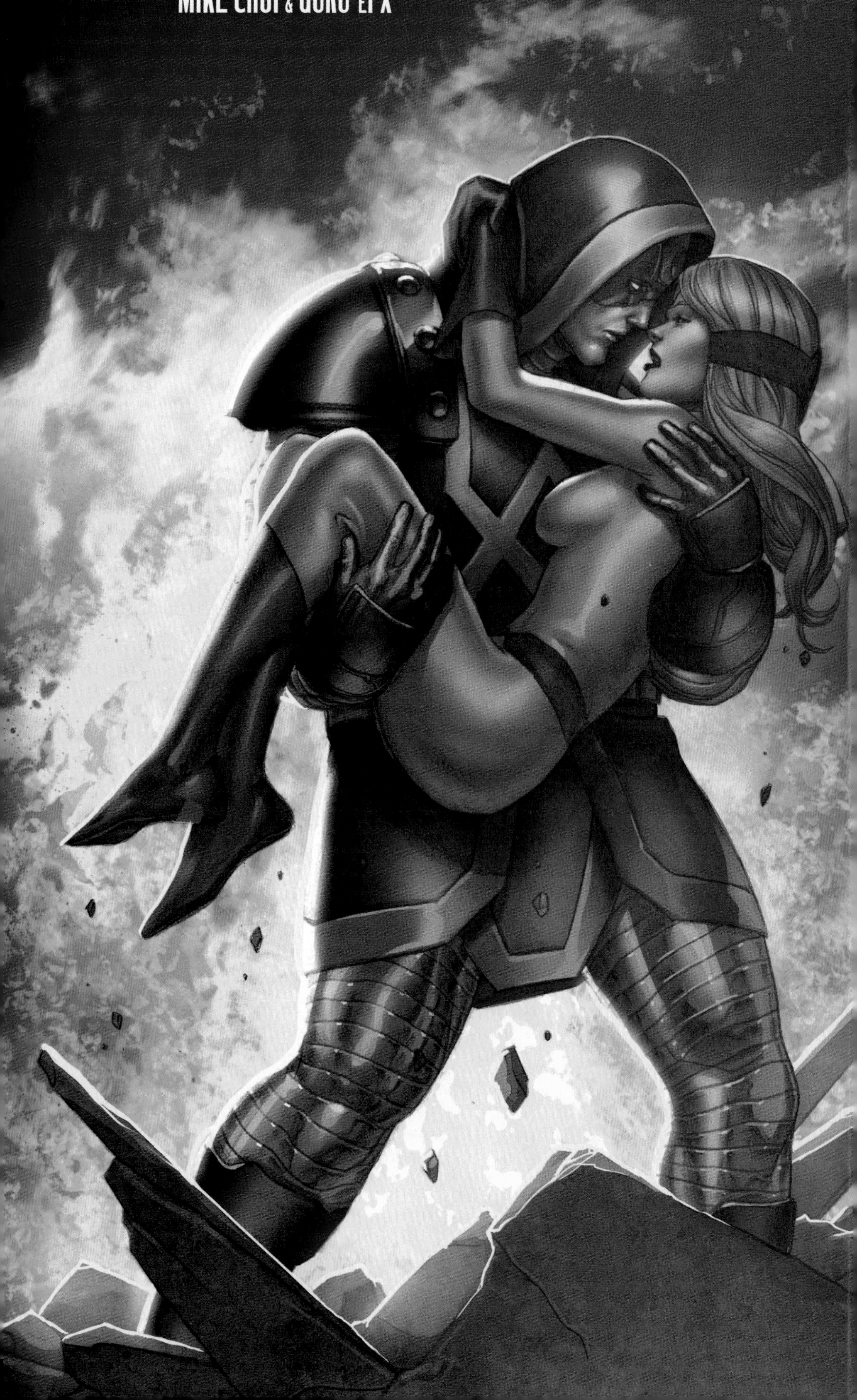

#22 COVER: RYAN STEGMAN & MARTE GRACIA

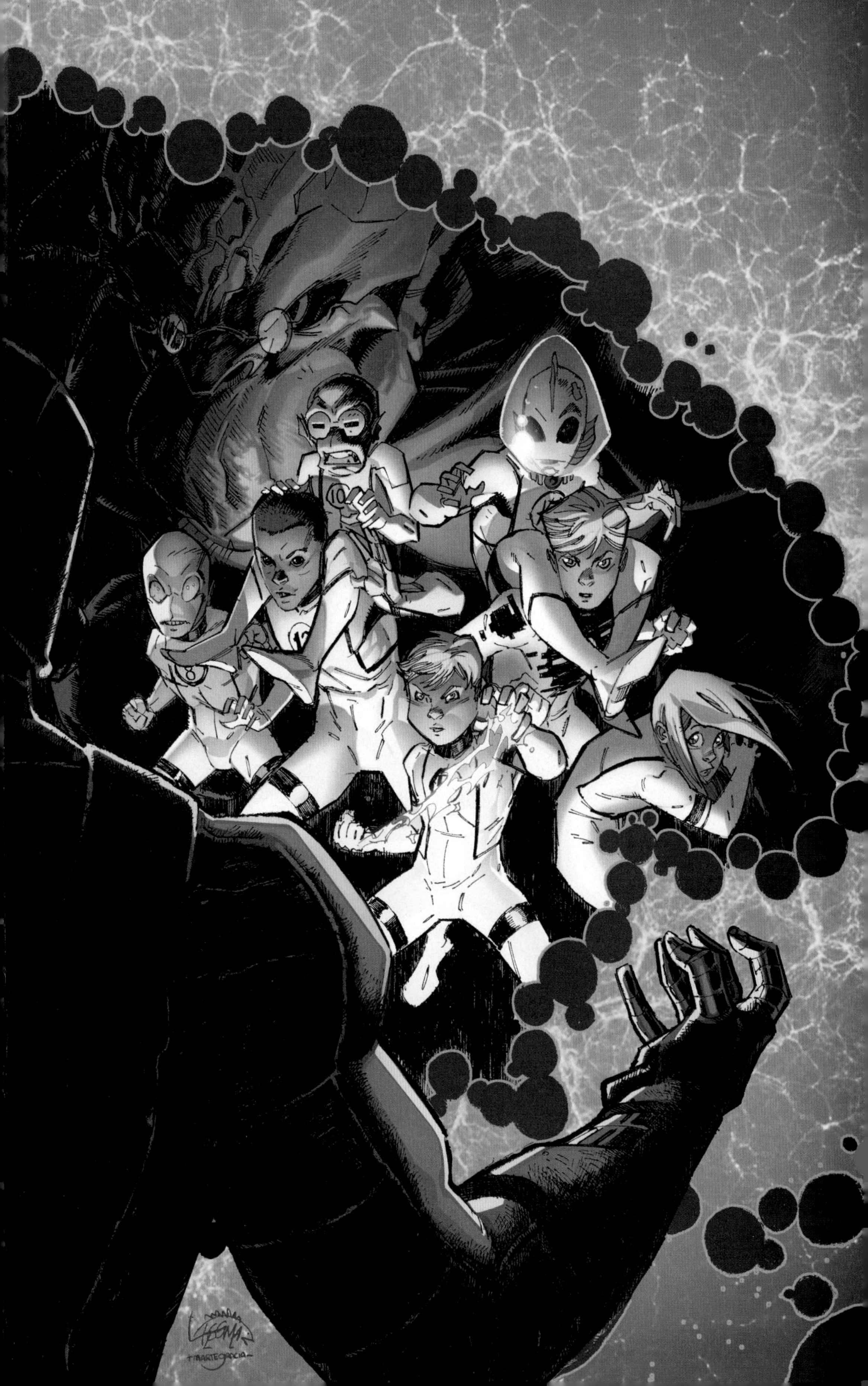

#23 COVER: **KALMAN ANDRASOFSZKY**

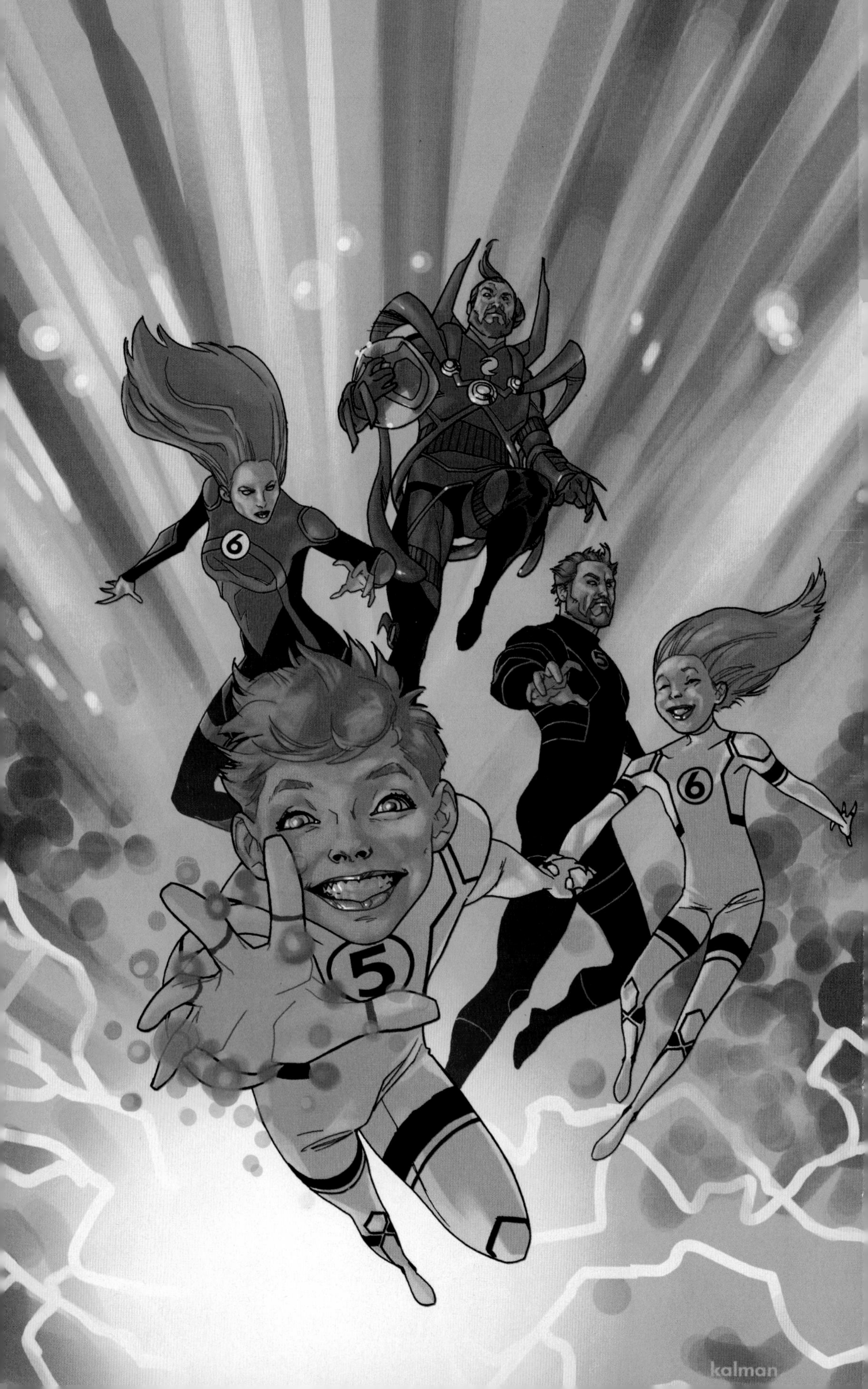

kalman